The Butterflies of Manitoba

P. Klassen
A.R. Westwood
W.B. Preston
W.B. McKillop

Manitoba Museum of Man and Nature, Winnipeg, 1989

ISBN-0-920704-16-6

Preface

This book is intended to serve as an identification guide to the butterflies known to occur in the province of Manitoba. Its intended audience is both amateur and professional entomologists and others interested in our butterfly fauna. We have attempted to bring together as much information as possible on the butterflies occurring in our province, drawing from various publications and other sources as well as personal experience.

There are many excellent publications on butterflies, some continent-wide in their coverage, and others covering limited regions of North America. Our intent is not to replace any of these but to supplement them by focusing on Manitoba. For information on butterflies on a wider scale we recommend the books by Klots (1951), Howe (1975), Opler and Krizek (1984), Scott (1986) and Royer (1988) and any of the publications listed in the reference section.

In preparing this book we found there is much to be learned about the biology of butterflies in Manitoba. It is our sincere hope that this book will help the user gain a greater appreciation for our butterfly fauna.

We would like to acknowledge the help, advice and encouragement of the following people and organizations: G. Ayre, Agriculture Canada, Winnipeg; G.T. Austin; R. Barrow; E. Becker, CanaColl Foundation, Ottawa; Mr. and Mrs. A.D. Brady; J.M. Burns, Smithsonian Institution; R. Cannings and C. Guppy of the Royal British Columbia Museum; P. Catling; J. Christie; W. Christie; P.J. Conway; J. Corkett; R. Dana; R. Dmytriw; J. Dubois; T.C. Emmel; T.D. Galloway, University of Manitoba; K. Giesbrecht, City Press; B. Glassey; G.B. Graphics; R. Gray; W.W. Gregory; the late R.J. Heron; D. Hopper; R.R. Hooper; K. Johnson; G. Jones, Little Northern Museum; D. Kritch; W. Krivda; N. Mackie, Image Color; Manitoba Heritage Federation; Manitoba Museum of Man and Nature Foundation; T. McIntyre; L. Nelson; D.K. Parshall; J. Polusny; F. Preston; J. Preston; J.D. Reist; F.H. Rindge, American Museum of Natural History; K. Roney, Saskatchewan Museum of Natural History; J.A. Scott; O. Shields; J. Spence; F. Sperling; D. Spitzer, Image Graphics; P. Taylor; The Entomological Society of Canada; The Entomological Society of Manitoba; The Manitoba Naturalists Society; J. Troubridge; E. Vystrcil; D.M. Wright; and F. Zawislak. We also extend a special note of appreciation to all who have contributed to this work, to the Manitoba Museum of Man and Nature and to Rohm and Haas Canada Inc. who supported the authors in this endeavor.

We are grateful to R.E. Wrigley and V. Hatten who served on the editorial committee for this book, and to P.A. Opler for his valuable suggestions and advice.

Lastly, we extend special thanks to F. Martin Brown, Colorado Springs and J.D. Lafontaine, Canadian National Collection; for their valuable suggestions and assistance in reviewing the manuscript.

Paul Klassen
Richard Westwood
Bill Preston
Brian McKillop

Table of Contents

Introduction

Butterflies in Perspective

In order to understand the genetic and evolutionary relationships of animals, those with similarities are grouped together into a systematic hierarchy. Depending upon the authority, animals are arranged into approximately 26 major groups or phyla (singular – phylum) based mainly upon their body structure. Those with a segmented body and an external skeleton (exoskeleton) are placed in the Phylum Arthropoda (jointed-legged animals), which contains about 75 percent of the Animal Kingdom and is further subdivided into two groups. One group includes horseshoe crabs, arachnids (spiders and relatives), and sea spiders, while the other contains insects, crustaceans, millipedes, centipedes, and a few others. The Class Insecta is characterized by a body divided into three sections (head, thorax and abdomen), three pairs of walking legs, and one pair of antennae. Many insects also possess wings – a marvelous adaptation which greatly expands the organism's mobility and range of possible habitats.

Among the countless kinds of animal life, insects are by far the most abundant, with approximately 1.5 million described species. Some entomologists estimate that there may be five to ten times more that have yet to be discovered. Recent research on tree-canopy insects in South American rain forests, however, has led some entomologists to revise this figure upward to 30 or even 50 million species. Unfortunately, at the present rate of worldwide destruction of tropical rain forests, many of these insects may never be known to science.

The Class Insecta is divided into 31 orders, usually characterized by the type of mouth parts and wings, and often named for the latter. The order Lepidoptera (from the Greek words *lepis* = scale and *pteron* = feather or wing) to which butterflies and moths belong, is characterized by having the mouth parts of the adult usually reduced to a coiled proboscis for sucking liquid food, and scales covering the wings. Orders are further subdivided into families and these into genera (singular – genus) each including one or more species. Species may be further subdivided into subspecies or geographic races, often based on differences in appearance.

The order Lepidoptera is one of the largest insect orders, only exceeded in number of species by the Coleoptera (beetles) and possibly the Diptera (flies). Approximately 200,000 species of Lepidoptera have been described, of which about 17,500 are butterflies and skippers, and the remainder are moths. Butterflies are classified into two superfamilies, Papilionoidea (true butterflies) and Hesperioidea (skippers). In North America north of Mexico, there are nearly 700 species of butterflies and skippers with 272 in Canada and 144 in Manitoba. A few of these are strays or occasional visitors, brought northward from their breeding areas by strong southerly winds.

Depending upon the classification used, up to eight families of butterflies are represented in Manitoba: Hesperiidae (skippers); Papilionidae (swallowtails); Pieridae (whites and sulphurs); Lycaenidae (gossamer-winged butterflies, including harvesters, coppers, blues, elfins and hairstreaks); Heliconiidae (long-wings); Nymphalidae (brush-footed butterflies); Satyridae (browns); and Danaidae (milkweed butterflies). Many authors include the Heliconiidae with the Nymphalidae, and the Satyridae and Danaidae are also sometimes placed as subfamilies of the Nymphalidae by some authors.

Butterfly Names

Common names of plants and animals have never been universally accepted, and often vary from place to place. However numerous attempts have been made to standardize them, the most success having been attained with birds.The system of scientific names, first proposed for animals by Carl von Linnaeus in 1758, has been accepted as the standard by scientists throughout the world. Referred to as binominal or binomial nomenclature, it consists of a combination of two names for every species. The first name, or genus, always begins with a capital, while the second name is the species, actually a descriptive adjective, and is not capitalized. These names are usually derived from Latin or latinized Greek roots, and frequently describe the species in question. Sometimes the name may honor the person who first collected the species, or it may indicate the locality where it was first collected. The scientific name is always italicized or underlined in manuscripts to indicate italics. Following the species name is the author's name – the name of the person or persons who first described that particular species. If, through further study, it has been found necessary to change the genus name, the author's name is placed in parentheses. For example, the Silvery Blue, *Glaucopsyche lygdamus* (Doubleday), was first described by Doubleday under a different genus, *Polyommatus*.

Many species occur in recognizably different populations, in which case a third name – the subspecies or race – is applied, making the name a trinominal or trinomial. For example, in Manitoba there is at least one subspecies of the Silvery Blue, *Glaucopsyche lygdamus couperi* Grote, and possibly another, *Glaucopsyche lygdamus afra* (W.H. Edwards) in the western part of the province. These two subspecies are described by different authors, *couperi* by Grote under the genus *Glaucopsyche*, and *afra* by W.H. Edwards under a different genus. The author's initials are used if there are two or more authors with the same surname.

The reader may note that scientific names vary among publications. The names used in many older works, for example Holland (1905) and Klots (1951), have been outdated due to revisions in which species have been combined or split into several species, older species names discovered and used, and the combining or dividing of genera. With advanced technology additional relationships may be disclosed, necessitating further name changes. We have tended to follow the checklist by Klassen (1984), with revisions from recent literature and from personal communication with a number of authorities, including Opler (in preparation). In an attempt to alleviate confusion we include a short synonymy for every species where more than one name is in current use. For example, while most authors accept *Polites coras* as the scientific name for Peck's Skipper, some lepidopterists prefer *Polites peckius*. Such species known by more than one scientific name are presented as follows:

Peck's Skipper

Polites coras (Cramer), 1775
= *Polites peckius* (W. Kirby), 1837

Butterflies and Moths

The order Lepidoptera includes both butterflies and moths. The difference between them may at first seem obvious, moths being dull coloured and nocturnal and butterflies on the other hand being brightly coloured and diurnal. While this is generally true, there are many moths that rival butterflies in colour and there are also many day-flying species of moths. Butterflies do not fly at night, although occasionally some species may be attracted to lights at night and some butterflies are dull coloured. One of the most reliable methods to distinguish butterflies from moths is examination of the antennae. All butterflies have clubbed antennae. Those of skippers, while not noticeably clubbed, are swollen near the tip with a hooked or curved tip above the swollen portion. The antennae of moths may be thread-like or feather-like, and at most swollen, never clubbed near the tips at least in North American species. Butterflies tend to have slender bodies which are lightly to moderately covered in hair-like scales, whereas moths usually have thicker bodies often covered in dense tufts of hair-like scales. Skippers have bodies that are intermediate in appearance between butterflies and moths.

The Life History of Butterflies

Butterflies and moths belong to the group of insects that are holometabolous, that is those with complete metamorphosis. In this group, which also includes the Coleoptera (beetles), Neuroptera (lacewings), Mecoptera (scorpionflies), Diptera (flies), Siphonaptera (fleas), Trichoptera (caddisflies) and Hymenoptera (ants, bees and wasps), the larvae are different in appearance from the adults. The remaining insect orders are either ametabolous, in which the immatures resemble the adults except for size and development of sexual organs (silverfish), or hemimetabolous, in which the immatures (nymphs) resemble the adults, but lack wings and sex organs (cockroaches). This latter group is referred to as having incomplete metamorphosis.

Butterflies lay their eggs either singly or in groups on or near a particular food plant. In some species the eggs overwinter before the larvae hatch (e.g., hairstreaks in the Lycaenidae). In many species however, it is one of the larval stages or the pupal stage that overwinters and for each particular species it is the same stage. A few overwinter in the adult stage. Upon hatching, the young larvae often eat the egg shells. The larvae of Lepidoptera, known as caterpillars, represent the primary feeding and growing stage of the life cycle. During growth the larvae will moult or shed their skin a fixed number of times. The stage between each moult is called an instar and most Manitoba butterflies have five larval instars. In addition to the three pairs of legs on the first three body segments, the thorax, which later develop into the adult legs, there are five pairs of prolegs on the abdomen, which serve as the main walking legs for the larvae.

On reaching maturity the larva ceases feeding and moults, forming a pupa, which in butterflies is called a chrysalis – from the Greek word *chrysos* = "gold" because of the metallic gold colouring often present. The pupal stage has frequently been referred to as a resting stage, however there is intense biological activity occurring as the larval tissues are reorganized into the adult organs and structures.

Many authors, including Klots (1951), Howe (1975), Pyle (1981) and Scott (1986) provide in depth descriptions of butterfly anatomy, wing venation and sex determination. The reader is urged to consult these works for additional information on butterfly biology and anatomy.

Many butterfly species have one generation per year, for example the Great Copper (*Lycaena xanthoides*). Some species may have two generations per year in warmer areas of their geographic range, but only one in cooler northern localities, (e.g., the angle-wings, *Polygonia spp.*). Others like the Cabbage Butterfly (*Pieris rapae*) may have several generations per year. There are some species that require two years to complete their life cycle, such as Macoun's Arctic (*Oeneis macounii*) in which adults are present only in even-numbered years in southeastern Manitoba. Here the larvae of Macoun's Arctic hatch in an even-numbered summer, feed, and hibernate over their first winter. The larvae resume feeding in the second summer and hibernate once again during their second winter, pupating in the spring and emerging as adults shortly thereafter. In the western part of the province adults appear in odd-numbered years.

Manitoba as an Environment for Butterflies

The province of Manitoba, 650,000 square kilometres in area, is situated between 49 degrees and 60 degrees north latitude and the meridians of 89 degrees and 102 degrees. The province is bordered on the south by North Dakota and Minnesota, on the east by Ontario, on the west by Saskatchewan, and on the north by the Northwest Territories and Hudson Bay. Topographically the province is very flat, tilting from sea level along the Hudson Bay coast in the northeast to generally over 600 metres elevation in the southwest.

The largest, and also the oldest, part of Manitoba consists of the Precambrian Shield, which extends from the southeast corner northward along the east side of Lake Winnipeg, swinging westward beyond the north end of the lake, but excluding the lowlands immediately south of Hudson Bay. The Precambrian Shield, seldom exceeds 30 metres in relief and lies between 120 metres elevation in the southeast and 240 metres in the northwest.

The Hudson Bay Lowlands, south of Hudson Bay, consist of an undulating plain overlain with marine clays deposited when this area was submerged beneath the sea. The area is poorly drained, much of it being low and swampy. The Lowlands are underlain by Paleozoic limestones and represent

Map 1: Manitoba Biomes: Vegetation Zones

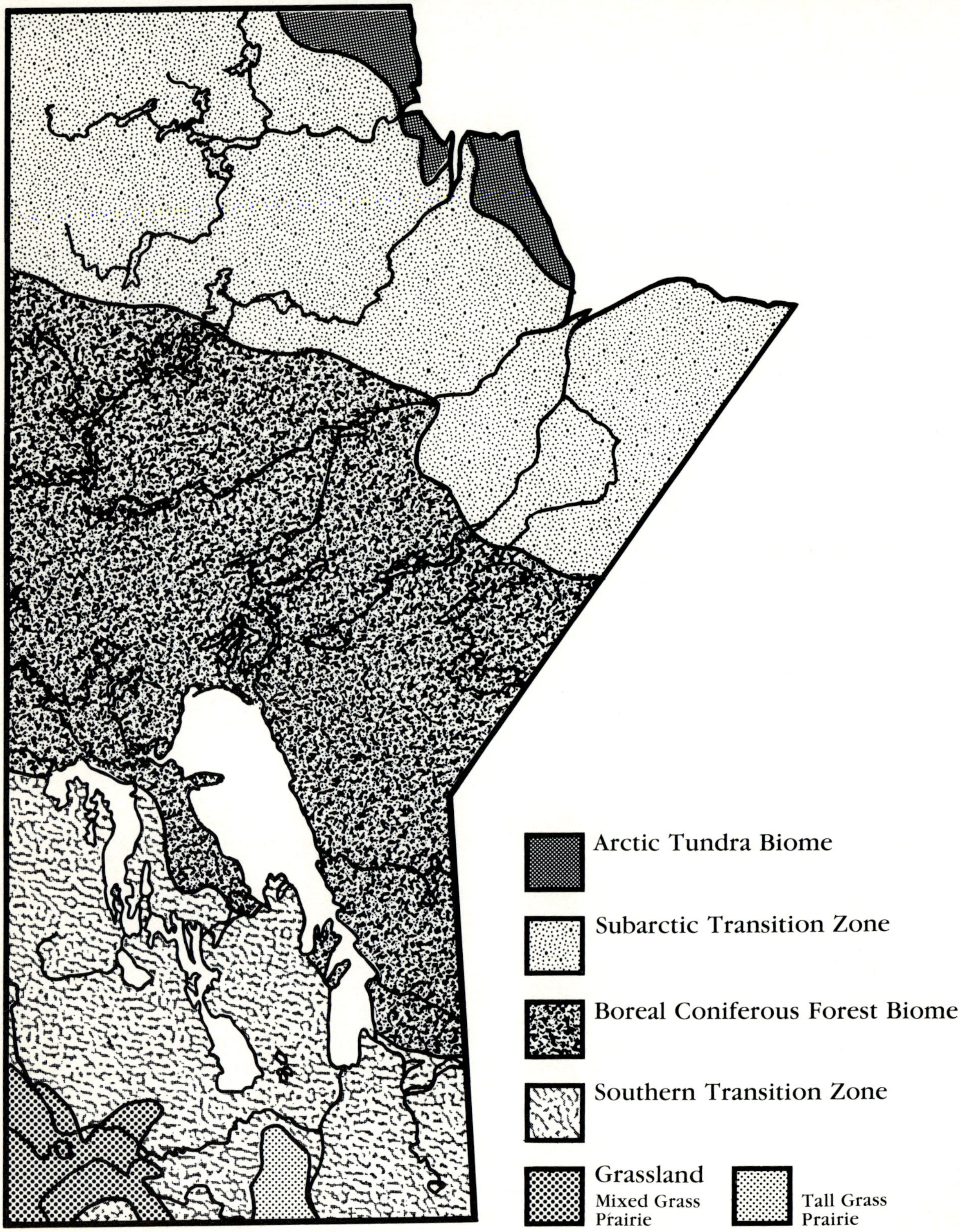

Hudson Bay Lowlands

the second-oldest geological formation in the province.

The Manitoba Lowlands, the flattest part of the province, with a relief of generally less than eight metres, lie in the central part of the province between Lake Winnipeg, Lake Winnipegosis and Lake Manitoba, and extend west of the latter. These lakes are the remnants of glacial Lake Agassiz which once covered much of south and central Manitoba. Like the Hudson Bay Lowlands the Manitoba Lowlands are also underlain by Paleozoic limestones. The elevation here is generally between 210 and 270 metres.

The greatest relief is provided by the Southwestern Upland, which is underlain with Mesozoic rocks and Pleistocene morainal deposits. Four hills in this region rise above 600 metres in elevation. Three of these hills, Porcupine, Duck and Riding Mountains, form the Manitoba Escarpment, with the highest point at 839 metres in the Duck Mountains. Turtle Mountain, at 757 metres, is an erosional remnant, capped by rocks of the Eocene age and by Pleistocene morains.

Approximately 12,000 years ago, the glaciers retreated from southwestern Manitoba and the melt water formed glacial Lake Agassiz. Great volumes of sand were deposited in a delta by the Assiniboine River and winds shaped the delta sand into dunes in the area now occupied by Spruce Woods Provincial Park.

The climate of Manitoba is cool, with mean annual temperatures ranging from -7.9 °C in the northeastern corner to 2.9 °C in the south-central and southwestern regions. In July, the warmest month, the mean daily temperature ranges from 12.5 °C in the northeast corner to 20 °C in the south-central region. Probably of more importance to butterflies, however, is the length of the growing season, which ranges from 70 frost-free days in the northeast to 120 frost-free days in the south-central region.

The mean annual precipitation, including snowfall equivalents, ranges from 356 mm (with 178 mm between June and August) in the north to 559 mm (with 229 mm between June and August) in the southeastern corner of the province. The mean annual precipitation in the southwest is between 406 and 457 mm with approximately 229 mm of this occurring between June and August. The mean potential evapo-transpiration, or the potential amount of water lost through evaporation and transpiration by plants, ranges from 406 mm in the northeast to 559 mm in the south-central and southwestern regions, most of which occurs during the summer. The greatest moisture deficit, and therefore the driest region of the province is in the southwestern corner.

Reflecting the climate are the vegetational types of the province, represented by three biomes or major ecological communities (Map I). Along the coast of Hudson Bay, in the northeast corner, is the Arctic Tundra Biome. Sedges, rushes and lichens predominate, with grasses in the drier areas.

There are scattered groups of stunted spruce, tamarack, willows and birches. A profusion of flowers covers the tundra during the short summer. This area is still largely untouched by civilization and contains a number of species of butterflies found nowhere else in the province. Typical species of the Arctic Tundra Biome include: Arctic, Nastes and Giant Sulphurs; Arctic Blue; Polaris, Frigga and Purple Lesser Fritillaries; Ross' and Theano Alpines; Arctic Grayling; and Melissa and Polixenes Arctics.

To the south of the Arctic Tundra lies the Subarctic Transition Zone (forest-tundra), characterized in upland areas by scattered black spruce, low shrubs and an underlying mat of lichens. Large areas are covered by bog and muskeg. This zone merges with the Boreal Coniferous Forest Biome, also known as taiga, which occupies the middle third of the province. The taiga is dominated by black spruce, white spruce, tamarack, jack pine and balsam fir. Numerous lakes, rivers, streams and bogs, as well as rock outcrops, are interspersed through the boreal forest. Like the tundra, this area is largely uninhabited. Typical butterflies include the Grizzled Skipper; Old World Swallowtail; Veined White; Ausonides Marble; Giant, Pink-edged and Palaeno Sulphurs; Dorcas Copper; Spring Azure; Frigga and Freija Fritillaries; Green and Hoary Commas; Disa and Red-disked Alpines and Jutta Arctic.

Southward, the Boreal Coniferous Forest Biome merges through a Southern Transition Zone of mixed woodlands and parklands, with the Grassland Biome. Important trees in the transition zone include trembling aspen, paper birch, Manitoba maple, burr oak in sandy areas, and green ash, American elm, willow and cottonwood along the rivers. Much of the area has been cleared for agriculture, although extensive stands still remain along rivers. Further south, stands or "bluffs" of trembling aspen are interspersed with grassland, forming a parkland. Typical butterflies of the Southern Transition Zone include the Northern Cloudy Wing; Dreamy, Sleepy and Juvenal's Dusky Wings; Tawny-edged, Hobomok, Dun, and Roadside Skippers; Tiger Swallowtail; Pink Edged Sulphur; Dorcas Copper; Brown, Hoary and Pine Elfins; Western Tailed, Silvery and Greenish Blues; Great Spangled, Atlantis, Aphrodite, Meadow and Silver-bordered Fritillaries; Silvery and Harris's Checkerspots; Pearl Crescent; Gray Comma; Compton and Milbert's Tortoiseshells; Mourning Cloak; White Admiral; Little Wood Satyr; Northern Pearly Eye; Common Alpine and Macoun's Arctic.

Once more extensive than at present, the grassland has been encroached upon by the aspen parkland, which was once limited by prairie fires and by the grazing of large herds of bison. Native grassland is represented by tall-grass prairie in the Red River Valley and by mixed-grass prairie in the more arid southwest. Intensive agriculture has left only remnants of these prairie communities, especially the tall-grass prairie. Virgin prairie is the most endangered habitat in Manitoba and several butterfly species are more or less limited to this habitat. Typical butterflies include the Long Dash; Pawnee, Assiniboia, Garita, Peck's and Dusted Skippers; Western Checkered White; Common Sulphur; Alfalfa Butterfly; Great, Bronze and Purplish Coppers; Orange Bordered, Greenish and Arctic Blues; Variegated and Aphrodite Fritillaries; Gorgone Checkerspot; Eyed Brown; Prairie Ringlet; Common Wood Nymph, and Alberta and Uhler's Arctics.

In the southeastern corner of the province, elements from a fourth biome, the Eastern Deciduous Forest Biome, are represented through a zone of transition between the boreal coniferous forest and the deciduous forest. Further information on Manitoba geography, climate and vegetation can be found in Davies *et al.* (1962), Kendrew and Currie (1955), Longley (1972), Manitoba Resources Division (1979), Thomas (1953), Weir (1960) and Teller (1984).

Distribution

Several factors affect the distribution of butterflies in Manitoba. Temperature is important, since there are many more species in the south than the north. Moisture is another restrictive factor, as the dry southwestern corner of the province has fewer butterfly species than the wetter southeastern region. Scott (1986) divided North American butterflies into a number of faunas. Manitoba butterflies appear to be derived mainly from three of these: the Arctic/Alpine Fauna, the Boreal Forest Fauna, and the Great Plains Fauna. There is also some representation from the

Eastern Deciduous Forest Fauna, for example the Harvester, Banded Hairstreak, Henry's Elfin, and Baltimore. Our butterfly distribution ultimately depends upon the distribution of larval food plants, which in turn is governed by environmental factors such as temperature, moisture, and soil type.

The Southern Transition Zone contains the greatest number of butterfly species – 132, of which 22 species occur only in this area. The Grassland and Boreal Coniferous Forest Biomes each have 82 species, with 2 species restricted to the former and none to the latter. The Arctic Tundra Biome has 47 species with 6 species restricted to it, while the Subarctic Transition Zone has 44 species with none restricted to it. Two families in particular, the Pieridae and the Satyridae, are well-represented in the Arctic Tundra Biome and the Subarctic Transition Zone. Due to limited accessibility species distribution records are poor for the east side of Lake Winnipeg and the northern part of the province, with the exception of the Churchill area.

Conservation

Butterflies are closely associated with their food plants, especially the larvae or caterpillars. Some species are host specific, that is the caterpillar can feed on one plant genus or species only. Such butterfly species may be very limited in their distribution. For example, the larva of the Bog Copper (*Lycaena epixanthe*) feeds only on cranberry (*Oxycoccus* sp.), which occurs in isolated bogs in Manitoba. However these bogs occur in areas that are buffered from environmental disturbance and the food plant, cranberry, is common within the bogs. Conversely, a species whose habitat is extremely limited and easily disturbed is very susceptable to extinction. For example, the development of the San Francisco Peninsula in California destroyed the sand dune habitat of the Xerces Blue, resulting in the extinction of this butterfly in 1943. The Xerces Society, active in the conservation of terrestrial arthropods and their habitats, takes its name from this butterfly. Destruction of habitat through development is currently affecting a number of other butterfly species.

Collecting is not known to have ever resulted in the extinction of an invertebrate species. By far the greatest threat is habitat destruction, due either to human or natural causes. There is little value in protecting endangered or threatened species unless the habitat is protected as well, and usually, for invertebrates, this may be all that is required. The most threatened habitats in Manitoba are virgin prairie, including both mixed-grass and especially tall-grass prairie. A number of species are confined to this habitat, including the Dakota Skipper, Pawnee Skipper, Dusted Skipper, and Riding's Satyr. Although none of these species appears to be extirpated as yet, Riding's Satyr has not been reported from Manitoba since 1953.

The Lepidopterists' Society, in response to a request from its membership, has produced a set of guidelines intended to encourage ethical practices in the collection of Lepidoptera. These guidelines are reproduced in Appendix VI courtesy of the Lepidopterists' Society.

The Study of Butterflies

> "As the laws of nature must be the same for all beings, the conclusions furnished by this group of insects must be applicable to the whole organic world; therefore the study of butterflies – creatures selected as the types of airiness and frivolity – instead of being despised, will some day be valued as one of the most important branches of Biological science."
>
> Henry Walter Bates, 1864 in *The Naturalist on the River Amazons.*

The classical method of studying butterflies was simply to collect them. Collecting is still important, especially in remote, seldom-visited areas, as there is yet much to be learned from butterfly distribution. It is, however, not necessary to kill butterflies in order to study them. Investigations have been conducted by identifying butterflies with binoculars, or netting and releasing them after identification (Knapton 1977). Individuals can also be caught with a net, put into separate glassine envelopes, and transported safely to one's home or laboratory for study. After identification they should be released at the capture site. In this way, as well as through the building of a reference collection, one can become familiar with the butterfly species of a given area. Much can be learned by watching butterflies and observing their behavior and ecological relationships. Lepidopterists make observations on many facets of butterfly behavior; e.g., flower preferences, how activity is affected by time of day and temperature, the effect of wind and other climatic factors. Butterfly counts may be conducted in a particular locality from year to year and results used to construct a calendar of butterfly activity (Preston 1979), to indicate population trends from year to year (Preston and Westwood 1981), or to list butterflies of a particular area (Huber 1981). Lepidopterists often carry out marking studies to estimate population densities or movements. Mapping of butterfly species in limited localities can indicate the presence or absence of critical habitat types.

Rearing and life history studies of butterflies are extremely important for better understanding of butterfly biology and behavior. Photography may be used to document the life stages of butterflies. For a more in-depth discussion on various approaches to the study of butterfly biology the reader is referred to Brewer and Winter (1986), Pyle (1974, 1984), and Scott (1986).

Instructions on pinning and spreading butterflies are given in Appendix I. In addition there are many excellent books on the collection and preservation of butterflies including Bland and Jaques (1978), Brewer and Winter (1986), Erhlich and Erhlich (1961), Klots (1951), Martin (1977) and Tilden and Smith (1986). It is most important to emphasize that essential data (collection date, locality and collector's name) accompany each specimen if it is to have any scientific value. Additional data such as behavioral, ecological, or biological observations are desirable. Collections should be well cared for and protected from light (which can fade specimens), humidity (which can result in mold), and the ravages of pests such as dermestid beetles (McKillop 1978, 1986).

Collecting, between Gillam and Thompson, Manitoba. L-R: B. Glassey; R. Dmytriw; B. McKillop; W. Preston. July 1986.

Early Lepidopterists in Manitoba

The first actual list of insects collected in what is now the province of Manitoba contained 38 species, including 22 butterflies and 16 beetles. This list was published as an appendix to the Biological Survey of Canada in 1880 and documented collections around the Churchill and Nelson Rivers and God's and Island Lakes. The report covered explorations by Dr. Robert Bell, but the insects were actually collected by Archdeacon Kirkby.

One of Manitoba's earliest lepidopterists was E. Firmstone Heath, a farmer who settled near Cartwright in 1882 (Wolley Dod 1916). Heath made a fine collection of the local species and upon his death in 1914 the Manitoba Government purchased his collection and turned it over to the Winnipeg Board of Trade to place in its museum. When the building containing the museum was dismantled, the collection was sent to the Agricultural College in Fort Garry, Winnipeg. It presently resides in the J.B. Wallis Museum, Department of Entomology, University of Manitoba.

Norman Criddle, who settled with his parents at Aweme near Treesbank, Manitoba in 1882, became a renowned naturalist with special interests in botany and entomology. Much of his collection is in the Canadian National Collection, Bio-systematics Research Centre in Ottawa, while some remains in the Manitoba Museum of Man and Nature and at the Agriculture Canada Research Station on the University of Manitoba campus.

During the period of 1883 to 1900, A.W. Hanham of Winnipeg amassed a sizable collection of Lepidoptera which today is in the Royal British Columbia Provincial Museum. At the same time A.J. Dennis of Beulah also began collecting butterflies. Disabled during the World War I, his activity was confined to the immediate area around Beulah. Upon his death in 1946, G. Shirley Brooks purchased the collection and later transferred it and his own collection to the Manitoba Museum.

J.B. Wallis, a school teacher, began collecting insects in 1893 and continued collecting until his death in 1962. Wallis published "A Colour Key to the Manitoban Butterflies" in 1927, believed to be the first comprehensive listing of Manitoba butterflies. Most of his collection is housed in a small museum bearing his name at the Department of Entomology, University of Manitoba. Other specimens are in the Canadian National Collection, the Manitoba Museum of Man and Nature, and the Agriculture Canada Research Station, University of Manitoba campus.

L.H.D. Roberts, who worked for the Canadian National Railway, settled in Manitoba in 1913 and collected beetles and butterflies extensively. Today a small part of his collection is held at the Manitoba Museum of Man and Nature. G. Shirley Brooks, who also worked for the C.N.R., collected from the early 1920's through to the late 1940's near Victoria Beach (Brodie 1969) and made a series of collecting trips to Gillam and Churchill. For several years before his death he was curator of insects at the Manitoba Museum. In 1942 Brooks published "A Check List of the Butterflies of Manitoba", based in part on the collection and listings prepared by D.H. Brodie of Winnipeg. Today both collections are in the Manitoba Museum of Man and Nature.

J.F. May was a forest ranger at Riding Mountain National Park during the 1930's and was an enthusiastic collector of Lepidoptera. He amassed a large collection and gathered worldwide representation through specimen exchange. After moving to Colorado Springs, Colorado, May established a private museum which is still in existence. From the 1930's to the 1950's collections of forest lepidoptera were made across Canada by the Forest Insect Survey. Butterfly species detrimental to forests were reported with accompanying distribution maps and lists of host plants (McGugan 1958). Other collectors from this era include F.H. and R.L. Chermock (Chermock and Chermock 1940).

By the early 1950's, D. Mackie had prepared a significant collection which he donated to the University of Manitoba. During 1954 and 1955, C.D. Bird collected extensively in Whiteshell Provincial Park (Bird 1940; 1956). Bird was the first to discover breeding populations of the Bog Copper (*Lycaena epixanthe*) in Manitoba. Today specimens from his collection can be found in the American Museum of Natural History, Brandon University, Agriculture Canada Research Station, University of Manitoba, and at the Museum of Man and Nature. H.A. Gibbon of Miniota, Manitoba made a fine collection of butterflies and moths, and through exchange and purchase expanded the collection. Today most of this collection forms part of the Canadian National Collection in Ottawa. A sizable collection of both exotic and local specimens was made from the 1940's to the mid 1970's by C.S. Quelch of Winnipeg and was purchased after his death by J. King, also a collector. Most of Quelch's collection was donated to the Transcona Museum in Winnipeg after King passed away in 1987. Some of the specimens collected by Quelch are held in the Agriculture Canada Research Station collection and in the private collection of P. Klassen.

During the early seventies J.H. Masters made several collecting trips to Manitoba and published lists of butterflies taken in various provincial parks and forests (Masters 1971a; 1971b; 1972b; 1972c; 1972d; 1972e). Lastly, the late Dr. R.J. Heron collected in the mid 1970's at Riding Mountain National Park and together with Dr. A.G. Robinson, prepared a report entitled "The Butterflies and Skippers of Riding Mountain National Park, Manitoba". Dr. Heron's collection is held at the Parks Canada office in Wasagaming.

Additional information on Manitoba lepidoptera may be found in Allen (1923), Chermock and Chermock (1968), Hooper (1969), Reeks (1959), Riegert (1980) and Wallis (1954); while information on currently active local lepidopterists may be obtained by writing: The Curator of Entomology, Manitoba Museum of Man and Nature, 190 Rupert Avenue, Winnipeg, Manitoba, R3B ON2.

Superfamily

HESPERIOIDEA: SKIPPERS

Family

HESPERIIDAE

Adult skippers are usually small or medium in size with large heads and stout bodies. The wings of both males and females are often dull coloured and usually black, orange or white. There are over 3000 species of skippers worldwide with approximately 250 occurring in North America, 64 in Canada and 33 in Manitoba.

Skippers have eyes and antennal bases widely separated, generally with many brush-like eyelashes at the base of the antennae. The end of the antenna has a club shaped like a hook with pointed terminally curved segments called the apiculus. The thorax has well developed tegulae over the forewing bases and males often have a divided flap covering the ventral surface of the abdomen. The front legs have a spur called the epiphysis while the middle and hind legs have at least one pair of terminal tibial spurs (Howe 1975). Wings are short and narrow, often with folds, pockets, or hair-like tufts and forewing veins are unbranched arising from the discal cell at the wing base. Although wing patterns are generally reliable for identification, examination of palpi, antennae, legs or genitalia may also be necessary.

The eggs are hemispherical and often covered with finely sculptured patterns. Eggs are usually laid singly on or near the food plant. Mature skipper larvae have large heads, narrow thoraxes and tapering abdomens. The first segment of the thorax is particularly narrow and gives skipper caterpillars the appearance of having a neck. Although naked in appearance all are covered with minute hairs. Most larvae rest in silk and leaf shelters by day and feed at night, often some distance from the shelter. The pupae are smooth and elongate, often with long tongue cases. Larvae pupate within a silken cocoon either within the larval shelter or exposed and attached to the food plant by a silk pad or silk girdle. Skippers feed at flowers, rotting substances or mud.

Subfamily

PYRGINAE: PYRGINES

Skippers belonging to the subfamily Pyrginae are small to medium in size. Members of this subfamily rest with their wings outstretched unlike the Hesperiinae. Adults are checkered black and white or brown to black in colour. Antennae are long, often

Thymelicus lineola

with long and curved clubs. The tibia in the fore and middle legs lack spines (Howe 1975). Males may have a costal fold along the front of each forewing but lack a patch of dark scales known as a forewing brand which occurs in some Hesperiinae. In addition males may also have a dense tuft of hairs on the hind tibia and a divided flap on the thorax covering the base of the abdomen.

Male Pyrgines often perch and some species actively patrol in search of females. Mating occurs in the afternoon and females oviposit from noon onward (Opler and Krizek 1984).

The eggs are ovoid or drum shaped and ribbed both vertically and horizontally. Larvae form folded shelters, feeding only at night. The mature larva have heart-shaped head capsules, often with two eye-spots in front. Most members of this subfamily overwinter as nearly mature larvae within shelters and pupate the following spring in loose cocoons.

Silver-spotted Skipper

Epargyreus clarus (Cramer), 1775

Plate 1 No. 1, 2, 3

Description: 47-53 mm. Our largest skipper has pointed forewings and lobed hindwings, dark brown above with a broad yellowish-orange translucent band on the forewings. Below, the forewings resemble the upperside except for paler outer margins, while the hindwings have a large silvery-white spot in the middle. Males have a costal fold in each forewing.

Life Cycle: Larvae feed on various legumes including False Indigo (*Amorpha fruticosa*), Wild Pea (*Lathyrus palustris*), Beggar's-lice (*Desmodium canadense*), and Hog-peanut (*Amphicarpa bracteata*), all of which are found in Manitoba. Females lay round, ridged green eggs on a plant near the food plant. The larvae move to the food plant after hatching and construct loose nests. The mature larvae are lemon yellow to greenish-brown and marked with green lines and spots. The brown head capsules have two large, round, orange-red spots on the front. The brown pupae are enclosed in loosely constructed cocoons located in litter on the ground (Howe 1975; Ferris 1981; Opler and Krizek 1984). Silver-spotted Skippers overwinter as mature larvae or pupae in tightly-spun shelters (Klots 1951; Pyle 1981).

In Manitoba this species is probably single brooded and adults have been recorded from May 1 to July 22.

Habitat: Scrubby areas in or near open woods, meadows, disturbed areas, river and creek banks where the larval foodplant is present.

Range: Southern British Columbia across southern Canada to New Brunswick and southward through the United States to South America (Howe 1975; Ferris and Brown 1981; Pyle 1981).

Manitoba Records: Brandon, Carberry, Cartwright, Cowan, Culross, Deleau, Kelwood, Killarney, Lyleton, McCreary, Miami, Miniota, Overflowing River, Roseisle, Sand Ridge, Selkirk, Souris, Spruce Woods Provincial Park, Victoria Beach, Whiteshell Provincial Park and Winnipeg.

Subspecies: Two subspecies are recognized. One of them, *Epargyreus clarus clarus* (Cramer), 1775, occurs in southern Canada and all of the United States except Arizona and New Mexico (Howe 1975; Miller and Brown 1981).

Remarks: This large and conspicuous skipper is generally not common in Manitoba but occasionally may be seen in moderate numbers. Adults feed on a wide variety of flowers including Buffalo Berry, Alfalfa, Fleabane, Swamp Milkweed, Thistles, Red Clover and Joe-pye weed. Males often perch on low branches, shrubs or weeds periodically leaving to intercept intruders or other males, later returning to the same perch. Both males and females are very wary and difficult to approach even when feeding.

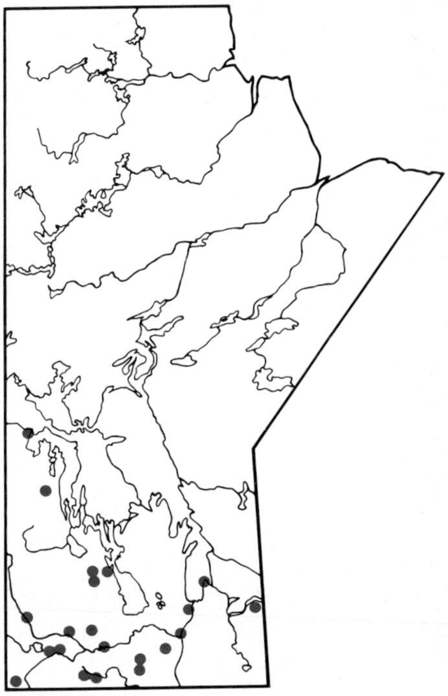

Northern Cloudy Wing

Thorybes pylades (Scudder), 1870

Plate 1 No. 4, 5, 6

Description: 32-40 mm. The wings are an even dark brown above with a number of small, angular, white translucent spots on the forewings. Below, the wings are brown, outwardly suffused with gray and marked similarly to the upper side; two faint dark bands run across the middle of the hindwings. Males have a costal fold in each of the forewings.

Life Cycle: Larval food plants include various legumes including Tick-trefoil (*Desmodium* sp.), Clover (*Trifolium* sp.), Alfalfa (*Medicago sativa*), Milk Vetch (*Astragalus* sp.), Wild Pea (*Lathyrus* sp.), Trefoil (*Lotus* sp.) and Lead plant (*Amorpha* sp.) (Howe 1975).

The round, ridged, white or pale greenish eggs are laid singly on the food plant and hatch in about ten days. The larvae build silken shelters on the food plant where they hide when not feeding. Mature larvae are dark green to dull orange mottled with maroon and have a maroon dorsal stripe with a pink-orange stripe on each side of the body. The cuticle is covered in fine short hairs arising from minute tubercles. Pupation takes place in a silken shelter. The pupae are dark brown with buff wing pads. Northern Cloudy Wings overwinter as mature larvae or pupae (Emmel and Emmel 1973; Howe 1975; Ferris and Brown 1981; Pyle 1981; Opler and Krizek 1984). Adults have been recorded from May 18 to July 17 in Manitoba, being most common in early June. Females appear about a week after the males.

Habitat: Adults can be found in openings or clearings in forested areas or in scrubby areas along forest edges. Forest roads are preferred resting or feeding places.

Range: Across southern and central Canada from the Northwest Territories to Nova Scotia and southward through the United States to south-central Mexico.

Manitoba Records: Agassiz Provincial Forest, Belair, Beulah, Birds Hill, Birtle, Carberry, Cartwright, Cowan, Cranberry Portage, Culross, Denbeigh Point, Duck Mountain, Elm Creek, Flin Flon, Fort Alexander, Gypsumville, Hadashville, Kelwood, Lauder, Marchand, McCreary, Miami, Miniota, Pine Ridge, Riding Mountain, Sandilands Provincial Forest, Selkirk, Stead, Teulon, The Pas, Thompson, Treesbank, Victoria Beach, Wabowden, Whitemouth Lake, Whiteshell Provincial Park and Winnipeg.

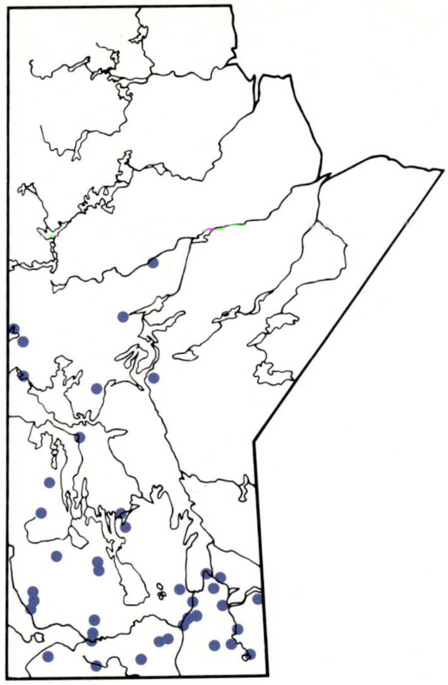

Subspecies: No subspecies are recognized.

Remarks: The Northern Cloudy Wing is wide-spread in Manitoba. Adults frequently perch on or near the ground along forest roads, ditches and the edges of clearings. Because they have a very swift flight adults are best observed while sipping moisture from mud puddles or visiting flowers. They prefer white, pink, purple or blue flowers (e.g. Dogbane, Common Milkweed, Red Clover, Crown Vetch, Purple Vetch or various Thistles).

Dreamy Dusky Wing

Erynnis icelus (Scudder and Burgess), 1870

Plate 1 No. 7, 8, 9

Description: 24-32 mm. This species has short, blunt wings that are blackish to grayish-brown above. The forewings are outwardly suffused with hoary gray and contain a band of darkly outlined spots. The hindwings are dark brown and contain marginal and submarginal rows of pale tan spots. Below, both pairs of wings are dark brown and contain marginal and submarginal rows of pale tan spots. Males have a tibial tuft on each hind leg and a forewing costal fold. Females are generally paler and have more contrasting markings. Dreamy Dusky Wings lack the white, translucent forewing spots found in several other members of this genus.

Similar Species: The Sleepy Dusky Wing is larger, a little less hoary gray with more completely developed forewing bands and less developed tan spots. The palpi of the Sleepy Dusky Wing are shorter, antennal clubs more blunt and males lack tibial tufts; however, examination of the male genitalia may be the only way to differentiate the Sleepy from the Dreamy Dusky Wing.

Life Cycle: Larval food plants include species of Poplar (*Populus* sp.), Willow (*Salix* sp.), and Birch, (*Betula* sp.). The tall, rounded pale green eggs turn pinkish after several days and are laid singly on young suckers or saplings of the food plant. The larvae construct webbed shelters of leaves where they hide when not feeding. When mature, the larvae have stout bodies tapering toward each end and covered with fine, short hairs arising from tiny white tubercles. The head capsules are black, concave on the dorsal surface and covered with reddish and yellowish spots. The mature larvae overwinter in webbed shelters and pupate early the following spring. The pupae are dark brown or greenish in colour.

Adults have been recorded from May 8 to July 11 in Manitoba, being most common in late May in southern Manitoba and later further north. There is one generation a year in Manitoba (Howe 1975; Ferris and Brown 1981; Pyle 1981; Opler and Krizek 1984).

Habitat: Forest edges, clearings, meadows, roads and trails. Also found in scrubby areas on the prairie or where forests have been recently cleared.

Range: The Dreamy Dusky Wing occurs from the southern Northwest Territories and British Columbia across Canada to Nova Scotia and southward to New Mexico (Hooper 1973; Howe 1975).

Manitoba Records: Agassiz Provincial Forest, Aweme, Beulah, Birds Hill, Brokenhead, Carberry, Cartwright, Cowan, Culross, Deleau, Duck Mountain, Elm Creek, Gillam, Gypsumville, Kelwood, Lynn Lake, McCreary, Melbourne, Miniota, Narcisse, Neepawa, Norway House, Pasquia, Pine Ridge, Riding Mountain, Sandilands Provincial Forest, Selkirk, The Pas, Thompson, Turtle Mountain, Victoria Beach, Wabowden, Winnipeg and Whiteshell Provincial Park.

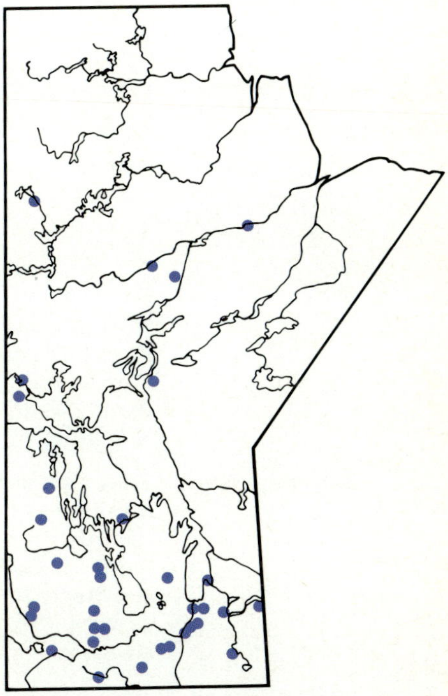

Subspecies: No subspecies are recognized (Dos Passos 1964; Miller and Brown 1981).

Remarks: Dreamy Dusky Wings are common and widespread in southern Manitoba. In spring they are especially common along forest roads, sometimes congregating in large numbers at mud puddles. Specimens seen in oak woods are easily confused with the similar but much less common and more local Sleepy Dusky Wing (which also frequents oak woods). Dreamy Dusky Wings will feed at a variety of flowers, especially legumes and also Blueberry, Strawberry, Vetch, Dogbane and Labrador Tea.

Sleepy Dusky Wing

Erynnis brizo (Boisduval and Leconte), 1834

Plate 1 No. 10, 11, 12

Description: 31-37 mm. The wings are dark brown above, with forewings containing two broken bands of darkly outlined markings suffused with hoary gray scales. The inner band may be poorly defined. The hindwings contain two rows of pale tan spots which may be poorly developed. Below, both pairs of wings are dark brown and contain one to two rows of more or less developed tan spots. Females tend to be slightly larger and paler with more distinct markings.

Similar Species: Dreamy Dusky Wing differs as described under that species.

Life Cycle: The larval food plants of the Sleepy Dusky Wing are various species of oak. In Manitoba the Bur Oak (*Quercus macrocarpa*) is the food plant.

Early stages are similar to those of the Dreamy Dusky Wing. In Manitoba, adults have been recorded from May 1 until June 17 but are most common in mid to late May. There is one generation per year.

Habitat: Dry, open, sandy ridges containing scattered oak trees and open areas (e.g. sandy flats, clearings or roads) in oak forests.

Range: Saskatchewan across to Ontario and southward through most of the United States to northern Mexico (Howe 1975; Opler and Krizek 1984).

Manitoba Records: Agassiz Provincial Forest, Aweme, Beulah, Birds Hill, Birtle, Brandon, Carberry, Cartwright, Elm Creek, La Riviere, Margaret, Narcisse, Pine Ridge, Riding Mountain, Sandilands Provincial Forest, Selkirk, Spruce Woods Provincial Park, Whiteshell Provincial Park and Winnipeg.

Subspecies: Four subspecies are recognized.The nominate subspecies *Erynnis brizo brizo* (Boisduval and Leconte), 1834, occurs from Saskatchewan to Massachusetts southward to Florida, Texas and north-eastern Mexico (Dos Passos 1964; Miller and Brown 1984).

Remarks: The Sleepy Dusky Wing is largely restricted to oak woods and is seldom found far from this habitat. This species is uncommon in Manitoba but when found it is often in association with the Dreamy Dusky Wing feeding at mud puddles. The Sleepy Dusky Wing may also be seen perched on dry ground or low vegetation, basking in the sun. Adults will frequent the flowers of Silver-berry, Dandelion or Blueberry growing in sunny areas on the edges or in clearings of Oak woods.

Juvenal's Dusky Wing

Erynnis juvenalis (Fabricius), 1793

Plate 1 No. 13, 14, 15

Description: 34-40 mm. Above, the forewings are blackish-brown with triangular dark spots and white translucent spots. The hindwings are also dark brown, having long dark hairs that partially obscure two rows of tan spots. Below, both fore and hindwings are dark brown with markings similar to the upper surface, except that the hindwings frequently have two whitish spots in the outer third of the apical area. Females are paler, more brownish, and have more distinct markings and larger white spots. The males have costal folds on the forewings and lack tibial tufts on the hind legs.

Similar Species: The Mottled, Columbine and Persius Dusky Wings are smaller in size, have smaller white spots and lack the two whitish spots on the outer third of the apical area on the underside of the hindwing.

Life Cycle: In Manitoba, the larval food plant is Bur Oak (*Quercus macrocarpa*). The early stages are similar to those of the Dreamy Dusky Wing.

Adults have been recorded from May 13 to June 28 in the province and are most abundant in late May. There is one generation per year in Manitoba.

Habitat: Juvenal's Dusky Wing can be found in openings, clearings, meadows, and on roads adjacent to stands of Bur Oak. They can also be found on dry, sandy, grassy ridges containing Bur Oak or on Hazel bushes surrounding stands of Bur Oak.

Range: Saskatchewan through southern Canada to Nova Scotia and southward through most of the United States, except the Rocky Mountains (Opler and Krizek 1984).

Manitoba Records: Beulah, Birds Hill, Birtle, Brandon, Cartwright, Elm Creek, La Riviere, Margaret, Melbourne, Morden, Pine Ridge, Riding Mountain, Sandilands Provincial Forest, Turtle Mountain, Victoria Beach, Whiteshell Provincial Park and Winnipeg.

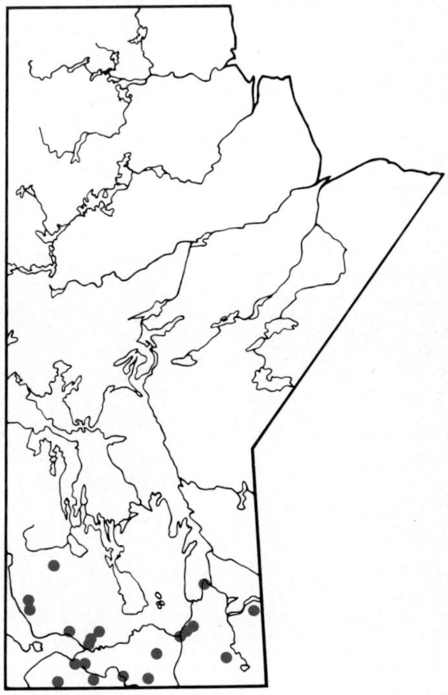

Subspecies: Two subspecies are generally recognized. *Erynnis juvenalis juvenalis* occurs in eastern North America from Saskatchewan to Nova Scotia, southward to Florida and Texas. It is distinguished by having whitish ventral hindwing spots and brown hindwing fringes. The other subspecies, *Erynnis juvenalis clitus*, has white hindwing fringes and usually lacks the whitish ventral hindwing spots.

Remarks: Juvenal's is the largest Dusky Wing found in Manitoba. Adults will visit flowers such as Silverberry, Dandelion and Blueberry for nectar. Although quite wary they perch on the ground or bask in the sun on the more exposed limbs of shrubs or on plants.

Mottled Dusky Wing

Erynnis martialis (Scudder), 1869

Plate 1 No. 16, 17, 18

Description: 27-33 mm. The wings are short and brown and on the upper side are heavily mottled with black. Newly emerged specimens have a purplish sheen. In addition, the forewings have tiny translucent white spots and the hindwings small diffuse tan spots. Below, the wings are brown, mottled with darker brown and small tan spots. Both sexes are similar in appearance, although males have a costal fold and lack tibial tufts. The heavy mottling distinguishes this skipper from all other Dusky Wings found in Manitoba.

Life Cycle: Various species of the genus *Ceanothus* serve as larval food plants including New Jersey Tea (*Ceanothus ovatus*) which occurs in southeastern Manitoba (Scoggan 1957).

The early stages are similar to those described under the Dreamy Dusky Wing. The adult flight period is from May 16 to June 16 in Manitoba and probably consists of a single generation. Two generations have been reported for eastern North America while there is probably one generation per year for the western half of the Mottled Dusky Wing's range.

Habitat: Open wooded areas and scrubby fields. In Sandilands Provincial Forest adults were found along forest roads.

Range: Southern Manitoba, Ontario and Quebec in Canada, southward to Georgia, Mississippi and Texas. The Mottled Dusky Wing has also been recorded from the Black Hills, South Dakota and Colorado (Howe 1975; Opler and Krizek 1984).

Manitoba Records: Falcon Lake, Marchand, Sandilands Provincial Forest and Whiteshell Provincial Park.

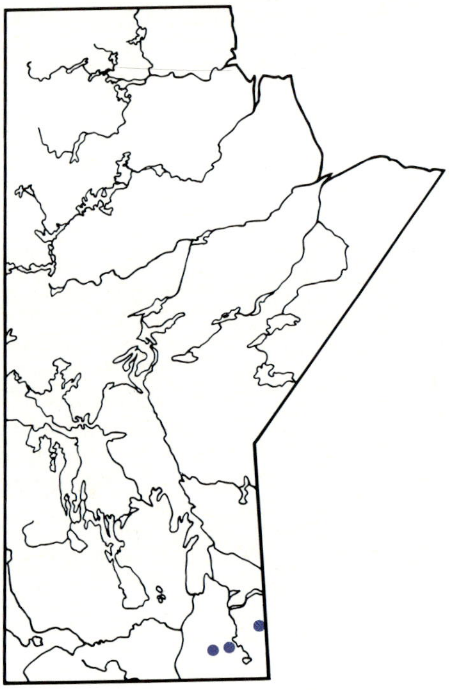

Subspecies: There are no subspecies recognized (Miller and Brown 1981).

Remarks: This species is probably the most easily recognized Dusky Wing found in the province. The first specimen was collected by Mr. and Mrs. C.S. Quelch on June 12, 1964 in Sandilands Provincial Forest. All other Manitoba specimens (14 by P. Klassen and two by R. Westwood) are from Sandilands Forest or the nearby Whiteshell Provincial Park. Specimens were collected along forest roads, mostly at mud puddles and often in association with the more abundant Dreamy Dusky Wing.

Columbine Dusky Wing

Erynnis lucilius (Scudder and Burgess), 1870

Plate 1 No. 20, 21

Description: 22-32 mm. This species has short, rounded wings which are blackish-brown basally and paler brown toward the outer margins. The forewings contain a dark band with white translucent spots. The hindwing bands contain more or less suffused tan spots. Below, the wings are brown with two rows of tan spots. Males have a tibial tuft on each hind leg.

Similar Species: The Persius Dusky Wing is larger, has longer wings and in males the forewings contain raised hairs that partially obscure the basal markings (giving the wings a soft appearance). Often examination of genitalia is essential for accurate identification.

Life Cycle: Larvae have been reported to feed only on Columbine (*Aquilegia* sp.). The preferred species of food plant in southern Manitoba is the Wild Columbine (*Aquilegia canadensis*), while in northern Manitoba the Small-flowered Columbine (*Aquilegia brevistyla*) may serve as the host plant.

Early stages are similar to those described for the Dreamy Dusky Wing. In Manitoba, adults have been recorded from June 22 to July 27. This species has two or three generations, probably dependent on geographical location (Howe 1975; Opler and Krizek 1984).

Habitat: Gullies and ravines in deciduous or mixed forests and along rocky outcrops bordering forested areas.

Range: Manitoba and Minnesota eastward to Quebec and southward to New Jersey, Pennsylvania and Kentucky (Howe 1975; Pyle 1981).

Manitoba Records: Gillam, Mile 349 and Mile 412 on the Hudson Bay Railway, Sandilands Provincial Forest, Thompson and Whiteshell Provincial Park.

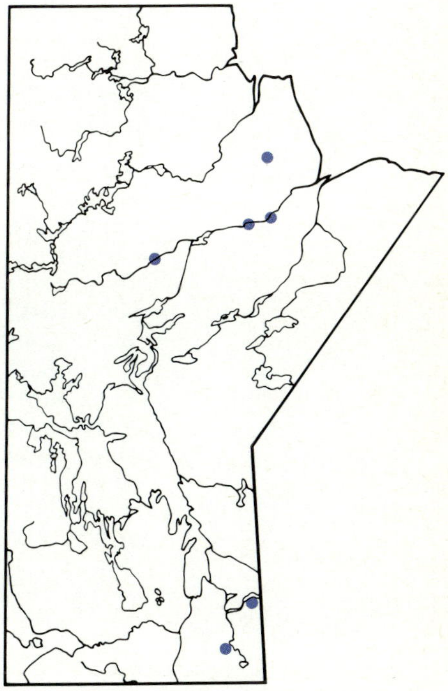

Subspecies: No subspecies are recognized (Howe 1975; Miller and Brown 1981).

Remarks: *Erynnis lucilius* is Manitoba's smallest Dusky Wing and it is most easily differentiated from similar species by its close affinity for its food plant. This skipper has rarely been found in Manitoba and is best looked for along forest roads, trails and openings, often on bare ground or at mud puddles.

Persius Dusky Wing

Erynnis persius (Scudder), 1863

Plate 1 No. 19, 23, 24, 25, 26

Description: 28-33 mm. Adults are dark brown above. Raised hairs on the forewings of the males partially obscure the darker markings at the base of the wings. In both sexes, the forewings have a series of small white translucent dots and the hindwings have two rows of suffused tan spots. Below, the wings are brown, with tan spots similar to those of the upper side. Males have a basal hind tibial tuft and a costal fold on each forewing. Females are generally paler and have more distinct markings.

Similar Species: Columbine Dusky Wing differs as described under that species.

Life Cycle: Willow (*Salix* sp.) and Poplar (*Populus* sp.) are probably the larval food plants in Manitoba. Early stages are similar to those described for the Dreamy Dusky Wing (Howe 1975; Opler and Krizek 1984).

In Manitoba, adults occur from May 21 to July 14. There is one generation per year.

Habitat: Openings and edges of boreal forests. In Manitoba, forest trails and roads are preferred, especially those passing through boggy areas.

Range: Alaska, Yukon and Northwest Territories across Canada to Quebec, southward to Virginia, New Mexico, Arizona and California (Howe 1975; Opler and Krizek 1984).

Manitoba Records: Beulah, Birtle, Churchill, Cowan, Duck Mountain, Gillam, Leaf Rapids, Riding Mountain, Sandilands Provincial Forest and Thompson.

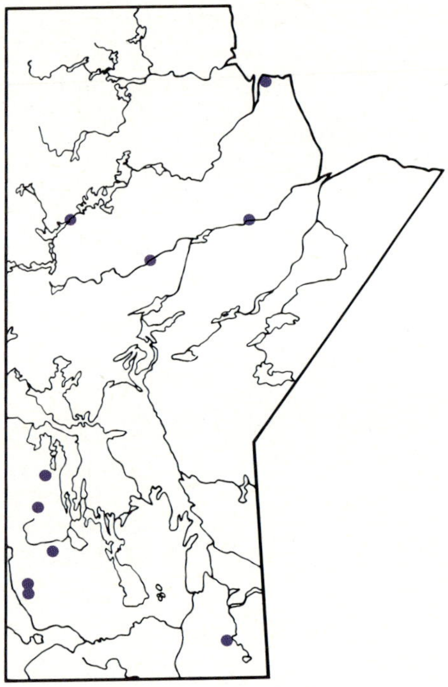

Subspecies: Three or four subspecies are recognized. The status of some of the subspecies is still under investigation. Specimens from Manitoba are *Erynnis persius fredericki* (Dos Passos 1964; Howe 1975; Miller and Brown 1981).

Remarks: The Persius Dusky Wing has been collected in small numbers in Manitoba. It may have been overlooked because it is often found together with the more abundant Dreamy Dusky Wing from which it is difficult to distinguish. The Persius Dusky Wing is sometimes locally common in the Riding Mountain area where individuals may be seen along roads and trails, perched on bare ground, sipping at mud puddles or visiting flowers. In areas of virgin prairie, it also flies along the edges of poplar groves, taking nectar at Locoweed (Hooper 1973).

Grizzled Skipper

Pyrgus centaureae (Rambur), 1840

Plate 2 No. 1, 2, 3

Description: 24-28 mm. Above, the wings are brownish-black with angular white spots and checkered fringes. The white spots are suffused on the hindwings. Below, the wings are paler, with more extensive white markings forming several complete bands on each hindwing. Males have a narrow costal fold and a hind tibial tuft.

Similar Species: The Common Checkered Skipper is larger with more extensive white areas (the white spots form continuous bands) on the upperside. Below, the wings of the Common Checkered Skipper are olive coloured with extensive white bands.

Life Cycle: Little is known about the early stages of the Grizzled Skipper, especially the subspecies occurring in Manitoba. The host plant is Cloudberry (*Rubus chamaemorus*), and probably Wild Strawberry (*Fragaria virginiana*) (Pyle 1981; Opler and Krizek 1984; Scott 1986).

In Manitoba, adults have been recorded from May 19 until July 15, usually being most common in early July. The species is common in odd-numbered years in Manitoba, and very rarely seen in even-numbered years. The Grizzled Skipper may require two years to complete its life cycle here.

Habitat: Forest edges and openings as well as mixed scrub/heath tundra. At Churchill, the Grizzled Skipper occurs mostly in the taiga zone, adjacent to or in boggy areas, or less commonly in scrubby willow thickets on the tundra.

Range: Europe and Asia and in North America from Alaska through subarctic Canada to Newfoundland and southward in the Rocky Mountains to New Mexico (Opler and Krizek 1984).

Manitoba Records: Churchill, Cowan, Duck Mountain, Falcon Lake, Gillam, Lynn Lake, Pikwitonei, Porcupine Provincial Forest, Sandilands Provincial Forest, The Pas and Whiteshell Provincial Park.

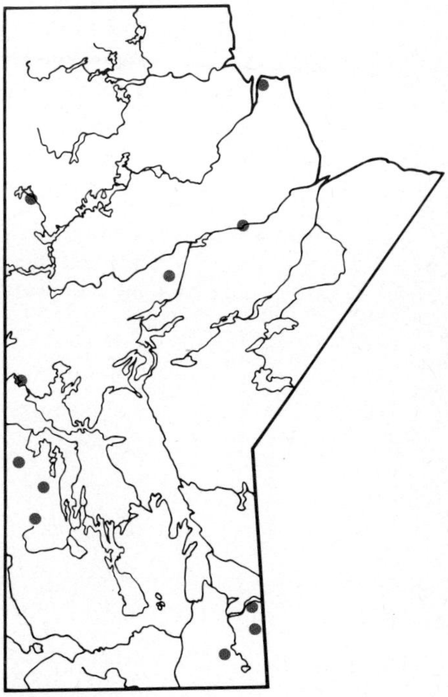

Subspecies: Two subspecies are recognized in Eurasia and three in North America. Only *Pyrgus centaureae freija* occurs in Manitoba and is characterized by having larger "squarish" white spots above, and more distinctly marked black and white areas below in comparison to the other North American subspecies. It is mainly confined to the boreal forests and taiga areas of Canada (Howe 1975).

Remarks: The Grizzled Skipper is quite local in occurrence. Although this skipper has been collected in small numbers at Churchill, it is rare in southern Manitoba. Adults reportedly feed on Canada Cinquefoil, Wild Strawberry, Blueberry and other low growing flowering plants. Those at Churchill have not been observed at flowers. In the Yukon adults were observed at mud puddles or on bare ground but rarely at flowers. When disturbed, they fly into nearby underbrush and often reappear on the wing some distance away, eventually returning to the original perch (Oosting and Parshall 1978; Opler and Krizek 1984).

Common Checkered Skipper

Pyrgus communis (Grote), 1872

Plate 2 No. 4, 5, 6

Description: 26-34 mm. The wings are brownish-black above, extensively marked with bands of white spots. Below, the forewings have gray and/or olive-gray bands (the olive-gray colour is generally confined to the wing tip). Olive-gray bands are also found on the hind wings. Females are larger and darker than males, with less extensive white markings on the upper surface. Males have a costal fold but lack hind tibial tufts.

Similar Species: The Grizzled Skipper differs as described under that species.

Life Cycle: The larvae feed on Mallows (Malvaceae), including Scarlet Mallow (*Malvastrum coccineum*), Rose-mallow (*Hibiscus* sp.), Curled Mallow (*Malva verticillata*) and Round-leaved Mallow (*Malva rotundifolia*) (Scoggan 1957; Howe 1975; Opler and Krizek 1984).

The rounded, hemispherical eggs are greenish-white, turning to cream prior to hatching. When not feeding, the larvae rest in shelters made of a host plant leaf tied together with silk. The mature larvae are yellowish-white to brownish with one dark and two brown dorsal stripes and two white lateral stripes. The cuticle is covered with tiny tubercles, containing small, white hairs. The head capsules are black and thickly covered in yellowish-brown hairs. *Pyrgus communis* overwinters as a mature larva. The pupae are pale green with light brown abdomens streaked and spotted with black (Howe 1975).

In Manitoba, adults have been recorded from May 21 to October 1 and may be encountered sporadically any time between those dates. There are probably two or three staggered generations per year in Manitoba.

Habitat: Disturbed open areas, weedy fields, meadows, farmyards and gardens. The Common Checkered Skipper may also be found in open Pine woods and other areas with bare ground and low vegetation.

Range: British Columbia eastward to Ontario and New York state. Southward through the United States to Argentina.

Scarlet Mallow,
Malvastrum coccineum.

Manitoba Records: Aweme, Beulah, Birtle, Cartwright, Culross, Glenboro, La Salle, Lyleton, Miami, Riding Mountain and Winnipeg.

Subspecies: Generally one subspecies is recognized in North America, that being the nominate *Pyrgus communis communis*. *Pyrgus albescens* occurring in the southern United States and Mexico, is considered a subspecies of the Common Checkered Skipper by some lepidopterists (Dos Passos 1964; Emmel and Emmel 1973; Miller and Brown 1981).

Remarks: Although not common in Manitoba this species can be found in lawns and gardens, perched on the grass or feeding on flowers. Adults prefer white-flowered composites such as Fleabane, Aster and Shepherd's Needle in natural areas. Like the Grizzled Skipper this species is easily overlooked, being inconspicuous in flight and when perched on the ground.

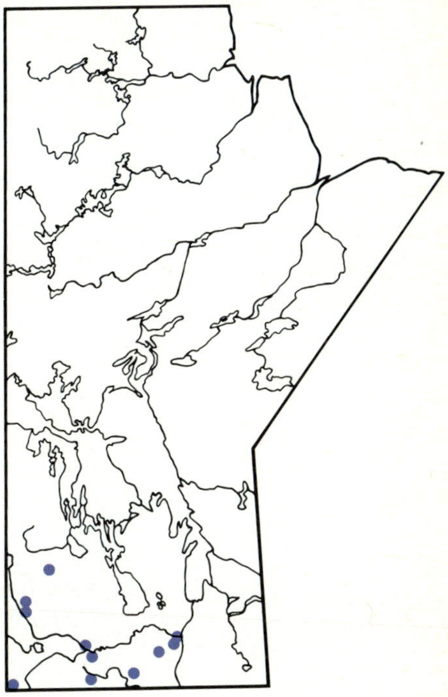

Subfamily

HETEROPTERINAE: DELICATE SKIPPERS

There are two genera within the subfamily Heteropterinae in North America and many others in the Old World. The only species of Heteropterinae that occurs in Manitoba is the Arctic Skipper. F.M. Brown (personal communication) notes that the two genera stand apart from the rest of the Family Hesperiidae in size, shape and structure. In general, Heteropterinae are more delicate and have more slender bodies with abdomens extending beyond the hindwings.

Arctic Skipper

Carterocephalus palaemon (Pallas), 1771

Plate 2 No. 10, 11, 12

Description: 22-29 mm. Above, the wings are dark brown with distinct orange patches and spots. Below, the forewings are orange with brown or dull blackish spots. The hindwings are yellowish-orange to brownish-orange with conspicuous brown-edged cream coloured spots. Markings vary between individuals. Females are larger and darker than males, who lack a stigma (or brand) on the upper forewings. The antennal clubs of both sexes are blunt.

Life Cycle: The larvae of the Arctic Skipper will feed on a wide variety of grasses, preferring broad-leaved species. Females have been known to oviposit on Purple Reedgrass (*Calamagrostis purpurascens*) in California and will lay eggs on Kentucky Blue Grass (*Poa pratensis*) in captivity. In Europe, the Arctic Skipper prefers Brome grasses (*Bromus* sp.) as host plants (Howe 1975; Opler and Krizek 1984). In Manitoba, Kentucky Blue Grass and several species of Brome grass are quite common, while Purple Reedgrass is uncommon, known only from Nueltin Lake (Scoggan 1957).

The greenish-white eggs are laid directly on the food plant and the larvae construct webbed leaf shelters. After the fourth instar molt the larvae move from the shelter and lie exposed on the leaves of the host plant. The mature larvae are green to cream coloured with a dark green dorsal stripe and a pale, yellowish lateral stripe with a row of black spots below the lateral stripe. Head capsules are whitish or green. Arctic Skippers overwinter as mature larvae (Howe 1975; McCabe and Post 1977; Morris 1980; Ferris and Brown 1981; Opler and Krizek 1984).

In Manitoba, adults are on the wing from May 19 until July 9 and most common in mid-June in southern parts of the province. There is one generation per year.

Habitat: Trails, roads, glades and openings in forests or on forest edges.

Range: Asia, Europe and in North America from Alaska eastward through the forested areas of Canada to Newfoundland. From Newfoundland, southward to Pennsylvania and then westward to California (Howe 1975; Ferris *et al.* 1983).

Manitoba Records: Agassiz Provincial Forest, Aweme, Brandon, Brokenhead, Cartwright, Cowan, Duck Mountain, Elm Creek, Fort Alexander, Gimli, Grand Rapids, Kelwood, Lake William, Miami, Norway House, Pine Ridge, Porcupine Provincial Forest, Riding Mountain, Roseisle, Rounthwaite, Sandilands Provincial Forest, Selkirk, Seven Sisters, Souris, The Pas, Thompson, Victoria Beach, Vivian, Whiteshell Provincial Park and Winnipeg.

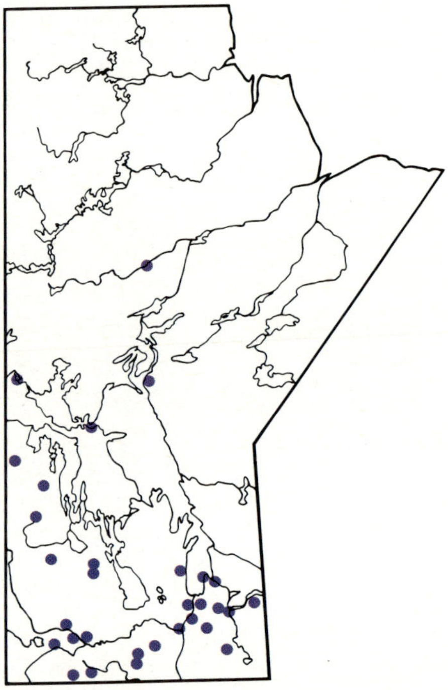

Subspecies: Generally one subspecies is recognized in North America, namely *Carterocephalus palaemon mandan* (Dos Passos 1964; McCabe and Post 1977; Miller and Brown 1981). It is of interest to note that the North American subspecies was named from specimens found on the outskirts of Winnipeg, at Pine Ridge by W. H. Edwards in 1863.

Remarks: The Arctic Skipper is locally common in Manitoba, but seldom is seen in large numbers. Adults can be encountered along forest roads and trails perched on low grass or visiting flowers nearby. Unlike most of the Manitoban skippers, the Arctic Skipper has a slow flight and alights quite often. Agassiz Provincial Forest is a good area to look for this species.

Subfamily

HESPERIINAE: BRANDED SKIPPERS

This subfamily includes small orange or brown skippers. Males often have a "brand" of specialized scales on the upperside of the forewings, but never a costal fold or a hind tibial tuft. Many species in the Hesperiinae may have spines on the mid or hind tibia. The antennal clubs end in a sharply curved apiculus, palpi are short and blunt and the proboscis is often as long or longer than the forewings. Mating and oviposition usually occur from mid to late afternoon. Members of the Hesperiinae readily visit flowers including those with deep sources of nectar. When resting adults frequently separate the hindwings from the forewings.

Larvae generally feed on monocotyledons, predominantly grasses and sedges. The eggs are hemispherical, with the width much greater than the length. The surface of the eggs may be smooth or finely pitted, but never ribbed. Larvae feed at night within a silk and leaf shelter or at the base of the food plant clump. The mature larvae will often overwinter and pupate in the leaf shelter. Last instar larvae have narrow egg-shaped head capsules, narrow bodies and often several lateral stripes (Howe 1975; Opler and Krizek 1984).

Assiniboia Skipper on mud near Rivers, Manitoba. August 1988.

Least Skipper

Ancyloxypha numitor (Fabricius), 1793

Plate 2 No. 13, 14, 15

Description: 21-25 mm. The upper side of the Least Skipper's forewings is dark brown suffused with golden-orange basally and along the costal margin; the underside is black with an orange upper margin and apex. Males lack forewing brands. The hindwings are golden-orange with wide brownish-black borders above and uniformly orange below. The antennae are short with blunt clubs and the abdomens are long and slender.

Life Cycle: The larval food plants are various grasses, including Blue Grass (*Poa* sp.) and Rice Cutgrass (*Leersia oryzoides*).

The eggs are bright yellow when laid, with an orange-red band appearing around the middle prior to larval hatch. The mature larvae are pale grass-green, covered with short, fine hairs and have dark brown head capsules, mottled with light spots. The pupae are cream coloured with brown stripes and spots and have wide blunt heads (Harris 1972; Howe 1975).

In Manitoba, the adult flight period extends from June 24 to August 26. The Least Skipper is most common in early July. Two or three generations per year are reported for this species in its southern range, so there may be one or two generations per year in this province.

Habitat: Moist areas containing tall grasses and sedges, such as stream and river banks, ditches, lake margins or marshes. In Manitoba, adults have been found on overgrown roads or trails passing through wet areas of mixed forest.

Range: Saskatchewan to Nova Scotia, southward to Florida, the Gulf States and Texas (Opler and Krizek 1984).

Manitoba Records: Agassiz Provincial Forest, Aweme, Berens River, Beulah, Birtle, Dawson Bay, Katimik Lake, Husavik, Ninette, Oak Hammock, Overflowing River, Pine Ridge, Riding Mountain, Sandilands Provincial Park, Selkirk, Tolstoi, Victoria Beach, Whiteshell Provincial Park and Winnipeg.

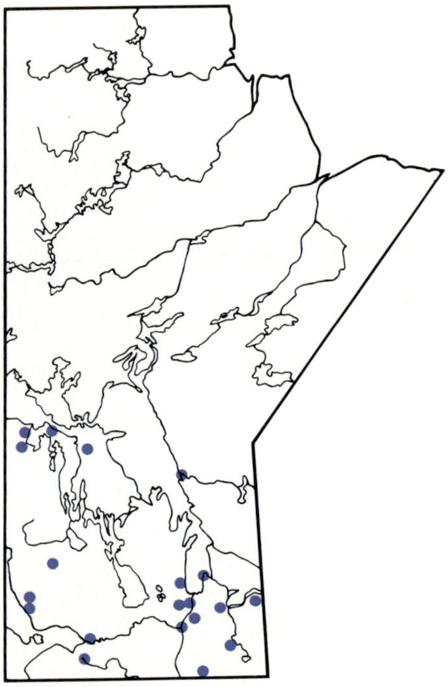

Subspecies: No subspecies are recognized.

Remarks: The Least Skipper is easily overlooked because of its small size and habit of flying weakly down among tall grasses. Adults usually occur near water where they perch on tall grasses and visit various flowers including Arrow Wood, Fleabane, Dogbane and White Clover. The Least Skipper is locally common along the forest roads of Agassiz Provincial Forest.

Powesheik Skipper

Oarisma powesheik (Parker), 1870

Plate 2 No. 16, 17, 18

Description: 25-32 mm. The wings are dark brown on the upper side. Forewings are suffused with golden orange along the upper margin while below, they are black with orange suffusion along the upper margins and near the apex. The hindwings are grayish with conspicuous silvery-white veins and with the inner third of the margins marked in black. The antennae are short and have blunt clubs. Males lack a forewing brand.

Similar Species: The Garita Skipper is smaller, with longer antennae and is mostly orange below lacking the black inner margin of the hindwings. It is also on the wing earlier in the season than the Powesheik Skipper.

Life Cycle: The larvae of the Powesheik Skipper have been reported to feed on Slender Spike-rush (*Eleocharis elliptica*) in Michigan. Scott (1986) stated that females laid eggs on sedges (Cyperaceae) and larvae feed on the same in the laboratory.

The pale yellowish-green hemispherical eggs are laid on the leaves of the food plant and hatch in approximately nine days. The fifth instar larvae are pale, grass-green with a darker green dorsal stripe and seven thin cream coloured lines along each side. The head capsules are also green. The fifth instar larvae overwinter by clinging to the underside of food plant leaves. They resume feeding the next spring prior to pupation in late May or early June (McCabe and Post 1977; Opler and Krizek 1984).

This skipper has been found in Manitoba from June 23 to July 8. In North Dakota, adults have been recorded from June 12 to July 30. Females generally emerge later than males.

Habitat: Virgin mixed-grass or tall-grass prairie, old fields and moist meadows.

Range: Manitoba, Minnesota, Michigan, Wisconsin, North and South Dakota, Iowa and Nebraska (Howe 1975).

Manitoba Records: Gardenton, Stuartburn, Tolstoi and Vita.

Subspecies: There are no subspecies recognized.

Remarks: Although the Powesheik Skipper was reported prior to 1985 from Manitoba, these records were actually misidentified Garita Skippers. In 1985, during a brief survey of southeastern Manitoba, Catling and Lafontaine (1986) found Powesheik Skippers to be locally abundant near Vita, Stuartburn and Gardenton, in tall grass prairie separated by stands of oak, aspen and hazel. Three hand-caught specimens were the first documented record for the Powesheik Skipper in Canada. Powesheik Skippers fly low over grassy areas and readily visit flowers. When not feeding, adults perch on grasses or plants of medium height or on the ground.

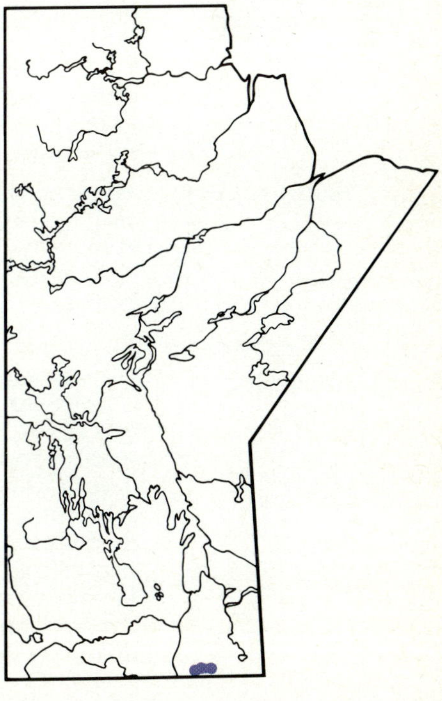

Garita Skipper

Oarisma garita (Reakirt), 1866

Plate 2 No. 19, 20, 21

Description: 21-25 mm. Above, the wings are brown and more or less suffused with orange scales giving the wings a golden-brown appearance. Below, the forewings are orange with a dark brown or black inner margin. The inner marginal third (anal fold) of the hindwing is orange, suffused with black or dark brown. The remaining two-thirds of the hindwings are pale-grayish brown with faintly outlined silvery-gray veins. Females and males are similar in appearance but males lack a forewing brand.

Similar Species: The Powesheik Skipper may resemble dark specimens of the Garita Skipper but the inner marginal third of the hind wings is entirely black whereas in the Garita Skipper there is always at least a streak of orange.

Life Cycle: The larvae feed on various grasses including Kentucky Blue Grass (*Poa pratensis*).

The eggs are creamy white and marked with a fine network of ridges. The larvae are grass green with a white stripe dorsally, and seven pale lines on each side. The head capsules are pale green. Garita Skippers overwinter as partially grown larvae (Hooper 1973; Howe 1975; Ferris and Brown 1981).

In Manitoba, adults are present from June 2 until August 5, being most common from late June until early July. There is one generation per year.

Habitat: Dry and moist virgin prairie, meadows and roadsides. On dry prairie they are usually found in the hollows or at the base of hills.

Range: British Columbia to Manitoba, southward to South Dakota, Nebraska and into Mexico (Howe 1975).

Manitoba Records: Agassiz Provincial Forest, Asessippi Provincial Park, Aweme, Beulah, Birds Hill, Birtle, Carberry, Cartwright, Culross, Deleau, Elm Creek, Gypsumville, Inwood, Komarno, Lundar, Miniota, Oak Lake, Pierson, Pine Ridge, Riding Mountain, Sand Ridge, Spruce Woods Provincial Park, Tolstoi, Victoria Beach and Winnipeg.

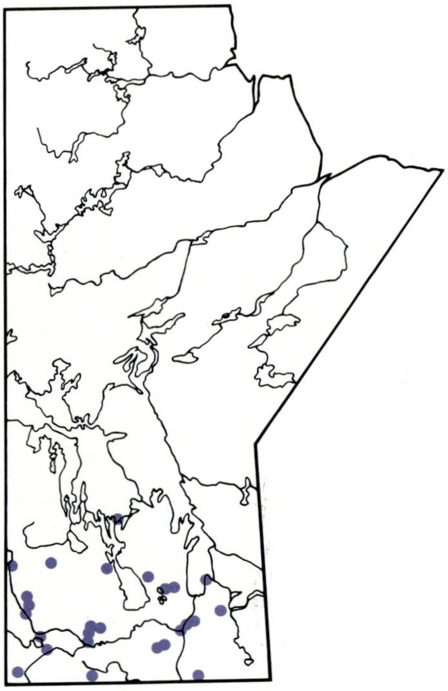

Subspecies: There are two subspecies, one in Mexico and the other occurring northward to Manitoba, which is the nominate, *Oarisma garita garita* (Miller and Brown 1981).

Remarks: Although still quite common and widespread in southern Manitoba, the Garita Skipper is restricted to a shrinking habitat of undisturbed grasslands. It is seldom found in disturbed grasslands, despite the presence of food plants. In Manitoba adults have been recorded feeding on Shrubby Cinquefoil, Harebell, Coneflowers, Black-eyed Susan, Locoweed and Gaillardia. When disturbed they fly low over grassy areas before dropping down into the undergrowth.

European Skipper

Thymelicus lineola (Ochsenheimer), 1808

Plate 2 No. 22, 23, 24

Description: 22-26 mm. The European Skipper is brassy orange above with narrow black borders. The veins are often outlined in black toward the outer margin of the wings. Below, the forewings are orange and the hindwings are pale grayish-brown. Females usually have a faint vertical dark line at the end of the discal cell. The antennae of both sexes are short and end in blunt clubs. Occasionally very pale forms occur but they are common within Winnipeg populations.

Similar Species: The Delaware Skipper is larger, with narrower wings. Female Delaware Skippers have wider dark borders on the wing margins and males lack the forewing brand.

Life Cycle: The preferred larval food plant is Timothy (*Phleum pratense*), but Redtop (*Agrostis alba*) and other grasses may also serve as host plants.

The whitish eggs are hemispherical and flattened dorsally. In late summer eggs are laid in rows of 25 to 30 under the leaf sheath or on the dried seed heads of the host plant, where they remain until the following spring. The mature larvae are greenish with a dark stripe along the back. The head capsules are pale brown with yellowish stripes extending over the front. Prior to pupation, the larvae tie the lower stems of host plants together with silk to form enclosures to hold the pupae. The pupae have green thoraxes, yellowish-green abdomens with a dark stripe along the dorsal surface and a horn projecting toward the head (Muller 1969; Howe 1975; Morris 1980).

In Manitoba, the adult flight period has been recorded from June 7 to August 5. Adults are most common before mid-July. There is one generation per year.

Habitat: Forest clearings, open grassy spaces, meadows, pastures and along roads and railway lines.

Range: Europe; introduced and spreading in North America, from southern Manitoba to Newfoundland, south to Virginia, North Carolina, Tennessee and Missouri. Also in British Columbia (Morris 1980; Opler and Krizek 1984).

European Skipper nectaring at Alfalfa, Winnipeg, Manitoba. July 7, 1986.

Manitoba Records: Agassiz Provincial Forest, Arborg, Birds Hill, Camp Morton, Culross, Elm Creek, Eriksdale, Gimli, Hecla Island, Komarno, Lundar, Northwest Angle Provincial Forest, Oak Hammock, Rathwell, Rennie, Sandilands Provincial Forest, Selkirk, Seven Sisters, Teulon, Whiteshell Provincial Park and Winnipeg.

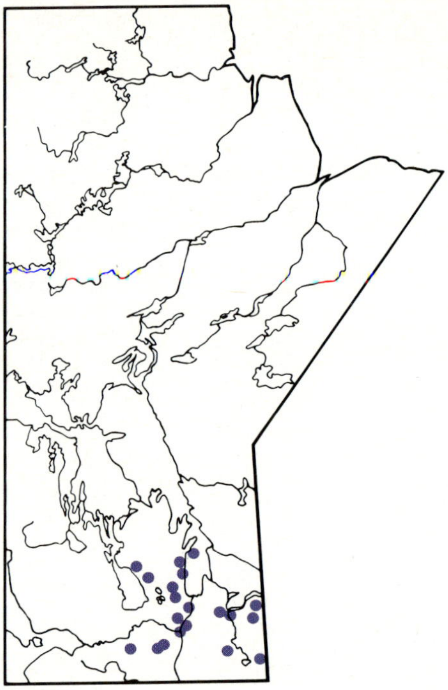

Subspecies: The North American subspecies is *Thymelicus lineola lineola* (Miller and Brown 1981).

Remarks: The first European Skipper was seen in North America at London, Ontario in 1910, apparently having been inadvertently introduced from Europe. It has since spread south to Tennessee and west to Manitoba. There is also an isolated colony in British Columbia. Some authors believe it could have been spread in hay fodder containing eggs. In Manitoba the first specimens known to be collected were taken by R. Westwood on July 12, 1972 in Winnipeg along the Red River, where the European Skipper is now locally common most years. Four specimens were collected in Sandilands Provincial Forest on July 19, 1972. In 1974 the European Skipper was seen sporadically in Agassiz Provincial Forest and now is locally common. It has since been found on Hecla Island in 1979, at Eriksdale and Elm Creek in 1986, and at Culross and Lundar in 1987. In most areas populations fluctuate dramatically, the species being very abundant some years and scarce in others. On July 24, 1984 the European Skipper was the most abundant butterfly species occurring in an area of mixed forest and meadows south of Highway 44, in Agassiz Provincial Forest (Howe 1975; Krivda 1976; Preston and Westwood 1981). Interestingly, one specimen was collected by F. Zawislak on September 30, 1984 at Seven Sisters.

The European Skipper has a weak flight, usually keeping close to the ground. It will visit a variety of flowering plants for nectar including Red and White Clover, Alfalfa, Dogbane, Thistle species, Fleabane and Milkweed.

Uncas Skipper

Hesperia uncas W.H. Edwards, 1863

Plate 2 No. 25, 26, 27

Description: 26-35 mm. Above, the wings are dull tawny-orange in the middle and grayish brown at the bases and margins. Several white spots occur at the forewing apex. Often the tawny-orange is restricted to a trace (mainly the hindwings) in the female. Below, all four wings are olive-gray. The forewings have white spots near the tip and the hindwings contain spots elongated at the veins and joined to form a complete band. The band on the underside of each hindwing is rimmed with dark brown and crossed by white veins, a distinctive feature of the Uncas Skipper. Females are larger, darker and more extensively marked than males, who have a slender black brand.

Life Cycle: In Colorado the larval food plant is Blue Grama Grass (*Bouteloua gracilis*) which is also found in Manitoba.

The smooth eggs are greenish-white. The young larvae form shelters by holding leaves or stems of the food plant together with silk. The mature larvae are pale brown with a narrow dark stripe along the dorsal surface and two pale stripes laterally. The head capsules are dark brown. Pupation occurs in a loosely constructed cocoon found among plant litter often some distance from the larval shelter (McCabe and Post 1977; Howe 1975).

The only adult record which can be accurately verified in Manitoba is June 29. In Saskatchewan adults occur from June 2 until July 22 and in North Dakota from June through September. In North Dakota emergence is staggered throughout the season. There is probably one generation per year in Manitoba (Hooper 1973; McCabe and Post 1977).

Habitat: Dry sandy prairie hillsides and pastures.

Range: Oregon and Alberta to Manitoba and Minnesota, southward to Texas and Arizona (McCabe and Post 1977).

Manitoba Records: Beulah, Brandon, Carberry, Glenboro and Westbourne.

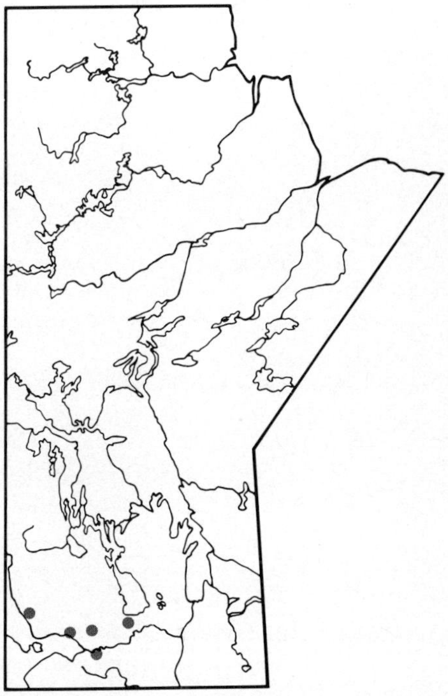

Subspecies: Three or four subspecies are recognized north of Mexico. The Manitoba subspecies is *Hesperia uncas uncas* (Miller and Brown 1981).

Remarks: Early authors recorded the Uncas Skipper from Brandon, Beulah and Westbourne, but the only specimens available are from a small colony discovered near Carberry in 1978. The Carberry population occupied several small knolls in a well-grazed pasture. Adults were either perched on the bare ground or feeding on Milk Vetch or less commonly on Gaillardia. They were very wary and left nectaring sites when disturbed, only to return to the same plant shortly afterward. Since 1978 no individuals have been found in the Carberry area. This species is uncommon in Saskatchewan and appears sporadically in North Dakota.

Comma Skipper

Hesperia comma (Linnaeus), 1758

Three subspecies of the Comma Skipper occur in Manitoba. These are the Assiniboia, Manitoba and Laurentian Skippers. We have treated the pale prairie subspecies *assiniboia* and the dark woodland subspecies *laurentina* and *manitoba* as distinct subspecies because of their large differences in appearance, behaviour and habitat. Future research may show that the prairie and boreal subspecies actually constitute two separate species.

Assiniboia Skipper

Hesperia comma assiniboia (Lyman), 1892

Plate 3 No. 1, 2, 3, 4, 5

Description: 25-33 mm. Above, females are dark brown, marked with variable yellowish-orange spots and blotches. Males are dull pale yellowish-orange with wide diffuse brown borders and black forewing brands. Below, both sexes are yellowish-green or grayish-green with inconspicuous yellowish or occasionally, white spots. These spots are often small and sometimes lacking, especially in males. Females are larger than males.

Similar Species: The Nevada Skipper is paler with narrower borders and has a more suffused pattern above. Below, it is less green and in the hindwing bands the lowest spots are out of line, located toward the base of the wings.

Life Cycle: The larval food plants for the various subspecies of *Hesperia comma* include Needle Grass (*Stipa* sp.), Blue Grass (*Poa* sp.), Fescue (*Festuca* sp.), Brome Grass (*Bromus* sp.), Rye Grass (*Lolium* sp.) and June Grass (*Koeleria gracilis*). The Assiniboia Skipper probably feeds on Needle Grass or June Grass in Manitoba, which are the food plants in North Dakota (McCabe and Post 1977; Pyle 1981; Opler and Krizek 1984).

Larvae inhabiting pasture areas often form silken burrows beneath dried cattle droppings in which they reside when not feeding (McCabe and Post 1977).

In Manitoba, adults have been recorded from July 31 to September 14, being most common in mid-August east of the Red River and in early August in western Manitoba. Manitoba records for June 22 to July 11 are questionable, but may constitute an unusually early generation. North Dakota records for June are uncommon (McCabe and Post 1977).

Habitat: Dry sandy virgin prairie and prairie hillsides, including grazed native pastures.

Range: *Hesperia comma* is found in most of Europe, northern Africa, temperate Asia and in North America. The subspecies *Hesperia comma assiniboia* occurs from Alberta to Manitoba and Minnesota southward to New Mexico (Hooper 1973; Howe 1975).

P. Klassen collecting near Miniota, Manitoba. August 1986.

Manitoba Records: Aweme, Beulah, Bowsman, Carberry, Cartwright, Cypress River, Deleau, Fort Alexander, Kelwood, Melbourne, Miami, Miniota, Pine Ridge, Riding Mountain, Sand Ridge, Sandilands Provincial Forest, Spruce Woods Provincial Park, Stockton, Teulon, The Pas, Victoria Beach and Winnipeg.

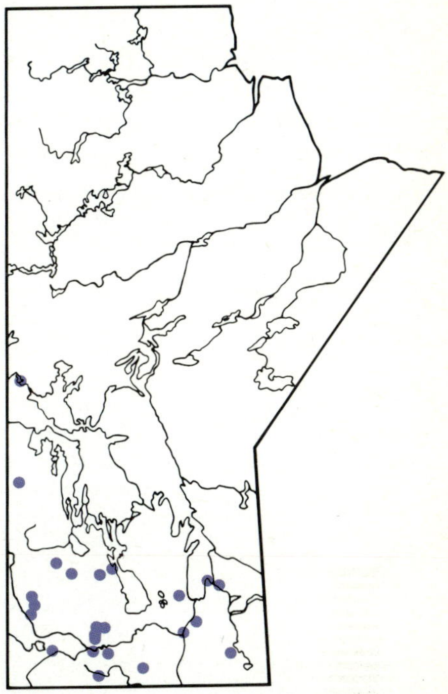

Subspecies: There are up to 14 intergrading subspecies of *Hesperia comma* recognized in North America (Howe 1975; Miller and Brown 1981).

Remarks: Although *Hesperia comma assiniboia* does occur in forested areas, it is usually restricted to dry sandy grassy areas. The Assiniboia Skipper was probably widespread and common in southwestern Manitoba before the area was turned over to large scale agriculture. It is now limited to the remaining tracts of virgin prairie and native grass pastures providing they are not seriously overgrazed. This species is still common around the Birds Hill and Pine Ridge areas near Winnipeg and although less prevalent can be found in the Carberry Hills and Spruce Woods Provincial Forest.

Adults are usually found on dry knolls or ridges, perching on bare patches of ground or on low plants, especially Blazing Star. Both sexes visit flowers frequently, including Blazing Star, Goldenrod, Aster, various Thistles and Sunflower.

Manitoba Skipper

Hesperia comma manitoba (Scudder), 1874

Plate 3 No. 6, 7, 8

Description: 25-29 mm. Above, female Manitoba Skippers have dark brown wings, marked with variable orange spots and blotches. The males have dull orange wings with wide dark brown borders which sometimes cover the greater part of the wings. The orange may be reduced to diffuse spots in the hindwings of the males. Below, the wings are golden brown to dark brown, usually with a greenish tinge. The wings also contain conspicuous, glistening white spots frequently edged with black and often joined to form bands. Males have a black forewing brand.

Life Cycle: The larval food plant for this subspecies is not known, but it is probably one or several of the grass species used by other subspecies of *Hesperia comma*.

In Manitoba, adults are on the wing from June 24 until August 15. *Hesperia comma manitoba* is most common in mid-July at Churchill in even numbered years, and is rarely seen in odd numbered years. This subspecies most likely requires two years to complete a generation in northern Manitoba.

Habitat: Openings and clearings including roads and railway lines passing through boreal forests and open rocky outcrops in pine woods.

Range: The Manitoba Skipper occurs throughout the boreal forest from Alaska to Manitoba where its range overlaps with that of the the Laurentian Skipper, *Hesperia comma laurentina*. The latter ranges from New Brunswick and Maine westward to southeastern Manitoba and northwestern Minnesota.

Manitoba Records: Churchill, Gillam, Lynn Lake, Pikwitonei, The Pas, Thompson, Wabowden and Whiteshell Provincial Park.

Subspecies: There is some confusion concerning the status of the Manitoban boreal forest populations of *Hesperia comma*. Three different subspecies have been assigned to these boreal forest populations: *Hesperia comma borealis* from the Labrador area, *Hesperia comma laurentina* from eastern and central Canada and *Hesperia comma manitoba* from northwestern North America. In Manitoba there is considerable overlap between the two subspecies *laurentina* and *manitoba*. Generally *laurentina* is brighter and more reddish-brown above and has smaller whitish spots below than *manitoba*. (Klots 1951; Howe 1975; Oosting and Parshall 1978; Opler and Krizek 1981; Scott 1986).

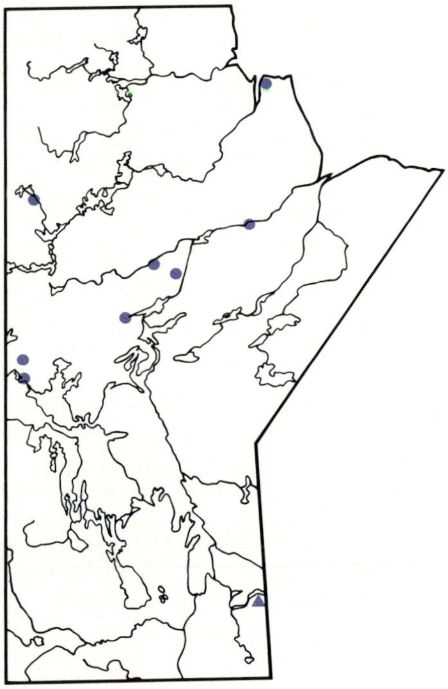

● *H.c. manitoba*
▲ *H.c. laurentina*

Remarks: Despite the confusion among subspecies, both *Hesperia comma manitoba* and *Hesperia comma laurentina* are quite distinct from *Hesperia comma assiniboia*. The subspecies *manitoba* may be more closely related to European subspecies of *Hesperia comma*. At Churchill the Manitoba Skipper is found south of the tree line in exposed areas with individuals perching on bare rock, basking in the sun or visiting flowers. In southeastern Manitoba (Whiteshell Provincial Park), *laurentina* can be found in open pine woods on rocks, exposed gravel or at mud puddles. Adults are wary and have a swiftly darting flight. It is very difficult to distinguish specimens of *manitoba* and *laurentina* in Manitoba where their ranges overlap.

Laurentian Skipper

Hesperia comma laurentina (Lyman), 1892

Plate 3 No. 9, 13

For discussion of the Laurentian Skipper see the Manitoba Skipper.

Ottoe Skipper

Hesperia ottoe W.H. Edwards, 1866

Plate 3 No. 10, 11, 12

Description: 32-41 mm. Females have a faded or "washed-out" appearance, even when newly emerged. Above, they are yellowish-orange with wide diffuse borders, more or less diffused pale tawny spots in the hindwings and a whitish, usually rounded translucent spot in the center of each forewing. Below, females are pale buff to yellow with a few small darker spots. Males are smaller than females (Howe 1975; McCabe and Post 1977). They are dull yellowish-orange with diffuse narrow, dark borders on the upper side and with blackish or gray centered bands on the forewings. Below, males are a uniform pale golden-orange.

Similar Species: The females of the Pawnee Skipper are darker, with more distinct markings; the white translucent spot in each forewing is angular and nearly square. The Pawnee Skipper is also on the wing later. The Dakota Skipper is smaller with more rounded wings (Pyle 1981).

Life Cycle: The larval food plants include various species of grasses. In Iowa, females oviposit on Little Blue Stem (*Andropogon scoparius*), which also occurs in Manitoba (Opler and Krizek 1984).

The smooth white hemispherical eggs are laid singly on or near the food plant. In Minnesota, females lay eggs on Purple Coneflower. Once the larvae hatch and eat their egg shells they drop from the Purple Coneflower to feed on the grass below. After the first molt the larvae construct shelters by tying grass leaves together. To feed, they remove leaves from the host plant and consume them in the safety of the shelters. The mature larvae are pale greenish-brown, with dark brown head capsules and black collars surrounding the prothoraxes. Ottoe Skippers overwinter as mature larvae (Nielsen 1958; Dana 1981).

In Manitoba, adults have been recorded in late July. North Dakota records show that the Ottoe Skipper is on the wing from June 15 to August 6. Females emerge a week or more after the first males. There is one generation per year.

Habitat: Virgin prairie with grasses of medium height, moist short grass prairie, open areas within scrub oak woods and old farmland where native grasses have re-established themselves.

Range: Montana and Manitoba to Michigan, southward to Texas and Colorado.

Mixed-grass prairie near Treesbank, Manitoba. Assiniboine Corridor Wildlife Management Area. July 1988.

Manitoba Records: Aweme, Spruce Woods Provincial Park and Treesbank.

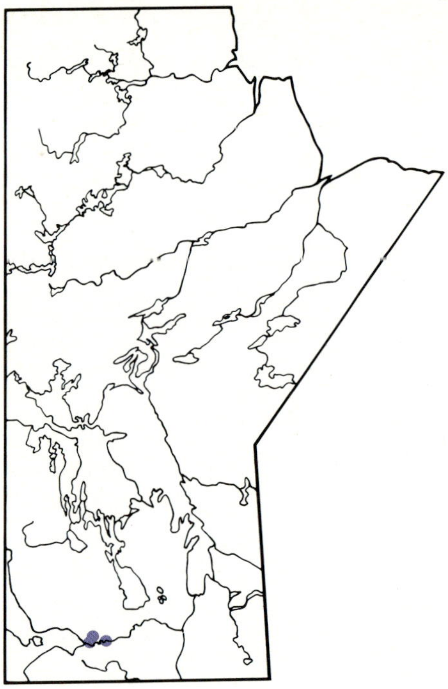

Subspecies: None are recognized.

Remarks: Manitoba is thc only province in Canada where the Ottoe Skipper has been found. The Ottoe Skipper has been confused with the Pawnee Skipper in some of the Manitoba records. The only reliable records are from Treesbank, Aweme and Spruce Woods. Wallis (1927) collected this species on a dry riverbank and stated that males were locally common. R. Westwood collected several specimens adjacent to mixed forest in Spruce Woods Provincial Park. Individuals have been observed on damp roads after rain showers. In North Dakota, the Ottoe Skipper is uncommon in most of the state. It should be searched for in virgin prairie in southern Manitoba, especially in the western part of the province. The Ottoe Skipper is wary and has a swift flight. Adults have been observed feeding on Coneflower, Blazing Star, Thistles, Alfalfa, Vetch, Sunflower, Milkweed and some species of Cactus.

Leonardus Skipper

Hesperia leonardus Harris, 1862

Plate 3 No. 14, 15, 16, 17

Description: 27-35 mm. Above, the Leonardus Skipper has blackish-brown wings, with fulvous orange spots and bands. In males, the orange is more extensive and surrounds the forewing brands. The underside of both sexes is golden brown with spots and bands similar to the upper side. In the hindwings, the spots are very distinct, usually white or occasionally cream coloured. Males have forewing brands, while females are larger and darker.

Life Cycle: In Manitoba, the larvae of the Leonardus Skipper feed on several grass species including Bent Grass (*Agrostis* sp.), Switch Grass (*Panicum virgatum*), and Poverty Oat Grass (*Danthonia spicata*).

The immature stages of the Leonardus Skipper are similar to those of other members of the genus. The eggs are greenish-white when laid. Mature larvae are finely mottled pale reddish-brown, tinged with green. The head capsules are black with two cream coloured patches and two cream coloured stripes on the front. These skippers overwinter as first or second instar larvae. The pupae are generally brown to green in colour (Howe 1975; Opler and Krizek 1984).

In Manitoba, adults are on the wing from August 5 to August 24. They are most common in mid-August. There is one generation per year.

Habitat: Clearings and open grassy areas in mixed forests. Open pine woods and roads and trails within woods. Adults also prefer moist or boggy areas and areas which receive considerable sunlight.

Range: Manitoba eastward to Nova Scotia, south to Maine, North Carolina, Louisiana and Missouri (Howe 1975; Opler and Krizek 1984).

Manitoba Records: Sandilands Provincial Forest, Victoria Beach and Whiteshell Provincial Park.

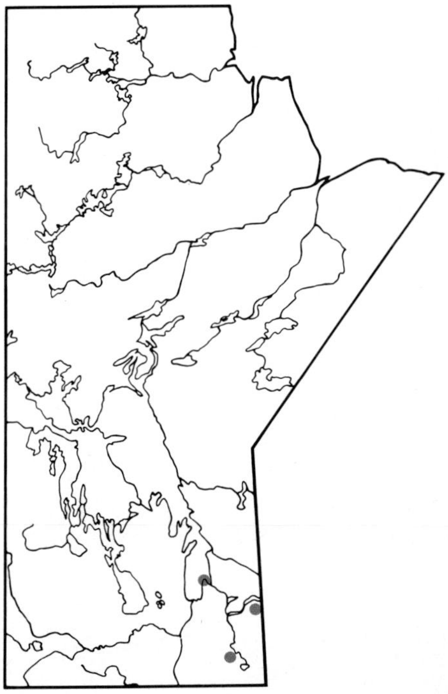

Subspecies: Some authors now consider *Hesperia pawnee* a subspecies of *Hesperia leonardus* (Scott and Stanford 1981; Miller and Brown 1981). In Manitoba, these species are quite distinct both in appearance and habitat preference. Until future research establishes the relationship between these two skippers, we will consider them separate species.

Remarks: The Leonardus Skipper occurs only in the southeastern part of Manitoba. It is locally common in the Whiteshell Provincial Park, where it can be seen seeking nectar from Wood Aster and a variety of Thistle species. Individuals have been observed perching on plants about a metre in height or on the bare ground along trails within the provincial park.

Pawnee Skipper

Hesperia pawnee Dodge,1874

Plate 3 No. 18, 19, 20, 21

Description: 30-37 mm. Above, females are brown, variably suffused with fulvous scales. The forewings have a pale yellowish band and pale yellowish spots, including a translucent spot. The hindwings have a suffused orange band. The males are orange above, with dull brown borders which may vary in width between individuals. Below, the wings of both sexes are buff coloured with the forewings becoming brown basally. The hindwings may have diffuse cream spots that are most developed in females. Females are larger than males, who have a forewing brand.

Similar Species: The Ottoe Skipper differs from the Pawnee Skipper as described under that species. The Dakota Skipper is smaller and pale grayish-brown to grayish-orange below. Female Dakota Skippers have more diffused spots and males have narrower borders and forewing brands. In *Hesperia comma*, the underside of the hindwings has a greenish hue with pale spots at the base. Leonardus Skipper females can be distinguished from dark Pawnee females by their darker underwings. The spots on the underside of the hindwings of the Leonardus Skipper are distinct and angular in shape compared to the rounded, diffuse spots of the Pawnee Skipper.

Life Cycle: The larval food plant of the Pawnee Skipper is Spear Grass (*Stipa comata*) in North Dakota and Blue Grama Grass (*Bouteloua gracilis*) in Colorado. Both these species occur in Manitoba. The larvae are similar in appearance to those of the Leonardus Skipper but have lighter head capsules (McCabe and Post 1977; Ferris and Brown 1981).

Adults have been recorded from July 30 to August 23, being most common in mid-August. Females usually emerge a week or more after the males. There is one generation per year in Manitoba.

Habitat: Dry, sandy virgin prairie including native grass pastures if they are not overgrazed.

Range: Saskatchewan and Manitoba, southward to Minnesota, Iowa, Kansas and Colorado.

Manitoba Records: Aweme, Carberry, Cartwright, Melbourne and Spruce Woods Provincial Forest.

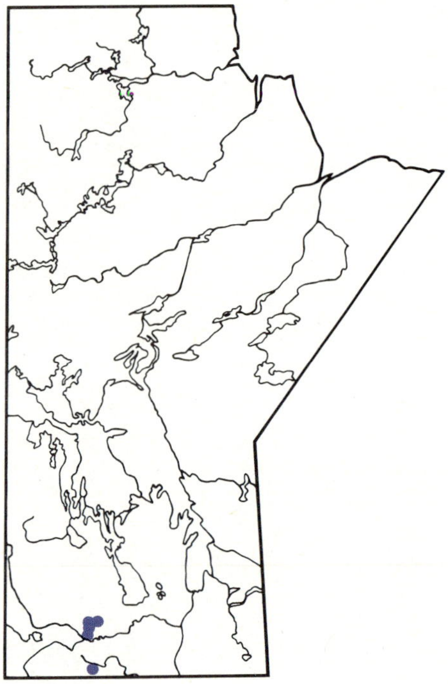

Subspecies: Scott (1986) considers *Hesperia pawnee* to be a subspecies of *Hesperia leonardus*. Miller and Brown (1981) and Tilden and Smith (1986) consider *Hesperia pawnee* a separate species.

Remarks: Although the Pawnee Skipper is locally common in southwestern Manitoba there are only a few records for the province. Adults frequent hilltops and knolls on open, dry, sandy prairie. They prefer Blazing Star, Thistles, Alfalfa, Goldenrod, and Joe-pye weed as nectar sources. The Assiniboia Skipper often flies in association with the Pawnee Skipper. The Pawnee Skipper is quite common in the Carberry Hills and Spruce Woods Provincial Forest in some years. These skippers are quite wary and can be best seen while feeding on flowers, especially Blazing Star.

Dakota Skipper

Hesperia dacotae (Skinner), 1911

Plate 3 No. 22, 23, 24, 25

Description: 26-33 mm. Female Dakota Skippers are dull grayish-buff to brown above. They also have suffused spots which are more distinct in dark individuals. Males are yellowish-orange above with narrow, diffused pale brown borders and short, black forewing brands. Below, the females are grayish-brown and may have obscure spots in the hindwings, whereas the males are grayish-orange occasionally with pale spots.

Similar Species: The Indian Skipper is much darker with larger spots (especially on the underside of the hindwings); the male Indian Skipper has wider borders than the male Dakota Skipper. The Assiniboine Skipper is on the wing considerably later in the season than the Dakota Skipper.

Life Cycle: The larvae of the Dakota Skipper have been reared on a wide variety of grass species in captivity. Scott (1986) indicated that food plants include Little Blue Stem (*Andropogon scoparius*), Kentucky Blue Grass (*Poa pratensis*) and Panic Grass (*Panicum* sp.). Pyle (1981) stated that females lay their eggs near the ground on blades of grass and that host plants included Grama Grass (*Bouteloua* sp.) and Three-awn (*Aristida* sp.). McCabe and Post (1977) noted that females lay their eggs on broad leaved plants e.g. Milk Vetch. Larvae hatch in approximately ten days and move downward into the grass below. The larvae will then build grass tube-like shelters, enlarging them as they mature. The larvae feed at night and seldom leave the tubes entirely. Dakota Skippers overwinter as fourth instar larvae and resume feeding the following spring. The head capsules and the three pairs of true legs are black. (McCabe and Post 1977; McCabe 1981).

In Manitoba, adults have been recorded from June 23 to July 14. In North Dakota adults occur from June 18 to July 30 (McCabe 1981).

Habitat: Low moist or dry virgin prairie where Camas grows.

Range: Manitoba, Minnesota, Illinois, Iowa and the Dakotas.

Manitoba Records: Brandon, Inwood, Lundar, Miniota, Stuartburn, Tolstoi and Winnipeg.

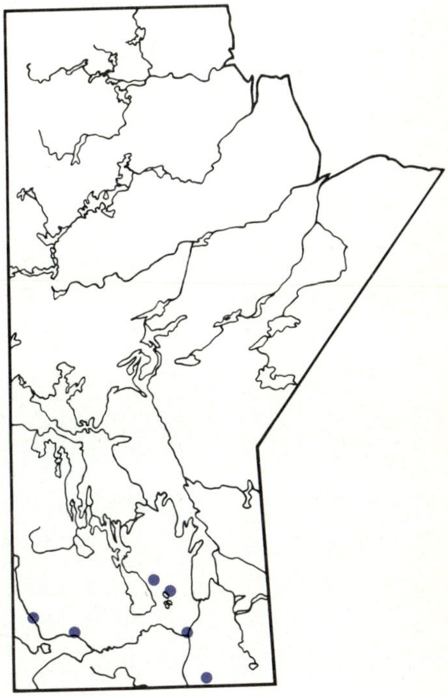

Subspecies: No subspecies are recognized.

Remarks: Prior to 1982 only a few records were available for the Dakota Skipper in Manitoba. Three males and two females were collected near Lundar in 1982 in a lightly grazed grassland area. Subsequently, a number of colonies have been found in ungrazed virgin prairie. The Dakota Skipper prefers alkaline prairie and is rarely found on heavily grazed areas. Adults in the Lundar area were frequently seen perched on Camas plants, used by males as vantage points to seek unmated females. The Dakota Skipper flies in association with Peck's Skipper, Long Dash and Garita Skipper in the Lundar area. The habitat for the Dakota Skipper is shrinking and efforts should be made to find healthy populations in areas that can be protected. Tilden and Smith (1986) noted that proposals have been made to place the Dakota Skipper on the endangered species list in the United States.

Indian Skipper

Hesperia sassacus Harris, 1862

Plate 3 No. 26, 27, 28, 29

Description: 27-33 mm. The Indian Skipper is orange above with wide, dark brown borders, indented along the inner margins. In Manitoba, females are darker than males, often brown with large orange spots and patches. Below, the wings are yellowish-olive to yellowish-brown. The hindwings also have a band of pale yellowish spots which are elongated along the veins of the wings. Males have black forewing brands.

Similar Species: The Dakota Skipper differs as described under that species. Females of the Long Dash have a contiguous, although sometimes faint, band on the underside of the hindwings.

Life Cycle: Howe (1975) and Opler and Krizek (1984) noted that the larva of the Indian Skipper feed on several grass species including Little Blue Stem (*Andropogon scoparius*), Panic Grass (*Panicum* sp.), and Red Fescue (*Festuca rubra*).

Early stages of the Indian Skipper are similar to other members of the genus. In Manitoba, adults are on the wing from June 2 to July 27. There is one generation per year.

Habitat: Forest clearings, pastures, rocky barrens and abandoned fields. In Manitoba, the Indian Skipper is primarily a woodland species, preferring pine forests where it can be found in glades and clearings. The Indian Skipper is a ''poor soil'' species found where grassy vegetation is sparse.

Range: Manitoba to New Brunswick, southward to Maine, Virginia and North Carolina (Opler and Krizek 1984).

Manitoba Records: Agassiz Provincial Forest, Rennie, Sandilands Provincial Forest and Schist Lake.

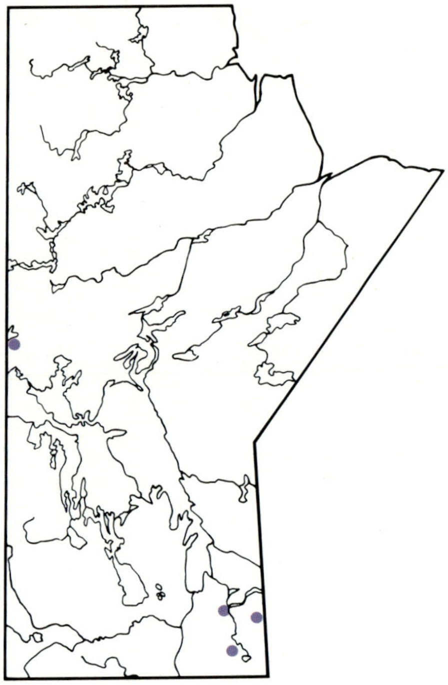

Subspecies: Some authors recognize two subspecies of the Indian Skipper. The darker form, *Hesperia sassacus manitoboides* is the subspecies that occurs in Manitoba, northwestern Ontario and Minnesota (Klots 1951; Miller and Brown 1981).

Remarks: The Indian Skipper is the most widespread and abundant member of the *Hesperia* in northeastern North America, but southeastern Manitoba seems to be near the edge of its range. Usually only one or two individuals are seen per season. The habitat occupied by the Indian Skipper although extensive in southeastern Manitoba, has been poorly surveyed and the skipper may be more abundant and wider ranging than present records indicate. For example, one specimen was taken farther north at Schist Lake by F. Zawislak in the summer of 1983.

Nevada Skipper

Hesperia nevada (Scudder), 1874

Plate 3 No. 30, 31, 32

Description: 25-35 mm. Adults are pale yellowish-orange above, with narrow or wide brown borders diffused inwardly. Females may be more yellowish-brown, with pale orange areas sometimes reduced to spots or patches. Both males and females are greenish-gray below with silvery white spots. The submarginal bands on the underside of the hindwings are irregular with the lowest spots offset basally. Males have short, black forewing brands.

Similar Species: The Assiniboia Skipper differs as described under that species.

Life Cycle: The Nevada Skipper feeds on bunch grasses including Sheep Fescue (*Festuca ovina*) and Western Needle Grass (*Stipa occidentalis*). Although Western Needle Grass does not occur in Manitoba, there are several other species of Needle Grass that may serve as host plants for the Nevada Skipper (Pyle 1981).

Early stages of the Nevada Skipper are similar to other members of the genus. The eggs are creamy-white when laid and change to greenish-white prior to larval hatch. The mature larvae are olive in colour with black head capsules covered in pale brown and whitish patches (Howe 1975; Dornfeld 1980).

In Manitoba, the adults are on the wing from June 18 to June 24 with one late record of August 5. In Saskatchewan adults have been recorded from June 6 to July 4 and August 10 to 21. The Nevada Skipper has one generation per year and may have a second in some years as indicated by the August records.

Habitat: In Saskatchewan, this species prefers virgin shortgrass prairie and hilltops, while in the western mountains it frequents grassland areas (Hooper 1973; Ferris and Brown 1981).

Range: British Columbia eastward to Manitoba and south to New Mexico and California.

Manitoba Records: Beulah

Subspecies: No subspecies are recognized.

Remarks: The Nevada Skipper which is uncommon in southern Saskatchewan, has only been recorded from Beulah in Manitoba. Several authors, including Hooper (1973) and Masters (1973) state that the species occurs in Manitoba. Adults seen in August may be confused with *Hesperia comma*. Although much of the virgin prairie around Beulah no longer exists, the Nevada Skipper may still breed in isolated pockets in the western half of the province. Hooper (1973) noted that the adults will take nectar from Milk Vetch.

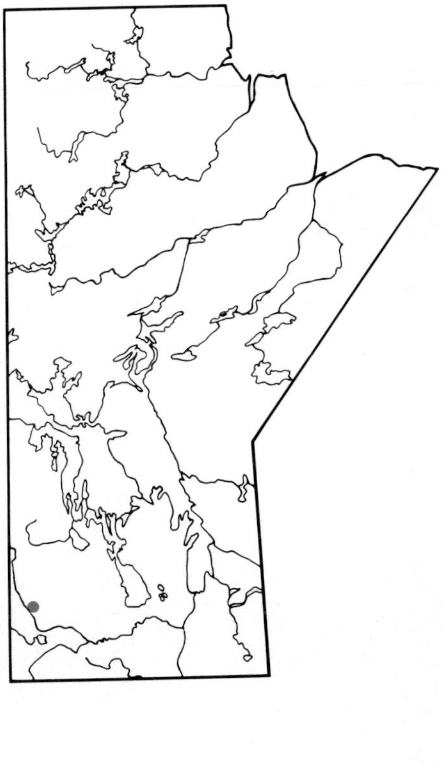

Peck's Skipper

Polites coras (Cramer), 1775

Plate 4 No. 1, 2, 3, 4

Description: 23-28 mm. Above, the wings are dark brown with orange or yellowish-orange patches and spots and a large darkly veined orange patch on both hindwings. Males have a dark grayish-brown spot next to the outer edge of each forewing brand, which resembles a long thin "S". Below, the forewings are similar to the upperside. The hindwings have a conspicuous irregular buff patch surrounded by golden brown borders. This hindwing patch helps distinguish Peck's Skipper from other Manitoba skippers.

Life Cycle: The larval food plant is Rice Cutgrass (*Leersia oryzoides*). The round eggs are flattened at the base and are pale green in colour at the time of oviposition. The larvae are dark maroon mottled with pale brown and the head capsules are black with white spots and two white lines on the front. Where there is one generation per year, Peck's Skippers overwinter as partly grown larvae. In more southern areas of the skippers' range where there are at least two generations per year they overwinter as pupae. The pupae are dull reddish-purple with white wing cases and appendages. The lateral sides of the abdomen of the pupae have a bluish bloom (Howe 1975; Morris 1980; Ferris and Brown 1981; Opler and Krizek 1984).

In Manitoba, adults have been recorded from June 21 to August 5. There is probably one generation per year in Manitoba.

Habitat: Roadsides, damp meadows, pastures, forest clearings and marshes.

Range: British Columbia eastward to Newfoundland, south to Georgia, Texas and California.

Manitoba Records: Agassiz Provincial Forest, Berens River, Beulah, Birtle, Cartwright, Culross, Elm Creek, Flin Flon, Fort Alexander, Husavik, Kelwood, Leaf Rapids, Lundar, Morden, Norris Lake, Riding Mountain, Sandilands Provincial Forest, Selkirk, Teulon, The Pas, Thompson, Tolstoi, Victoria Beach, Whiteshell Provincial Park and Winnipeg.

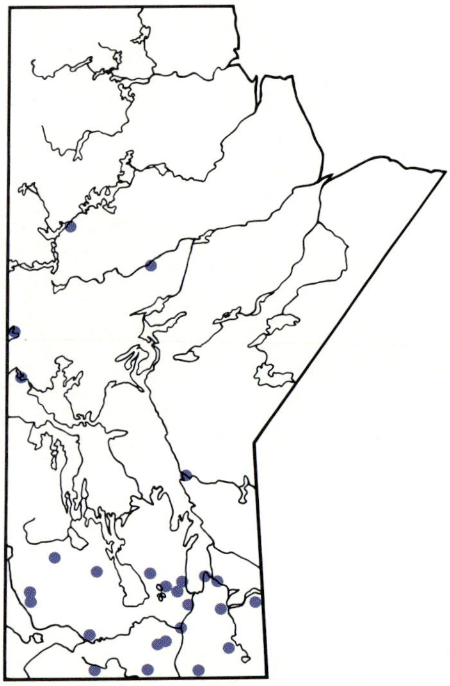

Subspecies: No subspecies are recognized.

Remarks: This skipper has undergone several specific name changes, from *Polites coras* to *Polites peckius* and back to *Polites coras*. Peck's Skipper is more common in the northern part of its range than in the south. This skipper has successfully exploited the intensely farmed areas of the Red River Valley in Manitoba, using the roadside ditches as breeding habitat. Peck's Skipper prefers grassy areas and may be easily overlooked while perching on grass or other plants. Adults will visit Alfalfa, Red Clover, Vetch, Thistles, Dogbane and Milkweed for nectar. The Tawny-edged Skipper and the Long Dash are frequently seen in association with Peck's Skipper.

Tawny-edged Skipper

Polites themistocles (Latreille), 1824

Plate 4 No. 5, 6, 7, 8

Description: 22-30 mm. The Tawny-edged Skipper is dark brown above with an orange patch along the upper margin of each forewing. This orange patch may extend to the lower margin, especially in males. Females also have a band of yellowish spots on the forewings. Below, the wing markings are similar to the upperside, while the ground colour is golden brown. Males have a forewing brand shaped like an elongated "S". Tawny-edged Skippers from eastern Manitoba are generally darker in colour, often with an almost indiscernible forewing orange patch and a vague band on the underside of the hindwings. The unmarked upperside of the hindwings distinguishes the Tawny-edged Skipper from other Manitoba skippers.

Life Cycle: The larval food plants include Panic Grass (*Panicum* sp.), and Blue Grass (*Poa* sp.).

The eggs are pale greenish when laid. The mature larvae have a thin dark brown stripe dorsally and a dark brown stripe along each side of the body. The cuticle is mottled with dark brown, especially between the stripes. The head capsules are black with two white spots and two short white stripes on the front. Tawny-edged Skippers probably overwinter as partly grown larvae or in the pupal stage in Manitoba.

In Manitoba, adults are on the wing from June 7 to July 27, being most common in mid-July. There is one generation per year in this province and two generations in the southern part of the range (Howe 1975; McCabe and Post 1977; Dornfeld 1980).

Habitat: Moist or dry meadows, fields, roadsides, forest openings and other areas where medium to tall grasses occur.

Range: British Columbia eastward to Prince Edward Island and south to Florida, Texas and California.

Manitoba Records: Agassiz Provincial Forest, Anola, Aweme, Beulah, Birds Hill, Birtle, Carberry, Cartwright, Cowan, Culross, Elm Creek, Fort Alexander, Gimli, Lundar, Miami, Northwest Angle Provincial Forest, Oak Lake, Riding Mountain, The Pas, Tolstoi, Westbourne, Whiteshell Provincial Park and Winnipeg.

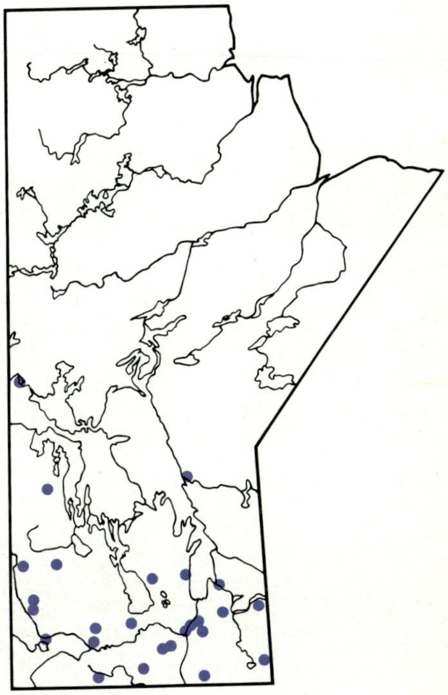

Subspecies: No subspecies are recognized. Forest populations from eastern Manitoba are noticeably darker than those from prairie areas.

Remarks: Like Peck's Skipper the Tawny-edged Skipper is more common in the northern parts of its' range than in the south. It ranges widely into drier prairie habitats even though it is more common in moist areas of tall grass. Adults feed at Red Clover, Sweet Clover, Vetch, and Dogbane and in agricultural areas may be common in roadside ditches.

Long Dash

Polites mystic (W.H. Edwards), 1863

Plate 4 No. 9, 10, 11, 12, 13

Description: 24-32 mm. Above, the wings of the Long Dash are yellowish-orange with wide brown to dark brown borders. Females may be mostly brown with the orange reduced to spots or bands. Both sexes have a dark spot near the forewing tips and in males this spot is joined to the forewing brands causing the brands to appear elongated. The common name is derived from the appearance of the elongated forewing brands. Below, the wings are pale golden brown and the hindwings usually contain a pale band and basal spot.

Similar Species: The Indian and Dakota Skippers differ as described under those species. The Delaware Skipper is brighter with narrower borders. Dark Delaware Skipper females can be distinguished from Long Dash females by the yellow-orange unmarked undersides of the hindwings.

Life Cycle: The larval food plants of the Long Dash include various grass species including Quack Grass (*Agropyron repens*), Barnyard Grass (*Echinochloa crusgalli*) and Timothy (*Phleum pratense*). In Pennsylvania, they have been noted to feed upon Blue Grass (*Poa sp.*).

The eggs are pale green when laid and Long Dashes overwinter as partly grown larvae. The mature larvae are brown, mottled with dull white with a dark brown stripe dorsally and short spines arising from numerous tubercles on the cuticle. The head capsules are roughly textured with numerous short hairs.

In Manitoba, adults are on the wing from June 3 until August 14. There is one generation per year in this province, and at least two in southern areas of the Long Dash's range.

Habitat: Roadsides, meadows, abandoned fields, and openings in mixed forest. The Long Dash is most common in medium and tall grass prairie (Howe 1975; Opler and Krizek 1984).

Range: British Columbia to Nova Scotia, southward to New Jersey, Virginia, Iowa, Colorado and Washington (McCabe and Post 1977).

Manitoba Records: Agassiz Provincial Forest, Anola, Beulah, Birds Hill, Birtle, Carberry, Cartwright, Cowan, Cranberry Portage, Culross, Duck Mountain, Elm Creek, Fort Alexander, Husavik, Kelwood, Killarney, Libau, Lundar, Lyleton, Miami, Norris Lake, Oak Hammock, Oak Lake, Overflowing River, Pikwitonei, Pine Ridge, Porcupine Provincial Forest, Riding Mountain, Sandilands Provincial Forest, Sandy Hook, Selkirk, Spruce Woods Provincial Park, Stuartburn, Teulon, The Pas, Thompson, Tolstoi, Victoria Beach, Westbourne and Winnipeg.

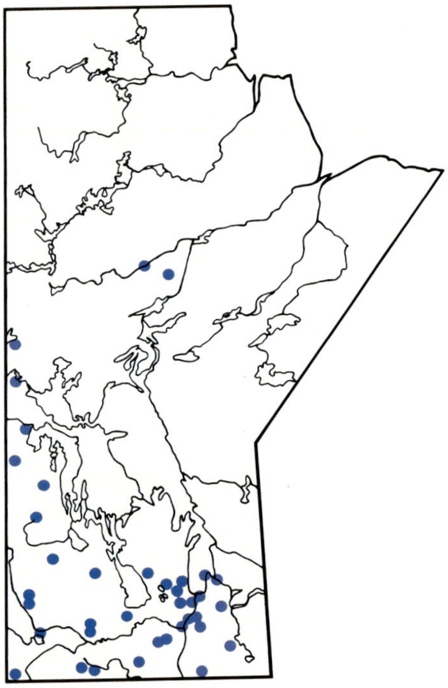

Subspecies: There are two subspecies of the Long Dash. The pale prairie form, where the ground colour is usually no darker than the band on the underside of the hindwing is *Polites mystic dacotah*. Darker specimens from eastern Manitoba resemble the subspecies *Polites mystic mystic* in appearance (Howe 1975).

Remarks: The Long Dash is probably Manitoba's most common prairie skipper. It has adapted to disturbed habitat and is common in heavily farmed areas. Adults perch on grasses and other plants and feed avidly on a wide variety of flowers including Alfalfa, Red, White and Yellow Sweet Clover. The less common Peck's and Tawny-edged Skippers are often found with the Long Dash.

Delaware Skipper

Atrytone logan (W.H. Edwards), 1863
= *Atrytone delaware* (W.H. Edwards), 1863

Plate 4 No. 14, 15, 16

Description: 27-35 mm. Above, the wings are bright golden orange with dark brown borders which are narrow in males and broader in females. The wing veins are dark brown, especially in the forewings. In general females are darker than males. Below, the wings are uniformly golden orange with no markings, except dull black lower margins in the forewings. The males do not have a forewing brand and the proboscis of both sexes is longer than in other Manitoba Hesperiinae.

Similar Species: The Long Dash and European Skipper differ as described under those species.

Life Cycle: The larvae of the Delaware Skipper feed on a variety of grasses including Wooly Beard Grass (*Erianthus divaricatus*), Switch Grass (*Panicum virgatum*) and Bluestem (*Andropogon* sp.). In addition, females have been observed ovipositing on Big Bluestem (*Andropogon gerardi*) (Howe 1975; McCabe and Post 1977).

The eggs of the Delaware Skipper have two red rings and are laid on the leaves of the host plant. Often females will lay 4 or 5 eggs per clump of grass. At maturity the larvae are bluish-white, thickly covered with small black tubercles and have a crescent shaped black band on the posterior abdominal segments. The head capsules are white and covered with several black stripes. The pupae are greenish-white with blunt, bristly black heads. The Delaware Skipper overwinters in either the larval or pupal stage. (Klots 1951; Howe 1975; McCabe and Post 1977).

From the few Manitoba records available for the Delaware Skipper, adults are on the wing from June 21 to July 21. In North Dakota, adults occur from June 19 until July 30. There is probably one generation per year in Manitoba and two or more in the southern part of the Delaware Skipper's range (Opler and Krizek 1984).

Habitat: Dry and moist prairie, roadsides, ditches, marshy areas and pond or stream edges. Adults have also been observed frequenting abandoned fields and lightly grazed pastures.

Range: Southern Alberta to Ontario, southward to Maine, Florida, Texas and New Mexico.

Vegetated dunes, Spruce Woods Provincial Park. August 1970.

Manitoba Records: Aweme, Culross, Rathwell and Spruce Woods Provincial Park.

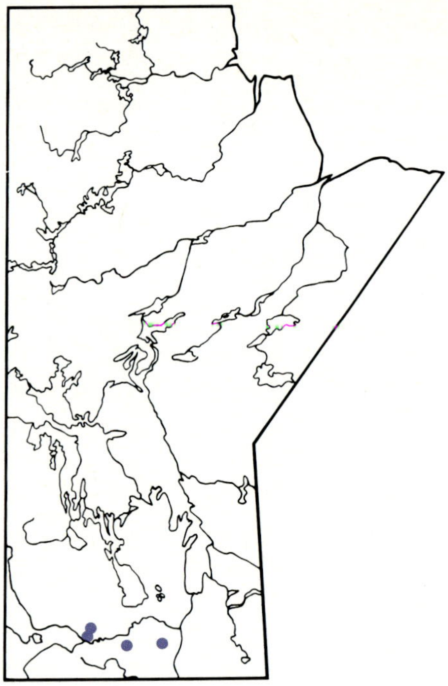

Subspecies: Two subspecies are recognized. The paler prairie subspecies is *Atrytone logan lagus* and the dark subspecies, which occurs east of the Great Plains, is *Atrytone logan logan*. The prairie subspecies has narrow pale borders and lacks the dark bar at the end of the dorsal forewing cell. Both subspecies are thought to occur in Manitoba.

Remarks: Although the Delaware Skipper is widespread it is not common in Manitoba. Apparently the first specimen collected in Manitoba was by Norman Criddle in 1921 at Aweme. Wallis (1927) stated that the Delaware Skipper was found on sandy prairie in the sandhills which are now the Spruce woods Provincial Park area. In 1985 a small colony was found near Culross in a grass-filled ditch in this intensively farmed area. Adults perched on short grasses among the taller grasses in moist places along the ditch. They preferred Red, Sweet and Alsike Clover as a nectar source and flew in association with the Long Dash, Peck's and the Tawny-edged Skipper. When flying together the Delaware Skippers were recognized by the bright golden flash of their wings. Later that year several females were observed in the Spruce woods area.

Hobomok Skipper

Poanes hobomok (Harris), 1862

Plate 4 No. 17, 18, 19, 20, 21, 22

Description: 25-33 mm. Above, the wings are orange with wide blackish-brown borders. The forewings have a small bar at the end of the discal cell and the hindwing veins are dark in colour. Below, the pattern is similar to the upper side. The hindwings have a conspicuous yellow patch and the margins are grayish-brown or purplish. Sometimes female Hobomok Skippers are encountered that are blackish-brown above rather than orange, with obscure pale yellow spots on the upper side and grayish-brown underwings. Males lack forewing brands.

Life Cycle: Female Hobomok Skippers have been observed ovipositing on several grass species, including Blue Grass (*Poa* sp.) and Panic Grass (*Panicum* sp.) (Ferris and Brown 1981; Opler and Krizek 1984).

Partially grown larvae are dark green to brown with rows of black tubercles containing short black spines. The head capsules are shiny black with white hairs. The Hobomok Skipper overwinters in either the larval or pupal stage (Klots 1951; McCabe and Post 1977; Pyle 1981).

In Manitoba, adults have been recorded from May 18 to July 20 and are most common in mid-June. Females usually emerge seven to ten days later than males. There is one generation per year in Manitoba, but as in much of the Hobomok Skipper's range the period of adult emergence is extended over a month or more.

Habitat: Forest edges, clearings, meadows, and alongside trails and roads. The Hobomok Skipper may also be found in garden or farmyard environments.

Range: Across southern Canada from Saskatchewan to Prince Edward Island and southward to Georgia, Arkansas, Kansas and New Mexico.

Manitoba Records: Agassiz Provincial Forest, Aweme, Beulah, Birds Hill, Birtle, Bowsman, Brandon, Brokenhead, Camp Morton, Cartwright, Cowan, Culross, Cypress River, Duck Mountain, Elm Creek, Erinview, Fort Alexander, Husavik, Kelwood, McCreary, Miami, Miniota, Ninette, Oak Hammock, Pine Ridge, Riding Mountain, Sand Ridge, Sandilands Provincial Forest, Selkirk, Seven Sisters, The Pas, Turtle Mountain, Victoria Beach, Whiteshell Provincial Park and Winnipeg.

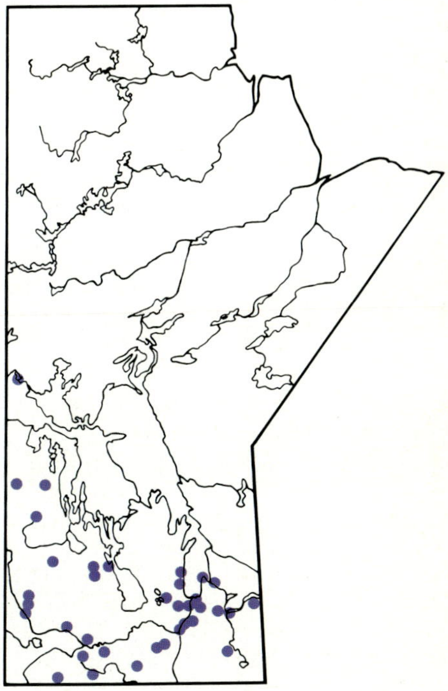

Subspecies: No subspecies are recognized (Miller and Brown 1981).

Remarks: The Hobomok Skipper is common in or near wooded areas in southern Manitoba but is scarce on the open prairie. At one time the dark female form of the Hobomok Skipper was considered a different species. The dark form has been given the name Pocahontas (Plate 4 No. 19 and 22) by some authors to differentiate the two types. Dark females have been observed at Miami, Elm Creek, Culross, Winnipeg and Pine Ridge. Adults prefer to perch on shrubs several feet off the ground in sunny areas. Hobomok Skippers will take nectar from Clovers, Vetches, Alfalfa and many garden flowers.

Broad-winged Skipper

Poanes viator (W.H. Edwards), 1865

Plate 4 No. 23

Description: 32-44 mm. This skipper is relatively large for the genus. Above, the forewings are brown with orange spots and the hindwings are mostly orange, with wide brown borders and brown veins. Below, the forewings are similar to, but paler than, the upper side while the hindwings are light brown with a long, pale, orange-yellow streak and several pale spots. The female forewing tips are more pointed and the dorsal spots more whitish, than in the male. Males lack forewing brands.

Life Cycle: Larvae feed on sedges including Lakeshore Sedge (*Carex lacustris*) and Beaked Sedge (*Carex rostrata*), on grasses including Annual Wild Rice (*Zizania aquatica*) and Panic Grass (*Panicum* sp.) (Scott 1986). In North Dakota the adults have a short flight period, usually in July, and there is one generation per year (McCabe and Post 1977).

Habitat: Marshes and sloughs, especially where sedges grow.

Range: Manitoba to southern Quebec, south to Florida and Texas.

Manitoba Records: Whiteshell Provincial Park.

Subspecies: It is the northern subspecies *Poanes viator viator* that occurs in Manitoba.

Remarks: Although the Broad-winged Skipper has been reported for Manitoba by McCabe and Post (1977), its actual occurrence was not confirmed until June 28, 1987, when W. Christie collected a specimen near Red Rock Lake in the Whiteshell Provincial Park. In North Dakota this species is highly localized, but always found near sedges. Many marshes where it occurs lack flowers, and while the species has not been observed on flowers in North Dakota, it does visit them in other areas (McCabe and Post 1977; Opler 1986).

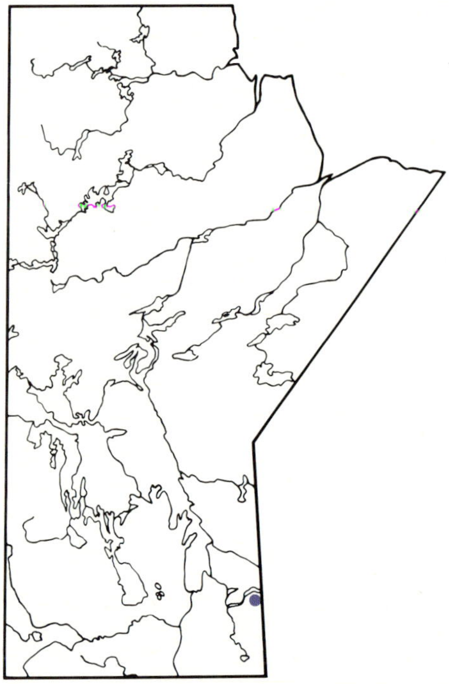

Dun Skipper

Euphyes ruricola (Boisduval), 1852
= *Euphyes vestris* (Boisduval), 1852

Plate 4 No. 24, 25, 26, 27

Description: 25-31 mm. The Dun Skipper is dark blackish-brown above and below. Males have a black forewing brand which is often obscured by the dark colour of the wings. Females have a band of small diffused whitish spots on both the upper and underside of the forewings and on the underside of the hindwings. Females have more rounded forewings than males.

Life Cycle: The host plants of the Dun Skipper include various grasses and sedges. The Dun Skipper feeds on Yellow Nut-grass (*Cyperus esculentus*) in Nebraska (this species does not occur in Manitoba). In Colorado, females were observed laying eggs on Hillside Sedge (*Carex heliophila*), which does occur in Manitoba. Tall Redtop (*Tridens flavus*) has also been reported in the literature as a larval food plant, but this species does not occur in this province.

The eggs are pale green when laid, and develop a red dorsal surface prior to hatch. The eggs are laid singly, usually on the underside of the leaf about halfway up the blade. Newly hatched larvae often eat their egg shells and construct a shelter from leaves and silk after they are partially grown. The mature larvae are pale translucent green with wavy lines and black dots. The head capsules are brown with two cream coloured stripes and a black dot on the front. Larvae pupate at the base of the host plant in a silk-lined tube constructed from leaves. In the laboratory Dun Skipper larvae required approximately 40 days from egg hatch to pupation (Heitzman and Heitzman 1974). Dun Skippers overwinter as partly grown larvae.

In Manitoba, adults have been observed from June 23 to August 17, being most common after mid-July. There is one generation per year in Manitoba and two generations per year in the southern part of the Dun Skipper's range.

Habitat: Forest edges, clearings, fields and roadsides (usually near wet areas).

Range: Across southern Canada from Saskatchewan to Nova Scotia and southward to Florida, Texas, Arizona and California (Opler and Krizek 1984).

Manitoba Records: Agassiz Provincial Forest, Aweme, Beulah, Birds Hill, Birtle, Carberry, Cartwright, Culross, Cypress River, Elm Creek, Grand Rapids, Hecla Island, Katimik Lake, Killarney, Komarno, Melbourne, Miami, Ninette, Norris Lake, Overflowing River, Riding Mountain, Sandilands Provincial Forest, Spruce Woods Provincial Park, Strathclair, Teulon, The Pas, Victoria Beach, Whiteshell Provincial Park and Winnipeg.

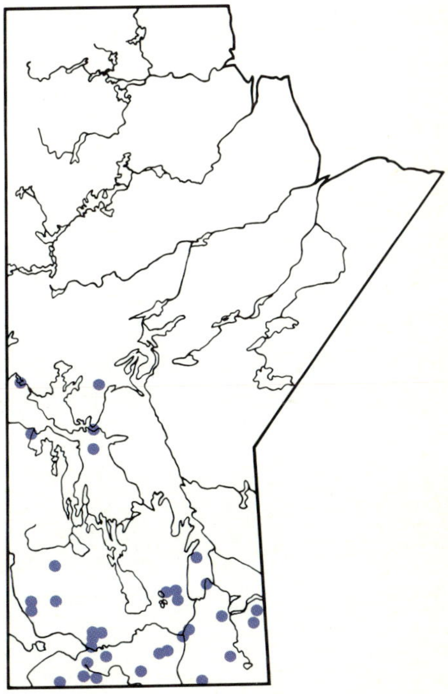

Subspecies: Two subspecies are recognized. In Manitoba, the subspecies is *Euphyes ruricola metacomet*, which is characterized by having the forewing brand almost the same colour as the rest of the forewing. The other subspecies which occurs west of Manitoba is *Euphyes ruricola ruricola*, in which the ground colour of the wing is lighter and the forewing brand is much more noticeable. (Howe 1975; Miller and Brown 1981; Tilden and Smith 1986).

Remarks: The Dun Skipper is commonly found through much of southern Manitoba, but it rarely occurs in large numbers, preferring wooded areas to open prairie. Agassiz Provincial Forest is an area where the Dun Skipper can be quite easily found. Adults have a swift flight but frequently perch either on low shrubs about half a metre above the ground, or on bare ground. They prefer to take nectar from Wild Bergamot, Thistle and Dogbane.

Dusted Skipper

Atrytonopsis hianna (Scudder), 1868

Plate 4 No. 28, 29, 30, 31

Description: 27-34 mm. Above, the wings of the Dusted Skipper are dark gray or grayish-brown. The forewings usually have a number of small but distinct translucent white spots. Below, the wings are brown at the base and dusted with pale gray outwardly. The underside of the forewings have spots similar to the upper side and the underside of the hindwings may also have several small white spots. The forewings are pointed and the males have no forewing brands. Females are larger and have wider forewings with more extensive white markings.

Similar Species: The Dun Skipper lacks the grayish dusting below and males have forewing brands. The Pepper and Salt and the Roadside Skipper are smaller with more rounded wings and have checkered fringes.

Life Cycle: The larval host plants of the Dusted Skipper include Big Bluestem (*Andropogon gerardi*) and Little Bluestem (*Andropogon scoparius*) (McCabe and Post 1977; Opler and Krizek 1984).

The flattened eggs are bright yellow when laid and later change to pale brown with a pinkish tinge dorsally. The larvae hatch in about seven to ten days. The larvae construct tube-like shelters by tying grass blades together and by the fifth instar the tubes can be seven to ten cm. in length. In the fall the larvae seal the ends of the tubes with silk and leaf pieces and overwinter in the shelters. The mature larvae pupate in the leaf tubes during the following spring. Prior to pupation the seventh instar larvae are pale pinkish-lavender dorsally with gray sides. The last abdominal segment is pale brown and depressed dorso-ventrally. The heads and upper thoraxes of the pupae are dark brown, while the first abdomen segments are orange, tinged with pink. The posterior abdominal segments are brown (Heitzman and Heitzman 1974).

In Manitoba, adults are on the wing from May 23 to June 25, being most common during the second week of June.

Habitat: Dry virgin prairie or lightly grazed pasture. Adults may also be found near forest edges.

Range: Southern Canada from Saskatchewan to Ontario, southward to New England, Georgia, Arkansas, Colorado and Wyoming (Howe 1975).

Manitoba Records Aweme, Birds Hill, Brandon, Brokenhead, Carberry, Cromer, Deleau, Miniota, Pine Ridge, Selkirk, Stead and Winnipeg.

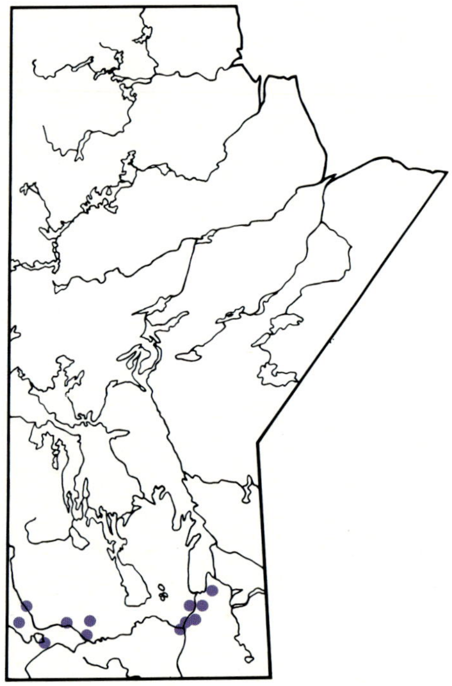

Subspecies: Two or three subspecies are recognized by various authors, but only *Atrytonopis hianna hianna* occurs in Manitoba.

Remarks: The Dusted Skipper which is now confined to the remnants of dry virgin prairie in the province is considered uncommon although where found it may occur in moderate numbers. Both Wallis (1927) and Brooks (1942) noted that the Dusted Skipper was uncommon in Manitoba. As the flight period is relatively short this species may have been overlooked in the past. Adults will visit a variety of flowers for nectar, including Red Clover, Locoweed, and Strawberry. They are best observed while perched or taking nectar as their rapid flight is difficult to follow.

Pepper and Salt Skipper

Amblyscirtes hegon (Scudder), 1864
= *Amblyscirtes samoset* (Scudder), 1864
Plate 4 No. 32, 33, 34

Description: 21-26 mm. The wings of the Pepper and Salt Skipper are dark grayish-brown above with diffuse whitish spots on the forewings. The underside of the wings is dusted with pale gray, with diffused whitish spots in the forewings and a whitish band in the hindwings. The veins on the underside of the hindwings are highlighted with whitish-gray and the wing fringes are checkered. The male forewing brands blend in with the dark grayish-brown colour of the forewings. Most specimens have a greenish-gray hue on the underside of the wings.

Similar Species: The Roadside Skipper is darker and the forewing markings are restricted to a group of three tiny spots near the upper margin. The veins on the underside of its hindwings do not contrast strongly with the ground colour and individuals never have a greenish tinge like that found in the Pepper and Salt Skipper. The Dusted Skipper differs as described under that species. The Dun Skipper is larger and lacks ventral gray dusting and checkered wing fringes.

Life Cycle: Larval food plants include Kentucky Blue Grass (*Poa pratensis*) and Indian Grass (*Sorghastrum nutans*).

The fully grown larvae are pale whitish green with dark green stripes dorsally and a white stripe laterally. The head capsules are dark brown with two vertical pale brown stripes on the front and a pale brown stripe on each side. The pupae are dull yellow tinged with green and have dull orange tongue cases (Howe 1975).

In Manitoba, adults have been recorded from May 14 to July 1, with most records occurring in early June. There is one generation per year.

Habitat: Forest roads, clearings, paths and glades.

Range: Southern Canada from Manitoba to Nova Scotia, southward to Georgia, Mississippi and Arkansas (Howe 1975).

Manitoba Records: Agassiz Provincial Forest, Beulah, Birds Hill, Brandon, Fort Alexander, McCreary, Pine Ridge, Riding Mountain, Sandilands Provincial Forest, Selkirk, Seven Sisters, Stony Mountain and Winnipeg.

Subspecies: No subspecies are recognized.

Remarks: The Pepper and Salt Skipper, strictly a woodland species is uncommon in southern Manitoba. In the wild it is difficult to separate the occasional Pepper and Salt Skipper from scores of similar Roadside Skippers, with which it is usually found. The Pepper and Salt Skipper is not a strong flier and lands often on roads, trails or low vegetation.

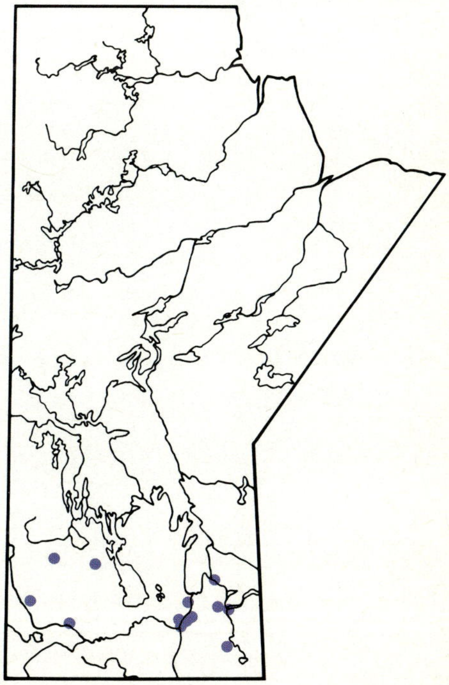

Roadside Skipper

Amblyscirtes vialis (W.H. Edwards), 1862

Plate 4 No. 35, 36, 37

Description: 22-27 mm. Above, the wings are dark grayish-brown with a group of small white dots near the upper margin of the forewings. In some specimens there may also be a small white dot in the center of each forewing. Below, the Roadside Skipper is grayish-brown and the forewing tips and most of the hindwings are dusted with purplish-gray. The dots found on the dorsal surface of the forewing also occur on the underside. The wings are rounded and have checkered fringes. Males have inconspicuous forewing brands.

Similar Species: The Pepper and Salt Skipper differs as described under that species. The Dun Skipper is larger and both it and the Common Sooty Wing lack the ventral grayish dusting and checkered wing fringes found in the Roadside Skipper.

Life Cycle: The larvae of the Roadside Skipper feed on several types of grasses including Kentucky Blue Grass (*Poa pratensis*), and Bent Grass (*Agrostis* sp.) (McCabe and Post 1977).

The newly laid eggs are pale green and upon hatching the larvae construct shelters from leaves of the food plant. After passing through several molts the larvae produce a waxy powder that covers the cuticle and head capsules. At this stage the larvae leave the protection of the shelter and rest fully exposed on the leaves of the food plant. The mature larvae are light green with a dotted cuticle. The head capsules are dull white with several brownish-red bands on the front. The pupae are green with yellow to red colouring on the heads and last abdominal segments. The Roadside Skipper overwinters in the pupal stage (Howe 1975).

In Manitoba, adults are found from May 12 to July 20, being most common in early to mid-June. There is one generation per year in this province and two in southern parts of its range.

Habitat: Forest edges, roads, trails and clearings.

Range: Across central and southern Canada from British Columbia to Nova Scotia and south to Florida and California (Howe 1975).

Manitoba Records Agassiz Provincial Forest, Aweme, Beulah, Birds Hill, Birtle, Brandon, Carberry, Cartwright, Cowan, Duck Mountain, Flin Flon, Gimli, Grand Rapids, Katimik Lake, Marchand, McCreary, Miami, Morden, Pine Ridge, Porcupine Provincial Forest, Riding Mountain, Sandilands Provincial Forest, Snow Lake, Stony Mountain, Victoria Beach and Winnipeg.

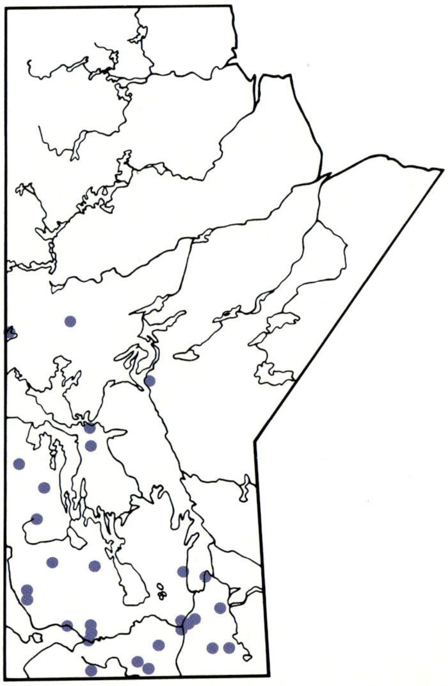

Subspecies: No subspecies are recognized.

Remarks: The Roadside Skipper is the most widespread skipper in North America. Although primarily a woodland species, it occurs in a variety of habitats including prairie areas. Adults will perch on bare ground and males often intercept intruders. Unlike other skippers this species seldom visits flowers, but when it does seek nectar, it prefers blue flowers such as Ground Ivy and Verbena.

Superfamily

PAPILIONOIDEA: TRUE BUTTERFLIES

Family

PAPILIONIDAE: SWALLOWTAILS AND PARNASSIANS

Members of this family are widely distributed in the tropical, temperate and boreal regions in all continents and on many islands. Six hundred or more species exist in the world, of which more than 500 occur in the tropics. Only about 19 species occur in Canada and six of these are found in Manitoba. Two of the three subfamilies of the Papilionidae are found in Canada. The Parnassians (Subfamily Parnassiinae) are primarily an Old World group and in Canada are only found in the western mountains. The Swallowtails (Subfamily Papilioninae) occur from coast to coast north to the tree line in the arctic.

Subfamily

PAPILIONINAE: SWALLOWTAILS

There are approximately 16 species of swallowtails in Canada. Members of the Papilioninae have long tails on the basal margins of the hindwings and are usually brightly coloured. Swallowtails have a spur on the tibia of their front legs (tibial spur or epiphysis) and a single vein near the inner hindwing margins. The forewings are well developed and the proboscis long. Adults readily visit flowers and are swift, strong fliers. The eggs are usually laid singly on the leaves of the host plant. Immature larvae resemble bird droppings and usually feed at night, resting under leaves or within a rolled leaf by day. Mature larvae have a smooth cuticle and in many species the third thoracic segment is enlarged and covered by eye-like spots. In addition, larvae have a pair of fleshy horns (osmeteria) which are situated behind the head capsule and can be extruded. These horns emit a pungent and often repelling odour. The pupae are green or brown and each is attached to a silken anchor pad by a circle of hooks at the posterior of the abdomen. The pupae also have a silk girdle spun around the middle of the thorax. Swallowtails overwinter in the pupal stage.

Papilio glaucus

Pipevine Swallowtail

Battus philenor (Linnaeus), 1771

Plate 5 No. 1

Description: 70-86 mm. The Pipevine Swallowtail is dark gray to coal black dorsally with conspicuous blue and greenish iridescent areas particularly in the hindwings. There is a submarginal row of whitish or yellowish spots in the hindwings and occasionally the pattern is repeated in the forewings. Ventrally the forewings are dull gray and the hindwings are metallic blue outwardly with a submarginal row of large orange spots and a marginal row of narrow whitish spots.

Similar Species: Female Black Swallowtails have an orange spot on the lower inner hindwing margin.

Life Cycle: The food plant, Pipe Vine (*Aristolochia macrophylla*), does not occur in Manitoba.

Habitat: Deciduous and tropical forests, open fields, gardens, roadsides and scrub areas (Opler and Krizek 1984).

Range: Southern Ontario, Great Lake states, southern Minnesota, southward through the southern United States.

Manitoba Records: Killarney

Remarks: The lone record for Manitoba was collected at Killarney, Manitoba by D.W. Morden on September 12, 1942 on a Zinnia flower. The nearest record to Manitoba is for Butterfield, Minnesota, over 800 km to the south.

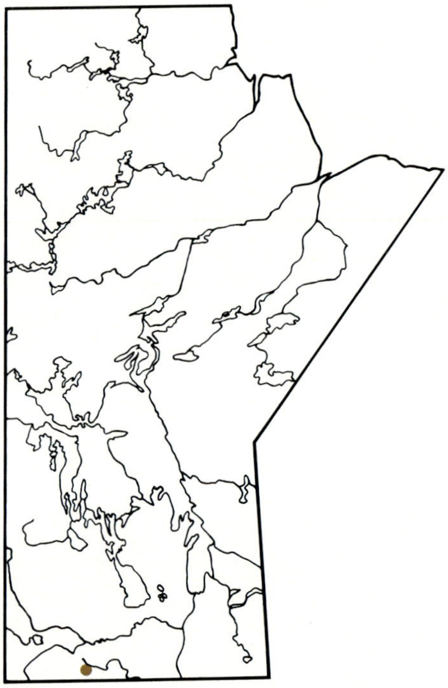

Black Swallowtail

Papilio polyxenes Fabricius, 1775

Plate 5 No. 2, 3, 4

Description: 60-85 mm. Above, there are two bands of yellow spots in each wing, with the inner band being reduced and diffused in the female and wider and bolder in the male. Between the yellow spots of the hindwings, there is a band of diffuse blue spots, large in females and smaller in males. At the base of the inner margin of each hindwing there is a conspicuous black-centered orange spot. The ventral surfaces of the wings are similar in coloration except that the spots in the bands are mostly orange or orange-red.

Similar Species: The yellow inner bands are larger than the outer bands in the Kahli Swallowtail. In addition, the spots form a contiguous band in the hindwings of Kahli Swallowtail males. The black in the orange eye-spots at the base of the hindwings is offset, usually occurring at the base of the eye-spot and frequently joined to the black inner margin of the wing. Below, the spots in the bands of the Kahli Swallowtail are mostly yellow, not orange.

Life Cycle: The larvae of the Black Swallowtail feed on many members of the Parsley Family (*Umbelliferae*). In Manitoba the preferred food plant is Heart-leaved Alexanders (*Zizia aptera*), garden Carrot, Parsley and Parsnip. Other food plants include Meadow Parsnip (*Thaspium barbinade*), Wild Parsnip (*Pastinaca sativa*), Water Hemlock (*Cicuta bulbifera*), Water Parsnip (*Sium suave*), and Sweet Cicely (*Osmorhiza* sp.) (Scott 1986).

Berenbaum (1978) stated that one or more pale green eggs are laid near the tip of a young leaf or flower bud. The young larvae resemble fresh bird droppings while the mature fourth instar larvae are mostly green, yellowish-green or bluish-green with black bands transversing the dorsal and lateral surfaces. These black bands contain yellow to reddish-orange spots. Like all members of the Swallowtail family the larvae have a pair of osmeteria. In captivity, egg hatch to pupation lasts approximately a month. The pupae are green to light brown, with several dark stripes along the dorsal and lateral surfaces.

In Manitoba, adults have been recorded from May 13 to September 2. There are two generations per year in this province. One very worn individual was observed on Sept. 26 by P. Taylor near Brokenhead.

Habitat: Open woods, meadows, gardens, roadsides and pastures.

Range: Southern Canada from Saskatchewan to Nova Scotia and southward to northern South America.

Manitoba Records: Altona, Arden, Aweme, Badger, Birtle, Brandon, Brokenhead, Carberry, Cartwright, Chatfield, Clanwilliam, Cowan, Cromer, Culross, Duck Mountain, Elm Creek, Elva, Gimli, Gladstone, Grand Beach, Gypsumville, Horod, Inwood, Lyleton, McCreary, Miniota, Mulvihill, Neepawa, Norgate, Oak Hammock, Pine Ridge, Riding Mountain, Russell, St. Claude, Sand Ridge, Sandilands Provincial Forest, Selkirk, Spruce Woods Provincial Park, Stonewall, Stuartburn, Teulon, Tolstoi, Turtle Mountain, Valley River, Victoria Beach and Winnipeg.

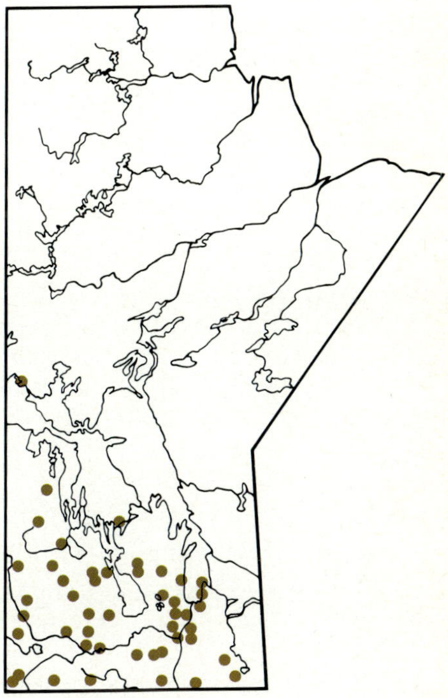

Subspecies: Four subspecies of the Black Swallowtail are recognized. The subspecies in Manitoba is *Papilio polyxenes asterius*.

Remarks: Although common in much of its range, the Black Swallowtail is scarce in Manitoba. This species may be encountered in a variety of habitats and both sexes commonly visit Thistle, Clover and Milkweed for nectar. Males frequently cover large areas in search of females. Larvae commonly feed on garden vegetables, but unlike some other areas they have never become a pest in Manitoba.

Kahli Swallowtail

Papilio kahli F. & R. Chermock, 1937

Plate 6 No. 1, 2, 3, 4, 5, 6

Description: 62-78 mm. Above, there are two bands of yellow spots in each wing with the inner bands usually wider than the outer. In males, the yellow spots of the hindwing often form a contiguous group with a band of diffuse blue spots between the yellow spots. At the base of the inner margin of each hindwing is a black centered orange spot. The black scales within the orange spot are usually offset and connected to the black of the inner margin of the wing. The markings on the ventral surface of the wings are similar to the dorsal side, but there may be an infusion of orange in some of the yellow spots.

Similar Species: The Black Swallowtail differs as described under that species. Rare individuals with extensive yellow bands may be hybrids resulting from Kahli and Old World Swallowtail crosses.

Life Cycle: The primary food plant is Heart-leaved Alexanders (*Zizia aptera*). Other members of the Parsley Family including Carrots, Parsley and Parsnip also serve as food plants in Manitoba.

The larval description and life cycle are similar to that described for the Black Swallowtail. Adults are on the wing from May 20 to August 14 in Manitoba. There are two generations in Manitoba, although some of the pupae from the first generation go into diapause and adults do not emerge until the following spring.

Habitat: Forest meadows, clearings, roadsides and open hills.

Range: Southern Saskatchewan and central and southern Manitoba.

Manitoba Records: Altona, Aweme, Birtle, Brandon, Cartwright, Cowan, Cromer, Culross, Duck Mountain, Elm Creek, Gimli, Gladstone, Kelwood, McCreary, Miniota, Moosehorn, Oak Hammock, Pine Ridge, Pine River, Riding Mountain, Russell, St. Claude, Sand Ridge, Sandilands Provincial Forest, The Pas and Winnipeg.

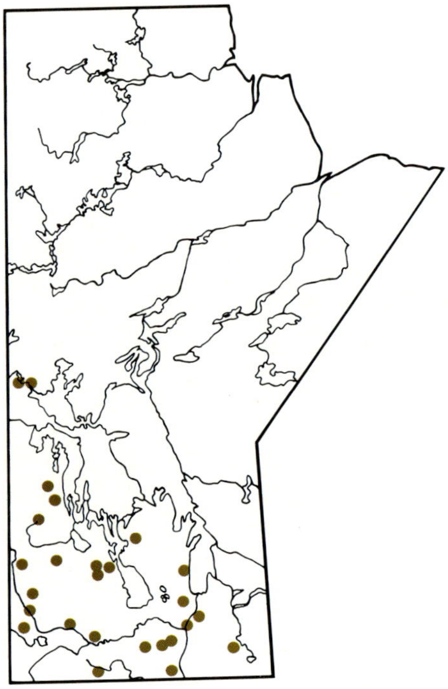

Subspecies: The status of *Papilio kahli* is in debate. Some authors consider the Kahli Swallowtail to be a subspecies of the Black Swallowtail. Sperling (1987) stated that the Kahli Swallowtail consists of an unstable breeding population originating from a *Papilio polyxenes/Papilio machaon* cross, freely interbreeding with its originators.

Remarks: The Kahli Swallowtail and its hybrids have often been misidentified in the past because of their great variability in appearance. Adults are rarely seen in Manitoba, so the best way to find the species is to look for eggs or larvae in the flower buds and heads of their food plant, Heart-leaved Alexanders. At Cowan, Manitoba adult Kahli Swallowtails have been observed flying together with Old World and Tiger Swallowtails. This species is most common in the Riding and Duck Mountains where the parental populations meet. Specimens from further south in Manitoba show some introgression of *machaon* genes, though these populations may be clinally connected to pure *Papilio polyxenes* (Sperling pers. comm.).

Old World Swallowtail

Papilio machaon Linnaeus, 1758

Plate 7 No. 1, 2, 3

Description: 54-78 mm. The upperside of each wing is yellow with wide black marginal bands that enclose a row of yellow submarginal spots. Adjacent to these spots is a row of diffuse blue spots. The forewings have black bases and several black bars near the upper margins. The hindwings have black inner margins. There is an orange-red eyespot at the bottom of each inner hindwing. Within the eyespot is a elongated black oval that is usually joined to the black inner margin of the wing. The wing veins are outlined in black. The markings on the ventral wing surfaces are similar to those of the dorsal but paler.

Life Cycle: In Manitoba the larval food plant is thought to be Palmate-leaved Colt's-foot (*Petasites palmatus*). Larvae of the Old World Swallowtail feed upon other species of *Petasites* and Sagebrush (*Artemisia* spp.) in the Northwest Territories and Yukon. The early stages of the Old World Swallowtail are not well known in Manitoba. Adults have been recorded from May 17 to July 27 in Manitoba, with most sightings occurring in June.

Habitat: Coniferous forest edges, forest clearings, roadsides, trails and open pine woods.

Range: Europe and Asia and in North America from Alaska, Yukon and Northwest Territories, southeastward through the boreal forests to northern Manitoba and northwestern Ontario. South to the shore of Lake Superior in Ontario, southern Manitoba, central Saskatchewan, Alberta and British Columbia (Howe 1975).

Coniferous forest edge, near Thompson, Manitoba. July 1986.

Manitoba Records: Berens River, Brandon, Churchill, Cowan, Denbeigh Point, Duck Mountain, Flin Flon, Gillam, Lynn Lake, Mafeking, Mile 200 and 412 of the Hudson Bay Railway, Miniota, Pine River, Porcupine Provincial Forest, Riding Mountain, The Pas and Thompson.

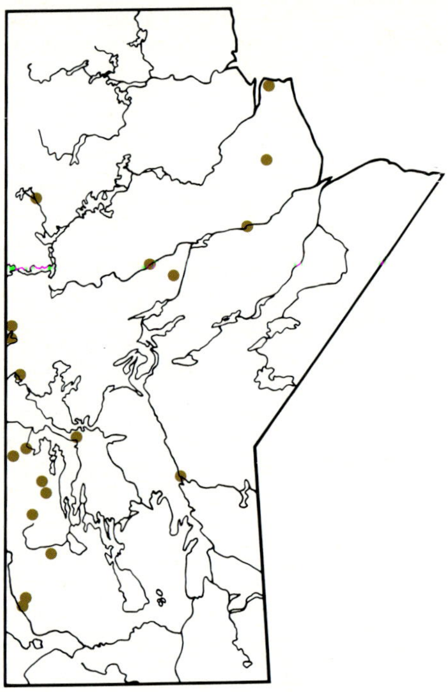

Subspecies: The Manitoba subspecies of the Old World Swallowtail is *Papilio machaon hudsonianus*.

Remarks: Although the Old World Swallowtail is widely distributed in Manitoba, it is usually only seen in small numbers and little is known about its biology. P. Klassen observed over 20 freshly emerged males at mud puddles in the Duck Mountains on June 24, 1975. Here they were associated with Tiger Swallowtails which occurred in much larger numbers. The Old World Swallowtail is locally common at Thompson on or near hillsides. Adults are wary of intruders, but may be observed while feeding upon such plants as Labrador Tea, Dandelion, Dogbane and Hawksbeard.

Giant Swallowtail

Papilio cresphontes Cramer, 1777

= *Heraclides cresphontes*

Plate 7 No. 4

Description: 84-140 mm. The Giant Swallowtail is dark brownish-black dorsally with two yellow spot-bands converging at the tip of the forewings and an orange spot at the end of the hindwings' inner margin. Ventrally the wings are yellow with black borders and veins. The hindwings have a band of blue crescents and an orange spot at the end of the inner margin.

Life Cycle: The larval food plants do not occur in Manitoba.

Habitat: Semi-open or brushy areas. In the northern part of its range the Giant Swallowtail prefers rocky and exposed hillsides near streams (Howe 1975).

Range: Ontario and Quebec, southward to Florida and the southwestern states and into South America.

Manitoba Records: Winnipeg.

Remarks: The Giant Swallowtail is most abundant in the tropics and southern United States and sporadically extends its range northward. Individuals have been found in Minnesota and North Dakota. N.R. Brandt collected one specimen in Winnipeg in August of 1961. W. Preston observed a Giant Swallowtail in Winnipeg on September 23, 1978, the day after a strong south wind.

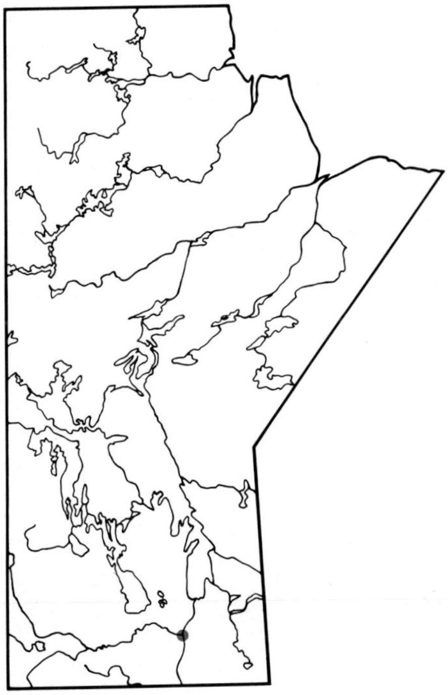

Tiger Swallowtail

Papilio glaucus Linnaeus, 1758
= *Pterourus glaucus*

Plate 8 No. 1, 2, 3

Description: 63-91 mm. Above, the wings are yellow with black margins enclosing a submarginal row of yellow spots. There are black "tiger-like" stripes across the fore and hindwings. Usually the top submarginal hindwing spot is orange and there are two marginal orange spots close to the tail of each hindwing. In addition, there is a band of diffuse blue spots traversing the hindwings. The undersides of the wings are similar to but paler than the upper surfaces. Females are larger than males and more extensively marked with black, orange and blue. Occasionally, females may be quite pale in appearance with cream-coloured forewings and rarely males are encountered with a orange tinge to the wings.

Similar Species: The Old World Swallowtail differs as described under that species.

Life Cycle: The Tiger Swallowtail has a great number of host plants including Trembling Aspen (*Populus tremuloides*), Balsam Poplar (*Populus balsamifera*), White Birch (*Betula papyrifera*), Wild Cherry (*Prunus* sp.), Green Ash (*Fraxinus pennsylvanica*), Maples (*Acer* sp.) and Western Mountain Ash (*Sorbus americana*).

The newly laid eggs are yellowish-green in colour and the early instar larvae are brown and white, resembling bird droppings. The larvae feed mostly at night and construct silken pads on leaves to rest upon when not feeding. As the larvae mature they construct curled leaf shelters for protection (Opler and Krizek 1984). The full grown larvae are green, approximately 5 cm long, with smooth cuticles. There are large orange and black eye-spots on the thoracic segments and posterior to the eye-spots is a yellow and black band. The pupae are mottled brown, tan or green and resemble twigs. They are attached by silken girdles to a tree trunk or branch where they overwinter.

In Manitoba, adults have been observed from May 17 to August 20. Females are on the wing later than males. There is one generation per year.

Habitat: Deciduous woods and less commonly coniferous forests, river and stream banks, roadsides, trails, meadows, gardens and farmyards.

Range: Alaska, Yukon and in every province across Canada and south throughout the United States east of the Rocky Mountains.

Manitoba Records: Agassiz Provincial Forest, Ashville, Aweme, Badger, Beresford Lake, Binscarth, Birds Hill, Brokenhead, Carberry, Cartwright, Churchill, Cowan, Cromer, Culross, Deleau, Denbeigh Point, Duck Mountain, Elm Creek, Flin Flon, Gillam, Gimli, Grand Beach, Grand Rapids, Gypsumville, Katimik Lake, Kelwood, Killarney, Lundar, Lyleton, Lynn Lake, Mafeking, Marchand, Melbourne, Miami, Mile 200 Hudson Bay Railway, Moosehorn, Neepawa, Norris Lake, Northwest Angle Provincial Forest, Norway House, Overflowing River, Pine Ridge, Porcupine Mountain, Riding Mountain, Rossburn, Rounthwaite, Sandilands Provincial Forest, Schist Lake, Sclater, Selkirk, Seven Sisters, Spruce Woods Provincial Park, The Pas, Thompson, Treesbank, Turtle Mountain, Victoria Beach, Wabowden, Wallace Lake, Whitemouth Lake, Whiteshell Provincial Park and Winnipeg.

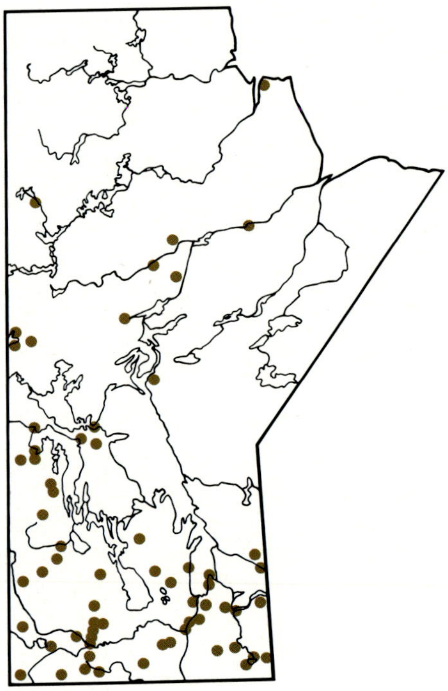

Subspecies: There are three subspecies recognized. In most of Canada the subspecies is *Papilio glaucus canadensis* (Howe 1975; Miller and Brown 1981).

Remarks: In the southern part of their range, female Tiger Swallowtails are either yellow or black and differ so greatly in appearance that they were once considered separate species. In Manitoba, only the Monarch exceeds the Tiger Swallowtail in size. Newly emerged males sometimes gather by the hundreds at mud puddles to feed. Both sexes will feed on animal excrement and avidly visit a wide variety of flowers for nectar. Adults have been observed feeding at the flowers of Dogbane, Thistle, Clover, Milkweed, Labrador Tea, Joe-pye Weed, Lilac and many garden plants. Females are generally more sedentary than males and remain closer to the forest.

Family

PIERIDAE: WHITES, MARBLES AND SULPHURS

There are approximately 1000 species within the family Pieridae. About 60 species occur in North America and 37 of these are found in Canada. There are 17 species of whites, marbles and sulphurs in Manitoba.

Members of this family occur on all continents, except the Antarctic. In Manitoba, the family Pieridae consists of medium sized white, yellow or orange butterflies with black markings. The colour pigments in the scales are formed from uric acid, unlike other butterfly families. The forelegs are fully developed in both sexes and lack an epiphysis; the tarsal claws are bifid. Males of Manitoba species actively search out females and mating generally occurs in the afternoon. Adults will frequently bask in the sun with wings tightly closed but occasionally perch with the wings partly opened. Members of this family readily feed on flowers and males often congregate at mud puddles.

The eggs are spindle-shaped and frequently ribbed. They are laid singly on the host plant. Most species of Pieridae larvae in Manitoba feed exposed on leaves, flowers and fruit of crucifers and legumes (several species feed on heaths and willow). Mature larvae are smooth and slender, often with numerous tiny tubercles bearing short, fine hairs. Larvae are green with yellow or white stripes. Pupae of many species have a projection on the head and are attached to the pupation site by a silk girdle. Three subfamilies within the family Pieridae occur in Manitoba.

Subfamily

PIERINAE: WHITES

These butterflies are usually white in colour and the antennae are long with wide clubs. Flight is slow but often quite erratic. Larvae within this subfamily are covered with down or tiny hairs and feed on leaves of members of the Cruciferae (Mustard Family).

Colias eurytheme

Checkered White

Pontia protodice
(Boisduval & Leconte), 1829
= *Pieris protodice*
Plate 9 No. 1, 2, 3, 4

Description: 37-47 mm. Above, the wings are white with charcoal or brown markings. In females the markings are brownish and much heavier, forming a submarginal band that is broken near the bottom of the forewings. There is a similar pattern on the underside of the forewings and the hindwings are lined with brown or yellowish-green in females and unmarked in males. Spring adults from overwintering pupae are smaller and darker than those from the summer generation: males have heavy dark scales bordering the veins on the underside of the hindwings and females tend to have darker scaling on both surfaces of the wings. Females are best identified by the large squarish black spot at the inner margin on the underside of the forewings.

Similar Species: The Western Checkered White males have more extensive black markings forming marginal and submarginal bands in the forewings and the veins on the underside of the hindwings are always outlined. Females have complete submarginal bands. In both sexes, the spot at the inner forewing margin is never large and squarish. Some specimens are very difficult to distinguish from the Checkered White.

Life Cycle: The Checkered White feeds on many members of the Cruciferae, including Cabbage, Turnip, Mustard and Shepherd's-purse (*Capsella bursa-pastoris*).

The mature larvae are covered in fine hairs and are alternately striped with greenish-purple and yellow. There are two generations per year and the Checkered White overwinters in the pupal stage. Adults have been recorded from July 2 to September 22, with most records occurring in August.

Habitat: Open fields, prairie hillsides and roadsides.

Range: Across the southern United States from California to Florida, northward to southern Quebec and westward to southern Alberta.

Prairie hillsides, southeast of Souris, Manitoba. July 1978.

Manitoba Records: Aweme, Beulah, Birds Hill, Birtle, Brandon, Carberry, Culross, Elm Creek, Glenboro, Riding Mountain, Sandilands Provincial Forest, Victoria Beach and Winnipeg.

Subspecies: No subspecies are recognized.

Remarks: This butterfly is also known as the Common White. In recent years there has been a decline in the population in eastern North America probably due to habitat loss rather than from competition from the Cabbage White as some authors have stated. The Checkered White is not common in Manitoba; Wallis (1927) stated that this species "is quite rare in the province". It is sometimes found in association with the more abundant Western Checkered White, feeding in alfalfa fields in southwest Manitoba.

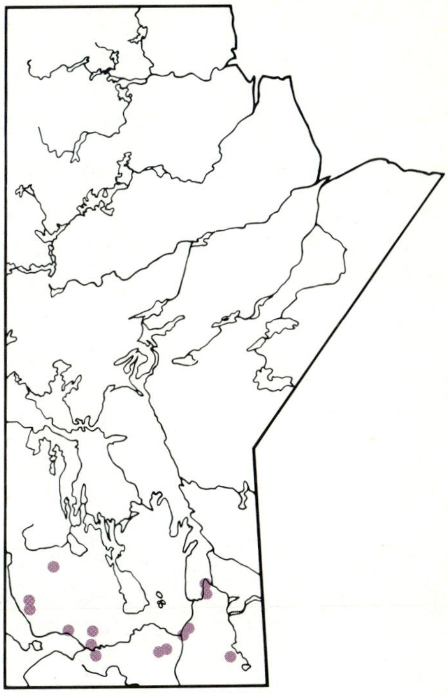

Western Checkered White

Pontia occidentalis (Reakirt), 1866

= *Pieris occidentalis*

= *Pieris callidice* Hübner, 1805

Plate 9 No. 5, 6, 7

Description: 35-47 mm. The dorsal surface of the wings is white with blackish or charcoal spots and bands. The markings are darkest toward the apex of the forewings. The pattern is repeated on the ventral surface of the forewings and in the hindwings the veins are lined with greenish-gray scales. Females generally have darker markings than males and adults from the overwintering generation are smaller, duller above and darker green below, than individuals from the summer generation.

Similar Species: The Checkered White as described under that species. Males of the overwintering generation of the Checkered White and Western Checkered White are more difficult to distinguish than those from the summer generation because both are heavily marked. Checkered White males of the summer generation are much lighter than those of the Western Checkered White.

Life Cycle: Larval food plants include Tumble Mustard (*Sisymbrium altissimum*), Stinkweed (*Thlaspi arvense*), Spider Plant (*Cleome serrulata*) and probably other members of the Mustard Family.

The eggs are yellow and spindle shaped. The mature larvae are dull green with alternate light and dark stripes running the length of the body (Scott 1986). The pupae are bluish-gray in colour and speckled with black. In Manitoba, the Western Checkered White overwinters in the pupal stage.

Adults are on the wing from April 28 to September 27 in Manitoba and there are two generations per year. Adults from the summer generation usually appear in late July and early August.

Habitat: Virgin prairie hillsides, open grassy areas, old fields and weedy abandoned farmyards.

Range: From Alaska and the Yukon to Ontario, southward in the western United States to Mexico.

Manitoba Records: Austin, Aweme, Berens River, Beulah, Birtle, Carberry, Churchill, Culross, Deleau, Duck Mountain, Elm Creek, Fort Alexander, Gillam, Hecla Island, Kelwood, Kola, Lauder, Lyleton, McCreary, Melbourne, Mile 412 Hudson Bay Railway, Miniota, Oak Lake, Partridge Lake, Pine Ridge, Riding Mountain, Sandilands Provincial Forest, Spruce Woods Provincial Park, Stony Mountain, Teulon, The Pas, Treesbank, Turtle Mountain Provincial Park and Winnipeg.

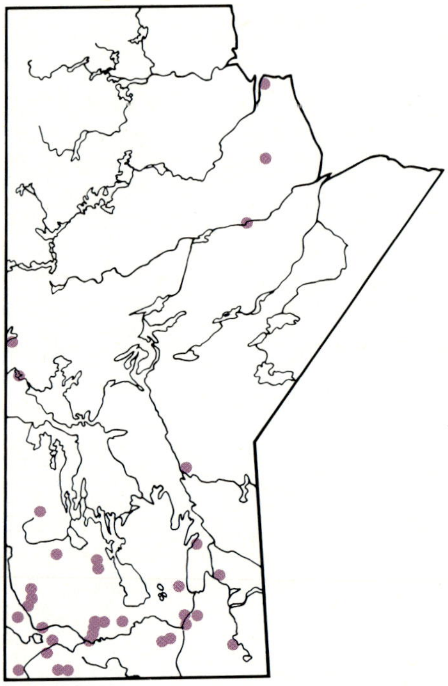

Subspecies: Two subspecies are recognized. In Manitoba the subspecies is *Pontia occidentalis occidentalis*.

Remarks: The Western Checkered White is most abundant in the southwestern corner of the province. If wild flowers are scarce adults will feed in alfalfa fields. In the Carberry area adult Western Checkered Whites fly in association with the Alfalfa Butterfly, Common Sulphur and the Cabbage Butterfly. The Western Checkered White seems to be most numerous during sunny, hot summers and scarce in cool wet summers.

Veined White

Pieris napi (Linnaeus), 1758
= *Artogeia napi*

Plate 9 No. 8, 9, 10, 11

Description: 34-44 mm. The wings of individuals from the summer generation are white above and pale cream below. There is an absence of spots or lines on both the upper and lower wing surfaces. Occasional females may have faint gray spots. Members of the spring generation are white above with light gray scales along the veins of the hindwings and those near the tip of the forewings. Below, the wings of the spring form are cream coloured with much darker gray scales along the veins of the hindwing and near the forewing tip. At Churchill only the dark-veined spring form occurs.

Similar Species: Occasionally Cabbage Butterflies are encountered where the upper surfaces of the wings are nearly devoid of markings. These individuals are dingy white above and usually have a faint gray spot on the ventral side of the forewings and lack the darkened veins of the Veined White.

Life Cycle: Larvae feed on various Cruciferae, including Rock Cress (*Arabis* sp.), Tower Mustard (*Arabis glabra*), Winter Cress (*Barbarea orthoceras*), Stinkweed (*Thlaspi arvense*) and Cabbage.

The pale green vase-shaped eggs are laid singly on the underside of the leaves of the food plant. Mature larvae are velvety-green with greenish-yellow stripes running along the dorsal and lateral surfaces of the body. Short, fine hairs cover the cuticle giving the larvae a velvet-like appearance. The pupae are green or tan, flecked with black. In Manitoba the Veined White overwinters in this stage.

Adults have been recorded from May 7 to August 31 and are most abundant in late June and July. There are two generations per year in southern Manitoba and one in the Churchill area.

Habitat: Open glades, roadsides, trails in coniferous and mixed woods.

Range: Europe, Asia and in North America from Alaska and the Yukon to Newfoundland, southward to New York, the Great Lakes states, Montana, Arizona and California.

Manitoba Records: Agassiz Provincial Forest, Austin, Aweme, Beulah, Birds Hill, Cape Tatnam, Cartwright, Churchill, Cowan, Duck Mountain, Flin Flon, Fort Alexander, Gillam, Glenboro, Grand Marais, Hadashville, Hecla Island, Husavik, Island Lake, Katimik Lake, Kelwood, Lynn Lake, McCreary, Mile 412 Hudson Bay Railway, Miniota, Northwest Angle Provincial Forest, Norway House, Onanole, Oscar Point, Pine Ridge, Rennie, Riding Mountain, Rosenburg, Sandilands Provincial Forest, Seven Sisters, The Pas, Treesbank, Victoria Beach, Wallace Lake, Whiteshell Provincial Park, Winnipeg, Winnipeg Beach and York Factory.

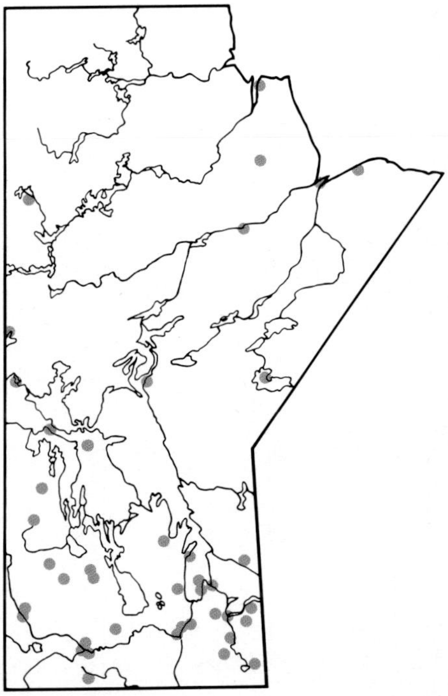

Subspecies: Nine subspecies of the Veined White are recognized in North America, although with future research some may prove to be separate species. The Manitoba subspecies is *Pieris napi oleracea* and its distribution includes Alberta east to Nova Scotia and the northeastern United States.

Remarks: The Veined White prefers cool, moist woodlands and seldom strays far from this habitat. It is common in boreal forest areas but scarce in the agricultural areas. Populations fluctuate on a yearly basis, but generally the summer generation is more plentiful than the overwintering generation. Yellow or white flowers of the Mustard Family are the preferred nectar sources. Adults have a weak flight and when disturbed on open trails or roadsides seek the protection of adjacent woodland. Adults of the overwintering generation are more confined to the forest than those of the summer generation which commonly venture out to open areas in search of flowers.

Cabbage White

Pieris rapae (Linnaeus), 1758

= *Artogeia rapae*

Plate 9 No. 12, 13, 14

Description: 34-47 mm. This butterfly is white or cream on the dorsal surface with a triangular gray or black patch at the tip of the forewings. There is one black spot in the forewings of the males, two in the females, and one at the upper hindwing margins of both sexes. Ventrally the spots are similar to those on the upper surface of the wings. The forewing tips are yellowish, and the hindwings are yellowish dusted with gray. Occasionally individuals from the overwintering generation lack black spots, but the veins are never darkly outlined as in the Veined White.

Life Cycle: The larvae of the Cabbage White feed on numerous species of crucifers, especially Cabbage, Cauliflower and Broccoli.

The surface of the vase shaped eggs is elaborately ribbed and the females usually oviposit on the underside of the food plant leaf. The green larvae are covered with short, fine hairs. They are dotted with black and have a thin yellow stripe along the dorsal surface and thin, broken yellow lateral stripes. The pupae are green, gray or brown and speckled with black. The pupae often resemble the colour of the substrate they are attached to and are the overwintering stage in Manitoba. Occasionally hundreds of eggs and larvae in different instars can be found on a single Cabbage plant.

Adults have been recorded from April 26 to October 14 in Manitoba. There are probably three or more staggered generations in this province, with adults being most common in July and August.

Habitat: Gardens, fields, forest clearings, farmyards, roadsides and other disturbed open areas.

Range: Europe, Asia and all of North America north to the Hudsonian Zone.

Manitoba Records: Widespread in southern Manitoba. Occurs northward to Churchill. In northern areas it is confined to areas in and around the scattered settlements.

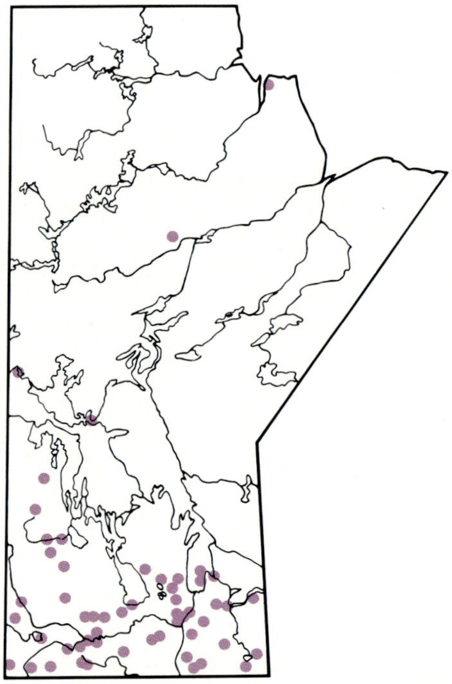

Subspecies: No subspecies are recognized in North America.

Remarks: This butterfly, also known as the European Cabbage Butterfly or Small White, was accidentally introduced to this continent in Quebec about 1860. It is of economic importance because of the larva, called the Cabbage worm, which can be a serious pest. Unlike many butterfly species, it has thrived on disturbed habitats; it has spread throughout the continent and is very common in southern Manitoba. Some authors have stated that the invasion of the Cabbage White has caused the decline of Checkered and Veined Whites, but the apparent decline of the latter two species is most likely due to habitat loss rather than competition. Adult Cabbage Whites avidly visit flowers and often a large number will visit a single plant. They also feed at moist earth and mud puddles, often sharing the site with Sulphurs. One specimen was collected March 28 but it is believed to have emerged indoors.

Subfamily
ANTHOCHARINAE: MARBLES AND ORANGE TIPS

This is a small subfamily and differs from the Pierinae in that the larvae feed solely on flowering parts of plants, while the Pierinae are leaf feeders; the male genitalia are also considerably different in structure. Manitoba species of Anthocharinae have green marbling on the underside of the wings. Orange Tips do not occur in this province.

The eggs are yellow when laid, turning a reddish-orange in less than 24 hours and are almost always laid on or near flowers of the food plant. The pupal period lasts approximately 10 months, with the adults emerging in spring. In Manitoba, adults are more wary than other whites and have a relatively swift, direct flight.

Creamy Marblewing
Euchloe ausonides (Lucas), 1852
= *Euchloe ausonia* (Hübner), 1803
Plate 9 No. 17, 18, 19

Description: 31-47 mm. The wings are creamy white above with a black bar at the end of the discal cell and black spots on the apex of the forewings. In the female, the hindwings may be cream to creamy-yellow. Below, the wings have yellowish-green marbling which occurs in separate bars and covers the hindwings and forewing tips. The marbling on the underside can be seen through the wings on the dorsal surface. Ventrally the hindwing veins are usually yellow and there is a black bar on each forewing. Females are generally larger than males, although individuals vary greatly in size and dwarf specimens are often encountered.

Similar Species: The Olympia Marble differs as described under that species.

Life Cycle: The larvae of the Ausonides Marble feed on a number of different crucifers, including Tower Mustard (*Arabis glabra*), Drummond's Rock Cress (*Arabis drummondii*), Tumble Mustard (*Sisymbrium altissimum*), Bird Rape (*Brassica campestris*) and Gray Tansy Mustard (*Descurainia richardsonii*).

The elongate, flask-shaped eggs are laid singly on the buds of the host plant. Usually only one egg is deposited per plant, but occasionally several are laid. The larvae feed on the young buds and may strip the entire plant. The mature larvae are dark green with a blue-gray stripe on the dorsal surface. Laterally the larvae are flanked by a grayish-green stripe and a yellowish stripe below. The Ausonides Marble overwinters in the pupal stage.

In Manitoba, adults have been recorded from May 2 to July 22. The flight period is variable, but adults are usually most numerous in late May and early June. There is one generation per year in this province (Howe 1975; Ferris and Brown 1981).

Habitat: Open pine forests, clearings, glades and meadows in mixed and boreal forests.

Range: Alaska, Yukon and the Northwest Territories to Ontario, southward to Michigan, Minnesota, New Mexico and California. Absent from the eastern and much of the central United States.

Manitoba Records: Agassiz Provincial Forest, Bellsite, Beulah, Brokenhead, Cowan, Churchill, Duck Mountain, Gillam, Grand Beach, Kelwood, McCreary, Mile 412 Hudson Bay Railway, Norway House, Oberon, Riding Mountain, Rosenburg, Sand Ridge, Sand River, Sandilands Provincial Forest, Victoria Beach, Whitemouth Lake and Whiteshell Provincial Park.

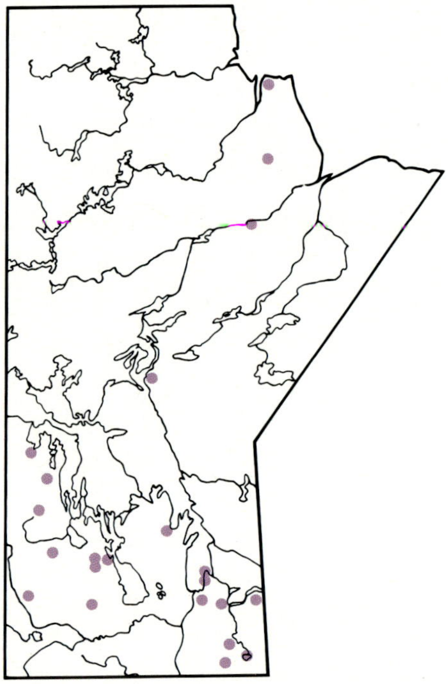

Subspecies: Howe (1975) refers all Manitoba specimens to *Euchloe ausonides mayi*. Brooks (1942) reported that *mayi* only occurred in Riding Mountain and that specimens from elsewhere in Manitoba belonged to the subspecies *coloradensis*. The authors feel that there is no appreciable difference between these populations and treat all Manitoba populations as *mayi*.

Remarks: Although widespread in distribution this butterfly is restricted to the forested areas in Manitoba. It is sporadic in appearance and populations fluctuate greatly from year to year. The Ausonides Marble is best sought in open pine forests where it flies low to the ground in a zig-zag pattern and often alights to feed at flowers. Riding and Duck Mountains and Sandilands Provincial Forest are areas where this marble may be most easily observed. At Sandilands it has been frequently observed nectaring at Tower Mustard.

Olympia Marble

Euchloe olympia (W.H. Edwards), 1871

Plate 9 No. 15, 16, 20

Description: 26-40 mm. The Olympia Marble resembles the Ausonides Marble, but is smaller and chalky white, not creamy, on the upper surface. The forewing tips have reduced gray markings. Below, the green marbling on the hindwings is restricted to three bands, the second and third band being joined together, with relatively large areas of white between them. There is usually a rosy flush on the underside of the hindwings, especially on newly emerged specimens.

Life Cycle: Larval food plants include Hedge Mustard (*Sisymbrium officinale*), Tower Mustard (*Arabis glabra*), Lyre-leaved Rock Cress(*Arabis lyrata*) and Drummond's RockCress(*Arabis drummondii*).

Females oviposit eggs singly on the unopened flower buds of the host plant. The larvae will feed exclusively on the flowering parts and subsequent seed pods. The mature larvae are green with gray stripes along the dorsal surface and a yellowish line laterally (which turns ash-gray prior to pupation). The pupae are rosy-purple initially, turning pale brown or tan with brown lines behind the head soon after formation. The Olympia Marble overwinters in the pupal stage (Opler and Krizek 1984).

The only reliable Manitoba collecting date record is for May 2. In Saskatchewan this species has been observed from May 24 to June 13. There is one generation per year (Hooper 1973).

Habitat: Dry knolls and hills in prairie areas, riverbank bluffs, woods and forests.

Range: Alberta to Quebec, southward to West Virginia and Texas, east of the Rocky Mountains (Howe 1975).

Manitoba Records: Aweme, Birtle and Riding Mountain.

Subspecies: There are no subspecies recognized.

Remarks: This species has rarely been observed in Manitoba. The authors were able to locate only two specimens, one collected by Norman Criddle at Aweme in 1896 and another collected by C.S. Quelch at Birtle on May 2, 1971. It has also been reported from Riding Mountain by J. Masters (Hooper 1973). The early flight period, local nature and restricted habitat of the Olympia Marble may be partly responsible for its rarity in Manitoba collections. Like the Ausonides Marble, the Olympia Marble flies close to the ground and readily visits a wide variety of flowers.

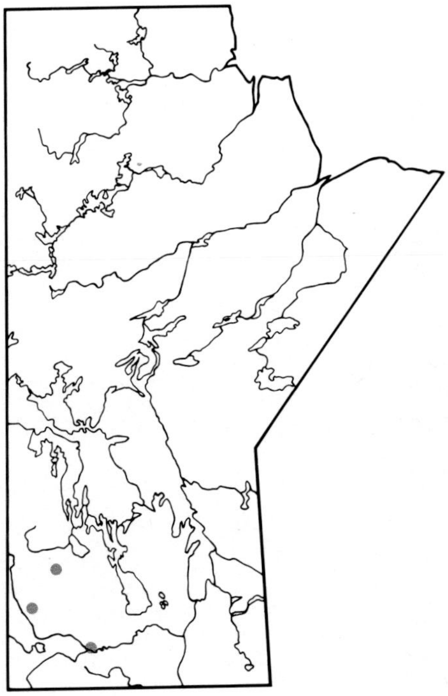

Subfamily

COLIADINAE: SULPHURS

In Manitoba, the members of this subfamily are medium sized yellow or orange butterflies usually with black borders, pink antennae and fringes along the wing edges. Adults are often sexually dimorphic and albino (white) females occur regularly in some of our species. Their antennae are shorter than those of the Whites (Pierinae) and they usually feed on legumes, although several species prefer willows and heaths as larval host plants.

Common Sulphur

Colias philodice Godart, 1819

Plate 10 No. 1, 2, 3, 4

Description: 34-47 mm. The dorsal surface of the wings of males is yellow with black borders, a black discocellular spot on each forewing and an orange spot on each hindwing. Beneath, the males have a silver spot ringed with red or pink on the hindwings, a black spot on the forewings and a row of submarginal dark spots on each wing. Females are similar, except that the black borders contain light spots. White or albino females are commonly encountered. Adults from the overwintering and last summer generations are smaller, with narrow black borders and considerable fucous or green dusting on the ventral side of the hindwings. This species is generally quite variable in size and appearance.

Similar Species: See the Alfalfa Butterfly.

Life Cycle: Larval food plants include White Clover (*Trifolium repens*), Alfalfa (*Medicago sativa*), Vetch (*Vicia* sp.), Hedysarum (*Hedysarum* sp.) and Locoweed (*Oxytropis* spp.).

The spindle-shaped eggs are laid singly on the leaves of the food plants. The eggs are yellowish-green and turn orange and dark red soon after they have been deposited. First instar larvae are pale with irregular bristles and dark head capsules. Mature larvae are yellowish-green with a darker stripe along the dorsal surface and a whitish line laterally, bordered by a variable black band containing a broken red line. The pupae are green and gradually lose their colour as the adults develop within. The Common Sulphur overwinters in the pupal stage.

This species had been recorded from May 7 to November 4 in Manitoba and is most common in July. There are generally three generations per year in Manitoba (Opler and Krizek 1984).

Habitat: Open fields, alfalfa fields, meadows and roadsides.

Range: Across the continent, through the territories and provinces of Canada, north to the Hudsonian Zone. Southward throughout the United States, but absent from Florida and western California (Howe 1975).

Manitoba Records: All of southern Manitoba, north to Flin Flon, Oscar Point, The Pas and Thompson.

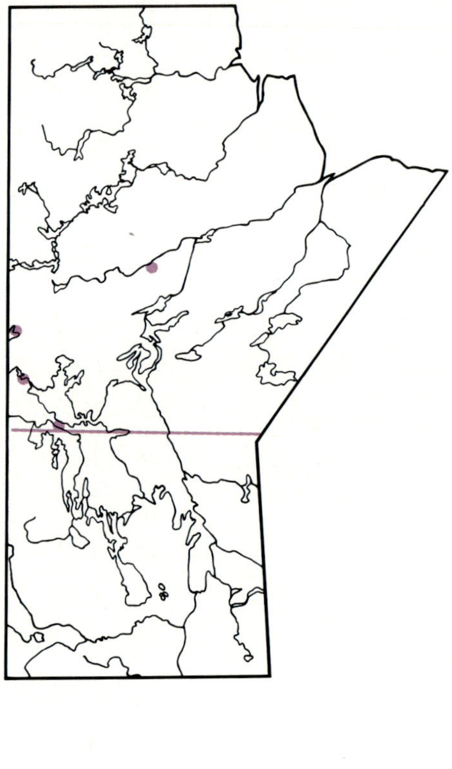

Subspecies: The Manitoba subspecies is *Colias philodice philodice* and occurs in the entire eastern part of the species range west of the Rocky Mountains.

Remarks: This is a common butterfly seen across the province. The Common Sulphur has benefited from the spread of agriculture in North America by utilizing introduced crops like alfalfa, clover and vetch as larval food plants. Adults visit a wide variety of flowers, including Dandelion, Alfalfa, Clovers, Goldenrod and Asters during the warmer hours of the day. Young males sometimes gather in large groups with Alfalfa Butterflies at mud-puddles or areas of moist soil.

Alfalfa Butterfly

Colias eurytheme Boisduval, 1852

Plate 10 No. 5, 6, 7, 8, 9, 10

Description: 37-56 mm. Above, the wings are orange or yellow with an orange tinge. The markings are similar to those of the Common Sulphur except that the black margins are usually wider. The orange colour often extends to the darkly dusted bases of the wings. Females may be orange, white or yellow (yellow individuals have at least a tinge of orange). The adults from the summer generation are larger and more brightly coloured than those from the spring generation.

Similar Species: The Common Sulphur is lemon yellow, without a tinge of orange and has a smaller wingspan. White females of both the Common Sulphur and Alfalfa Butterfly are very difficult to distinguish but usually the discal spot in the centre of the hindwings upper surface is orange in the Alfalfa Butterfly and yellow in the Common Sulphur. It has been suggested that the two species may hybridize. The Alexandra Sulphur has yellow wing bases and lacks the dark basal dusting common to the Alfalfa Butterfly.

Life Cycle: Alfalfa (*Medicago sativa*) is the primary host plant. Secondary host plants include White Clover (*Trifolium repens*), Late Yellow Locoweed (*Oxytropis campestris*) and possibly other legumes. The life history and immature stages are similar to that described for the Common Sulphur.

Adults have been observed from May 19 to November 15 in Manitoba. There may be up to three overlapping generations in this province, with the peak flight period occurring in July.

Habitat: Roadsides and open fields especially alfalfa fields. Infrequently found in heavily forested areas.

Range: British Columbia to Nova Scotia, northward to the Hudsonian Zone and southward to Mexico.

Manitoba Records: Across all of southern Manitoba, north to Churchill, Gillam, Oscar Point, Porcupine Provincial Forest, The Pas, Thompson and York Factory.

Subspecies: No subspecies are recognized at present.

Remarks: Apparently benefiting from the advent of agriculture, the Alfalfa Butterfly can often be found in great numbers in alfalfa fields. Adults avidly visit alfalfa flowers and males often congregate in large numbers at mud puddles.

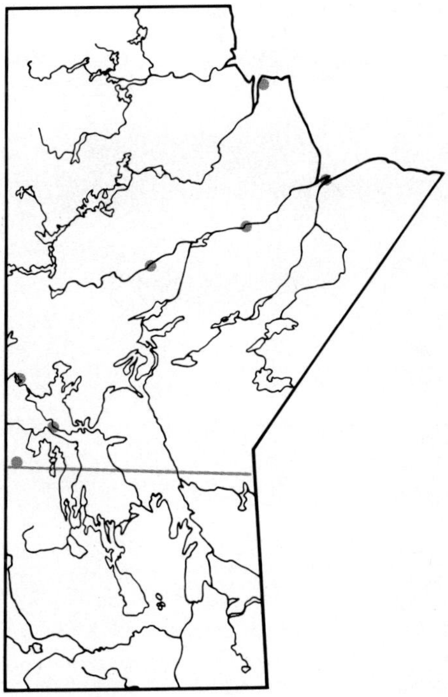

Christina Sulphur

Colias alexandra W.H. Edwards, 1863

Plate 10 No. 11, 12, 13, 14, 15

Description: 43-55mm. Above, males are orange, with yellow wing bases. The black margins at the edge of the wings are wide and there is a small cellular black spot in each forewing. Females are more yellowish than males sometimes nearly all yellow, or even white; the black wing borders are less developed, sometimes reduced to a black dusting or completely absent, especially on the hindwings. The submarginal row of dark spots on the underside of the wings are poorly developed and are usually absent entirely. Females are a little larger than males.

Similar Species: Alfalfa Butterfly differs as described under that species.

Life Cycle: Larval food plants include Milk Vetch (*Astragalus* sp.), Wild Pea (*Lathyrus* sp.), Alfalfa (*Medicago sativa*), Golden Banner (*Thermopsis* sp.) and Late Yellow Locoweed (*Oxytropis campestris*). Krivda (pers. comm.) has reared the Christina Sulphur on Hedysarum (*Hedysarum* sp.) at the The Pas, Manitoba and it may be the preferred food plant in the province.

The pitcher-shaped eggs are laid singly on the leaves of the food plant and hatch in about eleven days. The eggs are white when laid and turn pink several days later. Newly hatched larvae partially consume the eggshell. The larvae are green with stripes laterally and overwinter in the third instar in leaf litter at the base of the food plant. The larvae begin feeding again in the following spring and often whole plants are consumed, leaving only a withered stem. The pupal stage lasts approximately two weeks (Hooper 1973; Leslie 1980).

In Manitoba, adults have been recorded from June 12 to August 6. The males are more common in late June and females predominate in early July. There is one generation per year.

Habitat: Rolling prairie and hill-tops, forest openings, Jack Pine woods and rocky lake shores. In Manitoba, adults have been found along open forest roads and prairie roadside ditches.

Range: Alaska, Yukon, and the Northwest Territories southeastward to Manitoba, southwest to South Dakota and south to Baja California (Ferris and Brown 1981; Pyle 1981).

Open Jack Pine woods, near Grand Rapids, Manitoba. July 1986.

Manitoba Records: Beulah, Binscarth, Birtle, Buffalo Lake, Churchill, Duck Mountain, Fisher Branch, Grand Rapids, Gypsumville, Kelwood, Miniota, Moosehorn, Ponton, Riding Mountain, The Pas and Wabowden.

Subspecies: Generally six subspecies are recognized. The Manitoba subspecies is *Colias alexandra christina*.

Remarks: The scientific name that honours this butterfly was for Queen Alexandra, wife of Edward VII of England. The Christina Sulphur is relatively uncommon, but may have been more prevalent in southwestern Manitoba before the land was developed for agriculture. Records from 1898 to 1944 show that the Christina Sulphur was quite common in southwestern Manitoba and it is still commonly found on Hedysarum in eastern Saskatchewan and in the Riding and Duck Mountains in Manitoba. This species prefers undisturbed natural habitat. Adults visit flowers and males will congregate at mud puddles in association with the more common Alfalfa Butterfly (Masters 1975).

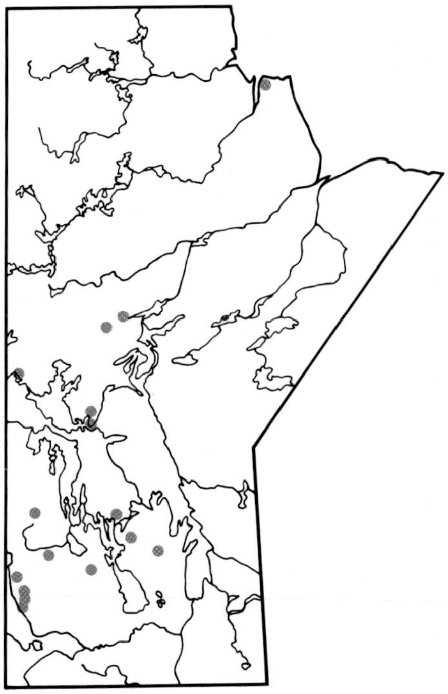

Arctic Sulphur

Colias hecla Lefèbvre, 1836

Plate 10 No. 16, 17, 18

Description: 37-44 mm. The dorsal surface of the wings is a solid, dull orange with wide black borders. There is a heavy greenish dusting on both the upper and lower surfaces of the wings.

Similar Species: The Alfalfa Butterfly, which rarely strays as far northward as the Churchill area, is larger and brighter.

Life Cycle: In Scandinavia the host plant of the Arctic Sulphur is Alpine Milk Vetch (*Astragalus alpinus*), also found across Arctic Canada.

The larvae are green, with pale stripes laterally and covered with numerous minute, bristly, black tubercles.

The flight period lasts from July 4 to August 10 in Manitoba. Although adults occur every year at Churchill, the life cycle may require two years to complete (Klots 1951; Howe 1975).

Habitat: Lush tundra meadows on well drained coastal or low tundra ridges and in sedge meadows on peat flats north of the tree line.

Range: The Arctic regions of Europe, Asia and North America. In North America, from Labrador to northern Manitoba, westward to central Alberta and northern British Columbia.

Manitoba Records: Churchill.

Subspecies: Three subspecies occur in North America. The subspecies found in Manitoba is *Colias hecla hela.*

Remarks: The Arctic Sulphur is more common farther north, but can be found infrequently at Churchill. Males have been observed patrolling the ditches beside the railway track southeast of Churchill and females can sometimes be found in the adjacent tundra. Adults are wary and have a strong, swift flight.

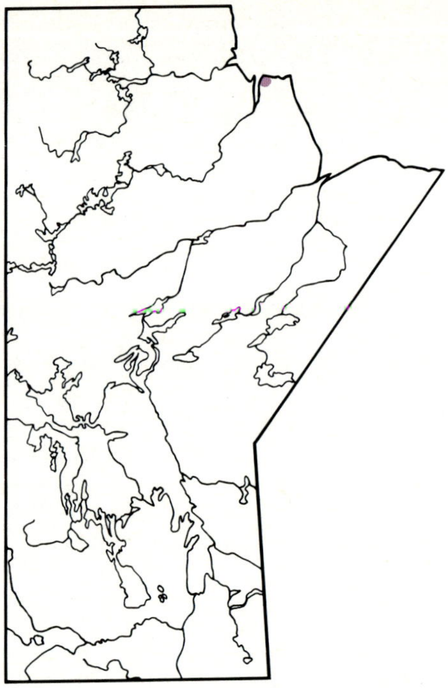

Nastes Sulphur

Colias nastes Boisduval, 1832

Plate 11 No. 1, 2, 3, 4

Description: 34-41 mm. The wings are greenish-yellow with a clouded appearance above. Below, the submarginal black spots are usually well developed. This Sulphur is best distinguished from other Manitoba sulphurs by the presence of light spots within the dark borders on the dorsal surface of the males. The Nastes Sulphur is quite variable: some males have solidly clouded forewings with many dark scales, while others have a light ground colour which contrasts with the dark borders. This sulphur is the smallest species found in Manitoba. Females are usually a little larger and paler than males.

Life Cycle: At Churchill several females were observed ovipositing on Late Yellow Locoweed (*Oxytropis campestris*) and they seem to favour low growing, nonflowering plants (Klots 1951).

In Europe, the mature larvae are dark moss-green with a pair of lateral yellow stripes, below which is a white, crimson-edged stripe. The cuticle is covered with tubercles which bear short black spines. The head capsule is a lighter green than the rest of the body. Larvae reared on Locoweed in Churchill went into an overwintering diapause during the third instar.

At Churchill, adults have been recorded from June 26 to August 13. Adult numbers usually peak in late June and females tend to emerge a week or two after males. There is one generation per year (Klots 1951; Howe 1975; Ferris and Brown 1981).

Habitat: Raised dry tundra flats north of the tree line where Milk-Vetches, Hedysarum and Locoweeds are found. Occasionally dry openings in coniferous forest.

Range: Circumpolar in the high arctic ranging southward in high, cold mountain ranges. In North America, from Alaska across northern Canada to Labrador, southward to northern Quebec and northern Manitoba. The range extends southward into southern Alberta, Montana and Washington within the Rocky Mountains.

Manitoba Records: Churchill.

Subspecies: Up to seven subspecies are recognized in North America. In the Churchill region, *Colias nastes moina* occurs.

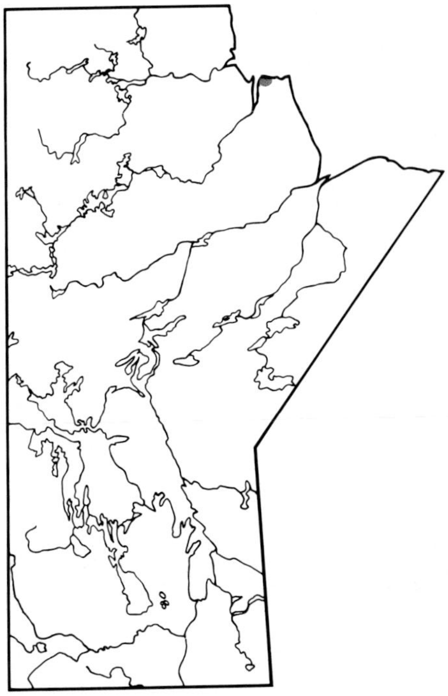

Remarks: Although the Nastes Sulphur is local in occurrence at Churchill occasionally it can be found in every available dry tundra habitat. Unlike many butterfly species of the far north, the Nastes Sulphur often flies in cool, windy and cloudy weather. Females usually are found near the food plant and both sexes take nectar from Milk-Vetches, Northern Hedysarum and Saxifrage. Adults fly swiftly near the tundra surface, frequently alighting to take nectar. When alarmed adults rise vertically in the air and fly swiftly downwind before alighting again.

Giant Sulphur

Colias gigantea Strecker, 1900

Plate 11 No. 5, 6, 7, 8

Description: 40-58 mm. Above, the males are yellow with relatively narrow black borders. Females vary from bright or pale yellow to white above with reduced borders which may be lacking entirely. Below, the wings of both sexes are dusted with gray scales and there are no submarginal dark spots. The discal spot on the underside of the hindwings is usually large and prominent, with a pearly centre and may be accompanied by a satellite spot.

Similar Species: The Pink Edged Sulphur is smaller, but males may be easily confused with small Giant Sulphur males. Generally the forewings of the Pink Edged Sulphur are more rounded, and the black borders are narrower near the base and quite jagged along the inner margin. The discal spot in the hindwings of the Pink Edged Sulphur is more prominent and the gray dusting on the wings is lighter. The Pink Edged Sulphur also has a weaker and less aggressive flight pattern.

Life Cycle: The larval food plant is Snow Willow (*Salix reticulata*). Klots (1951) observed females ovipositing on the leaves of Snow Willow in late July. Like the Nastes Sulphur, the larvae of the Giant Sulphur enter an overwintering diapause in August.

Adults have been observed from June 1 to August 9. In southern Manitoba male numbers peak in early July and in mid-July in the northern portions of the province. Females emerge about one week later.

Habitat: Moist areas of willow, including boreal forest and tundra. In southern Manitoba, this species is restricted to willow bogs or adjacent forest openings and roadsides.

Range: Alaska and the Yukon, eastward to Hudson Bay and southward to northwestern Ontario, northern Minnesota, Manitoba, Saskatchewan, Alberta, Wyoming and British Columbia (Hooper 1973; Howe 1975; Ferris and Brown 1981).

Manitoba Records: Assean Lake, Black River, Churchill, Cowan, Duck Mountain, Flin Flon, Gillam, Kettle Rapids, Leaf Rapids, Mile 200 Hudson Bay Railway, Norway House, Odei River, Orr Lake, Paint Lake, Pikwitonei, Ponton, Porcupine Provincial Forest, Riding Mountain, Sandy Hook, The Pas, Thompson, Wabowden, Whiteshell Provincial Park, William River and York Factory.

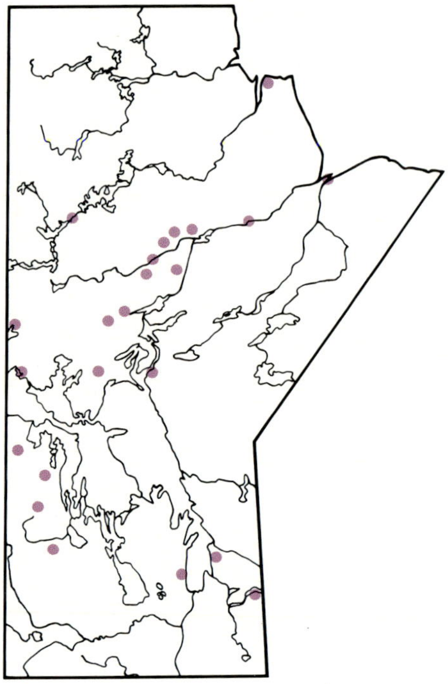

Subspecies: Three subspecies are recognized. *Colias gigantea gigantea* occurs in northern Manitoba and the larger and brighter *Colias gigantea mayi* occurs in southern and central Manitoba. Some lepidopterists do not consider these subspecies as valid, however the authors consider the two forms quite distinct. *Gigantea* and *mayi* form part of a cline, *gigantea* at the northern end and *mayi* at the southern end of the cline.

Remarks: Although the Giant Sulphur is common at Churchill, further south it becomes rarer and is confined mainly to willow bogs in boreal forests. Brooks (1942) stated that it is probably the most common *Colias* between The Pas and Churchill. The southern subspecies *mayi* was named for Jack May, a forest ranger from Riding Mountain National Park. The Giant Sulphur has a strong swift flight especially when disturbed. Males frequently patrol along roads and railways. Both sexes feed at a wide variety of flowers including Louseworts and Arctic Daisy.

Pink Edged Sulphur

Colias interior Scudder, 1862

Plate 11 No. 9, 10, 11, 12

Description: 40-52 mm. The Pink Edged Sulphur is yellow above, with a pink head and pink wing fringes. The males have narrow black borders and a poorly developed black spot (if developed this spot has a yellow centre) in each forewing; the hindwings have an orange spot. Females are quite variable, with the forewing borders usually restricted to the apex and sometimes reduced to a trace. Hindwing borders are usually lacking and if present occur as a few thin bars. White or albino females are rarely encountered. In both sexes the ventral surface of the wings is yellow with pink fringes. There is a silvery pink-edged hindwing spot and usually a small, yellow centered, black elongated forewing spot.

Similar Species: The Giant Sulphur differs as described under that species. The Common Sulphur is duller yellow, has more gray dusting and usually wider borders and more pointed wings. The dorsal forewing spot of the Common Sulphur is larger and ventrally there is a submarginal row of spots which is lacking in the Pink Edged Sulphur.

Life Cycle: Velvet Leaf Blueberry (*Vaccinium angustifolium* var *myrtilloides*) and Dwarf Bilberry (*Vaccinium caespitosum*) are the host plants for the Pink Edged Sulphur.

The pale, pitcher shaped eggs are laid singly on the food plant. Mature larvae are dark yellowish-green with lighter stripes on the dorsal surface and red-edged stripes on the sides. Larvae have been reported to overwinter in the first to third instar stage (Pyle 1981).

In Manitoba, adults are on the wing from June 9 to August 29. Males peak in abundance in early July and females in mid-July. There is one generation per year (Howe 1975).

Habitat: Open pine woods and forest openings, roads and trails, scrubby areas where Blueberries grow.

Range: Across Canada from Alberta and southern Northwest Territories eastward to Newfoundland and southward to New England, Virginia, Michigan and Minnesota.

Manitoba Records: Agassiz Provincial Forest, Brokenhead, Buffalo Lake, Cranberry Portage, Duck Mountain, Flin Flon, Grand Beach, Grand Rapids, Hargrave River, Island Lake, Katimik Lake, Kelwood, Lynn Lake, McCreary, Mile 200 Hudson Bay Railway, Northwest Angle Provincial Forest, Norway House, Ponton, Rennie, Riding Mountain, Sandilands Provincial Forest, Sandy Hook, Seven Sisters, The Pas, Thompson, Two Rivers Lake, Victoria Beach, Vivian, Wabowden, Whiteshell Provincial Park, William River and Winnipeg.

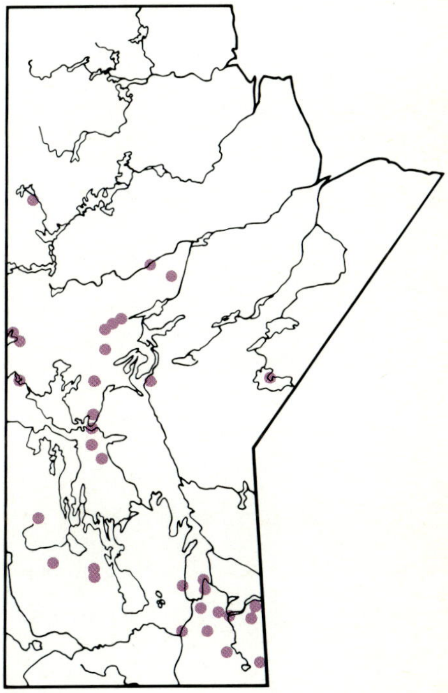

Subspecies: While there is little variation within the species some authors recognize three subspecies in North America. The subspecies found in Manitoba is *Colias interior interior*.

Remarks: The Pink Edged Sulphur, considered a Canadian zone butterfly is fairly common in Manitoba. Males will gather at mud puddles and use forest trails as flyways. Females are less active, staying closer to trees and their food plant. Both sexes visit Asters, Fireweed and other flowers for nectar. Sandilands and Agassiz Provincial Forests are areas where the Pink Edged Sulphur can be frequently found.

Palaeno Sulphur

Colias palaeno (Linnaeus), 1761

Plate 11 No. 13, 14, 15, 16, 17

Description: 31-44 mm. The upper surface of the males' wings is yellow. The hindwings are dusted with fucous, giving them a greenish-yellow appearance. The black borders are wide and the discal spot is nearly always small or absent on the forewings and very pale on the hindwings. Females have dark borders which are wide at the apex of the wings and gradually fade further down; in some females, the wing borders are reduced to small traces. In both sexes the ventral surface of the hindwings is heavily dusted with greenish-gray and the discal spot is small and rarely has a trace of a dark rim. White or albino females are common in the Churchill area. The Palaeno Sulphur is one of our smaller sulphurs, being only slightly larger than the Nastes Sulphur.

Similar Species: Other Manitoba Sulphurs have a dark rim around the white discal spot in each ventral hindwing.

Life Cycle: The primary host plant is Bog Bilberry (*Vaccinium uliginosum*). Dwarf Bilberry (*Vaccinium caespitosum*) may also be a food plant in Manitoba.

Females have been observed ovipositing on Bog Bilberry in early July. Howe (1975) reported that larvae reared on this plant fed until the third instar and then entered an overwintering diapause. The flight period is from June 21 to August 9. At Churchill mid-July is usually the peak flight period, with females emerging a little later than males.

Habitat: Shrubby areas at the edges and openings of spruce and tamarack forests and tundra ridges, usually where bilberry occurs.

Range: Arctic and subarctic regions of Europe, Asia and North America. In North America the range extends from Alaska through the Yukon, the Northwest Territories to Labrador, southward to Ontario, Manitoba, Saskatchewan, Alberta and British Columbia.

Manitoba Records: Assean Lake, Baralzon Lake, Churchill, Gillam, Jacam, Kettle Rapids, Leaf Rapids, Lynn Lake, Mile 200 Hudson Bay Railway, Orr Lake, Thompson and York Factory.

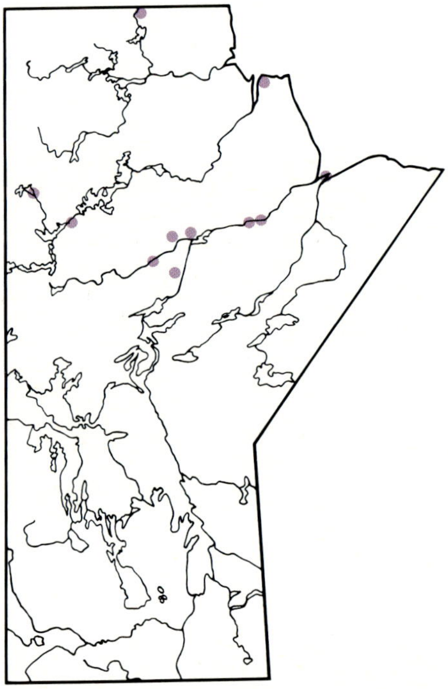

Subspecies: There are two subspecies in North America. *Colias palaeno chippewa* occurs in our area.

Remarks: This sulphur, occurring both north and south of the treeline, is one of the most common butterflies at Churchill. It is more common in the taiga areas than on the tundra. The Palaeno Sulphur prefers moist scrubby willow areas where Bilberry is found. Adults visit Louseworts, Arctic Daisy, Dandelion and other flowers for nectar. While records of this sulphur occurring in southern Manitoba are doubtful, it may have been overlooked in the past due to its resemblance to other species of sulphurs.

Baralzon Lake, Manitoba. July 1983.

Dogface Butterfly

Colias cesonia (Stoll), 1790
= *Zerene cesonia*
Plate 11 No. 18

Description: 48-64 mm. The wings are yellow dorsally with sharply pointed forewings containing a "dog head". The "head" is outlined by a black border and a conspicuous black spot forms the "eye".

Life Cycle: Larval food plants include False Indigo (*Amorpha fruticosa*), Clover (*Trifolium* sp.), Soybean (*Glycine* sp.) and Alfalfa (*Medicago sativa*).

Range: Across the southern United States, north to Wyoming, North Dakota, Manitoba, Iowa, Wisconsin, Minnesota, Michigan, Ontario and New York.

Manitoba Records: Aweme and Cartwright.

Remarks: Both Wallis (1927) and Brooks (1942) include this butterfly as a stray in their checklists. However, there have been no new records of this butterfly since the collection of two specimens at Aweme and Cartwright prior to 1942.

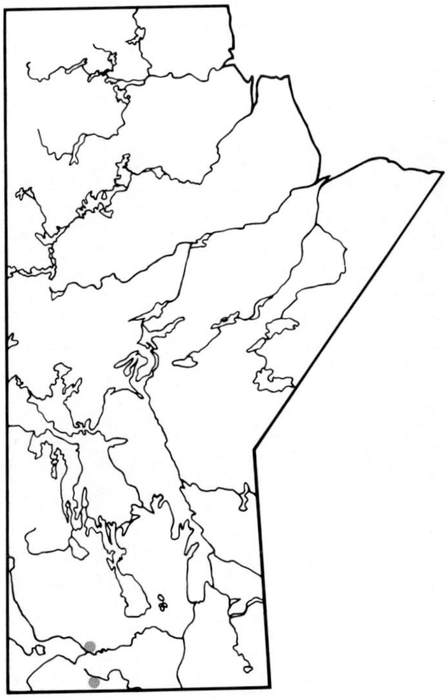

Mexican Sulphur

Eurema mexicana (Boisduval), 1836

Plate 11 No. 19

Description: 35-48 mm. Dorsally the wings are white with yellow along the top of the hindwings. There is a black outline of a "dog snout" on the forewings. The pointed hindwings distinguish this Sulphur from other Manitoban species.

Life Cycle: The food plant does not occur in this province. Five specimens have been collected in Manitoba between the dates of July 4 and September 29.

Range: Central America to the United States, straying as far north as southern Manitoba, Saskatchewan and Ontario.

Criddle Homestead, Aweme, Manitoba. May 1977.

Manitoba Records: Aweme, Cartwright, Riding Mountain and Stonewall.

Remarks: The Mexican Sulphur is an occasional stray.

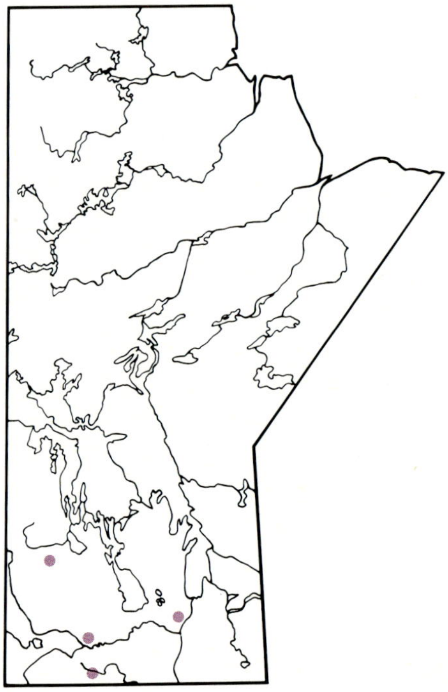

Dainty Sulphur

Nathalis iole Boisduval, 1836

Plate 11 No. 20, 21

Description: 19-29 mm. The Dainty Sulphur is yellow dorsally. The forewings have a wide black apex and a diffuse black bar across the bottom. The hindwings have a diffuse black bar across the top and are darkly edged at the bottom. The markings of the females are better developed than those of males. There may be a tinge of orange in the hindwings of the females. Ventrally the wings are yellow, variously marked with gray, black and often orange. The small size distinguishes the Dainty Sulphur from the other Manitoban species.

Life Cycle: Larval food plants include Beggarticks (*Bidens* sp.), Sneezeweed (*Helenium* sp.), Chickweed (*Stellaria media*) and Marigold (*Tagetes* sp.).

In Manitoba, adults have been recorded from July 25 to September 27.

Range: Central America and the southern United States north to South Carolina, Tennessee, Indiana, Iowa, Ontario, Manitoba, Saskatchewan and Wyoming.

Manitoba Records: Aweme, Cartwright, Culross, Sandilands Provincial Forest and Winnipeg.

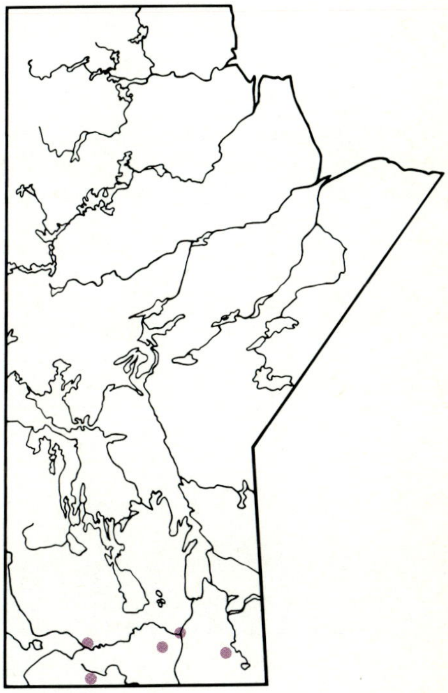

Remarks: This southern species migrates northward every year and occasionally reaches Manitoba. Six specimens have been collected in the province. A recently emerged female was found at Culross on July 25, 1966 by P. Klassen which may indicate that this species was breeding in the area, at least that summer.

Family

LYCAENIDAE: GOSSAMER WINGS

This is the largest family of butterflies, with an estimated world fauna of 7,000 species, of which 5,000 have been described to date. The North American fauna includes 100 species, with 59 in Canada and 27 in Manitoba. Butterflies representing this family in Manitoba include Harvesters, Coppers, Hairstreaks, and Blues. The family consists of small butterflies with eyes that are usually emarginate at the base of the antennae. The front legs are reduced in males and fully developed in females. Courtship, mating and egg-laying usually take place in the afternoon.

The eggs of members of this family are wider than long, often have a sculptured pattern and are laid singly. Larvae are usually green and have small head capsules and slug shaped bodies which taper at each end. The cuticle is covered with fine dense hair. The larvae have specialized abdominal nectar producing glands and are often attended by ants. Larvae are often hard to locate as they bore into the food plant or roll the leaves of the host plant around them while feeding. The pupae are usually brown, rounded at either end and often formed at the base of the food plant. Most species overwinter as eggs or partly grown larvae, rarely as pupae.

Subfamily

MILETINAE: HARVESTERS

= *Subfamily*

LIPHYRIDAE

Butterflies in this small subfamily are mainly confined to the Indo-Australian and African regions. There is only one species in North America. The larvae are carnivorous, feeding on soft-bodied insects, especially aphids.

Lycaena xanthoides

Harvester

Feniseca tarquinius (Fabricius), 1793

Plate 12 No. 1, 2, 3, 4

Description: 28-32 mm. This butterfly resembles a dull Copper. The wings are dull orange above, with dark brown markings that can vary greatly between individuals. There is a dark brown border, varying in width, on the forewings and the upper half of the hindwings. There are usually two to four submarginal spots on the lower edge of the hindwings. The discal area of the forewings is variably marked with blotches. On the ventral surface the forewings are dull orange with brown spots and the hindwings are brown with variable spots ringed with white.

Life Cycle: The larvae of the Harvester feed on Woolly Aphids (*Schizoneura* sp., *Pemphigus* sp., *Prociphilus* sp. and *Neoprociphilus* sp.). These aphids are found on Alder (*Alnus* sp.), Ash (*Fraxinus* sp.), Wild Currant (*Ribes* sp.), Witch Hazel (*Hamamelis* sp.), Hawthorn (*Crataegus* sp.) and Maple (*Acer* sp.).

The larvae reach maturity in the third instar, 10 to 12 days after hatching. The greenish-brown larvae feed by burying themselves beneath a mass of aphids. The larval body segments are prominent and covered with long hair (Klots 1951). The pupae are pale green ventrally and greenish-brown on the dorsal surface, which is covered in dark patches. This, along with the pupa's irregular shape make it resemble a monkey's head. The pupa is the overwintering stage.

In Manitoba, adults are on the wing from May 12 to August 17. The Harvester is most common in late May through mid-June. There are at least two generations per year in this province (Opler and Krizek 1984).

Habitat: Damp woodlands, swampy glades, forested riverbanks and forest roads and trails.

Range: Manitoba to Nova Scotia, southward to Florida and Texas.

Manitoba Records: Agassiz Provincial Forest, Brokenhead, Elm Creek, Sandilands Provincial Forest, Whitemouth Lake, Whiteshell Provincial Park and Winnipeg.

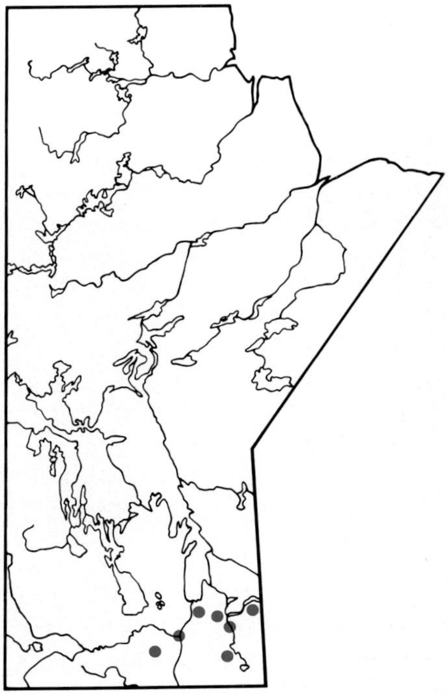

Subspecies: Two subspecies are recognized. The subspecies occurring in Manitoba is *Feniseca tarquinius tarquinius*.

Remarks: The Harvester is the sole North American representative of a tropical Old World group of carnivorous gossamer winged butterflies. It is quite local in Manitoba, seldom abundant and populations fluctuate from year to year. Adults have a weak fluttering flight and are usually seen flying about trees or shrubs harboring aphids. They will often alight and feed on honeydew secreted on the leaves or bask in the sun. In Sandilands Provincial Forest adults can be observed sitting on forest roads or trails, taking moisture from puddles especially after showers.

Subfamily

LYCAENINAE: COPPERS

The members of this subfamily have stout bodies. In Manitoba males are usually brown with a purple sheen and females are usually shiny orange or coppery brown above. Adults frequently feed at flowers and are capable of rapid flight. Males perch with wings partly opened and will readily intercept passing intruders. The eggs are laid on the underside of the host plant leaves and the larva will often pass the winter within the eggshell before hatching. Larval host plants include members of the Rose and Buckwheat Families. Our species are found in bogs, marshes and sloughs.

Great Copper

Lycaena xanthoides (Boisduval), 1852
= *Gaeides xanthoides*
Plate 12 No. 5, 6, 7, 8

Description: 32-41 mm. Both sexes are lustrous gray above, with a small bar and a spot in the end of the cell in the forewings. In the hind wings a marginal orange band (reduced in some individuals) encloses a row of black spots. Females have larger spots and an additional row of post-median dark spots on each wing. The hindwings have a well developed orange band and the forewings have an orange band at the base of the outer margins. Occasionally, females have orange scales present in the cell of the forewings.

Life Cycle: The larvae of the Great Copper feed on various species of Dock, including Curled Dock (*Rumex crispus*) and Western Dock (*Rumex occidentalis*).

The white eggs are laid singly on the underside of the leaves where they overwinter. Larvae hatch the following spring. The mature larvae are green, yellow-green or magenta with dark orange stripes dorsally. The pupae are formed within loosely woven cocoons at the base of the food plant (Pyle 1981).

Adults have been recorded in Manitoba from June 21 to August 18, being most common in mid-July. There is one generation per year in this province.

Great Copper, Winnipeg, Manitoba. July 1976.

Habitat: Restricted to marshes or sloughs and farming areas with roadside and drainage ditches.

Range: Central Alberta through southern Saskatchewan and Manitoba southward to Illinois, Iowa, Missouri and Colorado. Also found from Oregon to Baja, California in the west (Howe 1975).

Manitoba Records: Asessippi Provincial Park, Beulah, Birtle, Carman, Culross, Grand Beach, Husavik, Miniota, Riding Mountain, Rosebank, Sandilands Provincial Forest, Selkirk, Victoria Beach, Winnipeg and Winnipeg Beach.

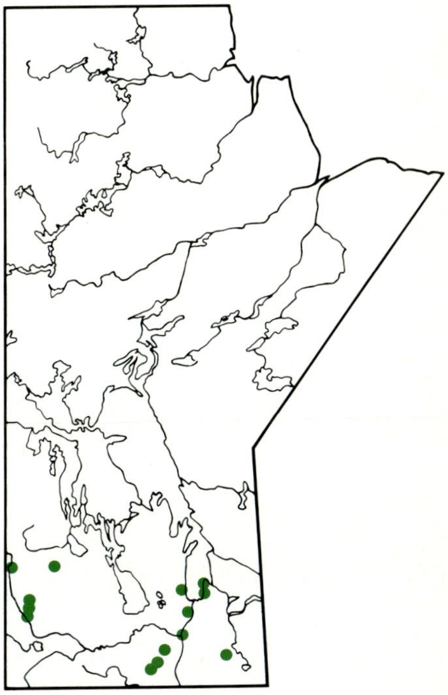

Subspecies: Two to three subspecies are recognized, of which *Lycaena xanthoides dione* is found in Manitoba.

Remarks: This is the largest Copper found in Manitoba; the Manitoba subspecies was formerly known as the Dione or Dione Copper. Although not common in the province it often can be found in disturbed areas such as roadside ditches where Dock plants occur. It was once common in Winnipeg along the Red River in the area that is now Juba Park. Adults seldom stray far from the host plant and will perch on marsh grasses or feed on Clover, Alfalfa, Milkweed and other flowers. The flight of the Great Copper is rapid and jerky, making adults difficult to observe if they are disturbed. The Great Copper is found in association with the Purplish and Bronze Copper, although the Great Copper tends to be more active later in the day than the other species.

Bronze Copper

Lycaena hyllus (Cramer), 1775
= *Hyllolycaena hyllus*
= *Lycaena thoe* (Guerin-Meneville), 1831

Plate 12 No. 9, 10, 11

Description: 28-39 mm. The males and females differ greatly in appearance. Males are copper-brown above, with a violet sheen to the wings. A submarginal orange band encloses a row of black spots on the hindwings. Females have orange forewings with prominent dark spots and brown margins. The hindwings are brownish-gray with small dark spots and wide orange margins that enclose black spots. Below, the forewings of both sexes are orange with pearly-white margins and prominent black spots. The hindwings are pearly-white with wide, bright orange margins and large black spots. Females are larger than males, sometimes approaching the Great Copper in size.

Life Cycle: The larval food plants include Curled Dock (*Rumex crispus*), Water Dock (*Rumex orbiculatus*), and Knotweed (*Polygonum* sp.).

The turban-shaped pale green eggs are laid on or near the food plant. The mature larvae are slug-shaped and bright yellowish-green with a dark stripe dorsally (Klots 1951). The pupae are pale orange-brown with darker patches. Eggs laid by second generation females overwinter and hatch the following spring.

In Manitoba, adults have been recorded from June 6 to September 15. There are two generations per year. Although peak abundance periods vary, first generation adults are most numerous in late June and second generation adults peak in late August.

Habitat: Wet meadows, marshes, prairie sloughs and ditches where Dock is found.

Range: Northwest Territories and Alberta eastward through Canada to Quebec, southward to New Jersey, West Virginia, Arkansas and Colorado (Opler and Krizek 1984).

Manitoba Records: Agassiz Provincial Forest, Beulah, Birtle, Cartwright, Culross, Dauphin, Elm Creek, Gimli, Grand Beach, Hecla Island, La Salle, Lauder, Miniota, Norris Lake, Oak Hammock, Onah, Pine Ridge, Rennie, Riding Mountain, Sandilands Provincial Forest, Selkirk, Stuartburn, The Pas, Thompson and Winnipeg.

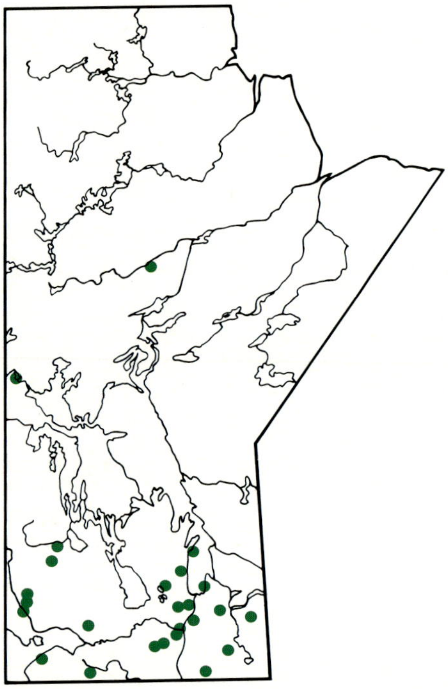

Subspecies: There are no subspecies recognized.

Remarks: The Bronze Copper is probably more widely distributed in Manitoba than present records indicate, although it is seldom abundant when found. Adults, especially females do not stray far from the food plant. The flight is swift and erratic and perching males will intercept Coppers or any other intruder flying near their perch. They are active earlier in the day than the Great Copper and often share the same habitat.

Bog Copper

Lycaena epixanthe

(Boisduval & Leconte), 1833

= *Epidemia epixanthe*

Plate 12 No. 12, 13, 14

Description: 22-25 mm. Males are dark brown above, with a purplish sheen to the wings. Both pairs of wings have inconspicuous dark borders and black spots; the hindwings feature one to several orange submarginal crescents which vary in size among individuals. Females are duller and somewhat grayish in appearance. Ventrally, the wings of both sexes are grayish-white with black spots and a row of submarginal reddish crescents, which may be quite faint.

Similar Species: In Manitoba, the Dorcas Copper is larger, more heavily marked with black spots and is dull pinkish-brown below.

Life Cycle: In Manitoba, Small Cranberry (*Oxycoccus palustris*), is probably the larval food plant. Wild Cranberry (*Oxycoccus macrocarpus*) is the food plant in other parts of the range but does not occur in Manitoba.

The dome-shaped eggs are laid singly on the underside of the leaf of the food plant. Females prefer to oviposit on Cranberries that are overgrown with Sedges near the edge of a bog (Scott 1986). The eggs overwinter on the leaves and can withstand flooding before hatching in the spring. Young larvae are green with a red stripe along the dorsal surface. The mature fourth instar larvae are solid green, lacking stripes and blend in well with the host plant. The pupae are green, speckled with black spots or occasionally solid purple in colour. Pupae are usually concealed beneath the Cranberry leaves near the ground. In New Jersey, freshly hatched Bog Copper larvae take from 52 to 60 days to reach adulthood.

Adults have been recorded in Manitoba from July 24 to August 8. The flight period lasts about four weeks and coincides with the flowering of Cranberries (Wright 1983).

Habitat: This species is confined to acid bogs where Cranberries are found. The Manitoba populations were found in Larch and Spruce bogs.

Range: Manitoba to Newfoundland, southward to New Jersey, Pennsylvania, Ohio, Michigan and Minnesota (Howe 1975).

Manitoba Records: Agassiz Provincial Forest, Northwest Angle Provincial Forest, Rennie (three miles northeast), Sandilands Provincial Forest and Telford.

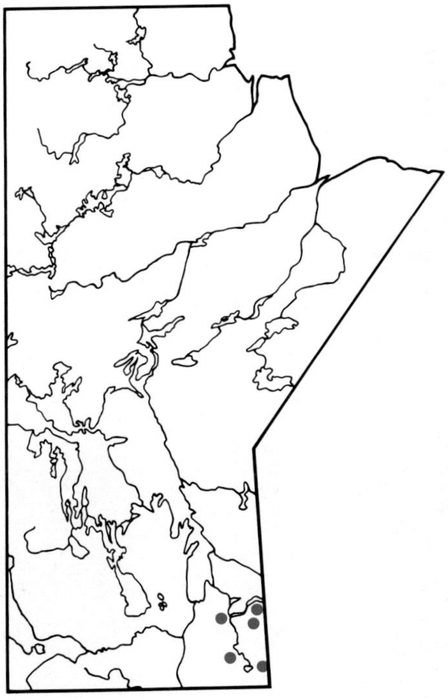

Subspecies: Three subspecies are recognized. The subspecies in Manitoba is *Lycaena epixanthe michiganensis*.

Remarks: The Bog Copper was first discovered in Manitoba in 1955 by C.D. Bird and A.B. Klots while collecting butterflies in Whiteshell Provincial Park. Masters (1968) found this species in several Manitoba bogs across the southern half of the province to Riding Mountain. P. Taylor photographed this butterfly near Milner Ridge in Agassiz Provincial Forest and P. Klassen collected two specimens at this locale in 1988. It is seldom found far from the host plant and adults take nectar almost exclusively from Cranberries.

Dorcas Copper

Lycaena dorcas W. Kirby, 1837
= *Epidemia dorcas*
Plate 12 No. 15, 16, 17, 18, 19, 20

Description: 23-28 mm. Above, the Dorcas Copper is dark brown with black spots and broad but inconspicuous dark borders. In addition, there are several red-orange submarginal crescents in the hindwings. Males have a purple sheen, which is usually absent in females. Females usually have buff or orange-buff patches (occasionally forming complete bands) in the forewings. Below, the forewings in both sexes are orange with prominent black spots. The hindwings are dull, pinkish-brown with tiny black spots (sometimes absent) and a thin scalloped submarginal red-orange line.

Similar Species: Bog Copper differs as described under that species. The Purplish Copper is much larger and brighter, usually has complete submarginal orange bands on the hindwing and has narrow borders.

Life Cycle: The larvae of the Dorcas Copper feed on Shrubby Cinquefoil (*Potentilla fruticosa*) in southern Manitoba.

The flattened greenish-white eggs are oviposited singly on the ventral side of the leaves of the food plant. The eggs remain on the leaves which fall to the ground in the fall. In the spring the larvae hatch and find their way to the host plant. Mature larvae are green, with yellow stripes dorsally and a white stripe laterally (Opler and Krizek 1984).

In Manitoba, adults have been recorded from July 4 to August 26 but are usually most common in late July and early August although their peak flights vary from year to year. Females emerge a few days after the males. There is one generation per year in Manitoba.

Habitat: Black Spruce or Tamarack bogs in glades and woodland meadows where Shrubby Cinquefoil is found. Occasionally along roads passing through boggy areas.

Range: Alaska, Yukon, Northwest Territories and all of the provinces of Canada. Southward to New Hampshire, Maine, Ohio, Michigan and Minnesota and in the mountains to New Mexico.

Shrubby Cinquefoil, Churchill, Manitoba.

Manitoba Records: Agassiz Provincial Forest, Assean Lake, Aweme, Berens River, Beulah, Churchill, Deer River (Mile 473 Hudson Bay Railway), Duck Mountain, Elm Creek, Fort Alexander, Gillam, Hecla Island, Hilbre, Jacam, Leaf Rapids, Libau, Lynn Lake, Mile 200 Hudson Bay Railway, Nueltin Lake, Orr Lake, Pikwitonei, Pine Ridge, Ponton, Rennie, Riding Mountain, Rounthwaite, Sandilands Provincial Forest, Telford, The Pas, Thompson, Tolstoi, Turtle Mountain, Wabowden, Whiteshell Provincial Park, William River and Winnipeg.

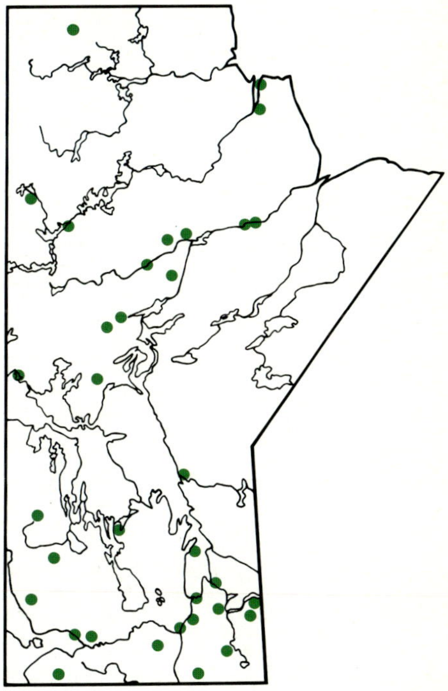

Subspecies: Up to seven subspecies are recognized by some authors. *Lycaena dorcas dorcas* is the subspecies in Manitoba.

Remarks: The Dorcas Copper is usually restricted to acid bogs of Spruce or Tamarack. In Agassiz Provincial Forest a small colony was located in a Black Spruce clearing overgrown with Fireweed and Cinquefoil. The Dorcas Copper seldom strays far from the host plant and readily visits it for nectar. When Cinquefoil is not in flower adults will visit other flowers including Clovers. The Dorcas Copper has a weak flight and is easily observed. Adults are more numerous in boggy areas, although occasionally they can be found near Shrubby Cinquefoil growing in dry upland areas.

Purplish Copper

Lycaena helloides (Boisduval), 1852
= *Epidemia helloides*

Plate 12 No. 21, 22, 23, 24

Description: 25-33 mm. The dorsal surface of males' wings is copper brown with a purplish sheen, narrow darkened borders and black spots. The hindwings have a narrow wavy submarginal orange band. The females have orange forewings with prominent black spots and brown borders. The hindwings are mostly brown with black spots and a narrow wavy submarginal orange band often with an adjacent orange spot. Rarely, females may be nearly all brown, with the orange reduced to submarginal bands and a few small patches.

Life Cycle: The larvae feed on species of Dock (*Rumex* sp.) and Knotweed (*Polygonum* sp.).

The slightly flattened white eggs are laid on the underside of the leaves or new shoots of the food plant. Occasionally females will oviposit in litter near the base of the host plant. The mature larvae are green with yellow dorsal stripes and one yellow stripe with many oblique yellow lines laterally. The cuticle is covered with many short whitish hairs. The short greenish-gray pupae are marked with gray and brown patches. Although the Purplish Copper is thought to overwinter in the pupal stage some authors have noted that the eggs were the overwintering stage in some areas (Howe 1975; Ferris and Brown 1981; Opler and Krizek 1984).

In Manitoba adults have been recorded from June 4 to September 25. The flight period often coincides with that of the Bronze Copper. Adults from the first generation are most numerous in mid-June and adults from the second generation are most abundant in late August. Males emerge a few days prior to females.

Habitat: Marshes, prairie sloughs, wet meadows, old fields and ditches.

Range: Southern British Columbia to Ontario southward to Illinois, Missouri, Iowa, Kansas, New Mexico and Baja, California (Howe 1975).

Manitoba Records: Anola, Aweme, Beulah, Berens River, Birtle, Brandon, Brokenhead, Cartwright, Culross, Elm Creek, Falcon Lake, Garson, Grand Beach, Hecla Island, Kelwood, Libau, Lundar, Marco, McCreary, Melita, Miniota, Ninette, Norris Lake, Northwest Angle Provincial Forest, Oak Hammock, Overflowing River, Riding Mountain, Roseisle, St. Claude, Sandilands Provincial Forest, Selkirk, Sprague, Stuartburn, The Pas, Victoria Beach, Vita, Whiteshell Provincial Park, Winnipeg and Winnipeg Beach.

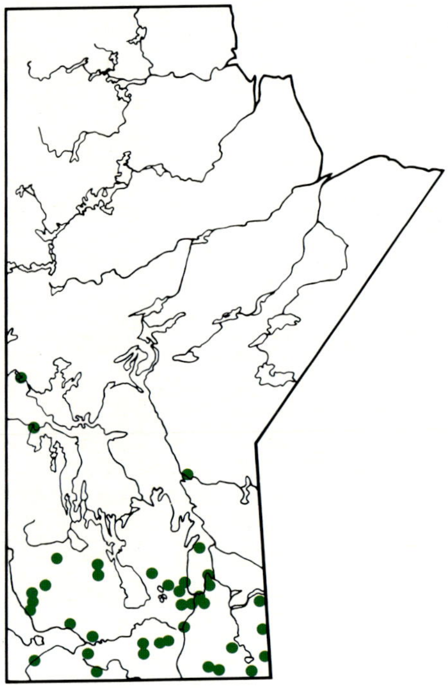

Subspecies: At present researchers have not agreed upon the correct nomenclature for subspecies of the Purplish Copper.

Remarks: The Purplish Copper is widespread in North America and is the most common copper in southern Manitoba. Populations vary in abundance from year to year. Unlike other species of coppers, the Purplish Copper is not closely tied to the food plant and adults will take nectar from flowers some distance from breeding areas. Adults visit many plants for nectar, including Small White Aster, Clovers and Milkweed. The Purplish Copper is usually more common in disturbed areas than natural habitats and is often observed in association with Bronze and Great Coppers.

Subfamily

THECLINAE: HAIRSTREAKS AND ELFINS

This subfamily is well represented in the tropics but becomes scarce in the northern parts of the North American continent. Adults of the species that occur in Manitoba are small and usually dark brown . Hairstreaks have a thin tail and often an adjacent red and black eye-spot (known as a "hecla spot") near the outer margin of the hindwings. The larvae of most species are leaf feeders while some species bore into fruits and flower buds. Some larvae are attended by ants and most species of Theclinae overwinter in either the egg or pupa stage. Adults are found in open forests, especially scrubby areas, usually fairly close to the host plant. They perch with closed wings, sometimes high in trees and have a swift, erratic flight.

Coral Hairstreak nectaring at Hairy Prairie Clover, *Petalostemum villosum.* **Lauder Sandhills Wildlife Management Area, Manitoba. July 1988.**

Coral Hairstreak

Harkenclenus titus (Fabricius), 1793
= *Satyrium titus*
Plate 12 No. 25, 26, 27, 28

Description: 25-33 mm. Males have angular wings and are gray-brown above. Females have rounded wings, usually with a row of submarginal reddish spots in the hindwings, which are occasionally also present in males. Females may also have submarginal red spots in the forewings and a suffusion of dull orange. Below, both sexes are gray-brown with small black spots and a prominent submarginal row of bright coral-red spots in the hindwings and occasionally in the forewings. There is considerable variation between individuals, even within adults of local populations. The Coral Hairstreak is the only Manitoban Hairstreak without a tail.

Life Cycle: The larvae of the Coral Hairstreak utilize several host plants including Wild Plums and Cherries (*Prunus* sp.). In Manitoba, the Coral Hairstreak prefers Sand Cherry (*Prunus pumila*) and Choke Cherry (*Prunus virginiana*). Other authors have reported Saskatoon (*Amelanchier alnifolia*) and Oak (*Quercus* sp.) as larva food plants (Ferris and Brown 1981; Opler and Krizek 1984).

The green eggs are laid on twigs of the food plant where they overwinter and hatch the following spring. The larvae consume both the flowers and fruit and are attended by ants that feed on the honeydew secreted by the larvae. The mature larvae are yellowish-green with dull rosy patches on the dorsal surface. The head capsules are black with dull white stripes on the front. The cuticle is covered in downy hairs and the larvae are slug-shaped. The pupae are covered in short brown hair and are light brown with black or dark brown speckles.

In Manitoba, adults have been recorded from June 26 to August 21. Adults are most common in July and there is one generation per year.

Habitat: Scrubby areas at forest edges and openings, meadows and roadsides where wild Cherries grow.

Range: British Columbia through southern Canada to New Brunswick, southward through most of the United States.

Manitoba Records: Agassiz Provincial Forest, Asessippi Provincial Park, Aweme, Beulah, Birds Hill, Birtle, Brereton Lake, Brokenhead, Carberry, Cartwright, Elm Creek, Glenboro, Libau, Lundar, McCreary, Melbourne, Miami, Miniota, Northwest Angle Provincial Forest, Pine Ridge, Prawda, Rennie, Riding Mountain, Russell, St. Malo, Sand Ridge, Sandilands Provincial Forest, Spruce Woods Provincial Park, Stockton, Stonewall, Tolstoi, Treesbank and Winnipeg.

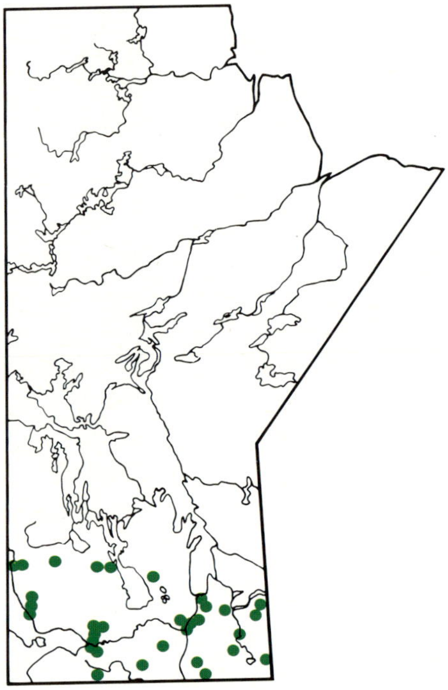

Subspecies: Four subspecies are recognized, two of which are found in Manitoba. *Harkenclenus titus immaculosus* occurs in the western half of the province and is characterized by a reduction or absence of the black spots on the underside of the wings. The subspecies *immaculosus* overlaps with the eastern subspecies *Harkenclenus titus titus* in the eastern half of Manitoba. There is often considerable variation among individuals, especially where the two subspecies interbreed. Hence, they are often difficult to distinguish (Miller and Brown 1981).

Remarks: The Coral Hairstreak is the most common Hairstreak in Manitoba. Males and females are often seen flying around isolated Sand Cherry plants or using them as perching sites. Both sexes visit flowers for nectar and have a rapid flight.

Acadian Hairstreak

Satyrium acadica (W.H. Edwards), 1862

Plate 13 No. 1, 2, 3,

Description: 28-35 mm. The Acadian Hairstreak is gray-brown above with an orange spot near the basal margins of the hindwings and pale slate-gray below with rows of black dots ringed with white. The ventral sides of the hindwings also have a submarginal wavy orange band and a blue spot near the tail at the outer margin. Both sexes are similar in appearance and have a thin tail at the bottom of the hindwings. Like many of the hairstreaks occurring in Manitoba, males have a thickened mass of scales (sex pad) near the upper margin of the dorsal side of the forewings.

Similar Species: The Banded Hairstreak is darker ventrally with white edged squarish spots that form discernible bands. Edwards' Hairstreak is duller, darker and browner below. In addition, Edwards' Hairstreak has less distinct markings and the submarginal band consists of several red crescents. The Acadian Hairstreak, unlike both the Banded and Edwards' Hairstreaks, has the blue spot on the hindwing underside "capped" with red as part of the red submarginal band.

Life Cycle: The larvae of the Acadian Hairstreak feed exclusively on Willow (*Salix* sp.). Sandbar Willow (*Salix interior*) is thought to be the preferred food plant in Manitoba.

This species overwinters in the egg stage. The mature larvae are grass-green with yellow or white oblique bars between two yellow stripes located on each side of the body. The head capsules are brown. The pupae are buff in colour and spotted with brownish-black flecks or blotches (Opler and Krizek 1984).

In Manitoba adults have been observed from June 18 to August 20, being most numerous in July. There is one generation per year.

Habitat: Damp meadows, fields, stream banks and drainage ditches in the farming areas of Manitoba.

Range: Eastern British Columbia to Prince Edward Island, south to New Jersey, Iowa, Colorado and Washington.

Manitoba Records: Agassiz Provincial Park, Aweme, Beulah, Birds Hill, Birtle, Carberry, Cartwright, Culross, Elm Creek, Hadashville, Melbourne, Miniota, Rathwell, Rennie, Riding Mountain, Rounthwaite, Sandilands Provincial Forest, Souris, Spruce Woods Provincial Park, Stuartburn, Teulon, Treesbank, Waskada, Whiteshell Provincial Park and Winnipeg.

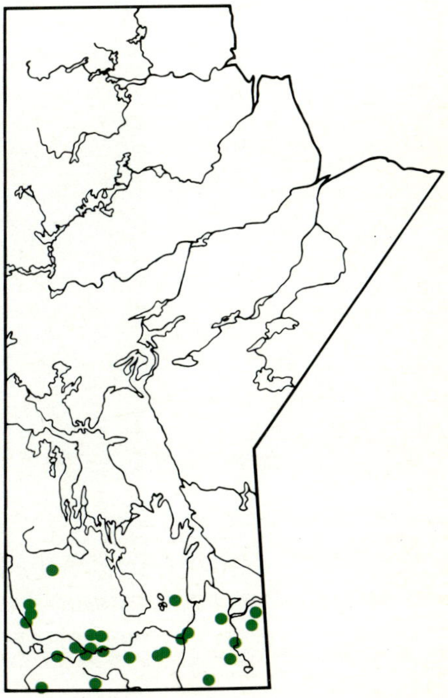

Subspecies: Four poorly defined subspecies have been described in the literature. The nominate subspecies, *Satyrium acadica acadica*, occurs from southwestern Manitoba to Ontario, south to New Jersey, Michigan and North Dakota. The more northern subspecies is *Satyrium acadica watrini*, and occurs in the southern parts of the Canadian zone (i.e. Quebec across northern Ontario to central Saskatchewan). Hooper (1973) reported finding *Satyrium acadica watrini* at Aweme and Riding Mountain in Manitoba. The northern subspecies is usually darker and more brownish below in comparison to *Satyrium acadica acadica*, although they are often difficult to distinguish.

Remarks: Although this Hairstreak is widespread in southern Canada, including Manitoba, it is never found in large numbers. Wallis (1927) stated that it was rarely found within the province. Acadian Hairstreaks are best observed in ditches where scrubby willows grow and where they can be found perched on the tall grasses adjacent to the trees. Adults will feed on a variety of flowers including Milkweed, White Clover, Thistle and Dogbane.

Edwards' Hairstreak

Satyrium edwardsii

(Grote & Robinson), 1867

Plate 13 No. 4, 5, 6,

Description: 25-28 mm. Edwards' Hairstreak is gray-brown above and below, occasionally with small diffuse dull orange spots near the basal margin of the dorsal surface of the hindwings. Ventrally the wings have bands of small, dark brown oval spots, often ringed in white. On the underside of the hindwings there is a relatively large blue patch with small orange spots on either side near the tail. Both sexes are quite similar in colouration. Males have an oval sex pad near the top margin of the forewings.

Edwards' Hairstreak on Dogbane, Winnipeg, Manitoba. July 1988.

Similar Species: The Acadian Hairstreak is paler gray below and the bands consist of sharply contrasting black spots. It also has more extensive orange bands in the hindwings. The Banded Hairstreak, with which Edwards' Hairstreak is most easily confused in Manitoba, has a continuous band of connected squarish spots, outlined in white at the outer edge, on the ventral surface of the wings.

Life Cycle: The larvae of Edwards' Hairstreak feed on species of Oak. In Manitoba, the host plant is Bur Oak (*Quercus macrocarpa*).

Females oviposit under next year's buds or on small twigs near the buds. The eggs remain there until the following spring. The larvae hatch in late May or early June and when mature are brown with pale brown markings and covered with small blackish tubercles bearing short brown hairs. The head capsules are black with a narrow white stripe. The darkly mottled, buff coloured pupae are attached to a dead leaf or other debris by a silk girdle (Klots 1951; Opler and Krizek 1984).

In Manitoba adults have been recorded from June 23 to August 27, usually being most common after mid-July. There is one generation per year in this province.

Habitat: Shrubby forest edges and openings, clearings and sandy areas where oaks predominate and especially in areas where oaks are small and intermixed with other tall shrubs.

Range: Saskatchewan to Nova Scotia, southward to Georgia and Texas.

Manitoba Records: Aweme, Birds Hill, Carberry, Lundar, Melbourne, Miami, Miniota, Pine Ridge, Riding Mountain, Roseisle, St. Malo, St. Norbert, Spruce Woods Provincial Park, St. Malo, St. Norbert, Stuartburn, Tolstoi and Winnipeg.

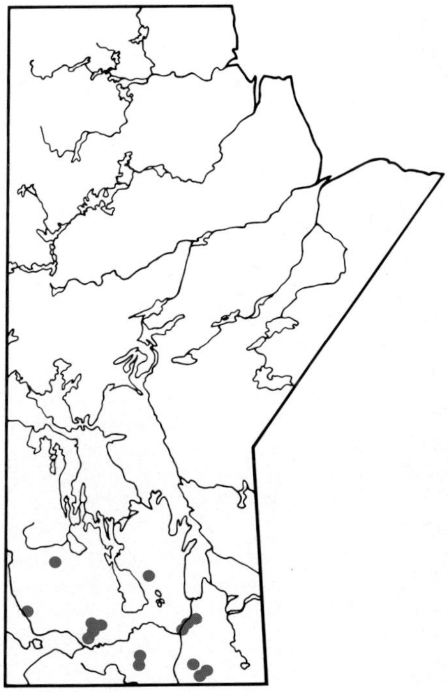

Subspecies: No subspecies are recognized.

Remarks: Edwards' Hairstreak is most common in eastern Canada, becoming scarcer in the south and southwestern part of its range. This Hairstreak is locally abundant in Manitoba and was previously overlooked by other lepidopterists because of its local nature and sporadic appearance. It seldom strays far from the host plant. Adults have a swift flight and males will leave their perching site to intercept other Hairstreaks. Frequently two or more males will engage in brief aerial encounters, rising vertically in the air. Adults have been observed feeding on Goldenrod, Sweet Clover, Spiraea and Dogbane. Edwards' Hairstreak was found flying in association with Striped Hairstreaks in the Melbourne area. At both Melbourne and Pine Ridge adults preferred sandy uplands at the edges of Oak stands, frequently perching on Hazelnut, Chokecherry and Oak.

Banded Hairstreak

Satyrium calanus (Hübner), 1809

Plate 13 No. 7, 8, 9

Description: 25-28 mm. Above, the Banded Hairstreak is brown, occasionally with diffuse orange spots above the tail. Below, males are brownish-black (females are a little paler) with a forewing band that consists of continuous squarish spots outlined in white on the outer edge. There is a blue patch near the tail, with small orange spots on either side. Both sexes are similar in appearance and have tails. Males also have a forewing sex pad.

Similar Species: Acadian and Edwards' Hairstreaks differ as described under those species. The Striped Hairstreak has more widely spaced broken white lines and a purplish sheen below; the orange submarginal band extends over the top of the blue spot on the hindwing underside.

Life Cycle: In Manitoba, the larvae of the Banded Hairstreak most likely feed on Bur Oak (*Quercus macrocarpa*). In the eastern part of their range larvae have been found on Walnut, Butternut, Hickory and other species of Oaks.

The pale green eggs are laid on the twigs of the host tree and hatch the following spring. Young larvae feed on catkins and move to young leaves in the later instars. The mature larvae are brown or green and marked with faint white oblique lines. They are covered with brownish, soft downy hair. The hairy pupae are mottled brown and suspended on or near the food plant by a silk girdle (Howe 1975; Pyle 1981).

In Manitoba, adults have been recorded from June 23 to August 28. There is one generation per year in this province.

Habitat: Deciduous forest edges and openings, clearings, oak thickets and roadsides.

Range: Southern Saskatchewan to Quebec, southeastward to the Atlantic states and south to Florida, Texas, New Mexico and Wyoming.

Manitoba Records: Aweme, Beulah, Birds Hill, Brandon, Cartwright, Culross, Elm Creek, Husavik, La Salle, Melbourne, Miami, Miniota, Riding Mountain, Rounthwaite, Tolstoi and Winnipeg.

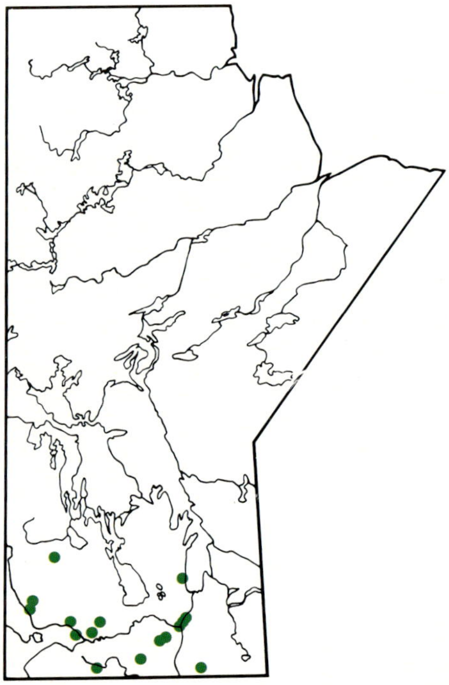

Subspecies: There are three or four subspecies recognized in North America. The subspecies found in Manitoba is *Satyrium calanus falacer*. At one time *falacer* was considered to be a separate species, but now most authors consider it a subspecies of *calanus*.

Remarks: The Banded Hairstreak is common in eastern North America, but has rarely been observed in Manitoba. Adults can be found perched on low branches of trees or near the top of small shrubs and they will visit various flowers for nectar, including Milkweed, Dogbane, Spiraea, and Sumac.

Striped Hairstreak

Satyrium liparops (Leconte), 1833

Plate 13 No. 10, 11, 12, 13

Description: 25-28 mm. This Hairstreak is brownish-black above, usually with a prominent brownish-orange patch of scales in the forewings. This patch varies greatly and may cover half the wings or in the occasional specimen be completely lacking. The ventral surface of the wings is dark brown with a purplish sheen and striped with broken fine, white lines, which may be inconspicuous, especially in the hindwings. In addition to the stripes there are blue and orange spots in the hindwings. Like the Acadian Hairstreak, the red spots of the submarginal band in the hindwing underside are continuous over the blue spot giving this spot a red "cap". Both sexes have tails and males have forewing sex pads. In Manitoba, the Striped Hairstreak is best separated from other Hairstreaks by the presence of the orange patches in the forewings.

Similar Species: The Banded Hairstreak differs as described under that species.

Life Cycle: The Striped Hairstreak utilizes a wide variety of host plants which include Heath (Ericaeae), Blueberry (*Vaccinium* sp.), Rose (Rosaceae), Choke Cherry (*Prunus virginiana*), Saskatoon (*Amelanchier alnifolia*), Hawthorn (*Crataegus* sp.), Apple (*Malus* sp.), Willow (*Salix* sp.) and Oak (*Quercus* sp.).

The eggs are laid singly on twigs of the food plant and hatch the following spring. The young larvae feed on flowers and fruit and older larvae feed on leaves. The mature larvae are grass-green, striped obliquely with yellow-green lines. The pupae are buff-brown with a reddish tinge and mottled with reddish-brown dots (Howe 1975).

In Manitoba, adults have been recorded from June 9 until August 12, being most common from early to mid-July. There is one generation per year.

Habitat: Forest edges and openings, patches of shrubbery, roadsides, backyards and pine woods.

Range: Alberta to Nova Scotia, south to Florida, Texas and Colorado (Hooper 1973; Opler and Krizek 1984).

Manitoba Records: Agassiz Provincial Forest, Aweme, Berens River, Beulah, Birds Hill, Birtle, Cartwright, Culross, Deleau, Elm Creek, Grand Beach, Husavik, Lauder, Melbourne, Miami, Miniota, Norris Lake, Northwest Angle Provincial Forest, Pine Ridge, Rennie, Riding Mountain, Rounthwaite, St. Malo, Sand Ridge, Sandilands Provincial Forest, Spruce Woods Provincial Forest, Tolstoi, Treesbank, Turtle Mountain, Victoria Beach, Whiteshell Provincial Park and Winnipeg.

Bur Oaks, Lauder Sandhills Wildlife Management Area, Manitoba. July 1988.

Subspecies: Four subspecies are recognized. The subspecies occurring from Alberta to Ontario is *Satyrium liparops fletcheri*.

Remarks: Although the Striped Hairstreak ranges over much of North America and has a wide variety of host plants it is seldom found in abundance. In Manitoba, the Striped Hairstreak is sporadic in appearance and local in distribution. Despite its local nature the Striped Hairstreak is more common than other members of the genus in Manitoba. Adults can be found near the host plants, for example in the Whiteshell Provincial Park they can be found in open pine woods perching on Blueberry and Saskatoon bushes; in Spruce Woods on Choke Cherry growing in sand dunes; and in Miami on Choke Cherry, Hazel and Saskatoon bushes at forest edges. Adults feed on a wide variety of flowers including White Sweet Clover, Dogbane, Goldenrod, Spiraea, Milkweed and Viburnum.

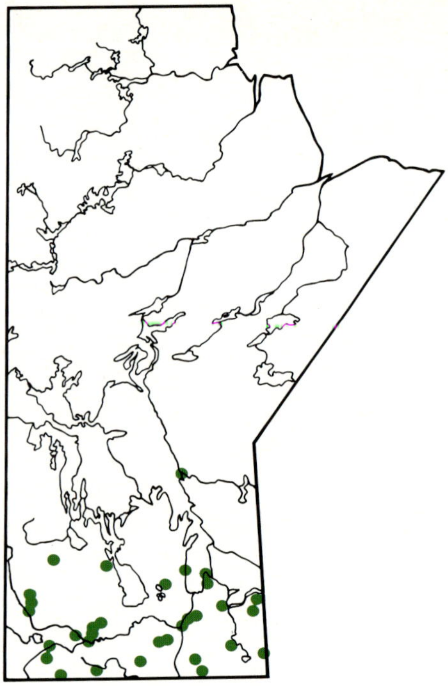

Brown Elfin

Callophrys augustus (W. Kirby), 1837
= *Incisalia augustus*
= *augustinus* (Westwood), 1852

Plate 13 No. 14, 15, 16

Description: 19-25 mm. The Brown Elfin is dark gray-brown above and rich chestnut brown below. In addition, the ventral surfaces of the wings are darker towards the base and more reddish toward the outer margins. The reddish-brown underside distinguishes this species from other Manitoba Elfins.

Life Cycle: The larvae feed upon Blueberry (*Vaccinium* sp.), Bearberry (*Arctostaphylos uva-ursi*), Labrador Tea (*Ledum groenlandicum*) and Leather Leaf (*Chamaedaphne calyculata*).

The greenish eggs are laid on or near the flower buds of the host plant. The young larvae bore into the buds and flowers and into the fruits as they mature. The slug-shaped larvae are bright green with a yellowish-stripe dorsally and oblique lines laterally. The larvae take approximately three weeks to reach maturity (three instars) and pupate in debris at the base of the host plant. The Brown Elfin overwinters in the pupal stage and adults emerge the following spring (Opler and Krizek 1984).

In Manitoba, adults have been observed from May 11 to June 29, with one very late record of July 19 at Lynn Lake. The Brown Elfin is most common in late May and there is one generation per year.

Habitat: Open woodland glades, bogs, open pine woods, forest edges, roads and trails.

Range: Alaska, Yukon and the Northwest Territories across all provinces of Canada to the Atlantic states southward to Virginia, and across to Michigan, New Mexico and Baja California.

Manitoba Records: Agassiz Provincial Forest, Aweme, Beulah, Brokenhead, Cartwright, Cowan, Duck Mountain, Fort Alexander, Gillam, Grand Beach, Lynn Lake, Mile 349 Hudson Bay Railway, Narcisse, Pikwitonei, Red Rock Lake, Richer, Riding Mountain, Sandilands Provincial Forest, Stony Mountain, Thompson, Victoria Beach, Wallace Lake and Winnipeg.

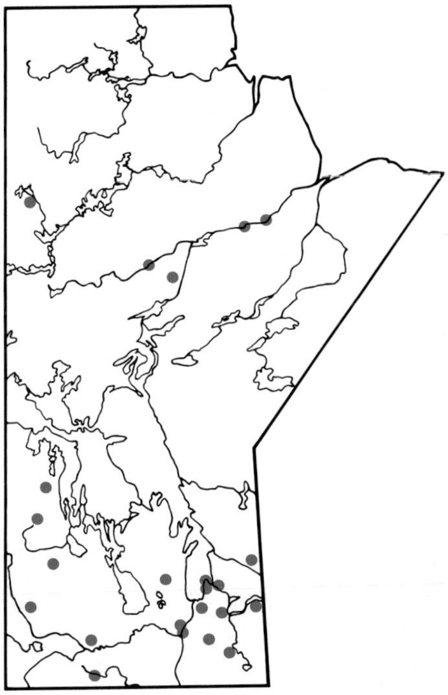

Subspecies: Five subspecies have been described for the Brown Elfin. The subspecies occurring in Manitoba is *Callophrys augustus augustus*.

Remarks: This is the most common Elfin in North America. In Manitoba it appears sporadically and populations fluctuate from year to year. The Brown Elfin is one of the first butterflies to emerge in the spring. In Sandilands Provincial Forest adults have been observed perching on roads and trails, sometimes taking moisture from puddles. Females often remain close to the host plant, e.g. Bearberry in Sandilands Provincial Forest. By flying low over surface vegetation, adults remain inconspicuous. They frequently fly in association with the more common Pine and Hoary Elfins.

Hoary Elfin

Callophrys polios (Cook & Watson), 1907
= *Incisalia polios*

Plate 13 No. 17, 18, 19

Description: 19-25 mm. The Hoary Elfin is dark gray-brown above and brown below. Ventrally the wings are darker basally and have hoary gray forewing margins. The outer half of the hindwings is also hoary gray. Occasionally faded and worn specimens resemble Brown Elfins but males can be distinguished by the conspicuous scent pads on the forewings which are paler than the ground colour.

Similar Species: Brown Elfins lack hoary clouding and are redder below. Male Brown Elfins have inconspicuous scent pads. Henry's Elfin has the outer margin of the hindwings scalloped.

Life Cycle: In Manitoba, Bearberry (*Arctostaphylos uva-ursi*), is the larval food plant.

The flattened eggs are laid at the bases of flower buds of the host plant. The newly hatched larvae are light green with long hairs and require about four weeks to reach maturity (three instars). The fully grown larvae are dark green and the pupae are dark brown. The Hoary Elfin overwinters in the pupal stage and adults emerge the following spring (Ferris and Fisher 1973).

In Manitoba, adults have been recorded from May 5 to June 27 and are most common in late May. There is one generation per year (Opler and Krizek 1984).

Habitat: Sandy forest edges and openings, sandy pine woods, rocky outcrops, where Bearberry occurs.

Range: Alaska, Yukon and all of the provinces to Nova Scotia, southward to New York, Virginia, Illinois, Minnesota, North Dakota, New Mexico and Oregon.

Manitoba Records: Agassiz Provincial Forest, Aweme, Beulah, Birds Hill, Brokenhead, Churchill, Cowan, Elm Creek, Gillam, Grand Beach, La Salle, Melbourne, Narcisse, Onah, Pikwitonei, Pine Ridge, Ponton, Riding Mountain, Sand Ridge, Sandilands Provincial Forest, Thompson, Victoria Beach, Whiteshell Provincial Park and Winnipeg.

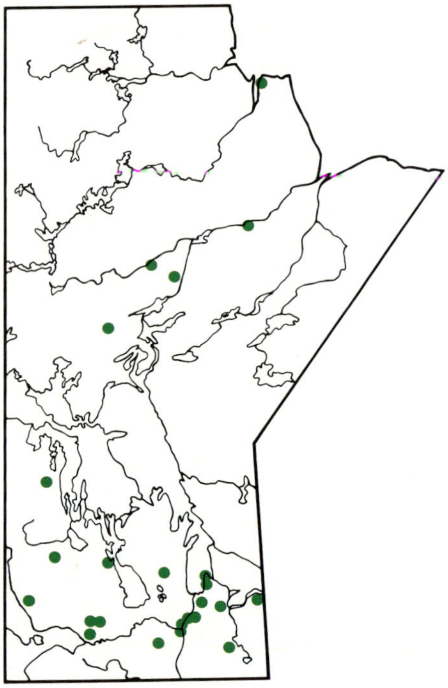

Subspecies: There are two subspecies of the Hoary Elfin, which overlap in Manitoba. Specimens found in eastern Manitoba are *Callophrys polios polios*, while specimens from western Manitoba are *Callophrys polios obscurus* (Ferris and Fisher 1973). The subspecies *polios* is generally rufous brown above and the male scent pad is pale or lighter than the ground colour. The subspecies *obscurus* is gray brown above and the male scent pad is black or darker than the ground colour.

Remarks: The Hoary Elfin is the most common Elfin species in the province. Like other Elfins, it is on the wing early in the spring and rarely strays far from its food plant, Bearberry. Individuals fly close to the ground and may perch on rocks or bare ground or take moisture from puddles. The Hoary Elfin is common in Sandilands Provincial Forest and can be observed by walking along roads or sandy trails.

Henry's Elfin
Callophrys henrici (Grote & Robinson), 1867
= *Incisalia henrici*
Plate 13 No. 20, 21, 22

Description: 22-28 mm. The wings are dark brown suffused with dull orange dorsally. Females have more orange than males. Below, the hindwings are deep dark brown at the base, sharply contrasting with the lighter outer area of the wings. The outer margins of the hindwings are hoary gray toward the bottom. There is a prominent lobe and short tail at the bottom of each hindwing and males lack forewing scent pads. This is the only Elfin in Manitoba with "tails".

Life Cycle: The larvae of Henry's Elfin feed upon Blueberry (*Vaccinium* sp.). The eggs are laid on the host plant and upon hatching the young larvae bore into the flower buds and fruit. As they mature larvae will also feed on the leaves. The fully grown larvae are about one centimetre in length, slug-shaped and light green with a paler stripe dorsally and oblique side stripes. Occasionally a reddish-brown larva is found with paler brown stripes. Pupation occurs at the base of the food plant about one month after eggs hatch. Henry's Elfin overwinters in the pupal stage and adults emerge in the spring.

Adults have been recorded from May 11 to June 12 in Manitoba. There is one generation per year.

Habitat: Forest edges, openings and clearings, open pine woods, brushy areas and forest roads or trails.

Range: Manitoba to Nova Scotia, southward to Florida, Texas, Illinois and Nebraska.

Manitoba Records: Sandilands Provincial Forest and Winnipeg.

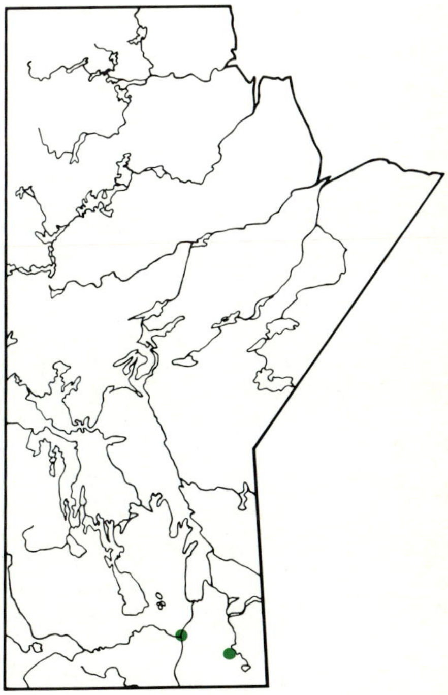

Subspecies: There are four subspecies of Henry's Elfin. *Callophrys henrici henrici* occurs in Canada and the northeastern United States.

Remarks: Henry's Elfin, although widespread in distribution is very local and rarely encountered. The first record for Manitoba consisted of six males found in an aspen glade in Sandilands Provincial Forest on May 28, 1967. Subsequently the Elfin has been found on roads at mud puddles and on bare forest trails within the provincial forest. Henry's Elfin flies in association with the much more numerous Hoary, Pine, and Brown Elfins, which is probably one reason why it has been overlooked. Usually no more than one or two individuals are observed in any one year.

Pine Elfin

Callophrys niphon (Hübner), 1823
= *Incisalia niphon*

Plate 13 No. 23, 24, 25

Description: 22-28 mm. The wings are dark gray-brown above, largely suffused with dull orange in the females. Below, the wings are mottled with gray and brown with two dark brown bars in the forewing cell. There is also a submarginal band of comparatively shallow angled chevrons and a faint hoary border in each hindwing. The fringes of the wings are checkered and those of the hindwings are slightly scalloped. The male scent pads blend in with the ground colour of the wing.

Similar Species: Western Pine Elfin differs as described under that species.

Life Cycle: In Manitoba, Jack Pine (*Pinus banksiana*) is the larval food plant.

Females usually oviposit on smaller trees and the larvae feed on young needles. At maturity the slug-shaped larvae are green and about one to one and a half cm. in length. The larvae have a whitish stripe along each side of the body. The cuticle is covered in downy yellow-brown hairs and the small head capsules are brown in colour. Pupae are black-brown with a yellowish-brown tinge. The Pine Elfin overwinters in the pupal stage and adults emerge in the spring (Klots 1951; Howe 1975; Opler and Krizek 1984).

In Manitoba, adults have been recorded from May 10 to June 17, usually being most abundant in late May. There is one generation per year.

Habitat: Open pine woods, glades, woodland borders and roads, especially in sandy areas where pines occur.

Range: Alberta to Nova Scotia, southward to Florida, Arkansas and Texas (Reist 1979).

Manitoba Records: Agassiz Provincial Forest, Beulah, Brokenhead, Cowan, Duck Mountains, Erinview, Grand Beach, Red Rock Lake, Riding Mountain, Sandilands Provincial Forest and Victoria Beach.

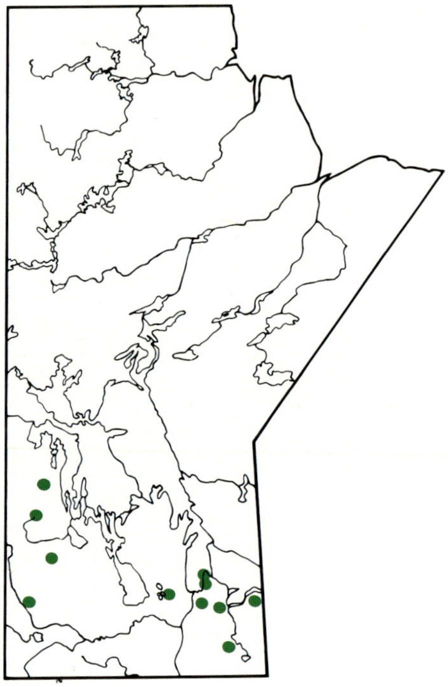

Subspecies: Two subspecies are recognized. The subspecies found in Manitoba is *Callophrys niphon clarki*.

Remarks: Also known as the Banded Elfin, this species is common in the coniferous forests of Manitoba. In Sandilands Provincial Forest Pine Elfins often sit on the bare sandy surface of trails and gravel roads. Adults occasionally move a considerable distance from pine trees to feed, preferring Bearberry and Dandelion. In the afternoon males often perch high up in pine trees. Although the first adults appear early in the spring, emergence is staggered over a period of weeks, which results in a longer flight period than in other Elfins. Populations of the Pine Elfin fluctuate from year to year in cycles that closely coincide with those of other Elfin species. These cycles can be readily observed in Sandilands Provincial Forest where a number of Elfin species occur.

Western Pine Elfin

Callophrys eryphon (Boisduval), 1852
= *Incisalia eryphon*

Plate 13 No. 26, 27, 28

Description: 22-28 mm. The Western Pine Elfin is similar in appearance to the Pine Elfin except that females usually are more extensively suffused with orange dorsally. There is usually one short bar at the end of each ventral forewing cell. The chevrons on the ventral surface of the hindwings of the Western Pine Elfin are deeply angled and enclose brown spots.

Similar Species: The Pine Elfin usually has an additional bar in the middle of each ventral forewing cell. The ventral surface of the hindwings has a hoary border and less deeply angled chevrons. It is sometimes difficult to separate the two species where their distributions overlap.

Life Cycle: The larvae of the Western Pine Elfin feed on Jack Pine (*Pinus banksiana*) in Manitoba.

The flattened chalk-white eggs are laid at the base of the needles of young shoots. Newly emerged larvae bore into the base of the needles as they feed and older larvae feed exposed on whole young needles. The mature larvae are one to one and half centimetres in length with tapered bodies and brown head capsules. The larvae are velvet green with four distinct yellowish stripes and a cuticle covered in fine short brown hairs. The larvae require about seven weeks from hatch to time of pupation. The stout pupae are dark brown and partly covered with fine hairs. The Western Pine Elfin overwinters in the pupal stage and adults emerge the following spring (Hardy 1959).

The few available Manitoba records are from June 16 to June 29. There is one generation per year in Manitoba.

Habitat: Pine forest edges and openings, forest meadows and spruce bogs.

Range: The Northwest Territories and British Columbia across Canada to Quebec, south to Maine, Michigan, Minnesota, North Dakota, New Mexico and California.

Manitoba Records: Churchill, Gillam, Lynn Lake and Pikwitonei.

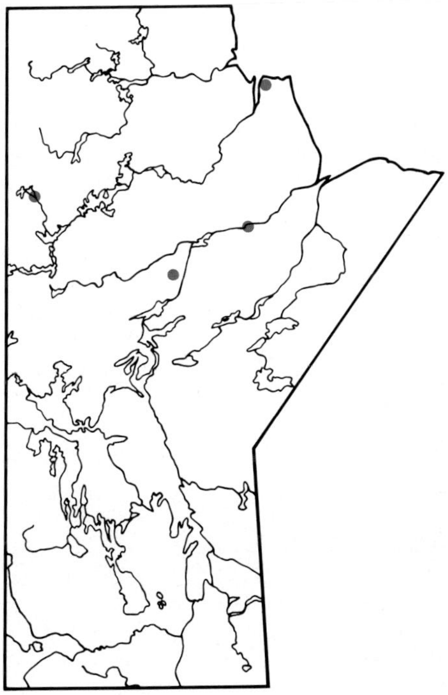

Subspecies: Two poorly defined subspecies have been described. The subspecies that occurs in Manitoba is *Callophrys eryphon eryphon*.

Remarks: In Manitoba, the first Western Pine Elfins were found at Gillam on June 16, 1949. In 1982 more were found near the edge of a mixed Jack Pine and Black Spruce forest along the railway that passes through Gillam. Both females and males were found perched on small pine trees or shrubs among the pines. The males frequently chased one another and often rose six to ten metres in the air before returning to their perches. Some were also found perched on bare ground, a behaviour that most other Elfin species exhibit. Adults are reported to visit Wild Rose and Willow catkins for nectar.

Gray Hairstreak

Strymon melinus Hübner, 1818

Plate 13 No. 29, 30, 31

Description: 25-32 mm. Dorsally the Gray Hairstreak is slate-gray, with a prominent orange spot on the hindwings. Below, the wings are a light gray with thin, orange and white-edged bands. The hindwings have a large orange patch and a few dark spots at the outer margin. The Gray Hairstreak has longer tails than other Manitoban Hairstreaks. Specimens vary in appearance both geographically and seasonally. Adults from the overwintering generation are smaller and darker ventrally than adults from the summer generation.

Life Cycle: The larvae of the Gray Hairstreak feed on a wide variety of plants, including Hops (*Humulus* sp.), Mallow (*Malva* sp.), Knotweed (*Polygonum* sp.), Beans (*Phaseolus* sp.), Hawthorne (*Crataegus* sp.), Oak (*Quercus* sp.), Cotton (*Gossypium* sp.), Strawberry (*Fragaria* sp.) and Mint (*Mentha* sp.).

The cuticle of the larva may be covered with short brownish hair or be naked and the head capsule is quite small in comparison to the body. Larvae are generally reddish-brown to green. When feeding, they bore into the fruits and seeds of the host plant. Laboratory reared larvae are often cannibalistic if overcrowded. The pupae are brown and heavily marked with deep brown spots. The Gray Hairstreak overwinters in the pupal stage (Howe 1975; Pyle 1981; Opler and Krizek 1984).

The only records for Manitoba are August 5 to 13, although Hooper (1973) states that adults have been found in Saskatchewan from May 20 to July 26. There are two generations in the northern part of this species range and three or more further south.

Habitat: Open deciduous woods, roadsides, old fields, parks, vacant lots and other open spaces.

Range: British Columbia to Nova Scotia, southward throughout the Untied States to Venezuela and Columbia.

Manitoba Records: Aweme, Brereton Lake, Carberry, and Winnipeg.

Subspecies: Six subspecies have been described. *Strymon melinus humuli* occurs in our area.

Remarks: Although the Gray Hairstreak is one of the most common Hairstreaks in North America it has rarely been seen in Manitoba. Adults visit a variety of flowers including Winter Cress, Dogbane, Milkweed, Mint, White Sweet Clover, Tick-trefoil and Goldenrod. The Gray Hairstreak has occasionally done economic damage to commercial Bean, Hop and Cotton crops in the United States.

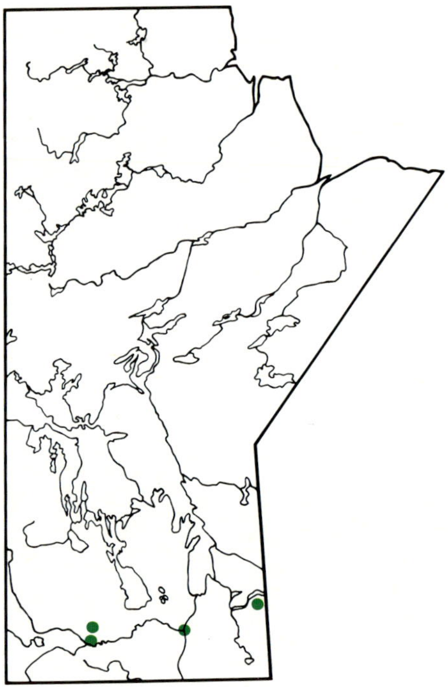

Reakirt's Blue

Hemiargus isola (Reakirt), 1866

Plate 14 No. 1, 2, 3

Description: 19-28 mm. This butterfly is purplish-blue dorsally with one or two submarginal black spots on the hindwings. Females are grayish outwardly. Ventrally the wings are brownish-gray with whitish wavy lines. The forewings have a row of prominent white-ringed round black spots and the hindwings have one or two black spots similar to the upper surface.

Life Cycle: The larval food plants do not occur in Manitoba. This species occurs farther south and on occasion probably migrates northward.

Habitat: Grasslands, fields and other open areas.

Range: British Columbia, Saskatchewan, Manitoba to Michigan and Ohio, southward to Mexico and Costa Rica.

Manitoba Records: No locality is given for the specimens collected in Manitoba.

Remarks: This tropical species regularly migrates northward and occasionally strays into the northern United States and Canada. Two specimens were collected in Manitoba in 1932 and 1933 and were deposited in the American Museum of Natural History.

Subfamily

POLYOMMATINAE: BLUES

= *Subfamily*

PLEBEJINAE

The Blues are widely distributed in temperate regions around the world with many more species occurring in the Old World than the New World. Members of this subfamily are small and include the smallest North American butterflies. Most adult males are blue in colour but females may be gray, brown or russet, usually with some blue at the base of the wings. Blues have a weak flight when not disturbed, most visit flowers and males sometimes congregate in large numbers at wet sand or mud.

The eggs are turban-shaped, flattened on the top and sculpted with ridges and depressions. They are usually laid on or near flower buds but sometimes on young growth or stems. Larvae are well camouflaged while they feed among the buds and seeds; most have honeydew producing glands and are sometimes attended by ants. Mature larvae are slug shaped and pupae are plump, egg shaped and often covered in short hair, bristles or spines. Pupae are attached to the substrate by a cremaster and silk girdle and can produce a "creaky" sound when disturbed.

Silvery Blues visiting moist gravel road, Agassiz Provincial Forest. May 1981.

Eastern Tailed Blue

Everes comyntas (Godart), 1824

Plate 14 No. 4, 5, 6

Description: 18-25 mm. The males are purplish-blue with dark borders; orange crescents and black dots lie above the hindwing tails. The females are dark slate-gray, more or less suffused with blue; they also have orange and black markings similar to the males. On the ventral surface the wings are grayish-white with distinct bands of grayish-black spots. There are conspicuous orange crescents (usually two) and black dots above a small thin tail at the bottom of each hindwing. The Eastern Tailed Blue is seasonally variable, with adults of the overwintering generation being smaller and brighter blue than the darker, more heavily marked individuals from the summer generations.

Similar Species: Western Tailed Blue differs as described under that species.

Life Cycle: Larvae feed on various species of legumes including Wild Pea (*Lathyrus* sp.), White Clover (*Trifolium repens*), Red Clover (*Trifolium pratense*), Alfalfa (*Medicago sativa*), Vetch (*Vicia* sp.), Milk Vetch (*Astragalus* sp.), Tick-trefoil (*Desmodium* sp.) and Beans (*Phaseolus* sp.).

The eggs are laid between the flower buds of the food plant. The larvae usually prefer to feed on the flowering parts of the host plant but will also consume leaves if flowering parts are absent. Although the larvae produce some honeydew they are seldom tended by ants. Mature larvae are dark green with a dark brown stripe dorsally, faint brownish oblique stripes laterally and covered with tiny tubercles bearing short hairs. The larvae pass through four instars and may be quite variable in appearance. They usually overwinter within the seed pod of the food plant and pupate in the spring. The pupae are buff or whitish-green with dark heads and thoraxes (Howe 1975; Opler and Krizek 1984).

In Manitoba, adults have been recorded from May 16 to September 6. There are probably three generations per year in this province.

Habitat: Forest edges, clearings and disturbed areas such as old fields, farmyards, roadsides and ditches.

Range: Manitoba to New Brunswick and New England, southward to Florida, Texas and Colorado. Also found in California, Oregon, Mexico and Central America.

Manitoba Records: Culross, Grand Beach, Northwest Angle Provincial Forest, Pine Ridge, Rathwell, Sandilands Provincial Forest, Whiteshell Provincial Park and Winnipeg.

Subspecies: Two subspecies are recognized. The subspecies found in Manitoba is *Everes comyntas comyntas*.

Remarks: The Eastern Tailed Blue is common in eastern North America and readily colonizes disturbed areas. This species is uncommon in Manitoba and most specimens were observed along roads in the Culross area from 1970 to 1975, where it has not been observed since. Adults in the Culross area stayed close to Red Clover, utilizing it for perching, nectar and probably as a larval host plant. When at rest, adults actively rub their wings together and will take nectar from a wide variety of flowers including Cinquefoils, Wild Strawberry, White Clover, Dogbane, Fleabane and Asters.

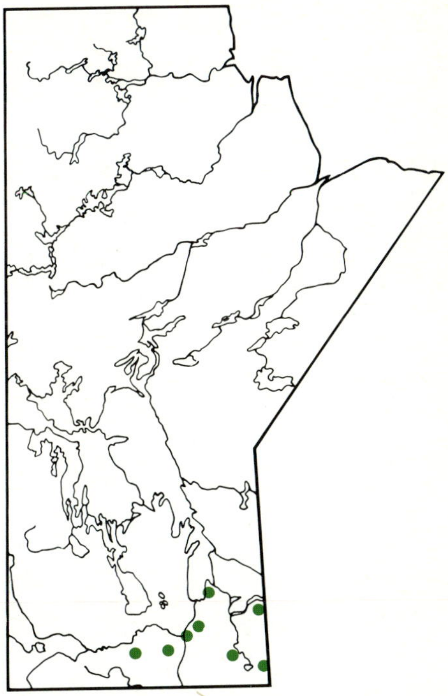

Western Tailed Blue

Everes amyntula (Boisduval), 1852

Plate 14 No. 7, 8, 9, 10

Description: 17-25 mm. The males are bright purplish-blue dorsally with very narrow dark borders. The females are grayish-black variably suffused with blue basally. Both sexes have one to two black dots above the tails and occasionally the dots may be faintly capped with orange in the females. Ventrally the wings are chalk-white with gray markings (often faint or absent) and there are usually one or more small orange spots above the tails.

Similar Species: The Eastern Tailed Blue is a duller colour, has more pronounced markings, wider borders on the dorsal surface and a grayish-white, not chalky-white ventral surface. Some specimens can only be distinguished from the Western Tailed Blue by genitalic examination.

Life Cycle: In Manitoba the preferred food plant of the Western Tailed Blue is thought to be Wild Pea (*Lathyrus* sp.). In other areas host plants include Milk Vetch (*Astragalus* sp.), Vetch (*Vicia* sp.), Locoweed (*Oxtropis* sp.) and Clover (*Trifolium* sp.).

The pale green eggs are laid singly on the flowers or developing seed pod of the host plant. The larvae will feed mostly on the developing seeds and overwinter within the seed pod. The larvae possess honeydew producing glands and are sometimes attended by ants. The mature larvae may be variable shades of green with pink or maroon markings and are covered with short, fine white hairs. Pupation occurs within the seed pod. The pupae can produce sounds with a stridulating organ located between the abdominal segments (Howe 1975; Opler 1981).

In Manitoba, adults have been recorded from May 13 to August 21. Adults are most common in June in southern Manitoba and in July at Churchill. There is one generation per year in northern Manitoba and probably two per year in southern Manitoba.

Habitat: Forest edges and clearings, meadows and roadsides.

Range: Alaska, Yukon and the Northwest Territories to Gaspé Penninsula, Quebec, southward to Minnesota, North Dakota, Colorado, Arizona and Baja California.

Manitoba Records: Agassiz Provincial Forest, Asessippi Provincial Park, Aweme, Bellsite, Berens River, Binscarth, Birds Hill, Brandon, Buffalo Lake, Carman, Cartwright, Churchill, Cormorant Lake, Cowan, Cranberry Portage, Culross, Duck Mountain, Elm Creek, Flin Flon, Gillam, Grand Beach, Grand Rapids, Gypsumville, Jacam, Kelwood, Lauder, Leaf Rapids, Little Limestone Lake, McCreary, Miami, Miniota, Mile 200 and 412 of the Hudson Bay Railway, Narcisse, Norway House, Orr Lake, Overflowing River, Pine Ridge, Pisew Falls, Riding Mountain, Riverton, Russell, Sandiands Provincial Forest, Selkirk, Souris, Split Lake, Teulon, The Pas, Thompson, Turtle Mountain Provincial Park, Victoria Beach, Wabowden, Whiteshell Provincial Park and Winnipeg.

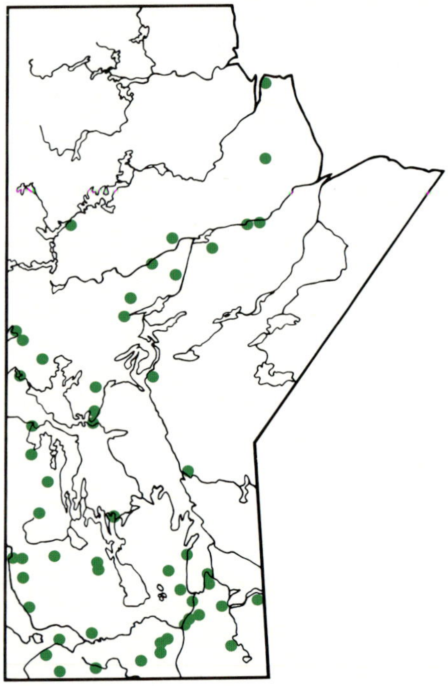

Subspecies: Four subspecies of the Western Tailed Blue are recognized. The northern subspecies, which occurs in Manitoba, is *Everes amyntula albrighti*.

Remarks: This species is common in Manitoba, largely replacing the Eastern Tailed Blue. While found mainly in or near forests it also occurs in agricultural areas. The Western Tailed Blue is closely associated with Wild Pea in Manitoba. The flight is weak and low to the ground. The Western Tailed Blue is common along roads and trails in Sandilands and Agassiz Provincial Forests.

Spring Azure

Celastrina argiolus (Linnaeus), 1758
= *Celastrina ladon* (Cramer), 1780

Plate 14 No. 11, 12, 16, 17, 18

Description: 18-26 mm. The dorsal surface of the wings is violet-tinged silvery blue, usually with checkered fringes. The males have narrow dark borders and the females have coal black forewing borders. Ventrally the Spring Azure is slate gray with fairly wide brownish-gray borders. Occasionally there is a large blotch in the hindwing as well as variable small spots in both wings.

Life Cycle: The larvae of the Spring Azure feed on a wide variety of plant species which include Blueberry (*Vaccinium* sp.), Meadowsweet (*Spiraea* sp.), Trefoil (*Lotus* sp.), Sumac (*Rhus* sp.), Viburnum (*Viburnum* sp.), Wild Cherry (*Prunus* sp.), Oak (*Quercus* sp.) and Dogwood (*Cornus* sp.).

The green, turban shaped eggs are oviposited among flower buds or on the leaves of the host plant. The larvae often feed on the flower buds only and are attended by ants seeking honeydew secretions. The mature larvae are predominately green with dark dorsal and lateral stripes, and a cuticle covered in soft white hair. The Spring Azure overwinters in the pupal stage (Howe 1975).

In Manitoba adults have been recorded from April 17 to Aug. 13 and are most common after mid-May in southern Manitoba and late June at Churchill. There is one generation per year in the northern part of the province and two in the south.

Habitat: Open forests, brushy areas, glades, clearings and roadsides. In spruce forests at Gillam and on tundra ridges just north of the treeline at Churchill, Manitoba.

Range: Europe, western Asia and in North America from Alaska to Labrador, south to Florida, Mexico and Panama.

Manitoba Records: Agassiz Provincial Forest, Aweme, Beulah, Birds Hill, Birtle, Carberry, Cartwright, Cowan, Churchill, Culross, Delta, Duck Mountain, Elm Creek, Fairford, Gillam, Grand Beach, Hargrave River, Kelwood, Lyleton, Lynn Lake, McCreary, Melbourne, Miami, Mile 412 Hudson Bay Railway, Miniota, Northwest Angle Provincial Forest, Norway House, Onah, Pikwitonei, Pine Ridge, Riding Mountain, Sandilands Provincial Park, Selkirk, Stony Mountain, The Pas, Thompson, Tolstoi, Victoria Beach, Wallace Lake, Whiteshell Provincial Park and Winnipeg.

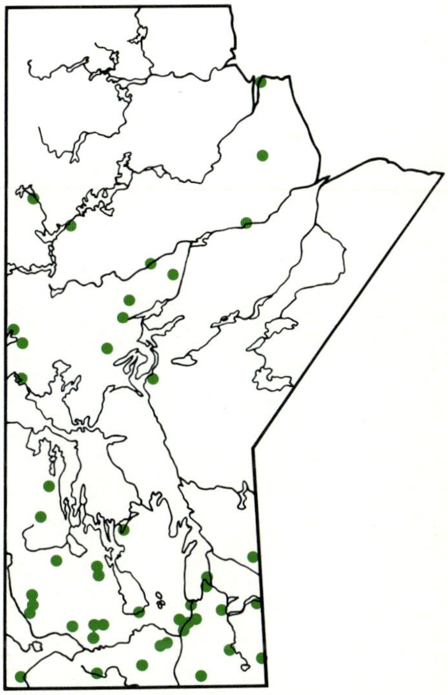

Subspecies: There are eight subspecies of the Spring Azure. *Celastrina argiolus lucia* occurs in Manitoba. *Celastrina argiolus* form *argentata*, with a chalk-white underside and generally uncheckered wing fringes, was formerly considered a subspecies, but is now regarded as a summer form. The ventral surface markings are greatly reduced and the male dorsal hindwings are pale. The ground colour of summer form females is mostly silvery white with bluish reflections.

Remarks: The Spring Azure is one of the first butterflies to emerge in the spring. It is common and widespread in the south and central areas of the province but scarce at Churchill. Adults will visit Saskatoon, Willow and Chokecherry when they are in flower in the spring. Adults from the summer generation usually prefer open, drier, less forested areas than individuals from the overwintering generation. The Spring Azure has a weak, leisurely flight and frequently sips moisture from mud puddles.

Silvery Blue

Glaucopsyche lygdamus (Doubleday), 1841

Plate 14 No. 13, 14, 15

Description: 21-28 mm. This butterfly is silvery blue above with narrow black borders in the males and variable wide, diffuse blackish borders in the females. Ventrally the wings are slate or brownish-gray with an irregular postmedian row of white-ringed black spots on each wing and several inconspicuous small spots basally. Occasionally individuals with reduced markings may be encountered. Adults may vary greatly in size.

Life Cycle: The larvae of the Silvery Blue feed on legumes including Wild Pea (*Lathyrus* sp.), Milk Vetch (*Astragalus* sp.), Vetch (*Vicia* sp.), Trefoil (*Lotus* sp.) and Locoweed (*Oxytropis* sp.). Sperling (pers. comm.) reared the Spring Azure on Northern Hedysarum (*Hedysarum boreale*).

The eggs are laid on the host plant and the larvae feed on the flowers and seed pods. Ants will tend larvae for their honeydew secretions. The mature larvae are slug-shaped, pale green, brown or purplish with a dark dorsal stripe and whitish lines laterally and on the head capsules. The pupae are formed in debris at the base of the plant. They are firmly attached to the substrate by a cremaster and silk girdle and are the overwintering stage in Manitoba (Howe 1975; Opler and Krizek 1984).

In Manitoba adults are on the wing from April 28 to August 11, being most abundant in early June in southern Manitoba and July at Churchill. Females emerge about a week after males. There is a single generation in Manitoba, but adult emergence is staggered over several months.

Habitat: Open woodlands and forest edges, but also found in brushy disturbed or burned over areas, and along streams and ditches in open terrain.

Range: Alaska to Nova Scotia and Newfoundland, southward to Georgia, Oklahoma, Arizona and Baja California.

Manitoba Records: Agassiz Provincial Forest, Aweme, Bellsite, Beulah, Birds Hill, Brandon, Brokenhead, Cape Tatnam, Carberry, Cartwright, Churchill, Cowan, Cranberry Portage, Cromer, Culross, Dawson Bay, Deleau, Delta, Duck Mountain, Elm Creek, Fairford, Flin Flon, Gillam, Grahamdale, Grand Beach, Grand Rapids, Gypsumville, Hadashville, Jacam, Kelwood, Kettle Rapids, La Riviere, Lauder, Lyleton, Marchand, McCreary, Miami, Mile 412 Hudson Bay Railway, Miniota, Narcisse, Neepawa, Ninette, Norris Lake, Northwest Angle Provincial Park, Oak Hammock, Onah, Onanole, Overflowing River, Pine Ridge, Pipun, Porcupine Provincial Forest, Riding Mountain, Russell, Sand Ridge, Sandilands Provincial Forest, Sanford, Selkirk, Seven Sisters, Shilo, Teulon, The Pas, Thompson, Victoria Beach, Whiteshell Provincial Park and Winnipeg.

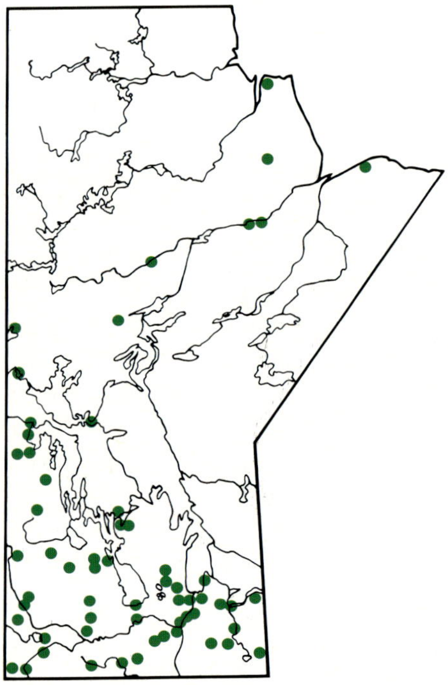

Subspecies: Up to eleven subspecies of the Silvery Blue have been described. The subspecies occurring in Manitoba is *Glaucopsyche lygdamus couperi*, although Hooper (1973) noted that specimens from western Manitoba may belong to the subspecies *Glaucopsyche lygdamus afra*. The latter is darker ventrally.

Remarks: The Silvery Blue is common throughout Manitoba. Adults have a relatively rapid flight and males will often congregate on areas of moist or wet soil. They visit a variety of flowers especially composites and legumes.

Northern Blue

Lycaeides idas Linnaeus, 1761
= *Plebejus idas*
= *Plebejus argyrognomon* (Bersträsser), 1779

Plate 14 No. 19, 20, 21, 22

Description: 22-28 mm. The males are purplish-blue above with narrow black margins (often with three or more small, obscure submarginal black dots in the hindwings). The outer half of the wings in females is gray-black, with blue confined to basal areas, and occasionally reduced to a trace. The hindwing dots are more developed in females than in males and may be capped with a trace of dull orange, sometimes forming a complete band of suffused spots in both fore and hindwings. Below, both sexes are grayish-white to slate gray with black spots and have a submarginal row of black-capped orange and silvery blue-green spots.

Similar Species: Orange Bordered Blue differs as described under that species.

Life Cycle: The early stages of the Northern Blue are not well known. Probable food plants in Manitoba include Dwarf Bilberry (*Vaccinium caespitosum*), Black Crowberry (*Empetrum nigrum*) and Labrador Tea (*Ledum groenlandicum*).

The pale gray-green eggs are laid singly on the food plant stems or on the litter beneath. The larvae are pea-green to brown with obscure lateral stripes (Pyle 1981).

In Manitoba adults have been recorded from June 27 to August 28 being most common in early July. There is one generation per year.

Habitat: Open areas, heaths, roads and trails in boreal forests. In Whiteshell Provincial Park the Northern Blue has been found in open pine woods and in small heaths in the Duck Mountains.

Range: Boreal regions of Europe, Asia and in North America from Alaska to Newfoundland, southward to Michigan, Wisconsin and Minnesota in the east and Colorado and California in the west.

Manitoba Records: Agassiz Provincial Forest, Bisset, Buffalo Lake, Churchill, Cowan, Duck Mountain, Gillam, Gypsumville, Hargrave River, Leaf Rapids, Lynn Lake, Mile 200 Hudson Bay Railway, Millwood, Norris Lake, Norway House, Ponton, Reed Lake, Riding Mountain, Sandilands Provincial Forest, Teulon, The Pas, Thompson, Victoria Beach, Whiteshell Provincial Forest, William River and Winnipeg.

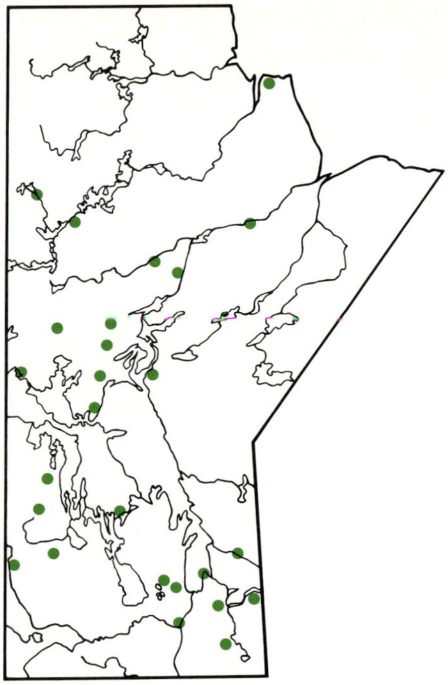

Subspecies: Twelve subspecies have been described for the Northern Blue. The subspecies *Lycaeides idas scudderi* occurs throughout Manitoba except east of the Red River and Lake Winnipeg where it is replaced by the subspecies *Lycaeides idas nabokobi* which is lighter and brighter ventrally.

Remarks: The Northern Blue (also known as Scudder's Blue) has been confused with the Orange Bordered Blue. In Manitoba there is some overlap between these species and because of their variability specimens have been incorrectly identified in the past. Generally in Manitoba the Northern Blue is confined to evergreen forests whereas the Orange Bordered Blue is found in dry, sandy prairie. The Northern Blue emerges later in the season than the other Blues and numbers fluctuate from year to year. Males frequently fly along forest roads or trails, congregate at mud puddles or patrol near larval food plants in search of females. Both sexes feed on the flowers of Clovers, Dogbane and Yarrow. Flight is relatively swift and low to the ground. Whiteshell Provincial Park and Duck Mountain are good areas to observe the Northern Blue.

Orange Bordered Blue

Lycaeides melissa (W.H. Edwards), 1873

= *Plebejus melissa*

Plate 14 No. 23, 24, 25

Description: 20-28 mm. The dorsal surface of the males is purplish-blue with very narrow black margins. Occasionally there are several inconspicuous small diffused black submarginal spots in the hindwings. The females are gray-brown above, usually with blue suffusion basally and a prominent orange border on each wing. Ventrally both sexes are grayish-white with black spots and an orange submarginal band in each wing, somewhat more developed in the hindwings and specially in females. In addition, there is a row of iridescent blue-green spots below the orange band on the hindwings.

Similar Species: Above, the Northern Blue males have narrower black margins. Ventrally the Northern Blue has a fainter marginal black line and the orange bands are reduced to disjunct spots. Occasionally genitalic examination is required to differentiate specimens of the two species.

Life Cycle: The larvae of the Orange Bordered Blue will feed on a variety of legumes including Alfalfa (*Medicago sativa*), Two-grooved Milk Vetch (*Astragalus bisulcatus*), Purple Locoweed (*Oxtropis lambertii*), Early Yellow Locoweed (*Oxtropis servicea*), Prairie Trefoil (*Lotus americana*) and Wild Licorice (*Glycyrrhiza lepidota*).

The white-ridged eggs are pale green and laid directly on the food plant or on objects nearby. The larvae feed on the leaves and produce honeydew which often attracts ants. There are five instars and the larvae overwinter in the third or fourth instar. The mature larvae are green, darker green dorsally with oblique lines laterally and covered in short hair. The pupae are green or brown with numerous translucent yellowish spots and are fastened to the substrate by a silk girdle and cremaster (Howe 1975; Opler and Krizek 1984).

In Manitoba adults have been recorded from May 15 to September 21. There are two generations per year. The adults from the overwintering generation usually begin to emerge in June, while the less numerous adults of the second generation occur in July or August. The rare September records of the Orange Bordered Blue may consist of adults from a third generation.

Habitat: Dry sandy virgin prairie, open meadows in woods and roadside ditches in agricultural areas.

Range: Southern Canada from British Columbia to Ontario, southward to New Hampshire and New York, the Great Lakes, the western plains and into Mexico.

Manitoba Records: Asessippi Provincial Park, Aweme, Beulah, Birds Hill, Birtle, Brandon, Carberry, Cartwright, Cowan, Cromer, Culross, Deleau, Glenboro, Grand Beach, Melbourne, Miami, Miniota, Onah, Pine Ridge, Porcupine Provincial Forest, Riding Mountain, St. Malo, Sand Ridge, Souris, Treesbank, Victoria Beach and Winnipeg.

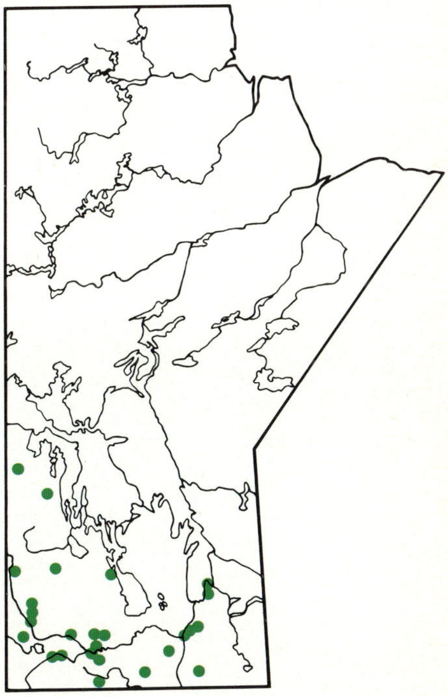

Subspecies: Five subspecies of the Orange Bordered Blue have been described. *Lycaeides melissa melissa* occurs in Manitoba.

Remarks: The Orange Bordered Blue is confined mostly to dry sandy prairie in Manitoba and is seldom found in forested areas. This species is uncommon in Manitoba, probably because some of its native habitat has been lost to agriculture, but Hooper (1973) noted that it is still common in southern Saskatchewan. In the Culross area the Orange Bordered Blue is occasionally abundant in roadside ditches where it is associated with Red Clover and Alfalfa. Adults have a swift low flight and are often difficult to observe if disturbed. Males regularly patrol along ditches, roads or hillsides and both sexes feed at a wide variety of flowers.

Greenish Blue

Plebejus saepiolus (Boisduval), 1852

Plate 14 No. 26, 27, 28

Description: 23-32 mm. The males are silvery-blue above with green reflections. The wing borders are suffused gray-black and sometimes contain small obscure dots in the hindwings. The females are mostly dark grayish-brown with variable blue suffusion basally. Occasionally there is a band of diffuse orange spots in the hindwings. Both sexes have a black bar, sometimes very faint, in each forewing. Ventrally the wings of both male and female are whitish-gray or gray. Females may be brownish-gray with small black spots. Occasionally there are one to two small black capped dull orange spots in the hindwings of both sexes. Females are quite variable in appearance but always with more pronounced markings than in males.Northern specimens are usually smaller than southern ones.

Life Cycle: Larvae of the Greenish Blue feed exclusively on clovers including Alsike Clover (*Trifolium hybridum*) and White Clover (*Trifolium repens*).

The eggs are oviposited in the flowers of the host plant. Larvae feed on the flowers and overwinter in the second or third instar. The mature larvae are green or reddish in colour (Howe 1975).

In Manitoba adults have been recorded from May 11 to July 21. The Greenish Blue is most common in June in southern Manitoba and July in northern areas. There is one generation per year.

Habitat: Forest edges and openings, glades, open meadows, roadsides and disturbed areas where clovers grow.

Range: Alaska and the Yukon to central and southern Canada to Newfoundland, southward to New Hampshire, Michigan, Minnesota, Nebraska, Colorado and California (Opler and Krizek 1984).

Manitoba Records: Agassiz Provincial Forest, Asessippi Provincial Park, Aweme, Berens River, Beulah, Brandon, Brokenhead, Cartwright, Churchill, Cowan, Cranberry Portage, Cromer, Culross, Deleau, Delta, Duck Mountain, Elm Creek, Eriksdale, Flin Flon, Fort Alexander, Gillam, Grand Beach, Grand Rapids, Grass River Provincial Park, Hazel Creek at Hwy. 15, Kelwood, Leaf Rapids, Lundar, Mafeking, McCreary, Millwood, Miniota, Neepawa, Ninette, Norway House, Oak Hammock, Onanole, Overflowing River, Pierson, Pikwitonei, Pine Ridge, Pisew Falls, Ponton, Porcupine Provincial Forest, Riding Mountain, Roblin, Sandilands Provincial Forest, Selkirk, Seven Sisters, Spruce Woods Provincial Park, The Pas, Thompson, Victoria Beach, Wabowden and Winnipeg.

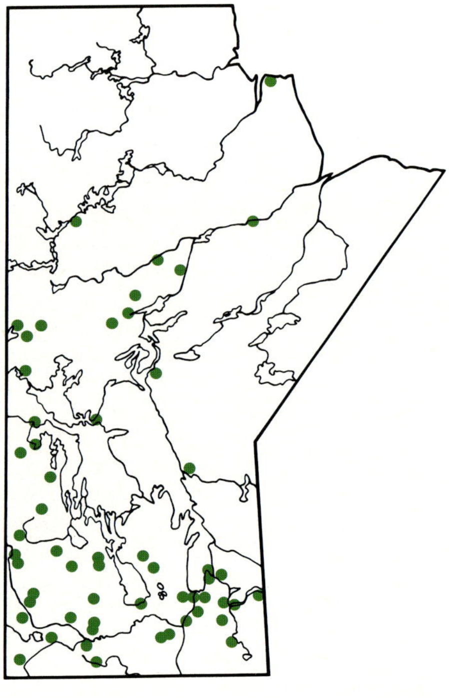

Subspecies: Six subspecies are recognized. The Manitoba subspecies is *Plebejus saepiolus amica*.

Remarks: The Greenish Blue, also known as the Saepiolus Blue, has moved eastward across southern Canada into the Maritimes over the last century. It is common in southern and central Manitoba, but scarce in the tundra zone. The Greenish Blue is on the wing very early in the spring. Males will congregate at moist areas of sand or soil, while females are more sedentary, staying close to the host plant. Both sexes visit a wide variety of flowers especially legumes.

Yukon Blue

Vacciniina optilete (Knoch), 1781
= *Plebejus optilete*

Plate 14 No. 29, 30, 31

Description: 19-22 mm. Dorsally the males are dark purple, while the females are mostly charcoal black with purple at the base of the wings. Both sexes are gray below, with prominent black spots ringed with white, and one orange spot in the submargin of the hindwings.

Similar Species: The Silvery Blue is larger and never has orange markings.

Life Cycle: Little is know about the life history of the Yukon Blue. In Manitoba the food plant is probably Grouseberry (*Vaccinium myrtillus*). The Yukon Blue overwinters in the larval stage (Howe 1975; Pyle 1981). Adults have been recorded in Manitoba from July 2 to July 26.

Habitat: Taiga and tundra, in or near bogs where cranberries are found and in wet areas beside roads or streams. At Churchill, adults have been found in the taiga zone, near wet cutover areas and along the railway line south of the town.

Range: This species occurs in the European Alps, arctic Europe, Asia and Japan. In North America it is limited to the subarctic regions from Alaska and the southern Yukon eastward to northern and central Manitoba.

Near Churchill, Manitoba. June 1982.

Manitoba Records: Caribou Lake, Churchill, Duck Mountain, Gillam, Lynn Lake, The Pas and Thompson.

Subspecies: The only subspecies found in North America is *Vacciniina optilete yukona*.

Remarks: Although common in Alaska and Yukon this butterfly is scarce in Manitoba. The first specimen found in this province was from Churchill on July 9, 1973. The Yukon Blue flies low over the ground or around shrubs and is often difficult to distinguish from the ground cover. This butterfly has a weak flight and regularly seeks moist areas from which to take water. The Yukon Blue is probably more common in Manitoba than is apparent from present records.

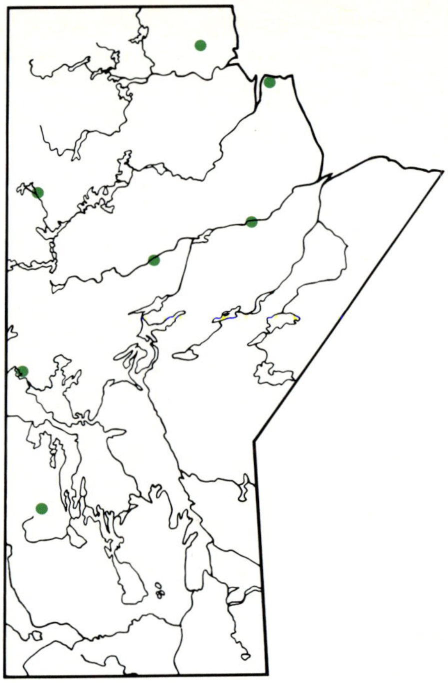

Arctic Blue

Agriades glandon (de Prunner), 1798
= *Plebejus franklinii* Curtis, 1798

Plate 14 No. 32, 33, 34, 35, 36, 37

Description: 20-25 mm. Dorsally the males are shiny gray-blue with dark, diffuse margins in the forewings and usually a marginal row of dots in the hindwings. The females are dark gray-brown with varying degrees of blue scaling basally. Both sexes usually have a dark bar in the middle of each wing (more developed in the forewing of the female). Ventrally the forewings are gray to light brown with white ringed black spots. The hindwings are light brown with white spots which may contain dark dots.

Life Cycle: Females have been observed ovipositing on Diapensia (*Diapensia lapponica*) on Baffin Island; on Rock Jasmine (*Androsace septentrionalis*) in Wyoming; on Shooting star (*Dodecatheon* sp.) in alpine areas and on Blueberry (*Vaccinium* sp.) in Newfoundland (Emmel 1970; Howe 1975). Larvae have also been found upon Purple Saxifrage (*Saxifraga oppositifolia*) and Prickly Saxifrage (*Saxifraga tricuspidata*). Little is known about the immature stages of the Arctic Blue in North America.

In Manitoba adults have been recorded from May 21 to Aug. 3 with a single record for August 19. In the southern part of the province adults are most common in June and in the Churchill area they fly in July. Females emerge about a week after males and there is one generation per year in Manitoba.

Habitat: Arctic dry tundra and meadows, forest meadows, ridges and rocky outcrops. In the Riding and Duck Mountains the Arctic Blue has been found in forest meadows and roadside ditches. In southern Manitoba this Blue occurs on dry virgin prairie or in roadside ditches.

Range: The Arctic Blue is circumpolar in distribution. In North America it is found from Alaska to Ellesmere Island and Labrador, southward through Newfoundland to southern Manitoba and South Dakota and in the west south to New Mexico.

Manitoba Records: Aweme, Bellsite, Beulah, Birds Hill, Birtle, Carberry, Cartwright, Churchill, Cormorant Lake, Cowan, Duck Mountain, Flin Flon, Grahamdale, Killarney, Norway House, Pine Ridge, Riding Mountain, Seal River, Stony Mountain, The Pas, Thompson, Treesbank and Winnipeg.

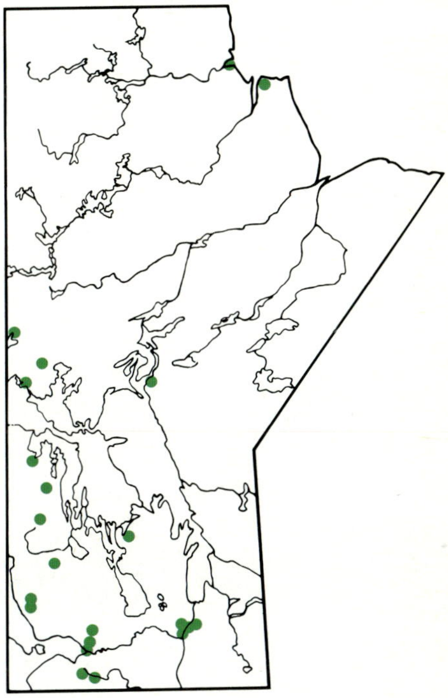

Subspecies: Six subspecies have been described for North America. Three of these are reported to occur in Manitoba. *Agriades glandon franklinii,* found at Churchill and Seal River, is small, seldom over 20 mm, dull coloured and quite distinct from the more southern subspecies. *Agriades glandon lacustris* is found in central Manitoba and is larger than *Agriades glandon franklinii*. Males have wider wing margins and are brighter while females are darker. The third subspecies *Agriades glandon rustica*, found in southern Manitoba, is distinguished by the pale ventral surface with large white spots often forming bands. Possibly all of the south and central Manitoba populations of the Arctic Blue should be assigned to the subspecies *rustica*.

Remarks: This is truly an arctic species, occurring northward to Ellesmere Island. When at rest adults blend in with the background and are easily overlooked. Adults fly very close to the ground. The Arctic Blue is scarce in Manitoba and is found only sporadically. The subspecies *rustica* has been found in the Carberry area and at Pine Ridge. *Franklinii* is common north of Churchill at Fort Prince of Wales where it occurs in association with Prickly Saxifrage (*Saxifraga tricuspidata*). This butterfly has been referred to as *Plebejus aquilo* by some authors.

Family

HELICONIIDAE: LONGWINGED BUTTERFLIES

With few exceptions, this family is mostly Neotropical. They have elongate forewings, reduced forelegs, a slender body, and a large head. As the larvae feed on the leaves of Passion Flower (Passifloraceae), the Heliconiids are thought to be distasteful to birds. According to some authorities, many butterflies mimic members of this group presumably to take advantage of this protection from potential predators.

Gulf Fritillary

Dione vanillae (Linnaeus), 1758
= *Agraulis vanillae*

Plate 15 No. 1

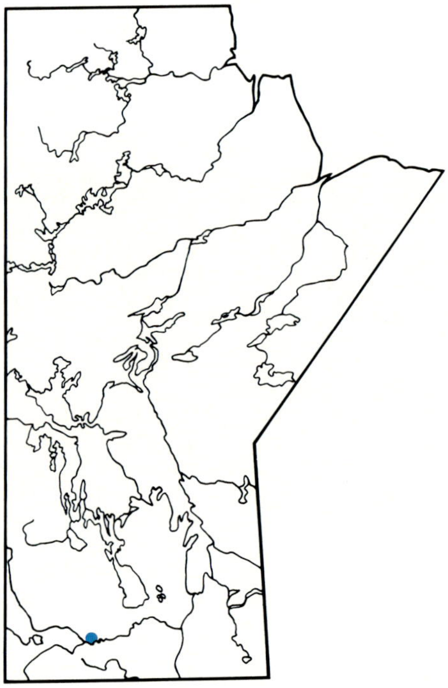

Description: 64-73 mm. This butterfly is bright brownish-orange dorsally with black veins widening near the margins. There are several black spots, some of which are white-centred, near the upper margin of the forewings. The hindwings have a black border containing a row of orange spots. Ventrally the forewings are similar to the upper surface with large silvery white spots near the tip. The hindwings are brown with large conspicuous elongated silvery white spots. The forewings are long and narrow.

Life Cycle: The larval food plants do not occur in Manitoba.

Habitat: Open fields, pastures and suburban gardens (Opler and Krizek 1984).

Range: Tropical America throughout the southern United States, north to New York, Pennsylvania, Wisconsin and Manitoba.

Manitoba Records: Aweme.

Remarks: At rare intervals this southern resident migrates northward to Wisconsin and Minnesota, having made its way to Manitoba at least once (Brooks 1942).

Family

NYMPHALIDAE: BRUSH-FOOTED BUTTERFLIES

There are approximately 3,000 species within the family Nymphalidae worldwide, with about 100 species known in North America, 63 in Canada and 40 in Manitoba. Members of this family occur on all continents, except Antarctica, from the arctic regions to the equator and from mountain summits to sea level.

The members of this family are characterized by having the forelegs reduced to stumps covered with long hairy scales. The antennae are strong, rigid, covered with scales and end in prominent clubs. Palpi are hairy and robust and the proboscis is relatively short. The cell in both fore and hindwings is usually open but sometimes enclosed by a weak vein. Adults feed on sap, dung, rotting fruit and take nectar from flowers.

The barrel-shaped eggs are laid singly or in groups on the underside of the leaves of the host plant or occasionally on nearby objects. Larvae usually have several rows of tubercles bearing spiny hairs, some have short dense hair, while a few have a smooth cuticle. Some species have forked "tails" and most have a pair of long spiny horn-like tubercles on the head capsule. In many species the larvae feed gregariously at night when young and frequently form silken or folded leaf shelters. Pupae hang free, suspended only by the cremaster. Most species overwinter as partly grown larvae or occasionally as adults.

Subfamily

ARGYNNINAE: FRITILLARIES OR SILVERSPOTS

Members of this subfamily are mostly medium to large orange butterflies with a fairly consistent pattern of black markings on the dorsal surface. The species within this subfamily are best distinguished by the ventral hindwings which often contain silvery white spots. The Lesser Fritillaries (*Boloria* sp.) are well represented in the northern and alpine regions of North America. They are small to medium sized butterflies and most are single brooded although some in the northern part of the continent require two years to complete their life cycle. The Greater Fritillaries are placed in the genus *Speyeria*. This is a complex group and it is

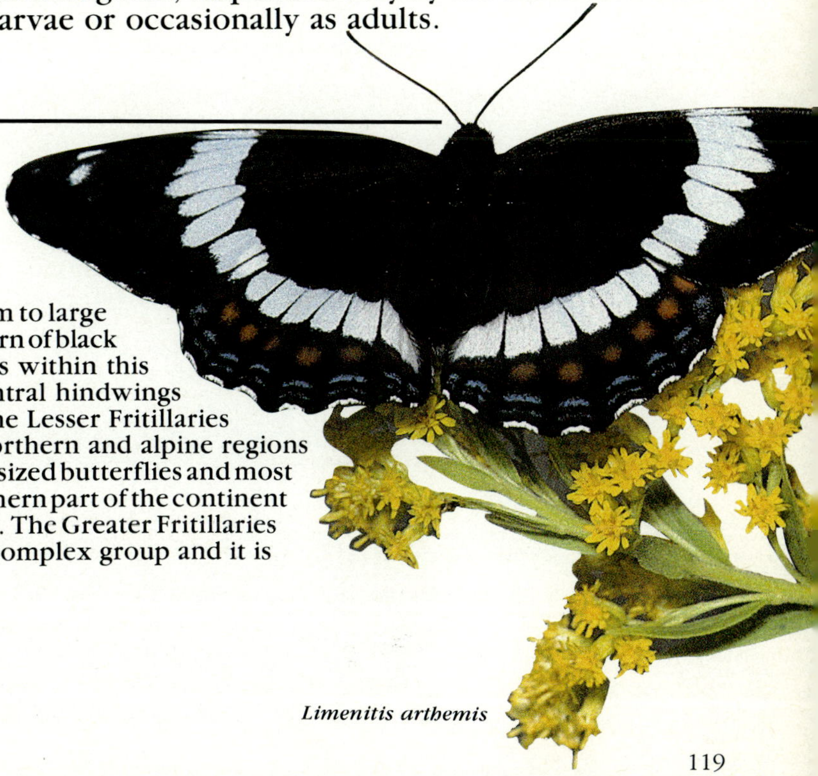

Limenitis arthemis

sometimes difficult to distinguish between species and especially hard to separate subspecies where the ranges overlap. Greater Fritillaries are medium to large in size and most of them are orange-brown with black markings and silver spots on the ventral surface. The cells of the hindwings are closed by a fine cross vein. Adults are strong fliers and visit a wide variety of flowers.

Variegated Fritillary

Euptoieta claudia (Cramer), 1775

Plate 15 No. 2, 3, 4

Description: 37-62 mm. Adults are variable in size but usually have a wingspan greater than 45 mm. Females are larger than males. Dorsally the wings are tawny brown, with a zig zag black line in the middle of both fore and hindwings. Outwardly there is a lighter band including a row of black spots in each wing. Ventrally the wings are whitish-brown, except the basal part of the forewings which is orange. The hindwings are mottled or variegated and never contain silver spots. The forewings are slightly elongated and both sexes are very similar in colour and pattern.

Life Cycle: Larval food plants include Violet and Pansy (*Viola* sp.), Yellow Flax (*Linum rigidum*), Purslane (*Portulaca* sp.), Stonecrop (*Sedum* sp.), Moonseed (*Menispermum canadense*) and Plantain (*Plantago* sp.). In Manitoba, Violets, Pansies and cultivated Flax are the preferred host plants.

Usually one to several ribbed cream coloured eggs are laid per plant. At Culross up to three larvae were found on individual pansy plants. In some cases they would consume the whole plant in 10 days and then seek another plant. When feeding on flax the larvae preferred the flowers, fruits and seeds. The mature larvae are orange-red, with black stripes and white spots laterally and four rows of black spines. The pupae are pale blue-green with orange, yellow and black spots and gold tubercles. The pupal period lasts from eight to 11 days. The Variegated Fritillary overwinters as an adult in frost free areas whereas Manitoba populations consist of new southern immigrants every spring.

In Manitoba adults have been recorded from May 20 to October 10. The Variegated Fritillary is most common in late July and August. There are several overlapping generations during the summer in Manitoba.

Habitat: Open fields, roadsides, gardens and forests. Especially flax fields in Manitoba.

Range: British Columbia to Quebec, including southern Northwest Territories. All of United States except Vermont and Rhode Island. Common in Mexico and also found in Jamaica, Central America and Argentina.

Flax field near Stockton, Manitoba. July 1988.

Manitoba Records: Agassiz Provincial Forest, Aubigny, Beulah, Birds Hill, Birtle, Boggy Creek, Brandon, Carberry, Cartwright, Cranberry Portage, Cromer, Culross, Dawson Bay, Deleau, Duck Mountain, Elm Creek, Flin Flon, Grand Rapids, Gypsumville, Inglis, Lauder, Lyleton, Margaret, Melbourne, Moosehorn, Morris, Ninette, Oak Hammock, Onanole, Oscar Point, Pine Ridge, Ponton, Porcupine Provincial Forest, Riding Mountain, Roblin, Russell, St. Adolphe, Sandilands Provincial Forest, Selkirk, Spruce Woods Provincial Forest and Park, Stockton, Stuartburn, Teulon, The Pas, Thompson, Thornhill, Tolstoi, Turtle Mountain, Victoria Beach, Wasagaming, Whiteshell Provincial Park, Whitewater Lake and Winnipeg.

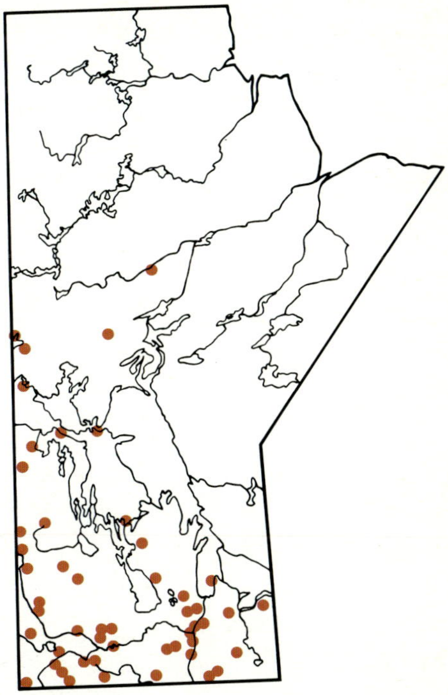

Subspecies: No subspecies are recognized.

Remarks: This migratory butterfly which probably originated in the tropics has spread across North America. In Manitoba the first southern migrants found in the spring are worn and battered. The Variegated Fritillary should be looked for along roadsides and ditches bordering Flax fields, especially when the Flax is in bloom. Adults visit many flowers including Asters, Sunflowers, Dogbane, Red Clover, Milkweed and Peppermint. In the fall when many wild flowers have gone adults move to flower gardens to seek nectar, preferring Marigolds. While quite variable in size, larger and darker individuals tend to be produced in cool, moist summers.

Great Spangled Fritillary

Speyeria cybele (Fabricius), 1775

Plate 15 No. 5, 6, 7

Description: 51-68 mm. Dorsally the males are orange while the females are pale yellowish-orange. The basal halves of the wings are dark brown and the borders are narrow. The female forewing borders are black with a row of whitish or yellowish spots. Ventrally the forewings are similar to the upperside, but coloured yellowish-orange with a few silvery spots at the tips. The hindwings are reddish-brown with large silvery spots and a wide submarginal yellow band. This species is one of Manitoba's largest resident Fritillaries.

Life Cycle: The larvae feed on various Violets (*Viola* sp.). The pale brown eggs are laid on or near the food plant in the late summer. Larvae hatch in the fall and enter into an overwintering diapause. In the spring larvae begin feeding at night on the new foliage. The mature larvae are velvety black dorsally, brown ventrally, and covered with orange based black spines. The pupae are dark brown, mottled with orange-red or light brown (Pyle 1981).

In Manitoba adults have been recorded from June 6 until August 22. Adults are most common in July and females emerge a week to ten days later than males. There is one generation per year in this province.

Habitat: Forest edges and meadows, open fields and roadsides. In Manitoba adults seldom stray far from forested areas.

Range: Southeastern British Columbia eastward to Nova Scotia and southward to Georgia, Nebraska and Arizona.

Manitoba Records: Agassiz Provincial Forest, Asessippi Provincial Park, Aweme, Balmoral, Beulah, Birds Hill, Birtle, Carberry, Cartwright, Culross, Delta, Duck Mountain, Elm Creek, Fort Alexander, Grand Beach, Hecla Island, Husavik, Inwood, Katimik Lake, Kelwood, Kinosota, Komarno, Libau, Lundar, Lyleton, McCreary, Melbourne, Miniota, Northwest Angle Provincial Forest, Norway House, Oak Lake, Pine Ridge, Porcupine Provincial Forest, Riding Mountain, St. Lupicin, St. Malo, Sand Ridge, Sandilands Provincial Forest, Sandridge, Sandy Hook, Selkirk, Sprague, Spruce Woods Provincial Forest, Stuartburn, Teulon, The Pas, Tolstoi, Turtle Mountain, Victoria Beach, Waugh, Whiteshell Provincial Park and Winnipeg.

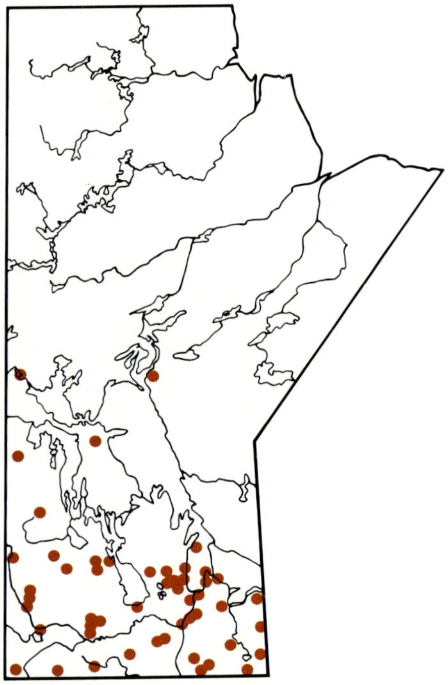

Subspecies: Nine subspecies are recognized. *Speyeria cybele pseudocarpenteri* is the one found in Manitoba.

Remarks: Wallis (1927) noted that this distinctive butterfly was a common sight in southern Manitoba. Due to loss of habitat it is now scarce in the intensively farmed areas of the province e.g. Culross and Elm Creek, but still common in many forested areas. The Great Spangled Fritillary prefers Thistle as a nectar source but will visit other flowers if thistles are absent. This species often flies in association with other Fritillaries. Adults have a fast flight but are easily observed while feeding. The Agassiz and Sandilands Provincial Forests, Carberry Hills and Riding Mountain area still have large populations of the Great Spangled Fritillary.

Aphrodite Fritillary

Speyeria aphrodite (Fabricius), 1787

Plate 15 No. 8, 9, 10

Description: 49-66 mm. Dorsally the wings are orange with black dots and dashes and narrow borders. The females are paler with yellower forewing margins dotted with whitish spots. Ventrally the forewings are similar to the upperside but paler and with silver spots at the wing tips. The hindwings are cinnamon brown to russet with a number of silver spots. The hindwing submarginal buff bands are narrow, being more or less suffused with the ground colour.

Similar Species: The Great Spangled Fritillary is larger, the ventral hindwing bands are wide and rarely suffused with the ground colour and the dorsal inner halves of both fore and hindwings are dark brown. See also Atlantis Fritillary.

Life Cycle: The larvae feed on Violets, including Nuttall's Yellow Violet (*Viola nuttallii*) in Manitoba.

The larvae resemble those of the Great Spangled Fritillary, except that the black dorsal spines have a yellow base rather than orange. The pupae are blackish-brown with yellow wing cases and gray abdomens (Howe 1975; Pyle 1981).

In Manitoba adults have been recorded from June 24 to September 14. Males are more numerous in early August and females are most common during the middle of August. There is one generation per year in Manitoba.

Habitat: Open wooded areas, wet meadows, dry fields, open oak woods, bogs, and glades. In Manitoba the Aphrodite Fritillary prefers forest edges and openings, open pine forests, dry prairie and roadsides.

Range: Southeastern British Columbia eastward to Nova Scotia and southward to Georgia, Nebraska and Arizona (Opler and Krizek 1984).

Manitoba Records: Agassiz Provincial Forest, Aweme, Balmoral, Beulah, Birds Hill, Brandon, Brokenhead, Carberry, Cartwright, Culross, Dauphin, Deleau, Duck Mountain, Elm Creek, Erinview, Flin Flon, Fort Alexander, Grand Beach, Hilbre, Husavik, Libau, Lyleton, Melbourne, Melita, Miniota, Neepawa, Northwest Angle Provincial Forest, Oak Hammock, Oak Lake, Onah, Onanole, Pine Ridge, Porcupine Provincial Forest, Rennie, Riding Mountain, Roblin, St. Malo, Sand Ridge, Sandilands Provincial Forest, Selkirk, Souris, Stuartburn, Telford, Teulon, The Pas, Tolstoi, Treesbank, Victoria Beach, Whiteshell Provincial Park and Winnipeg.

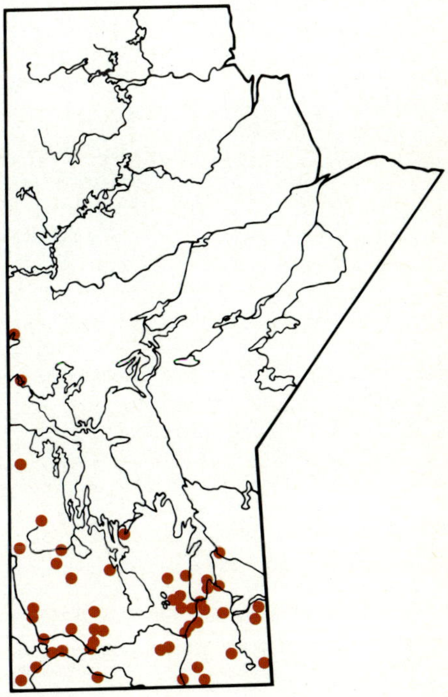

Subspecies: Eight subspecies have been recognized, but their distribution is still in question. At present Manitoba specimens of the Aphrodite Fritillary are probably best assigned to *Speyeria aphrodite manitoba* and the larger and darker specimens found in the southeast corner of the province to *Speyeria aphrodite aphrodite*.

Remarks: The Aphrodite Fritillary is common in many areas of the province. It has a long flight period and is often seen in association with the Great Spangled and Atlantis Fritillaries. Although fairly local in distribution it is often the most abundant Greater Fritillary species when found. Both sexes visit a variety of flowers and mating may take place right on the flowers. This species is frequently observed feeding at patches of Thistle in Sandilands and Agassiz Provincial Forests, Whiteshell Provincial Park and Pine Ridge near Winnipeg.

Regal Fritillary

Speyeria idalia (Drury), 1773

Plate 16 No. 1, 2

Description: 66-92mm. The Regal Fritillary is easily distinguished from other Manitoban Fritillaries by its large size, orange forewings and conspicuous whitish spotted black hindwings. Ventrally the hindwings are brown with large silver spots.

Life Cycle: Larvae feed on various species of Violets, (*Viola* sp.).

Habitat: Wet meadows and virgin tallgrass prairie (Ferris and Brown 1981).

Range: Montana to southern Manitoba, southern Ontario to Maine, southward to North Carolina, Arkansas and Colorado.

Manitoba Records: Aweme, Culross, Riding Mountain, Sandilands Provincial Forest and Winnipeg.

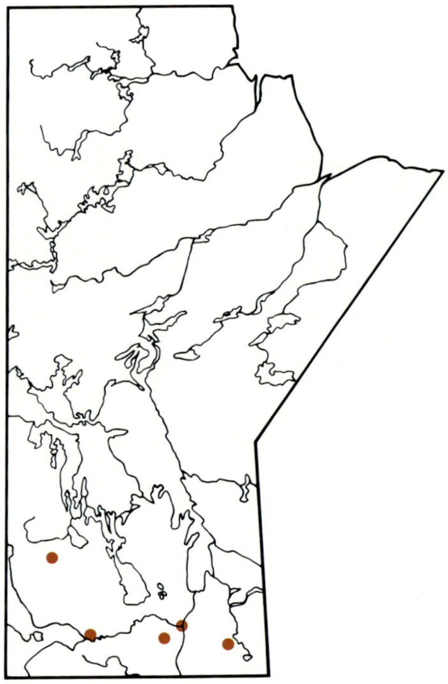

Remarks: There are six records of the Regal Fritillary entering Manitoba. The first specimen was collected by N. Criddle at Aweme on August 15, 1929; later B. Nero of Winnipeg collected one in the Assiniboine Forest on July 20, 1977. The most recent records were by P. Klassen in 1986 and 1987 at Culross where a freshly emerged female was collected, perhaps indicating the presence of a breeding colony in the area.

Edwards' Fritillary

Speyeria edwardsii (Reakirt), 1866

Plate 16 No. 3, 4

Description: 60-70 mm. These butterflies are orange above with moderately heavy markings in the males and heavy markings and wide borders in the females. Below, the forewings are reddish at the base and yellowish or buff outwardly, with black markings. The hindwings are greenish-brown and contain large showy elongated silver spots.

Similar Species: The Callippe Fritillary is smaller, paler and the black markings are reduced. The hindwings are pale grayish-green with yellow-edged veins and more sharply pointed submarginal silver triangles.

Life Cycle: Larvae have been reared on Nuttall's Yellow Violet (*Viola nuttallii*), although other species of Violet may also serve as host plants. Little is known about the biology of Edwards' Fritillary in Manitoba. It is thought that the first instar larvae enter into an overwintering diapause and resume feeding in the spring. There is one generation per year. In Manitoba adults have been recorded from June 15 to July 10. Females are on the wing up to two weeks prior to males.

Habitat: Grasslands, open pine forests and roadsides near mixed forests.

Range: Throughout the Rocky Mountain region and the adjacent plains from Alberta to southwestern Manitoba and southward to New Mexico.

Manitoba Records: Aweme, Beulah, Miniota, Riding Mountain and Winnipeg.

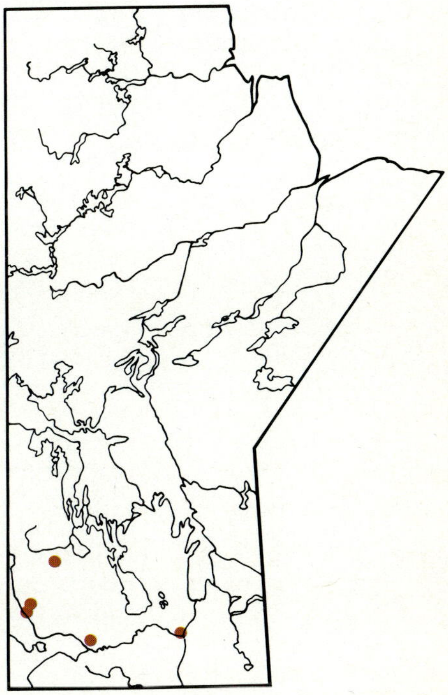

Remarks: Edwards' Fritillary is scarce in Manitoba and due to habitat loss may no longer breed here. The last specimen was collected at Miniota on July 10, 1934 by H. Gibbon. Wallis (1927) did not list this species, but Brooks (1942) reported it from Beulah and Miniota. However this species may still be present in western Manitoba as there are a number of isolated areas where little collecting has been done.

Callippe Fritillary

Speyeria callippe (Boisduval), 1852

Plate 16 No. 5, 6, 7

Description: 56-63 mm. The Callippe Fritillary is pale yellowish-orange dorsally, with heavier black markings in females. Ventrally the forewings are orange basally and grayish-green outwardly. The dorsal black markings are repeated on the underside. The grayish-green hindwings contain elongated triangular silver spots.

Similar Species: Edwards' Fritillary differs as described under that species. The greenish underside of the Callippe Fritillary distinguishes it from other Manitoba Fritillaries.

Life Cycle: The food plant of the Callippe Fritillary in Manitoba is Nuttall's Yellow Violet (*Viola nuttallii*).

The eggs are laid on objects close to the larval host plant. The mature larvae are gray with black patches and grayish bands. The cuticle is covered in orange and black spines. The Callippe Fritillary overwinters as a diapausing first instar larva (Pyle 1981).

In Manitoba adults have been recorded from June 16 to July 26. There is one generation per year in this province.

Habitat: Dry sandy prairies and hill-tops, sagebrush ranges and open pine forests (Hooper 1973; Howe 1975).

Range: British Columbia eastward to Manitoba and southward to California, Nevada and Colorado.

Manitoba Records: Aweme, Beulah, Birtle, Brandon, Carberry, Cartwright, Grand Beach, Kinosota, Miniota, Riding Mountain, Sandilands Provincial Forest and Victoria Beach.

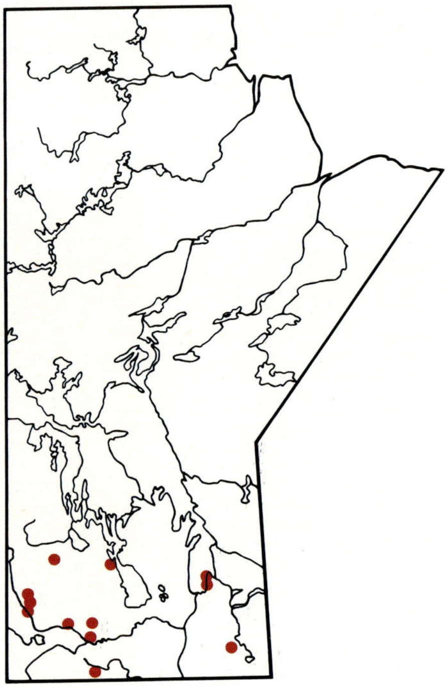

Subspecies: Sixteen subspecies of the Callippe Fritillary have been recognized to date. The Manitoba subspecies is *Speyeria callippe calgariana*.

Remarks: *Speyeria callippe calgariana* was named for the city of Calgary and is common in southern Saskatchewan but scarce in Manitoba. It may have been more common in southwestern Manitoba before much of the virgin prairie was destroyed by intensive agriculture or overgrazed by cattle. The Callippe Fritillary is a wary and swift flier, best observed when feeding on plants such as Thistles, Dogbane or Gaillardia. Riding Mountain and the Carberry Hills are good areas to observe this Fritillary.

Atlantis Fritillary

Speyeria atlantis (W.H. Edwards), 1862

Plate 17 No. 1, 2, 4

Description: 50-64 mm. Dorsally the wings are orange, darker basally and heavily marked with black. The outer margins of the wings are usually solid black. The forewing veins are edged with dark scales giving them a "thick" appearance. Ventrally the forewings are mostly orange with black markings and the hindwings are dark brown with narrow submarginal bands, sometimes suffused with the ground colour. The hindwings are covered with silver spots. There is often considerable variation in size.

Similar Species: The Aphrodite Fritillary is brighter and less heavily marked with black. The marginal border is rarely solid, usually consisting of two narrow lines and the veins are thin and not edged with dark scales. Ventrally the hindwings of the Aphrodite Fritillary are reddish-brown and the submarginal bands are wider. Some female Aphrodite Fritillaries may be very difficult to distinguish from female Atlantis Fritillaries.

The Great Spangled Fritillary is larger and the ventral hindwing bands are wide and rarely suffused with the ground colour. The dorsal inner halves of the wings are dark brown.

Life Cycle: The larval food plants are Violets including Early Blue Violet (*Viola adunca*).

The eggs are laid on objects close to the host plant. Atlantis Fritillaries overwinter as diapausing first instar larvae and resume feeding in the spring. The mature larvae are velvety dark brown with light brown to gray stripes and a cuticle covered in orange spines. The pupae are brown, speckled with black and mottled with light brown. The pupal period lasts approximately two weeks (Pyle 1981, Ferris and Brown 1981).

In Manitoba adults have been recorded from June 9 to August 22, being most abundant after the middle of July. Males emerge about a week before the females. There is one generation per year in Manitoba.

Atlantis Fritillary nectaring at Red Clover, Sandilands Provincial Forest. July 1976.

Habitat: Openings in deciduous and coniferous forests, glades, moist meadows, woodland streams and uplands.

Range: British Columbia to Newfoundland, northward to Yukon and Northwest Territories and southward to Pennsylvania and Minnesota.

Manitoba Records: Agassiz Provincial Forest, Assean Lake, Beulah, Birds Hill, Brokenhead, Buffalo Lake, Carberry, Cartwright, Cowan, Cromer, Cypress River, Duck Mountain, Eriksdale, Flin Flon, Fort Alexander, Gillam, Grand Beach, Grand Rapids, Grass River Provincial Park, Hazel, Katimik Lake, Kelwood, Lauder Sandhills, Lyleton, Lynn Lake, McCreary, Mile 200 Hudson Bay Railway, Miniota, Northwest Angle Provincial Forest, Norway House, Orr Lake, Oscar Point, Paint Lake, Porcupine Provincial Forest, Rennie, Riding Mountain, St. Anne, Sand Ridge, Sandilands Provincial Forest, Sandridge, Sandy Hook, Sprague, The Pas, Thompson, Two Rivers, Victoria Beach, Wabowden, Waugh, Whiteshell Provincial Park, William River and Winnipeg.

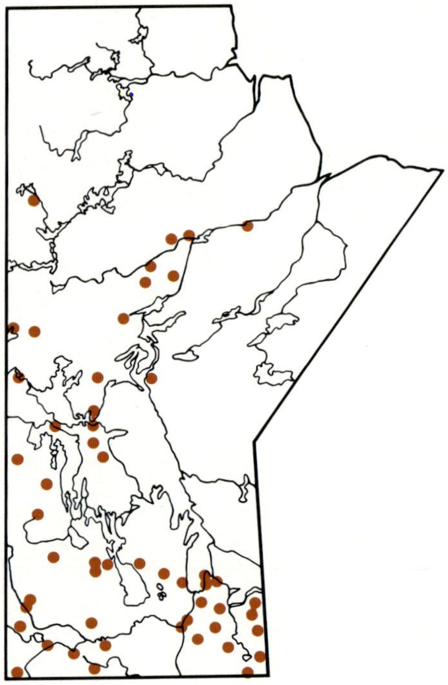

Subspecies: Two subspecies are recognized. *Speyeria atlantis hollandi* occurs in all of Manitoba except the extreme southeast corner of the province, where *Speyeria atlantis atlantis* is found. *Speyeria atlantis hollandi* males are smaller and darker dorsally, with more basal suffusion and narrower submarginal bands than *Speyeria atlantis atlantis* males. Female *hollandi* specimens are darker than *atlantis* specimens but they can be difficult to separate.

Remarks: The Atlantis Fritillary occurs farther north than most members of this genus, preferring moist, cool forested habitats. Males frequently fly along forest roads and trails. Females are less active but along with males readily visit a wide variety of flowers including Thistle and Alfalfa in Manitoba. The Atlantis Fritillary is very common in Sandilands and Agassiz Forests.

Northwestern Fritillary

Speyeria electa (W.H. Edwards), 1878

Plate 17 No. 3, 5, 6

Description: 44-55 mm. Dorsally the wings are orange with fine narrow black markings and with relatively little basal suffusion. Ventrally the wings are reddish-brown with small silver spots and relatively wide buff submarginal hindwing bands. Females, although similar to males in size and appearance, have a slightly paler ground colour and heavier, more distinct markings.

Similar Species: Aphrodite Fritillary is larger and darker, with heavier basal suffusion and heavier black markings dorsally. Ventrally the Aphrodite Fritillary is darker, usually with narrow hindwing submarginal buff bands. Some specimens of the Aphrodite Fritillary are very difficult to separate from the Northwestern Fritillary. The Aphrodite Fritillary is on the wing later.

Life Cycle: Larval food plants include species of Violets. The immature stages are as yet undescribed. In Manitoba adults have been recorded from June 5 to August 22, being most abundant in the first half of July. Males emerge a week or more before females.

Habitat: Forest openings and clearings, dry meadows and scrubby areas near short or tall grass prairie.

Range: Oregon, Washington and Alberta to central and southern Manitoba, south to New Mexico, Arizona and California.

Manitoba Records: Asessippi Provincial Park, Aweme, Beulah, Binscarth, Birtle, Boggy Creek, Brandon, Brokenhead, Cartwright, Duck Mountain, Grass River Provincial Park, Kelwood, Lauder Sandhills, Lyleton, McCreary, Melbourne, Miniota, Neepawa, Porcupine Mountain, Porcupine Provincial Forest, Riding Mountain, Sand Ridge, Sandilands Provincial Forest, The Pas and Winnipeg.

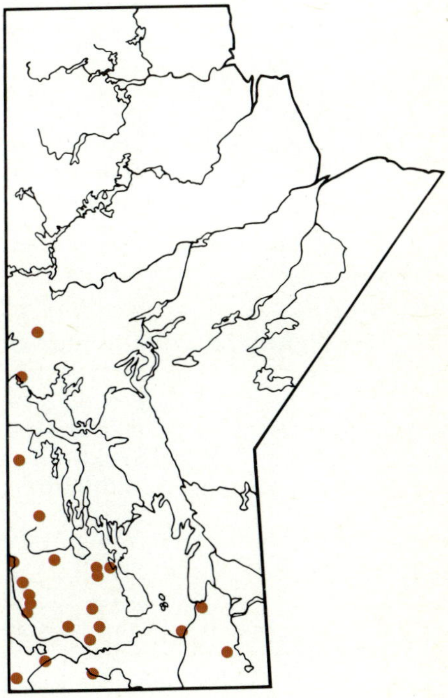

Subspecies: The taxonomic status of this species is in debate. Some authors consider *Speyeria electa* to be actually a subspecies of the Atlantis Fritillary and not a true species. Other researchers consider the Northwestern Fritillary a true species and attribute up to 17 subspecies to it. The subspecies *Speyeria electa dennisi* occurs in Manitoba but intergrades with *Speyeria electa lais* near the Manitoba-Saskatchewan border.

Remarks: The Northwestern Fritillary is found in the drier parts of the province and is on the wing earlier than our other greater Fritillaries. It is especially common in Riding Mountain National Park preferring drier, warmer and more open habitats than the Atlantis Fritillary. Males fly along roads and trails, but females are more sedentary. Both sexes take nectar from many flowers, preferring Thistle, Alfalfa, and Mint.

Mormonia Fritillary

Speyeria mormonia (Boisduval), 1869

Plate 17 No. 7, 8, 9

Description: 41-51 mm. This is Manitoba's smallest representative of the genus *Speyeria*. Dorsally both the fore and hindwings are pale orange and are narrowly outlined with dark scales along the veins, giving them a thin appearance. The submarginal crescents touch the marginal wing borders enclosing spots that are paler than the ground colour, especially in females. Ventrally the forewings are orange basally, yellowish outwardly and contain black markings similar to the upper side. The hindwings are buff and greenish or cinnamon brown and usually contain silver spots. The submarginal buff bands are fairly wide and distinct.

Similar Species: The Callippe Fritillary is larger with darker veins.

Life Cycle: Larvae feed on species of Violets. In Manitoba, Early Blue Violet (*Viola adunca*) is probably the host plant. The yellowish-brown eggs are oviposited on objects close to the food plant. The mature larvae are grayish-brown to yellowish brown with black stripes and numerous pale spines on the cuticle (Pyle 1981).

In Manitoba adults have been recorded from June 10 to August 21. In southwestern Saskatchewan the Mormonia Fritillary has two generations per year (Hooper 1973) whereas it probably has one generation per year in Manitoba.

Habitat: Open areas and forest edges. In Saskatchewan adults have been found in moist meadows adjacent to short grass prairie. In the mountains high and middle elevations are preferred.

Range: Alaska, southern Yukon, British Columbia, eastward to Manitoba, southward to California, Colorado and New Mexico.

Manitoba Records: Beulah, Birtle, Hamiota, Kelwood, Melita, Oak Lake, Rathwell, Riding Mountain and Sand Ridge.

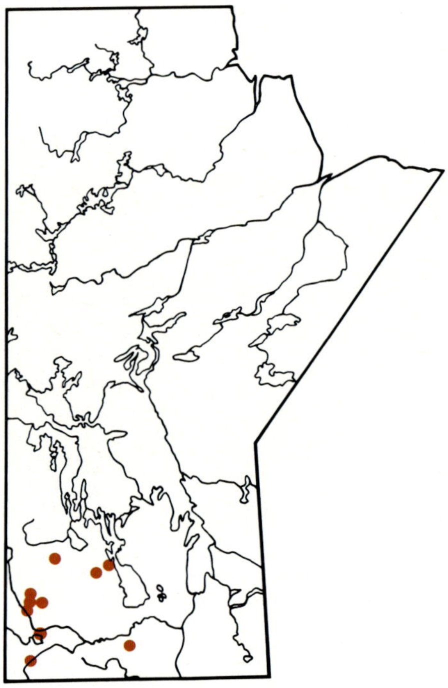

Subspecies: Up to 11 subspecies have been recognized in the literature. *Speyeria mormonia eurynome* occurs in Manitoba.

Remarks: The Mormonia Fritillary is not much larger than some lesser Fritillaries. This is a western species, common in the mountains, locally common in Saskatchewan but barely reaching Manitoba. Ten specimens had been recorded in Manitoba prior to 1938 and it was believed that the Mormonia Fritillary had ceased to breed in this province. On June 29, 1979 B. McKillop found a single specimen at Oak Lake and August 17, 1986 a viable colony was located on rolling prairie in the buffalo compound at Riding Mountain National Park. The males of the colony were quite worn as this was near the end of the flight period and were outnumbered by females. The Mormonia Fritillary flies close to the ground and will take nectar from a wide variety of flowers.

Bog Fritillary

Boloria eunomia (Esper), 1799
= *Proclossiana eunomia*
Plate 18 No. 1, 2, 3

Description: 32-40 mm. The Bog Fritillary is brownish-orange, more or less suffused with dark scales dorsally and with variable black markings. Ventrally the forewings are orange with marking similar to the upperside. The hindwing is brick-red and conspicuously marked with a marginal row of silvery white crescents. Along the bases of the hindwings are black edged white spots and a submarginal row of pearly white round spots ringed with dark brown. These latter spots distinguish this species from other Manitoban Lesser Fritillaries.

Life Cycle: The larvae of the Bog Fritillary feed on Alpine Smartweed (*Polygonum viviparum*) at Churchill and Violet (*Viola* sp.) and Willow (*Salix* sp.) in other areas (Klots 1951; Howe 1975).

The cream-coloured eggs are laid directly on the food plant. Mature larvae are reddish brown with numerous branched spines covering the cuticle. They enter into an overwintering diapause when partially grown and resume feeding during the following spring or early summer.

The flight period lasts from June 3 to August 16 and usually peaks in the middle of July at Churchill and after mid-June in southern Manitoba. There is one generation per year and females emerge several days later than males.

Habitat: Black spruce and tamarack bogs, usually found in more open areas or along the edges. At Churchill the Bog Fritillary also occurs in wet tundra and near ridges where willows grow.

Range: Circumpolar, in North America from Alaska across the arctic regions to Labrador,southward to Maine, Michigan, Wisconsin, Minnesota and Manitoba. Westward to British Columbia and southward to Colorado in the Rockies.

Manitoba Records: Baralzon Lake, Beaver Creek, Brokenhead, Caribou Lake, Churchill, Cormorant Lake, Duck Mountain, Fort Alexander, Gillam, Grand Beach, Kelwood, Kettle Rapids, Lynn Lake, Mile 332 Hudson Bay Railway, Norway House, Overflowing River, Pikwitonei, Rennie, Riding Mountain, Roblin, Sand Ridge, Sandilands Provincial Forest, Split Lake, The Pas, Victoria Beach, Whiteshell Provincial Park and Winnipeg.

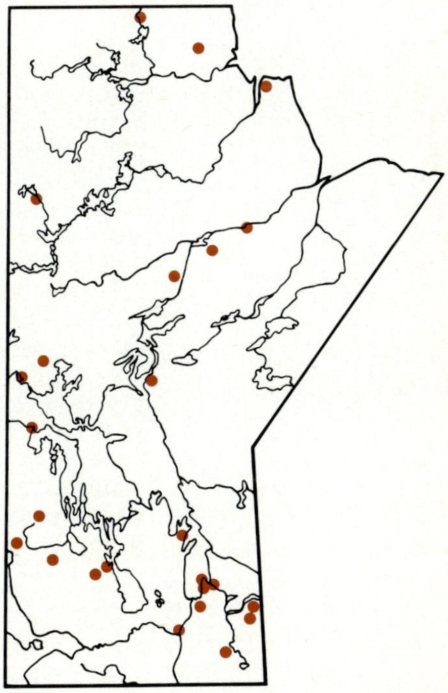

Subspecies: There are seven subspecies and that found in Manitoba is *Boloria eunomia dawsoni*.

Remarks: The Bog Fritillary is quite common and widespread in northern Manitoba, but is restricted to spruce and tamarack bogs in the southern part of the province. The flight period in southern Manitoba is probably less than two weeks in some years. Adults fly swiftly close to the ground or over heaths among tamarack and spruce trees. At Churchill, adults take nectar from Labrador Tea, White Mountain Avens, Dandelion and Arctic Daisy.

Silver Bordered Fritillary

Boloria selene

(Dennis and Schiffermüller), 1775

= *Clossiana selene*

Plate 18 No. 4, 7, 8

Description: 32-42 mm. This fritillary is orange dorsally, with black markings and variable black borders containing orange spots, which may be missing in some specimens. Ventrally the forewings are orange with black spots and a marginal row of silver spots. The hindwings are reddish-brown and buff with silver spots basally and along the outer margins. The metallic silver spotting on the underside of the hindwings distinguished the Silver Bordered Fritillary from other Lesser Fritillaries.

Life Cycle: The larvae feed on Violet (*Viola* sp.). The cream coloured eggs are laid on the food plant or on a nearby object. Mature larvae may be greenish-brown, dark gray or brownish-black, with greenish or yellowish mottling. The dorsal surface of the cuticle is covered with yellow barbed spines and there is a pair of black spines, longer than the others, projecting over the head. The pupae are tan with brown and green patches and a row of pointed spines along the dorsal surface of the abdomen (Opler and Krizek 1984).

In Manitoba the flight period lasts from May 26 to August 24. There are two generations per year. Adults from the overwintering population are most numerous in mid-June and adults from the summer generation peak in late July. Females emerge a week or more after the males.

Habitat: Meadows, marshy areas, roadsides and willow bogs, usually in or near forests.

Range: Europe and Asia and in North America from Alaska eastward to northern Manitoba, across to Newfoundland and southward to Michigan, Wisconsin and Colorado (Kohler 1977).

Manitoba Records: Agassiz Provincial Forest, Aweme, Beaver Creek, Beulah, Birds Hill, Birtle, Brokenhead, Carberry, Cartwright, Churchill, Cowan, Culross, Duck Mountain, Elm Creek, Flin Flon, Fort Alexander, Gillam, Gimli, Grand Beach, HeclaIsland, Kelwood, Komarno, Lundar, Lynn Lake, McCreary, McMunn, Melbourne, Miami, Mile 200 Hudson Bay Railway, Miniota, Nelson House, Norris Lake, Northwest Angle Provincial Forest, Norway House, Overflowing River, Pierson, Pikwitonei, Pine Falls, Pine Ridge, Ponton, Prawda, Rennie, Riding Mountain, Roseisle, Rounthwaite, Russell, St. Lazare, St. Malo, Sand Ridge, Sandilands Provincial Forest, Sandy Hook, Seven Sisters, Shilo, Sprague, Stuartburn, Teulon, Thompson, Victoria Beach, Wabowden, Wanipigow, Wanless, Whiteshell Provincial Park and Winnipeg.

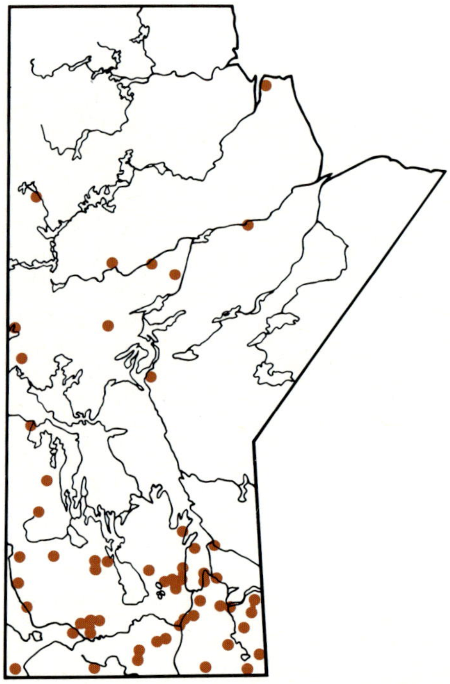

Subspecies: Five subspecies of the Silver Bordered Fritillary are recognized. The subspecies that occurs in Manitoba is *Boloria selene atrocostalis*.

Remarks: The Silver Bordered Fritillary occurs in most of Canada south of the treeline. It is common in the forested areas of Manitoba and was common in the tall grass prairie areas of the province before they were intensely farmed. Adults have a relatively swift flight but are easily observed while feeding on flowers including Asters, Thistle, Goldenrod, Black-eyed Susan and Red Clover.

Meadow Fritillary

Boloria bellona (Fabricius), 1775
= *Clossiana bellona*
= *Boloria toddi* (Holland), 1928

Plate 18 No. 5, 6, 9, 10

Description: 35-44 mm. The Meadow Fritillary is orange dorsally, with black markings heavier basally than marginally. Ventrally the forewings are mostly orange, purplish-brown near the tip, with black markings. The hindwings are brownish-purple outwardly with a band of orange-brown spots basally (the spot at the top is pointed and lightly dusted with white scales). This is the only Lesser Fritillary in which the outer margin of the forewings is angled outwardly below the tip, giving the apex a squared-off appearance. Adults can be extremely variable in both colouration and size.

Similar Species: The Frigga Fritillary may resemble dark specimens of the Meadow Fritillary but never has squared-off wing tips. The Purple Lesser Fritillary is more heavily marked with black, has checkered wing fringes, black marginal spots which are triangular dorsally and bolder ventral markings.

Life Cycle: Larvae feed on Wooly Blue Violet (*Viola sororia*) and Northern White Violet (*Viola pallens*). The greenish-yellow eggs are laid on or near the food plant.

Meadow Fritillaries overwinter as diapausing third or fourth instar larvae, which resume feeding the following spring. The mature larvae are dark shiny green with velvety bands laterally and dull yellowish-brown tubercles and spines on the cuticle. The pupae are yellowish-brown (Klots 1951; Ferris and Brown 1981).

In Manitoba adults have been recorded from May 2 to September 17. There are two generations per year in the southern part of the province, peaking in numbers first in late May and again at the beginning of August.

Habitat: Meadows, hay fields and pastures, usually near wooded areas. In Sandilands and Agassiz Provincial Forests it is common in open Jack Pine stands and along roads and trails.

Range: The Yukon, the Northwest Territories and British Columbia eastward to Newfoundland, southward to North Carolina, Missouri, Colorado and Washington.

Manitoba Records: Agassiz Provincial Forest, Aweme, Beresford Lake, Beulah, Birds Hill, Birtle, Brandon, Brokenhead, Carberry, Cartwright, Cowan, Cromer, Culross, Deleau, Duck Mountain, Elm Creek, Flin Flon, Gillam, Glenboro, Grand Beach, La Riviere, Libau, Lundar, Lyleton, Marchand, McCreary, Mile 332 Hudson Bay Railway, Miniota, Morden, Narcisse, Northwest Angle Provincial Forest, Norway House, Oak Lake, O'Hanly River at Hwy. 304, Pikwitonei, Pine Ridge, Porcupine Provincial Forest, Prawda, Rennie, Riding Mountain, Rosser, Russell, St. Lazare, St. Malo, Sandilands Provincial Forest, Stuartburn, Telford, Teulon, The Pas, Thompson, Tolstoi, Victoria Beach, Wabowden, Whiteshell Provincial Park, Whitemouth Lake and Winnipeg.

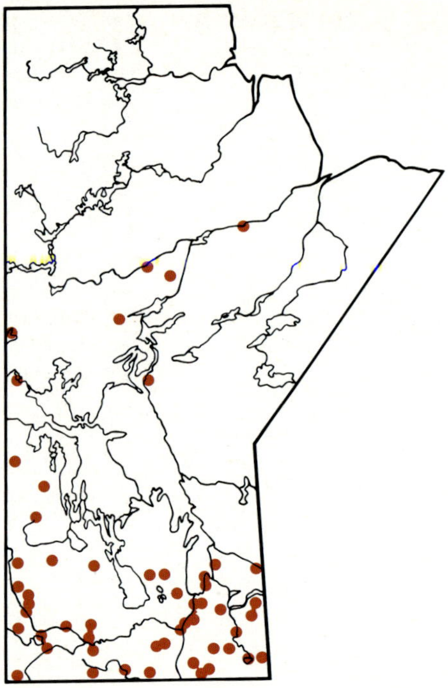

Subspecies: Three subspecies are recognized, two of which are found in Manitoba. *Boloria bellona toddi* occurs in southern Manitoba and *Boloria bellona jenistae* occurs in the northern part of the province southward to Beulah in the west and Whiteshell Provincial Park in the east. The basal portion of the wings are lighter and the ground colour has a reddish tinge in the northern subspecies. Where the ranges overlap specimens are quite variable in appearance.

Remarks: The Meadow Fritillary is the most widespread Lesser Fritillary in North America and in recent years seems to be expanding its range. Males fly in a zig-zag manner and venture far from host plants in search of nectar. Females are seen less frequently and seldom stray from the vicinity of the host plant. This is Manitoba's most common Lesser Fritillary and it prefers yellow flowers for nectar including Black-eyed Susan, Dandelion and Goldenrod.

Frigga Fritillary

Boloria frigga (Thunberg), 1791
= *Clossiana frigga*
Plate 18 No. 11, 12, 16

Description: 36-48 mm. Dorsally the wings are orange with a heavy suffusion of black at the base of the forewings and the inner half of the hindwings. Ventrally the wings are similar in appearance to those of the Meadow Fritillary but with a more distinct median band of spots and a more conspicuous white pointed spot near the upper margin of each wing. Females are noticeably larger than males.

Similar Species: The Meadow Fritillary differs as described under that species. The Freija Fritillary is smaller, has less basal suffusion and the ventral hindwings have a long, pointed white spot in the middle and a row of white "arrows" along the margins. The Polaris Fritillary is smaller, has a more suffused dorsal wing pattern and the ventral hindwings have a submarginal row of dark brown spots capped with white and a marginal row of white spots.

Life Cycle: The larval food plant in Manitoba is unknown. In Alaska a female was observed ovipositing on White Mountain Avens (*Dryas integrifolia*) and in Alberta larvae have been reared on Willow (*Salix* sp.) and Birch (*Betula* sp.). In Europe, Cloudberry (*Rubus chamaemorus*) is the primary food plant (Howe 1975; Ferris and Brown 1981; Opler and Krizek 1981). The Frigga Fritillary overwinters in the pupal stage.

In Manitoba adults have been recorded from May 23 to August 1. In the southern part of the province the flight period is short, peaking at the end of May or in early June. At Churchill in northern Manitoba the flight period lasts a number of weeks, peaking in early July. There is one generation per year.

Habitat: Willow thickets in the tundra and taiga at Churchill and in the boreal forest farther south in wet sphagnum and willow bogs.

Range: Europe and Asia. In North America across the arctic from Alaska to Newfoundland, north to Baffin Island and southward to Ontario, Michigan, Wisconsin, Minnesota and the prairie provinces and in the Rockies south to Colorado (Howe 1975).

Near Cape Tatnam, Manitoba. July 1982.

Manitoba Records: Birds Hill, Cape Tatnam, Churchill, Cowan, Duck Mountain, Fairford, Gillam, Hargrave River, Herchmer (Mile 412 Hudson Bay Railway), Kettle Rapids, Lynn Lake, McMunn, Norway House, Riding Mountain, Sandilands Provincial Forest, Sandy Lake, Split Lake, The Pas, Thompson, Treesbank and Wallace Lake.

Subspecies: Three subspecies are recognized in North America, of which the Manitoba subspecies is *Boloria frigga saga*.

Remarks: The Frigga Fritillary is common and widespread in the Churchill region but uncommon and local in southern Manitoba. This Fritillary is confined to sphagnum bogs in southern Manitoba and is very difficult to find. Males sometimes patrol the edges of bogs or occasionally, like the less active females, take nectar from nearby flowers.

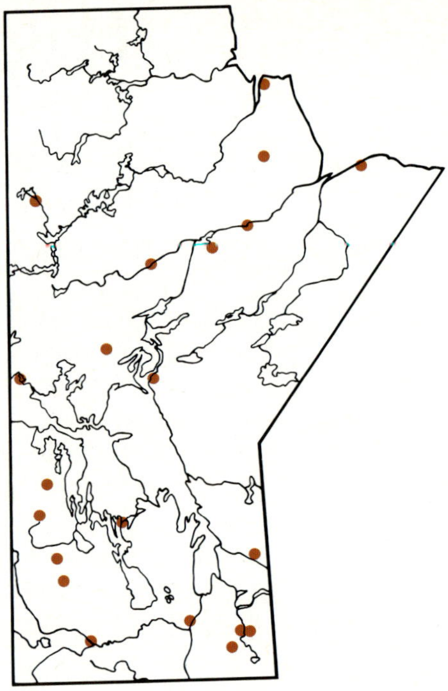

Polaris Fritillary

Boloria polaris (Boisduval), 1828
= *Clossiana polaris*
Plate 18 No. 13, 14, 15

Description: 32-38 mm. This Fritillary is dull orange dorsally, suffused with dark scales which are heavier basally than on the outer wing margins, giving the butterfly a dusky appearance. Ventrally the forewings are dull orange. The hindwings are reddish-brown, marked with a row of marginal white spots, a submarginal band of dark brown spots capped with white and a number of white spots basally.

Similar Species: The Frigga Fritillary differs as described under that species.

Life Cycle: Females have been observed ovipositing on White Mountain Avens (*Dryas integrifolia*) in Scandinavia and Bog Bilberry (*Vaccinium ulginosum*) at Churchill. Parshall (in Scott 1986) reported larvae fed on the latter in the laboratory.

In Manitoba adults have been recorded from June 17 to August 8, usually being most abundant in the latter part of June at Churchill. The Polaris Fritillary requires two years to complete its life cycle. In Manitoba this butterfly flies in odd-numbered years, rarely being found in even-numbered years (Oosting and Parshall 1978).

Habitat: Moist open tundra flats at Churchill.

Range: Circumpolar from Scandinavia to Greenland. In North America from Alaska across arctic Canada north of the treeline, to Labrador and north to the northern tip of Baffin Island and southward in the Rocky Mountains to central Alberta.

Manitoba Records: Caribou Lake, Churchill and Kettle Rapids.

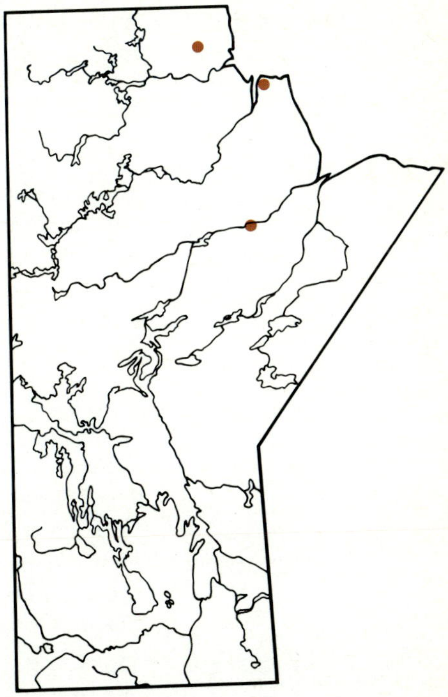

Subspecies: Two subspecies are recognized in the literature. The one in Manitoba is *Boloria polaris stellata*.

Remarks: This dusky, arctic butterfly thrives on the cold, windswept tundra. It has a swift, erratic flight and is difficult to follow when it flies low over the ground. When the butterfly alights it blends in with the background and is very wary.

Freija Fritillary

Boloria freija (Thunberg), 1791

= *Clossiana freija*

Plate 18 No. 17, 18, 19

Description: 31-37 mm. The Freija Fritillary is pale orange dorsally, basally suffused with dark scales. Ventrally the forewings are pale orange. The hindwings are yellowish-brown with a prominent, pearly-white, long, pointed spot in the centre and a narrow, wavy white or whitish band crossing the wings.

Similar Species: The Polaris and Frigga Fritillaries differ as described under those species. Some very worn specimens of these two species may be difficult to differentiate from similarly worn specimens of the Freija Fritillary. The Purple Lesser Fritillary from the Churchill area is similar but has wider dark borders with checkered fringes and less basal suffusion dorsally. Furthermore the ventral hindwings are reddish-brown, the white spots are less pronounced, the spot in the centre of the ventral hindwings is yellowish (not white as in the Freiga Fritillary) and the wavy white band present in the Freija Fritillary is lacking.

Life Cycle: In Europe larval food plants include Bearberry (*Arctostaphylos uva-ursi*), Crowberry (*Empetrum nigrum*), Cloudberry (*Rubus chamaemorus*) and Bog Bilberry (*Vaccinium ulginosum*). In Manitoba the larval host plant is probably Dwarf Bilberry (*Vaccinium caespitosum*). Oosting and Parshall (1978) observed female Freija Fritillaries ovipositing on Dwarf Bilberry at Churchill, Manitoba. Shepard in Howe (1975) stated that larvae were reared on Dwarf Bilberry in Washington.

The tan coloured eggs are laid around the food plant or directly on it. The mature larvae are brown with cream-coloured spots and many branching spines on the cuticle. The Freija Fritillary overwinters as a diapausing late instar larva.

In Manitoba the flight period extends from May 15 to July 21. The adult population peaks in late May or early June in the southern part of the province and in late June at Churchill.

Habitat: Willow bogs and open grassy areas in boreal forests. At Churchill adults occur on the tundra but are most abundant in the taiga zone.

Range: Arctic and subarctic regions of Eurasia. In North America from Alaska to Labrador and southward to Michigan, Wisconsin, Minnesota and the prairie provinces and further south through the Rockies to New Mexico.

Manitoba Records: Cartwright, Churchill, Cowan, Duck Mountain, Gillam, Herchmer, Kelwood, Kettle Rapids, Lynn Lake, McCreary, Mile 256 and 349 of the Hudson Bay Railway, Pikwitonei, Porcupine Provincial Forest, Riding Mountain, Sandilands Provincial Forest, SandyLake, Split Lake, The Pas, Thompson, Wabowden and Whiteshell Provincial Park.

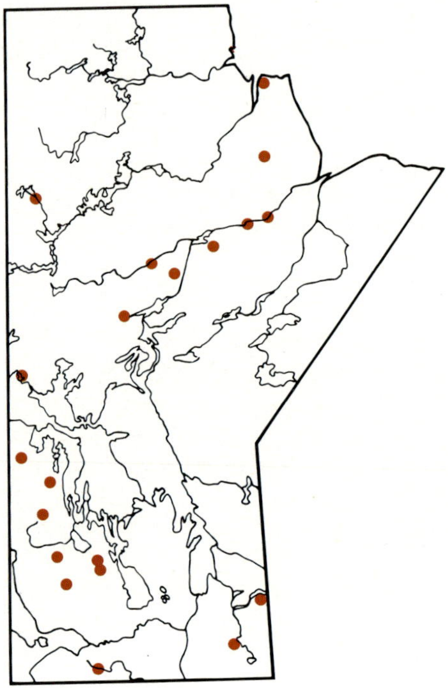

Subspecies: Five subspecies of the Freija Fritillary are recognized. The nominate subspecies *Boloria freija freija* occurs in Manitoba.

Remarks: This species is common at Churchill and usually uncommon further south. The Freija Fritillary is rarely seen in southeastern Manitoba, but can be found in modest numbers at Riding Mountain in the western part of the province. Here the flight period is short. Adults often leave the boggy breeding habitats for adjacent grassy areas in search of flowers.

Purple Lesser Fritillary

Boloria titania (Esper), 1793
= *Clossiana titania*

Plate 18 No. 20, 21, 22, 23, 24

Description: As the two subspecies of the Purple Lesser Fritillary found in Manitoba differ significantly in appearance they are described separately.

Boloria titania grandis: 37-44 mm. The wings are orange dorsally with heavy black markings, black borders and checkered fringes. Ventrally the forewings are orange with a purplish-brown apex and black spots. The hindwings are purplish-brown, intricately marked with purple, brown, buff, black and white (including a submarginal row of large, round black or dark brown spots and a marginal row of dark brown triangles). The females are larger than the males and the underside of the wings of both sexes can be quite variable.

Boloria titania boisduvalii: 33-38 mm. Dorsally the wings are less heavily marked with black and more extensively suffused with dark scales basally. Ventrally the black markings in the forewings are less extensive and the hindwings are reddish-brown variably marked with dark brown, buff and white. The spots in the submarginal row are small and brown and the marginal row of triangles is inconspicuous. The white markings on the hindwings are more extensive. Both subspecies are quite variable and intermediates are difficult to separate where the geographic ranges overlap.

Similar Species: The Freija Fritillary differs as described under that species.

Life Cycle: Larval foodplants include Alpine Smartweed (*Polygonum viviparum*) and Dwarf Willow (*Salix herbacea*) (Howe 1975; Scott 1986).

The tan eggs are laid near or on the food plant. The Purple Lesser Fritillary overwinters as a newly hatched diapausing larva (Pyle 1981).

In southern Manitoba adults have been recorded from June 6 to August 24 and from June 13 to August 4 at Churchill. In the south adult populations peak in early August whereas in the Churchill area the peak occurs in mid July. There is one generation per year.

Habitat: Openings in spruce and tamarack bogs, wet willow bogs, meadows and roadsides. The Purple Lesser Fritillary is common at Churchill in the taiga zone.

Range: Circumpolar. In North America from subarctic Alaska to Labrador in the subarctic, ranging southward to New Hampshire, Ontario, the prairie provinces, Washington and to New Mexico in the Rocky Mountains.

Manitoba Records: Agassiz Provincial Forest, Baralzon Lake, Churchill, Cowan, Flin Flon, Fort Alexander, Hecla Island, Kelwood, Lynn Lake, McCreary, Mile 214 Hudson Bay Railway, Northwest Angle Provincial Forest, Norway House, O'Hanly River at Hwy. 304, Orr Lake, Pikwitonei, Riding Mountain, Sand Ridge, Sandilands Provincial Forest, Sandy Hook, Sandy Lake, Seven Sisters, The Pas, Thompson, Turtle Mountain Provincial Park, Wallace Lake, Wanless, Whiteshell Provincial Park, Winnipeg and York Factory.

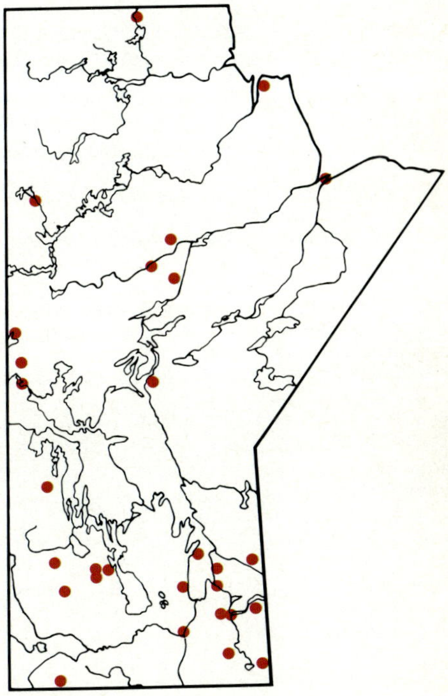

Subspecies: Six subspecies are recognized in North America. *Boloria titania grandis* occurs south of the Churchill area in Manitoba and *Boloria titania boisduvalli* is found at Churchill.

Remarks: The Purple Lesser Fritillary, generally found in boreal forests, is confined to wet bogs in southern Manitoba where it can become quite abundant. Adults fly into adjacent trails and roads to visit a variety of flowers including Thistle, Fireweed, Goldenrod and Aster. Agassiz Provincial Forest is a good area to observe the Purple Lesser Fritillary. At Churchill adults are more numerous after the other Lesser Fritillary species have been on the wing for some time. In the taiga around Churchill they prefer Labrador tea as a nectar source.

PLATE 1

1.	*Epargyreus clarus*	*M	D	Overflowing River	9	July	82
2.	*Epargyreus clarus*	F	D	Miami	9	July	75
3.	*Epargyreus clarus*	M	V	Deleau	20	May	77
4.	*Thorybes pylades*	M	D	Agassiz	11	June	82
5.	*Thorybes pylades*	F	D	Sandilands	11	June	84
6.	*Thorybes pylades*	M	V	Agassiz	11	June	82
7.	*Erynnis icelus*	M	D	Elm Creek	28	May	85
8.	*Erynnis icelus*	F	D	Elm Creek	31	May	86
9.	*Erynnis icelus*	M	V	Sandilands	17	May	85
10.	*Erynnis brizo*	M	D	Winnipeg	15	May	49
11.	*Erynnis brizo*	F	D	Elm Creek	28	May	85
12.	*Erynnis brizo*	F	V	Pine Ridge	14	May	85
13.	*Erynnis juvenalis*	M	D	Melbourne	23	May	84
14.	*Erynnis juvenalis*	F	D	Elm Creek	18	May	87
15.	*Erynnis juvenalis*	M	V	Elm Creek	7	June	86
16.	*Erynnis martialis*	M	D	Sandilands	16	June	83
17.	*Erynnis martialis*	F	D	Sandilands	12	June	75
18.	*Erynnis martialis*	M	V	Sandilands	12	June	75
19.	*Erynnis persius*	M	D	Churchill	27	July	78
20.	*Erynnis lucilius*	F	D	Thompson	28	June	82
21.	*Erynnis lucilius*	F	V	Gillam	18	June	86
22.	*Erynnis afranius*	F	D	Eastend, SK	16	June	79
23.	*Erynnis persius*	M	D	Duck Mountain	23	June	73
24.	*Erynnis persius*	F	D	Riding Mountain	6	June	83
25.	*Erynnis persius*	M	V	Riding Mountain	3	June	82
26.	*Erynnis persius*	F	V	Riding Mountain	14	June	84

*M = MALE F = FEMALE D = DORSAL V = VENTRAL

All butterfly specimens are shown life-size.

1
2
3
4
5
6
7
8
9
10
11
12
13
14
15
16
17
18
19
20
21
22
23
24
25
26

PLATE 2

1.	*Pyrgus centaureae*	M D	Churchill	8	July	77
2.	*Pyrgus centaureae*	F D	Churchill	4	July	77
3.	*Pyrgus centaureae*	F V	Falcon Lake	24	May	59
4.	*Pyrgus communis*	M D	Culross	15	July	86
5.	*Pyrgus communis*	F D	Culross	24	Aug.	81
6.	*Pyrgus communis*	M V	Culross	31	Aug.	75
7.	*Pholisora catullus*	M D	Oakland, NJ	3	July	67
8.	*Pholisora catullus*	F D	Oakland, NJ	3	July	67
9.	*Pholisora catullus*	M V	San Antonio, TX	27	May	72
10.	*Carterocephalus palaemon*	M D	Elm Creek	31	May	86
11.	*Carterocephalus palaemon*	F D	Duck Mtn.	24	June	75
12.	*Carterocephalus palaemon*	F V	Duck Mtn.	24	June	75
13.	*Ancyloxypha numitor*	M D	Overflowing River	9	July	82
14.	*Ancyloxypha numitor*	F D	Tolstoi	27	June	86
15.	*Ancyloxypha numitor*	M V	Agassiz	12	July	74
16.	*Oarisma powesheik*	M D	Tolstoi	27	June	86
17.	*Oarisma powesheik*	F D	Tolstoi	27	June	86
18.	*Oarisma powesheik*	M V	Stuartburn	28	June	86
19.	*Oarisma garita*	M D	Agassiz	2	June	76
20.	*Oarisma garita*	F D	Lundar	3	July	84
21.	*Oarisma garita*	M V	Pine Ridge	1	July	79
22.	*Thymelicus lineola*	M D	Agassiz	5	July	74
23.	*Thymelicus lineola*	F D	Agassiz	20	July	83
24.	*Thymelicus lineola*	M V	Agassiz	5	July	74
25.	*Hesperia uncas*	M D	Carberry	29	June	78
26.	*Hesperia uncas*	F D	Carberry	29	June	78
27.	*Hesperia uncas*	F V	Carberry	29	June	78

1
2
3
4
5
6
7
8
9
10
11
12
13
14
15
16
17
18
19
20
21
22
23
24
25
26
27

PLATE 3

1.	*Hesperia comma assiniboia*	M D	Pine Ridge	15	Aug.	79
2.	*Hesperia comma assiniboia*	F D	Carberry	5	Aug.	83
3.	*Hesperia comma assiniboia*	M V	Pine Ridge	15	Aug.	79
4.	*Hesperia comma assiniboia*	M V	Carberry	7	Aug.	85
5.	*Hesperia comma assiniboia*	F V	Pine Ridge	8	Aug.	83
6.	*Hesperia comma manitoba*	M D	Churchill	4	July	77
7.	*Hesperia comma manitoba*	F D	Churchill	23	July	78
8.	*Hesperia comma manitoba*	F V	Churchill	24	July	78
9.	*Hesperia comma laurentina*	M V	Brereton Lake	31	July	82
10.	*Hesperia ottoe*	M D	Slope Co., ND	22	June	86
11.	*Hesperia ottoe*	F D	Marshall, CO	10	July	73
12.	*Hesperia ottoe*	M V	Slope Co., ND	22	June	86
13.	*Hesperia comma laurentina*	F V	Brereton Lake	5	Aug.	84
14.	*Hesperia leonardus*	M D	Brereton Lake	5	Aug.	84
15.	*Hesperia leonardus*	F D	Brereton Lake	5	Aug.	84
16.	*Hesperia leonardus*	M V	Brereton Lake	20	Aug.	85
17.	*Hesperia leonardus*	F V	Brereton Lake	20	Aug.	85
18.	*Hesperia pawnee*	M D	Carberry	5	Aug.	83
19.	*Hesperia pawnee*	F D	Spruce Woods	11	Aug.	84
20.	*Hesperia pawnee*	M V	Carberry	5	Aug.	83
21.	*Hesperia pawnee*	F V	Spruce Woods	11	Aug.	84
22.	*Hesperia dacotae*	M D	Lundar	3	July	84
23.	*Hesperia dacotae*	F D	Lundar	8	July	85
24.	*Hesperia dacotae*	M V	Lundar	8	July	85
25.	*Hesperia dacotae*	F V	Lundar	8	July	85
26.	*Hesperia sassacus*	M D	Sandilands	11	June	84
27.	*Hesperia sassacus*	F D	Sandilands	1	July	79
28.	*Hesperia sassacus*	M V	Agassiz	17	June	75
29.	*Hesperia sassacus*	F V	Sandilands	16	June	83
30.	*Hesperia nevada*	M D	Albany Co., WY	28	June	75
31.	*Hesperia nevada*	F D	Albany Co., WY	28	June	75
32.	*Hesperia nevada*	F V	Chaffer Co., CO	25	June	73

1
2
3
4
5
6
7
8
9
10
11
12
13
14
15
16
17
18
19
20
21
22
23
24
25
26
27
28
29
30
31
32

PLATE 4

1.	*Polites coras*	M D	Tolstoi	27 June 86
2.	*Polites coras*	F D	Stuartburn	28 July 86
3.	*Polites coras*	M V	Carberry	9 July 81
4.	*Polites coras*	F V	Elm Creek	20 June 73
5.	*Polites themistocles*	M D	Carberry	29 June 78
6.	*Polites themistocles*	F D	Lundar	3 July 84
7.	*Polites themistocles*	M V	Miami	3 July 82
8.	*Polites themistocles*	F V	Tolstoi	7 July 86
9.	*Polites mystic*	M D	Carberry	5 July 79
10.	*Polites mystic*	F D	Lundar	3 July 84
11.	*Polites mystic*	M V	Culross	16 June 77
12.	*Polites mystic*	M V	Agassiz	5 July 74
13.	*Polites mystic*	F V	Carberry	24 June 80
14.	*Atrytone logan*	M D	Culross	12 July 85
15.	*Atrytone logan*	F D	Culross	14 July 86
16.	*Atrytone logan*	M V	Culross	9 July 86
17.	*Poanes hobomok*	M D	Sandilands	16 June 83
18.	*Poanes hobomok*	F D	Pine Ridge	18 June 84
19.	*Poanes hobomok*	F D	Culross	8 June 76
20.	*Poanes hobomok*	M V	Cowan	24 May 80
21.	*Poanes hobomok*	F V	Miami	15 June 73
22.	*Poanes hobomok*	F V	Miami	8 June 72
23.	*Poanes viator*	F D	Red Rock Lake	28 June 87
24.	*Euphyes ruricola*	M D	Agassiz	24 July 84
25.	*Euphyes ruricola*	F D	Agassiz	24 July 84
26.	*Euphyes ruricola*	M V	Agassiz	24 July 84
27.	*Euphyes ruricola*	F V	Agassiz	24 July 84
28.	*Atrytonopsis hianna*	M D	Pine Ridge	25 May 76
29.	*Atrytonopsis hianna*	M D	Pine Ridge	28 May 84
30.	*Atrytonopsis hianna*	F D	Pine Ridge	27 May 81
31.	*Atrytonopsis hianna*	F V	Pine Ridge	28 May 84
32.	*Amblyscirtes hegon*	M D	Sandilands	11 June 84
33.	*Amblyscirtes hegon*	F D	Agassiz	11 June 82
34.	*Amblyscirtes hegon*	M V	Agassiz	11 June 82
35.	*Amblyscirtes vialis*	M D	Sandilands	11 June 84
36.	*Amblyscirtes vialis*	F D	Agassiz	11 June 82
37.	*Amblyscirtes vialis*	F V	Agassiz	11 June 82

1
2
3
4
5
6
7
8
9
10
11
12
13
14
15
16
17
18
19
20
21
22
23
24
25
26
27
28
29
30
31
32
33
34
35
36
37

PLATE 5

1. *Battus philenor*	M	D	Hilton, CA	14	Aug. 71
2. *Papilio polyxenes*	M	D	Gypsumville	29	June 82
3. *Papilio polyxenes*	F	D	Culross	30	June 82
4. *Papilio polyxenes*	F	V	Riding Mtn.	2	July 78

1
2
3
4

PLATE 6

1.	*Papilio kahli*	M D	Culross	27	May	84
2.	*Papilio kahli*	M D	Riding Mtn.	20	June	
3.	*Papilio kahli*	F D	Culross	20	July	77
4.	*Papilio kahli*	F V	Culross	20	July	77
5.	*Papilio kahli X machaon*	M D	Riding Mtn.	26	June	55
6.	*Papilio kahli X machaon*	F D	Duck Mtn.	10	June	76

1
2
3
4
5
6

PLATE 7

1. *Papilio machaon*	M	D	Duck Mtn.	24 June 75
2. *Papilio machaon*	F	D	Thompson	28 June 82
3. *Papilio machaon*	M	V	Thompson	17 June 86
4. *Papilio cresphontes*	M	D	Upper Key Largo, FL	9 Apr. 72

1
2
3
4

PLATE 8

1. *Papilio glaucus*	M	D	Duck Mountain	23 June 73
2. *Papilio glaucus*	F	D	Cowan	11 June 86
3. *Papilio glaucus*	M	V	Cowan	11 June 86
4. *Papilio troilus*	M	D	Lake Co., OH	29 Aug. 72

1

2

3

4

PLATE 9

1.	*Pontia protodice*	M D	Carberry	4	Aug.	81
2.	*Pontia protodice*	F D	Melbourne	10	Aug.	84
3.	*Pontia protodice*	F V	Winnipeg	2	Sept.	70
4.	*Pontia protodice*	M V	Carberry	9	Aug.	81
5.	*Pontia occidentalis*	M D	Melbourne	7	Aug.	85
6.	*Pontia occidentalis*	F D	Melbourne	7	Aug.	85
7.	*Pontia occidentalis*	F V	Deleau	16	Aug.	86
8.	*Pieris napi*	M D	Sandilands	15	July	70
9.	*Pieris napi*	F D	Agassiz	24	June	77
10.	*Pieris napi* spring form	M V	Sandilands	25	May	82
11.	*Pieris napi* summer form	M V	Agassiz	16	July	71
12.	*Pieris rapae*	M D	Culross	27	Aug.	86
13.	*Pieris rapae*	F D	Culross	2	Aug.	84
14.	*Pieris rapae*	F V	Culross	27	Aug.	84
15.	*Euchloe olympia*	M D	Ipperwash, ON	11	May	80
16.	*Euchloe olympia*	F D	Ipperwash, ON	11	May	80
17.	*Euchloe ausonides*	M D	Riding Mountain	4	June	86
18.	*Euchloe ausonides*	F D	Riding Mountain	13	June	84
19.	*Euchloe ausonides*	F V	Sandilands	17	May	85
20.	*Euchloe olympia*	M V	Birtle	2	May	71

1
2
3
4
5
6
7
8
9
10
11
12
13
14
15
16
17
18
19
20

PLATE 10

1.	*Colias philodice*	M D	Spruce Woods	8 Sept. 86
2.	*Colias philodice*	F D	Riding Mountain	21 Sept. 86
3.	*Colias philodice*	F D	Spruce Woods	8 Sept. 86
4.	*Colias philodice*	M V	Riding Mountain	9 Sept. 86
5.	*Colias eurytheme*	M D	Spruce Woods	8 Sept. 86
6.	*Colias eurytheme*	M D	Sandilands	27 Aug. 85
7.	*Colias eurytheme*	F D	Culross	15 Aug. 72
8.	*Colias eurytheme*	F D	Riding Mountain	18 July 72
9.	*Colias eurytheme*	F D	Duck Mountain	1 July 76
10.	*Colias eurytheme*	M V	Miami	19 Aug. 75
11.	*Colias alexandra*	M D	Gypsumville	8 July 82
12.	*Colias alexandra*	F D	Riding Mountain	4 July 86
13.	*Colias alexandra*	F D	Riding Mountain	3 July 86
14.	*Colias alexandra*	F D	Riding Mountain	4 July 86
15.	*Colias alexandra*	M V	Duck Mountain	1 July 76
16.	*Colias hecla*	M D	Churchill	5 July 77
17.	*Colias hecla*	F D	Churchill	8 July 77
18.	*Colias hecla*	M V	Churchill	8 July 77

1
2
3
4
5
6
7
8
9
10
11
12
13
14
15
16
17
18

PLATE 11

1.	*Colias nastes*	M D	Churchill	15	July	79
2.	*Colias nastes*	M D	Churchill	17	July	76
3.	*Colias nastes*	F D	Churchill	27	July	78
4.	*Colias nastes*	F V	Churchill	27	July	78
5.	*Colias gigantea*	M D	Thompson	1	July	84
6.	*Colias gigantea*	F D	Duck Mountain	1	July	76
7.	*Colias gigantea*	F D	Churchill	25	July	78
8.	*Colias gigantea*	M V	Paint Lake	1	July	84
9.	*Colias interior*	M D	Grand Rapids	2	July	84
10.	*Colias interior*	F D	Agassiz	16	July	71
11.	*Colias interior*	F D	Agassiz	9	July	75
12.	*Colias interior*	M V	Riding Mountain	29	June	78
13.	*Colias palaeno*	M D	Churchill	15	July	79
14.	*Colias palaeno*	F D	Gillam	6	July	80
15.	*Colias palaeno*	F D	Churchill	12	July	87
16.	*Colias palaeno*	F D	Churchill	20	July	76
17.	*Colias palaeno*	M V	Churchill	15	July	78
18.	*Colias cesonia*	M D	Lake Co., IL	12	Sept.	71
19.	*Eurema mexicana*	M D	Bee Co., TX	2	May	76
20.	*Nathalis iole*	M D	Winnipeg	15	Aug.	70
21.	*Nathalis iole*	F D	Dunedin, FL	7	Aug.	75

1
2
3
4
5
6
7
8
9
10
11
12
13
14
15
16
17
18
19
20
21

PLATE 12

1.	*Feniseca tarquinius*	M D	Sandilands	11	July	72
2.	*Feniseca tarquinius*	M D	Elm Creek	11	June	72
3.	*Feniseca tarquinius*	F D	Sandilands	27	May	81
4.	*Feniseca tarquinius*	F V	Agassiz	11	June	82
5.	*Lycaena xanthoides*	M D	Culross	8	July	75
6.	*Lycaena xanthoides*	F D	Culross	15	July	81
7.	*Lycaena xanthoides*	F V	Culross	12	July	81
8.	*Lycaena xanthoides*	M V	Culross	15	July	81
9.	*Lycaena hyllus*	M D	Culross	22	June	71
10.	*Lycaena hyllus*	F D	Culross	12	July	85
11.	*Lycaena hyllus*	F V	Culross	24	Aug.	81
12.	*Lycaena epixanthe*	M D	Parry Sound, ON	25	June	77
13.	*Lycaena epixanthe*	F D	Chatsworth, NJ	27	June	71
14.	*Lycaena epixanthe*	F V	Kenne Bunk, ME	15	July	71
15.	*Lycaena dorcas*	M D	Gillam	12	July	87
16.	*Lycaena dorcas*	M D	Riding Mountain	20	July	86
17.	*Lycaena dorcas*	F D	Agassiz	24	July	84
18.	*Lycaena dorcas*	F D	Agassiz	24	July	84
19.	*Lycaena dorcas*	F D	Elm Creek	16	July	86
20.	*Lycaena dorcas*	M V	Agassiz	24	July	84
21.	*Lycaena helloides*	M D	Vita	27	Aug.	84
22.	*Lycaena helloides*	F D	Vita	27	Aug.	84
23.	*Lycaena helloides*	F D	Melbourne	11	Aug.	84
24.	*Lycaena helloides*	F V	Culross	12	June	76
25.	*Harkenclenus titus*	M D	Carberry	19	July	77
26.	*Harkenclenus titus*	F D	Sandilands	9	Aug.	82
27.	*Harkenclenus titus*	M V	Sandilands	4	Aug.	84
28.	*Harkenclenus titus*	F V	Carberry	9	July	81

1
2
3
4
5
6
7
8
9
10
11
12
13
14
15
16
17
18
19
20
21
22
23
24
25
26
27
28

PLATE 13

1.	*Satyrium acadica*	M D	Agassiz	24	July	84
2.	*Satyrium acadica*	F D	Stuartburn	24	July	87
3.	*Satyrium acadica*	F V	Stuartburn	24	July	87
4.	*Satyrium edwardsii*	M D	Pine Ridge	23	July	84
5.	*Satyrium edwardsii*	F D	Pine Ridge	23	July	84
6.	*Satyrium edwardsii*	M V	Roseisle	9	July	78
7.	*Satyrium calanus*	M D	Tolstoi	23	June	87
8.	*Satyrium calanus*	F D	Tolstoi	23	June	87
9.	*Satyrium calanus*	F V	Tolstoi	8	July	86
10.	*Satyrium liparops*	M D	Turtle Mountain	20	July	85
11.	*Satyrium liparops*	M D	Brereton Lake	6	July	75
12.	*Satyrium liparops*	F D	Tolstoi	8	July	86
13.	*Satyrium liparops*	F V	Beulah	17	July	75
14.	*Callophrys augustus*	M D	Sandilands	27	May	81
15.	*Callophrys augustus*	F D	Riding Mountain	3	June	82
16.	*Callophrys augustus*	M V	Riding Mountain	22	May	82
17.	*Callophrys polios*	M D	Riding Mountain	22	May	82
18.	*Callophrys polios*	F D	Duck Mountain	5	June	84
19.	*Callophrys polios*	M V	Riding Mountain	22	May	82
20.	*Callophrys henrici*	M D	Sandilands	25	May	82
21.	*Callophrys henrici*	F D	Sandilands	11	May	75
22.	*Callophrys henrici*	F V	Sandilands	15	May	80
23.	*Callophrys niphon*	M D	Sandilands	18	May	75
24.	*Callophrys niphon*	F D	Sandilands	28	May	84
25.	*Callophrys niphon*	M V	Sandilands	18	May	75
26.	*Callophrys eryphon*	M D	Gillam	25	June	82
27.	*Callophrys eryphon*	F D	Gillam	25	June	82
28.	*Callophrys eryphon*	F V	Gillam	25	June	82
29.	*Strymon melinus*	M D	Brereton Lake	13	Aug.	87
30.	*Strymon melinus*	F D	San Antonio, TX	12	May	73
31.	*Strymon melinus*	M V	Ledbetter, TX	8	May	74

1
2
3
4
5
6
7
8
10
11
12
9
13
14
15
16
17
18
19
20
21
22
23
24
25
26
27
28
29
30
31

PLATE 14

1.	*Hemiargus isola*	M D	Raymondville, TX	12	Apr.	70
2.	*Hemiargus isola*	F D	Beeville, TX	12	Apr.	70
3.	*Hemiargus isola*	F V	Brownsville, TX	27	June	69
4.	*Everes comyntas*	M D	Culross	29	July	75
5.	*Everes comyntas*	F D	Culross	3	Aug.	73
6.	*Everes comyntas*	M V	Culross	29	July	75
7.	*Everes amyntula*	M D	Sandilands	17	May	85
8.	*Everes amyntula*	F D	Pine Ridge	18	June	74
9.	*Everes amyntula*	F D	Elm Creek	18	May	87
10.	*Everes amyntula*	M V	Sandilands	25	May	82
11.	*Celastrina argiolus*	M D	Pine Ridge	13	May	73
12.	*Celastrina argiolus* spring form	F D	Sandilands	26	May	74
13.	*Glaucopsyche lygdamus*	M D	Cowan	7	June	83
14.	*Glaucopsyche lygdamus*	F D	Thompson	2	July	84
15.	*Glaucopsyche lygdamus*	M V	Spruce Woods	7	May	85
16.	*Celastrina argiolus* summer form	F D	Elm Creek	25	June	71
17.	*Celastrina argiolus* spring form	M V	Sandilands	17	May	85
18.	*Celastrina argiolus* summer form	M V	Elm Creek	25	June	71
19.	*Lycaeides idas*	M D	Riding Mountain	4	July	86
20.	*Lycaeides idas*	F D	Duck Mountain	21	July	86
21.	*Lycaeides idas*	M V	Riding Mountain	4	July	86
22.	*Lycaeides idas*	F V	Riding Mountain	20	July	86
23.	*Lycaeides melissa*	M D	Culross	21	June	77
24.	*Lycaeides melissa*	F D	Carberry	5	Aug.	83
25.	*Lycaeides melissa*	F V	Culross	21	June	77
26.	*Plebejus saepiolus*	M D	Culross	19	May	77
27.	*Plebejus saepiolus*	F D	Riding Mountain	12	June	86
28.	*Plebejus saepiolus*	M V	Ponton	1	July	84
29.	*Vacciniina optilete*	M D	Churchill	11	July	77
30.	*Vacciniina optilete*	F D	Churchill	11	July	77
31.	*Vacciniina optilete*	F V	Churchill	4	July	77
32.	*Agriades glandon rustica*	M D	Carberry	16	June	79
33.	*Agriades glandon rustica*	F D	Grahamdale	16	June	86
34.	*Agriades glandon rustica*	F V	Grahamdale	16	June	86
35.	*Agriades glandon franklinii*	M D	Churchill	22	June	78
36.	*Agriades glandon franklinii*	F D	Churchill	23	July	78
37.	*Agriades glandon franklinii*	F V	Churchill	10	July	77

1
2
3
4
5
6
7
8
9
10
11
12
13
14
15
16
17
18
19
20
21
22
23
24
25
26
27
28
29
30
31
32
33
34
35
36
37

PLATE 15

1.	*Dione vanillae*	M	D	Pasadina, CA	25	Mar. 53
2.	*Euptoieta claudia*	M	D	Elm Creek	18	Aug. 86
3.	*Euptoieta claudia*	F	D	Elm Creek	18	Aug. 86
4.	*Euptoieta claudia*	M	V	Culross	20	Aug. 84
5.	*Speyeria cybele*	M	D	Elm Creek	30	June 72
6.	*Speyeria cybele*	F	D	Elm Creek	2	Aug. 85
7.	*Speyeria cybele*	M	V	Agassiz	20	July 83
8.	*Speyeria aphrodite*	M	V	Culross	15	July 72
9.	*Speyeria aphrodite*	M	D	Pine Ridge	9	Aug. 82
10.	*Speyeria aphrodite*	F	D	Pine Ridge	2	Aug. 82

1
2
3
4
5
6
7
8
9
10

PLATE 16

1.	*Speyeria idalia*	F D	Culross	5	July 87
2.	*Speyeria idalia*	F V	Johnson Co. KS	16	June 71
3.	*Speyeria edwardsii*	M D	Larimer Co. CO	22	June 74
4.	*Speyeria edwardsii*	F V	Pike Nat. For., CO	1	Sept. 75
5.	*Speyeria callippe*	M D	Sandilands	19	July 64
6.	*Speyeria callippe*	F D	Carberry	16	June 80
7.	*Speyeria callippe*	F V	Riding Mountain	26	July 71

1

2

3

4

5

6

7

PLATE 17

1.	*Speyeria atlantis*	M D	Agassiz	24	June	77
2.	*Speyeria atlantis*	F D	Sandilands	20	July	73
3.	*Speyeria electa*	M V	Riding Mountain	29	June	78
4.	*Speyeria atlantis*	F V	Agassiz	4	July	76
5.	*Speyeria electa*	M D	Riding Mountain	9	July	81
6.	*Speyeria electa*	F D	Riding Mountain	16	June	80
7.	*Speyeria mormonia*	M D	Riding Mountain	17	Aug.	86
8.	*Speyeria mormonia*	F D	Riding Mountain	17	Aug.	86
9.	*Speyeria mormonia*	F V	Riding Mountain	17	Aug.	86

1
2
3
4
5
6
7
8
9

PLATE 18

1.	*Boloria eunomia*	M	D	Duck Mountain	18 June	78
2.	*Boloria eunomia*	F	D	Riding Mountain	6 June	77
3.	*Boloria eunomia*	M	V	Churchill	23 July	78
4.	*Boloria selene*	M	D	Riding Mountain	21 June	73
5.	*Boloria bellona*	M	D	Duck Mountain	24 June	75
6.	*Boloria bellona*	M	V	Sandilands	16 May	78
7.	*Boloria selene*	F	D	Agassiz	24 July	84
8.	*Boloria selene*	F	V	Brereton Lake	5 Aug.	84
9.	*Boloria bellona* (dark)	M	D	Sandilands	25 May	82
10.	*Boloria bellona*	F	D	Sandilands	11 June	84
11.	*Boloria frigga*	M	D	Churchill	25 July	78
12.	*Boloria frigga*	F	D	Churchill	14 July	78
13.	*Boloria polaris*	M	D	Churchill	14 July	77
14.	*Boloria polaris*	F	D	Churchill	14 July	77
15.	*Boloria polaris*	F	V	Churchill	14 July	77
16.	*Boloria frigga*	M	V	Riding Mountain	23 May	80
17.	*Boloria freija*	M	D	Riding Mountain	22 May	82
18.	*Boloria freija*	F	D	Riding Mountain	22 May	82
19.	*Boloria freija*	F	V	Riding Mountain	22 May	82
20.	*Boloria titania boisduvalii*	F	D	Churchill	23 July	78
21.	*Boloria titania*	M	D	Agassiz	11 Aug.	73
22.	*Boloria titania*	F	D	Sandilands	4 Aug.	84
23.	*Boloria titania*	M	V	Agassiz	2 Aug.	82
24.	*Boloria titania boisduvalii*	F	V	Churchill	25 July	78

1
2
3
4
5
6
7
8
9
10
11
12
13
14
15
16
17
18
19
20
21
22
23
24

PLATE 19

1.	*Chlosyne gorgone*	M D	Deleau	29	May	78
2.	*Chlosyne gorgone*	F D	Melbourne	4	June	86
3.	*Chlosyne gorgone*	M V	Stony Mountain	28	May	84
4.	*Chlosyne nycteis*	M D	Miami	3	July	72
5.	*Chlosyne nycteis*	F D	Pine Ridge	20	June	72
6.	*Chlosyne nycteis*	F V	Spruce Woods	26	June	76
7.	*Chlosyne harrisii*	M D	Elm Creek	11	June	72
8.	*Chlosyne harrisii*	M D	Pine Ridge	18	June	84
9.	*Chlosyne harrisii*	F D	Agassiz	4	July	76
10.	*Chlosyne harrisii*	F V	Agassiz	5	July	75
11.	*Phyciodes tharos*	M D	Oklahoma City, OK	8	Apr.	74
12.	*Phyciodes tharos*	F D	Lebenon, NH	17	June	71
13.	*Phyciodes tharos*	M V	Lebenon, NH	17	June	71
14.	*Phyciodes tharos*	F V	Oklahoma City, OK	8	Apr.	74
15.	*Phyciodes morpheus*	M D	Culross	3	July	74
16.	*Phyciodes morpheus*	F D	Agassiz	5	July	74
17.	*Phyciodes morpheus*	M V	Elm Creek	6	June	73
18.	*Phyciodes morpheus*	F V	Culross	20	June	80
19.	*Phyciodes batesii*	M D	Sandilands	16	June	83
20.	*Phyciodes batesii*	F D	Agassiz	2	Aug.	82
21.	*Phyciodes batesii*	M V	Elm Creek	7	June	86
22.	*Phyciodes batesii*	F V	Agassiz	1	July	73
23.	*Euphydryas phaeton*	M D	Agassiz	12	July	74
24.	*Euphydryas phaeton*	F V	Agassiz	12	July	74
25.	*Euphydryas anicia*	M D	Lake Laberge, YT	3	July	85
26.	*Euphydryas anicia*	M V	Lake Laberge, YT	3	July	85

1
2
3
4
5
6
7
8
9
10
11
12
13
14
15
16
17
18
19
20
21
22
23
24
25
26

PLATE 20

1.	*Polygonia interrogationis*	M D	Agassiz	14	Aug.	48
2.	*Polygonia interrogationis*	F D	Transcona	3	Aug.	78
3.	*Polygonia interrogationis*	M V	Culross	4	Aug.	77
4.	*Polygonia comma*	M D	Miami	8	July	71
5.	*Polygonia comma*	F D	Spruce Woods	21	July	85
6.	*Polygonia comma*	M V	Northwest Angle Forest	7	Aug.	78
7.	*Polygonia satyrus*	M D	Sandilands	11	July	72
8.	*Polygonia satyrus*	F D	Sandilands	20	July	73
9.	*Polygonia satyrus*	F V	Culross	14	July	75
10.	*Polygonia faunus*	M D	Spruce Woods	21	July	85
11.	*Polygonia faunus*	F D	Agassiz	24	July	84
12.	*Polygonia faunus*	M V	Spruce Woods	21	July	85
13.	*Polygonia gracilis*	M D	Lac Ste. Anne, PQ	7	Sept.	71
14.	*Polygonia gracilis*	M V	Lac Ste. Anne, PQ	7	Sept.	71
15.	*Polygonia faunus*	F V	Sandilands	17	May	85
16.	*Polygonia progne*	M D	Elm Creek	15	Aug.	85
17.	*Polygonia progne*	F D	Northwest Angle Forest	7	Aug.	78
18.	*Polygonia progne*	M V	Sandilands	4	Sept.	80

1
2
3
4
5
6
7
8
9
10
11
12
13
14
15
16
17
18

PLATE 21

1.	*Nymphalis vau-album*	M D	Northwest Angle Forest	7	Aug. 78
2.	*Nymphalis vau-album*	F V	Spruce Woods	21	July 85
3.	*Nymphalis californica*	M D	Transcona	15	Oct. 45
4.	*Nymphalis californica*	F V	Pioneer, CA	14	June 71
5.	*Nymphalis antiopa*	F D	Culross	7	Aug. 84
6.	*Nymphalis antiopa*	M V	Culross	25	Oct. 86
7.	*Nymphalis milberti*	M D	Brereton Lake	5	Aug. 84
8.	*Nymphalis milberti*	F D	Culross	27	Aug. 86
9.	*Nymphalis milberti*	F V	Culross	27	Aug. 86

1
2
3
4
5
6
7
8
9

PLATE 22

1.	*Vanessa virginiensis*	M D	Elm Creek	16	July	86
2.	*Vanessa virginiensis*	F D	Rennie	27	July	86
3.	*Vanessa virginiensis*	M V	Elm Creek	23	July	86
4.	*Vanessa cardui*	M D	Pine Ridge	8	Aug.	83
5.	*Vanessa cardui*	F V	Culross	25	July	73
6.	*Vanessa atalanta*	F D	Rathwell	20	July	85
7.	*Vanessa atalanta*	M V	Agassiz	11	Aug.	73
8.	*Junonia coenia*	M D	San Rafael, CA	11	Aug.	71
9.	*Limenitis arthemis*	M D	Reed Lake	30	June	84
10.	*Limenitis arthemis*	M V	Sandilands	31	May	77
11.	*Limenitis arthemis*	M V	Sandilands	12	June	72
12.	*Limenitis archippus*	M D	Culross	8	July	75
13.	*Limenitis archippus*	M V	Culross	8	June	76

1
2
3
4
5
6
7
8
9
10
11
12
13

PLATE 23

1.	*Enodia anthedon*	M D	Agassiz	24 June 77
2.	*Enodia anthedon*	F D	Agassiz	20 July 83
3.	*Enodia anthedon*	M V	Agassiz	5 July 75
4.	*Satyrodes eurydice*	M D	Culross	21 June 77
5.	*Satyrodes eurydice*	F D	Culross	22 July 84
6.	*Satyrodes eurydice*	M V	Oscar Point	9 July 82
7.	*Satyrodes eurydice*	F D	Culross	21 June 87
8.	*Megisto cymela*	M D	Elm Creek	19 June 84
9.	*Megisto cymela*	F D	Elm Creek	19 June 84
10.	*Megisto cymela*	M V	Elm Creek	19 June 84
11.	*Coenonympha tullia*	F V	Deleau	29 May 78
12.	*Coenonympha tullia*	M D	Deleau	21 May 77
13.	*Coenonympha tullia*	F D	Melbourne	13 June 84
14.	*Coenonympha tullia*	M V	Melbourne	13 June 84
15.	*Coenonympha tullia*	M D	Gillam	12 July 87
16.	*Coenonympha tullia*	F D	Gillam	12 July 87
17.	*Coenonympha tullia*	M V	Gillam	12 July 87
18.	*Cercyonis pegala*	M V	Culross	20 July 84
19.	*Cercyonis pegala*	M D	Culross	5 July 78
20.	*Cercyonis pegala*	F D	Culross	22 July 84
21.	*Cercyonis pegala*	F V	Culross	22 July 84

1
2
3
4
5
6
7
8
9
10
11
12
13
14
15
16
17
18
19
20
21

PLATE 24

1.	*Erebia rossi*	M	D	Churchill	5	July	80
2.	*Erebia rossi*	F	D	Churchill	4	July	80
3.	*Erebia rossi*	M	V	Churchill	14	July	78
4.	*Erebia disa*	M	D	Churchill	3	July	80
5.	*Erebia disa*	F	D	Sandilands	22	June	79
6.	*Erebia disa*	M	V	Churchill	6	July	80
7.	*Erebia discoidalis*	M	D	Sandilands	15	May	80
8.	*Erebia discoidalis*	F	D	Sandilands	17	May	85
9.	*Erebia discoidalis*	F	V	Sandilands	10	June	79
10.	*Erebia theano*	M	D	Churchill	27	July	80
11.	*Erebia theano*	F	D	Churchill	16	July	79
12.	*Erebia theano*	M	V	Churchill	27	July	80
13.	*Erebia epipsodea*	M	D	Riding Mountain	3	June	80
14.	*Erebia epipsodea*	F	D	Riding Mountain	5	June	77
15.	*Erebia epipsodea*	M	V	Duck Mountain	22	June	73
16.	*Erebia epipsodea*	F	V	Riding Mountain	6	June	77
17.	*Neominois ridingsii*	M	D	Grand Co., CO	5	July	81
18.	*Neominois ridingsii*	F	D	Fremont Co., CO	30	June	70
19.	*Neominois ridingsii*	M	V	Fremont Co., CO	22	June	69

1
2
3
4
5
6
7
8
9
10
11
12
13
14
15
16
17
18
19

PLATE 25

1.	*Oeneis macounii*	M D	Agassiz	11 June 82
2.	*Oeneis macounii*	F D	Riding Mountain	5 July 79
3.	*Oeneis macounii*	F V	Sandilands	11 June 84
4.	*Oeneis chryxus*	M D	Cowan	31 May 81
5.	*Oeneis chryxus*	F D	Cowan	31 May 81
6.	*Oeneis chryxus*	F V	Cowan	3 June 82
7.	*Oeneis uhleri*	M D	Carberry	16 June 79
8.	*Oeneis uhleri*	F D	Carberry	16 June 79
9.	*Oeneis uhleri*	F V	Elm Creek	24 May 85
10.	*Oeneis alberta*	M D	Carberry	3 June 79
11.	*Oeneis alberta*	F V	Pine Ridge	10 June 79
12.	*Oeneis alberta*	M D	Pine Ridge	21 May 75
13.	*Oeneis alberta*	F D	Carberry	7 May 85
14.	*Oeneis alberta*	F D	Pine Ridge	14 May 85

1
2
3
4
5
6
7
8
9
10
11
12
13
14

PLATE 26

1.	*Oeneis bore*	M D	Churchill	14 July 78
2.	*Oeneis bore*	F D	Churchill	13 July 78
3.	*Oeneis bore*	F V	Churchill	13 July 78
4.	*Oeneis jutta*	M D	Riding Mountain	3 June 80
5.	*Oeneis jutta*	F D	Sandilands	18 June 79
6.	*Oeneis jutta*	F V	Cowan	3 June 80
7.	*Oeneis melissa*	M D	Churchill	3 July 80
8.	*Oeneis melissa*	F D	Churchill	5 July 80
9.	*Oeneis melissa*	M V	Churchill	27 July 79
10.	*Oeneis polixenes*	M D	Churchill	3 July 80
11.	*Oeneis polixenes*	F D	Churchill	2 July 79
12.	*Oeneis polixenes*	M V	Churchill	1 July 80

1
2
3
4
5
6
7
8
9
10
11
12

PLATE 27

1.	*Danaus plexippus*	M D	Culross	5 Aug. 79
2.	*Danaus plexippus*	F D	Culross	15 Aug. 85
3.	*Danaus plexippus*	M V	Agassiz	8 Aug. 74

1

2

3

Subfamily

MELITAEINAE: CHECKERSPOTS AND CRESCENTS

This subfamily occurs all over the world and is most numerous in Eurasia and the tropics of South America. Manitoba species of this subfamily are small and predominantly orange with black or dark brown markings dorsally. The eggs are laid in clusters of a few to several hundred. Larvae feed communally, mostly on members of the Composite Family and are characterized by having rows of branching spines or tubercles. Most species overwinter in the larval stage and adults of this subfamily readily visit flowers for nectar.

Silvery Checkerspot caterpillar, Roseisle, Manitoba. June 11, 1976.

Gorgone Checkerspot

Chlosyne gorgone (Hübner), 1810
= *Charidryas gorgone*
Plate 19 No. 1, 2, 3

Description: 27-38 mm. Dorsally the wings are marked with orange and black bands and spots. The black forewing tips contain small conspicuous white spots and the hindwings have a row of submarginal black dots. Wings have checkered fringes. Ventrally the forewings are orange with black markings and grayish tips. The hindwings are silvery-gray or brownish-gray with a zig-zag pattern of white arrow heads across the middle, white marginal crescents and white basal bars. Females are larger than males.

Similar Species: The Silvery Checkerspot and Harris' Checkerspot lack the zig-zag pattern on the ventral surface of the hindwings.

Life Cycle: The larvae of the Gorgone Checkerspot feed on many species of composites including Sunflower (*Helianthus annuus*), Prairie Sunflower (*Helianthus petiolaris*), Ragweed (*Ambrosia trifida*), Sump-weed (*Iva xanthifolia*) and Loosetrife (*Lysimachia* sp.).

The cream coloured eggs are laid in clusters on the host plant. Larvae feed in a group until about half grown and then enter an overwintering diapause. The mature larvae are deep black, speckled with white or cream, with a red fulvous stripe dorsally and a white mottled stripe laterally. The cuticle is covered in black spines and bristles. The true legs are black, the prolegs grayish-brown and the head capsules black and hairy. The pupae are gray, mottled with lighter and darker spots (Brown 1974).

In Manitoba adults have been recorded from May 15 to July 3 usually being most common in early June. There is one generation per year.

Habitat: Dry sandy prairie and grassy hillsides.

Range: The Rocky Mountains and eastward to Manitoba, southward to New York, Georgia, Mexico and Colorado.

Manitoba Records: Beulah, Birds Hill, Birtle, Boissevain, Brandon, Carberry, Cartwright, Cromer, Culross, Deleau, Duck Mountain, Elm Creek, Grahamdale, Kelwood, La Riviere, Melbourne, Melita, Miniota, Neepawa, Norris Lake, Pine Ridge, Riding Mountain, Sand Ridge, Stockton, Stony Mountain, Teulon, Treesbank, Turtle Mountain, William Lake and Winnipeg.

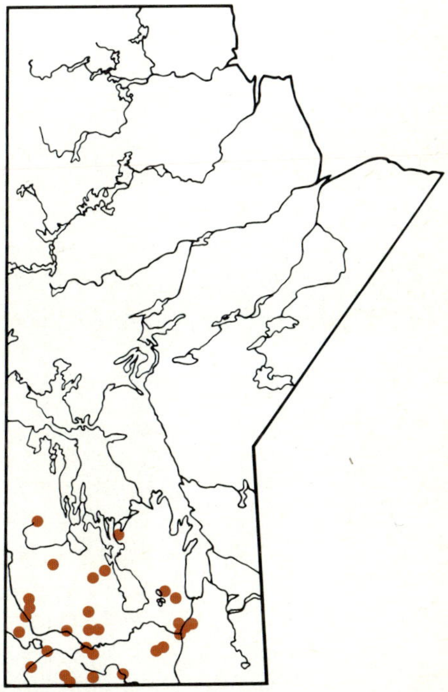

Subspecies: Two subspecies have been described, but only *Chlosyne gorgone carlota* occurs in Manitoba.

Remarks: The Gorgone Checkerspot is the darkest and smallest of the Checkerspots found here. In dry prairie areas this species can be found perched on isolated plants, visiting flowers and basking in the sun. It is quite wary and difficult to approach even while feeding at flowers. The Gorgone Checkerspot prefers to feed on yellow composites, but can also be found on Asters, Fleabane, Goldenrod, and Milkweed.

Silvery Checkerspot

Chlosyne nycteis

(Doubleday & Hewitson), 1847

= *Charidryas nycteis*

Plate 19 No. 4, 5, 6

Description: 35-44 mm. Dorsally adults are pale orange with black or dark brown markings and borders. The forewing borders are widest at the apex. The dorsal and ventral surfaces of the hindwings contain a submarginal row of dark spots, one or two of which have white centres. Ventrally the forewings are pale orange with a brown border and contain pale crescents. The hindwings have a median band of whitish or cream-coloured brown-edged oval spots, basal silvery white spots and a large brown patch which contains a prominent, silvery white crescent at the outer margin.

Similar Species: The Gorgone Checkerspot differs as described under that species. Harris' Checkerspot usually has a complete row of submarginal white crescents and a complete marginal orange band in each wing. In the Silvery Checkerspot the marginal band is inconspicuous, consisting merely of two thin lines.

Life Cycle: Larvae feed on a variety of plants including Jerusalem Artichoke (*Helianthus tuberosus*), Purple Stemmed Aster (*Aster puniceus*) and Tall Coneflower (*Rudbeckia laciniata*).

The ridged and pitted eggs are pale green and are laid in clusters of approximately 100 on the underside of the leaves of the host plant. The larvae feed as a group and spend the winter in diapause, resuming feeding in the spring. The mature larvae are velvety black with purplish streaks, and a dull orange stripe on each side. Dark brown or black tubercles with black and yellowish-brown bristles cover the cuticle. The pupae have five rows of conical tubercles on the abdomen and vary in colour from yellowish-green to pinkish- or grayish-brown. (Klots 1951; Howe 1975; Ferris and Brown 1981).

In Manitoba adults have been recorded from June 11 to July 15. There is one generation per year and females emerge later than males.

Habitat: Open areas in deciduous forests, moist meadows, along creeks and rivers, woodland trails and roadsides. This is a "poor soil" species of grassy barrens, sandy areas and old burns. In Manitoba the Silvery Checkerspot seems to be most abundant in scrubby cutover areas.

Range: Southeastern Canada from Manitoba to Nova Scotia, southward to Georgia, Texas, Arizona and Wyoming (not occurring west of Manitoba in Canada).

Manitoba Records: Agassiz Provincial Forest, Aweme, Beulah, Birds Hill, Cartwright, Elm Creek, Grand Beach, Holland, Lyleton, McCreary, Miami, Morden, Pine Ridge, Riding Mountain, Roseisle, Sand Ridge, Sandilands Provincial Forest, Spruce Woods Provincial Park, Tolstoi, Victoria Beach, Selkirk, Whiteshell Provincial Park and Winnipeg.

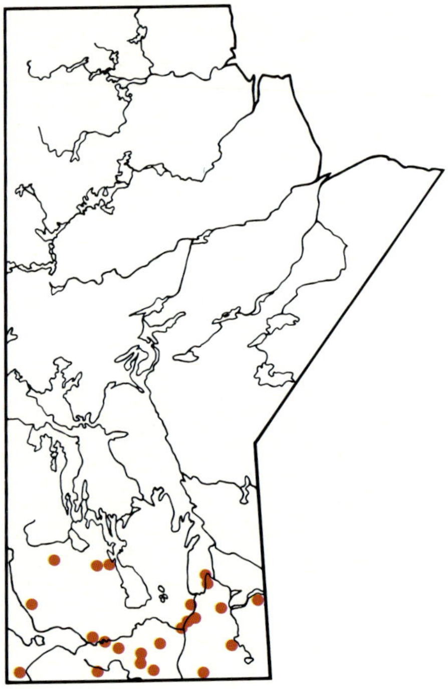

Subspecies: Three subspecies are recognized, two of which are found in this province. In southeastern and south-central Manitoba *Chlosyne nycteis nycteis* occurs. In the western part of the province e.g. Riding Mountain, *Chlosyne nycteis reversa* is found. In the subspecies *reversa* the dark dorsal markings are greatly reduced and the light areas are more extensive, giving the wing a "washed-out" appearance. Some specimens of *reversa* have been found as far east as Winnipeg and a number of Manitoba specimens appear to be intermediate between *reversa* and *nycteis*.

Remarks: The Silvery Checkerspot is widespread in southern Manitoba but is absent in intensively farmed areas. This species is common in the Agassiz Forest and in the Pembina Hills. The flight is slow, consisting of alternate flapping and gliding cycles. Males often patrol above low shrubs and will perch on shrubs or small trees. The females are less active and best seen when they visit flowers for nectar. Both sexes often bask in the sun with wings spread.

Harris' Checkerspot

Chlosyne harrisii (Scudder), 1864
= *Charidryas harrisii*
Plate 19 No. 7, 8, 9, 10

Description: 32-46 mm. This Checkerspot is pale orange dorsally with fairly wide black or dark brown borders. In females the dark markings are paler and less extensive than in males, often being suffused with the orange ground colour. There are usually submarginal, white centered dots both dorsally and ventrally, which are sometimes obscured by the dark wing borders. Ventrally the forewings are orange. The hindwings are light brown, with a median band of cream-coloured oval spots, basal cream and orange spots and a submarginal row of white crescents. Each wing has a narrow but complete marginal brown-edged orange band. Females are larger than males and markings can be quite variable in both sexes.

Similar Species: Gorgone and Silvery Checkerspots differ as described under those species.

Life Cycle: The usual larval food plant of Harris' Checkerspot is Flat-topped White Aster (*Aster umbellatus*) but occasionally Goldenrod (*Solidago* sp.) may serve as an alternate host.

The females lay groups of about 25 yellow eggs on the underside of White Aster leaves. The larvae feed communally after hatching and form a rough silken nest around the plant. Partially grown larvae move to the base of the plant in the fall and enter an overwintering diapause. They resume feeding in the spring. The mature larvae are deep orange-red with a black stripe dorsally and two cross stripes over each body segment. The last two abdominal segments are black with long, black branching spines. The white pupae are spotted with black, brown and orange and have several rows of black-tipped tubercles on the abdomen (Klots 1951; Opler and Krizek 1984).

In Manitoba adults have been recorded from June 3 to July 19, being most common in late June. Females emerge later than males and there is one generation per year.

Habitat: Forest openings, meadows and forest trails, usually preferring brushy areas in or near wet places.

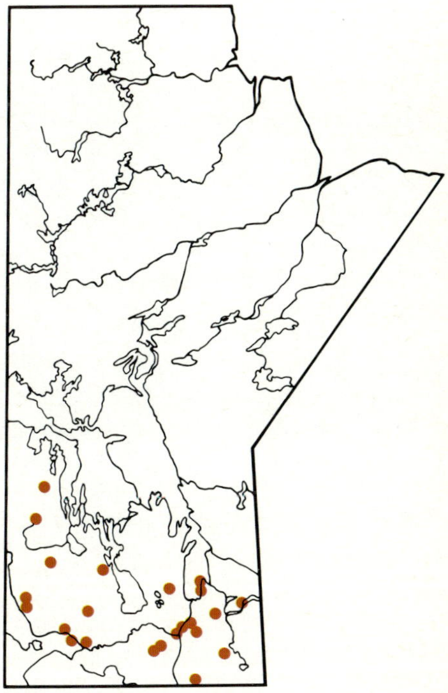

Range: Southern Canada from Saskatchewan to Nova Scotia southward to West Virginia, Illinois and North Dakota (Gregory 1975; Howe 1975).

Manitoba Records: Agassiz Provincial Forest, Anola, Aweme, Beulah, Birds Hill, Birtle, Brandon, Cowan, Culross, Duck Mountain, Elm Creek, Grand Beach, Komarno, Neepawa, Pine Ridge, Pointe du Bois, Riding Mountain, Rounthwaite, Sand Ridge, Sandilands Provincial Forest, Tolstoi, Victoria Beach and Winnipeg.

Subspecies: There is some disagreement between researchers as to the number of subspecies. Most of the Manitoba specimens are *Chlosyne harrisii hanhami*. Several specimens of the subspecies *Chlosyne harrisii harrisii* have also been found in southeastern Manitoba. The subspecies *harrisii* (Plate 19, No. 7) is heavily marked with black or dark brown dorsally. A dark band divides the orange discal area of the hindwings and the spots on the ventral side of the wings are clearly defined. The more common subspecies *hanhami* has a more extensive orange area on the upper surface of the wings, often suffused with the darker markings, which creates a washed-out pattern. The ventral spots in *hanhami* are paler and not as distinct as those in *harrisii*. There seems to be no clear geographical distinction between the two subspecies in Manitoba.

Remarks: Although localized and usually uncommon, this species occasionally becomes abundant. Local populations seem to fluctuate in size from year to year. Agassiz and Sandilands Provincial Forests are among the best areas to observe Harris' Checkerspot. Adults have a slow, leisurely flight and seldom wander far from the food plant. Both sexes visit flowers for nectar, bask in the sun and frequently perch on low plants.

Pearl Crescent

Phyciodes tharos (Drury), 1773

Plate 19 No. 11, 12, 13, 14

Description: 26-35 mm. The Pearl Crescent is uniformly orange dorsally, extensively marked with black lines and patches. Females usually have a jagged, whitish, thin submarginal line on the fore and hindwings. Individuals from the overwintering and the last summer generation have gray or grayish-brown ventral hindwings with an irregular pale stripe in the middle. The dorsal black areas are reduced and there is a submarginal pale line in the hindwings. The markings on both surfaces of the wings can be quite variable. The antennal clubs are usually black with some orange ventrally.

Similar Species: The Northern Pearl Crescent is larger; males have relatively large unbroken open orange areas dorsally while females usually lack the thin whitish submarginal line in the dorsal hindwings or if present, it is very dull. The Tawny Crescent has more distinct patterns and usually has pale buff bands on the forewings. Female Tawny Crescents lack the thin whitish submarginal line in the dorsal hindwings. Females of all Crescent species found in Manitoba are often difficult to distinguish and are best identified when associated with the more easily recognized males.

Life Cycle: The larvae of the Pearl Crescent feed on a wide variety of smooth-leaved asters. In Manitoba food plants include Many-flowered Aster (*Aster ericoides*), Smooth Aster (*Aster laevis*) and Small Blue Aster (*Aster simplex*).

The eggs are laid in small clusters (occasionally females will oviposit groups of up to 200 eggs) on the underside of the leaves of the host plant. A single female may lay up to 700 eggs in her lifetime. The larvae feed communally. Development from egg to pupa requires about 35 days in the summer. Larvae of the last summer generation enter into an overwintering diapause when they reach the third instar and resume feeding in the spring. The mature larvae are dark brown with a faint pale yellow stripe of broken dots along the dorsal surface and a yellow stripe laterally. The cuticle is covered in bristly blackish to yellowish-brown tubercles. The pupae are grayish or brownish, mottled with darker spots and stripes and have short tubercles on the abdomen (Oliver 1979; Opler and Krizek 1984).

In Manitoba adults have been recorded from June 5 to August 27. There are two or more overlapping generations per year dependent mostly on temperature and availability of food plants.

Habitat: Dry prairie hillsides, roads, pastures, fields, open pine forests or any open areas where asters grow (Hooper 1973).

Range: Southern Saskatchewan and Manitoba southward to New England, Florida and Mexico.

Manitoba Records: Beulah, Brokenhead, Elm Creek, Kelwood, McCreary, Miami, Miniota, Pine Ridge, Riding Mountain, Sand Ridge, Sandilands Provincial Forest, Spruce Woods Provincial Forest, Vita, Whiteshell Provincial Park and Winnipeg.

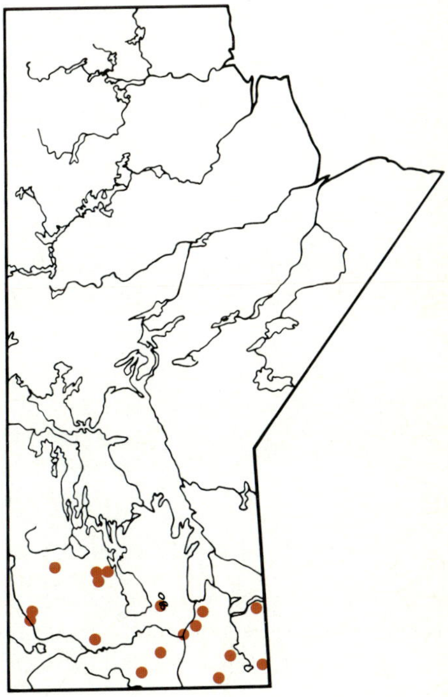

Subspecies: The Northern Pearl Crescent and the Pearl Crescent have only been regarded as separate species for a few years and research is needed to further define the relationships between the two species.

Remarks: This is one of the most common butterflies in eastern North America, yet the Pearl Crescent is uncommon in Manitoba. Some specimens once identified as Tawny Crescents have since been identified as Pearl Crescents. Adults congregate at moist areas along trails and roads and visit a wide variety of flowers.

Northern Pearl Crescent

Phyciodes morpheus (Fabricius), 1775
= *Phyciodes pascoensis* (W.G. Wright), 1905
= *Phyciodes selenis* (W. Kirby), 1837

Plate 19 No. 15, 16, 17, 18

Description: 28-37 mm. The wings are orange dorsally with wide black margins and black markings which are more extensive in the females. Ventrally, the forewings are orange with black spots. The hindwings are paler, frequently buff in colour, and sometimes containing a pearly crescent. The ventral tips of the antennae are orange. Females are larger than males and specimens from northern areas are smaller than those from the southern part of the province. Males are most readily identified by the large open orange area dorsally.

Similar Species: The Tawny and Pearl Crescents differ as described under those species.

Life Cycle: Small Blue Aster (*Aster simplex*) is probably the larval food plant in Manitoba.

Females lay small groups of eggs under the leaves of the host plant and upon hatching the larvae feed gregariously. During late summer, third instar larvae enter into an overwintering diapause. Feeding commences again in the spring. The mature larvae are dark brown with a pale brown dorsal stripe and gray or brown tubercles each containing light brown branching spines. The head capsules are covered in white spots. The pale gray or brown pupae are mottled with darker spots and lines and have short tubercles on the abdomen (Klots 1951; Oliver 1979).

Adults have been recorded from May 30 to September 5 in southern Manitoba. The Northern Pearl Crescent is most abundant in June. There are at least two generations per year in the southern part of the province but only one in the north.

Habitat: Forest openings, meadows, roadsides and stream banks.

Range: Across central Canada from the Yukon and British Columbia to Newfoundland, southward to New England, Virginia, Pennsylvania and in the Rockies to New Mexico.

Manitoba Records: Agassiz Provincial Forest, Assean Lake, Beulah, Birds Hill, Bowsman, Buffalo Lake, Buffalo Point, Carberry, Churchill, Cowan, Culross, Delta, Duck Mountain, Elm Creek, Flin Flon, Fort Alexander, Gillam, Gimli, Grand Marais, Grand Rapids, Hazel Creek at Hwy. 15, Hilbre, Husavik, Jacam, Katimik Lake, Kelwood, Kettle Rapids, La Rochelle, Libau, Lundar, Lynn Lake, Maskwa River, Melbourne, Miami, Mile 214 and 332 on the Hudson Bay Railway, Moosehorn, Northwest Angle Provincial Forest, Oak Hammock, Overflowing River, Patricia Beach, Pikwitonei, Pine Ridge, Pointe du Bois, Porcupine Provincial Forest, Rennie, Riding Mountain, Roseisle, St. Lazare, St. Lupicin, St. Malo, Sandilands Provincial Forest, Sandy Hook, Selkirk, Seven Sisters, Simonhouse Lake, Sprague, Spruce Woods Provincial Park, Stony Mountain, Stuartburn, Teulon, The Pas, Thompson, Tolstoi, Turtle Mountain, Victoria Beach, Wabowden, Wanless, West Shoal Lake, Whiteshell Provincial Park and Winnipeg.

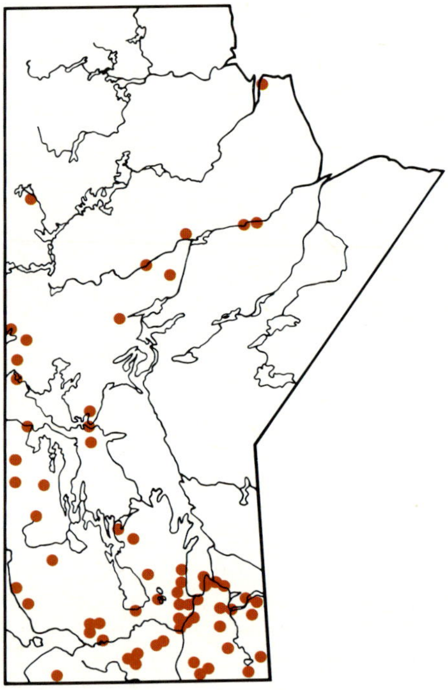

Subspecies: No subspecies are recognized.

Remarks: The Northern Pearl Crescent is perhaps the most abundant butterfly in Manitoba. After rain showers adults are sometimes found by the hundreds congregating at mud puddles. This butterfly visits almost any flower for nectar. Males are very pugnacious, frequently leaving their perch to intercept butterflies or other intruders. When undisturbed the flight consists of flaps and glides. This butterfly has a habit of moving its opened wings up and down several times after alighting.

Tawny Crescent

Phyciodes batesii (Reakirt), 1865

Plate 19 No. 19, 20, 21, 22

Description: 30-36 mm. Dorsally the wings are orange with wide black borders and are extensively marked with black lines and patches. The forewings have pale orange or buff bands, which are more prominent in females. Ventrally the forewings are orange and buff with black spots. The black spot at the bottom edge of each wing is wider than the one at the top. The ventral hindwings are a buff colour and at the bottom edge a pale crescent may be present within a brownish patch. The antennal clubs are black and white. The Tawny Crescent is best distinguished from other Crescents by its relatively distinct and clear-cut pattern.

Similar Species: Pearl Crescent males lack the pale forewing band and females have a thin whitish submarginal line on the hindwings. Occasionally specimens of the Tawny and Pearl Crescent may be very difficult to tell apart. The Northern Pearl Crescent differs as described under that species.

Life Cycle: In Manitoba the Small Blue Aster (*Aster simplex*) is probably the larval host plant for the Tawny Crescent.

The eggs are laid in clusters under the leaves of the host plant and larvae begin hatching within eight days. They feed gregariously and spin silken webs over the plant. Third instar larvae enter into an overwintering diapause and resume feeding in the spring. The mature larvae are brown, tinted with pink and with heavy black stripes. The cuticle is covered in light pinkish-brown tubercles containing brown bristles. The mottled pupae are light brown and more rounded in outline when compared to the pupa of *Phyciodes morpheus*.

Adults have been recorded in Manitoba from May 22 to August 16. August records are uncommon and may represent an occasional second generation in some years. Generally there is one generation per year in this province. Males are most common in June and females become more abundant in July.

Habitat: In or near wet areas in forest openings, meadows, trails and roadsides.

Range: Across southern Canada from Saskatchewan to Nova Scotia, southward to New England, Georgia, Pennsylvania and the in west to Colorado.

Sandilands Provincial Forest, east of Richer, Manitoba. June 26, 1988.

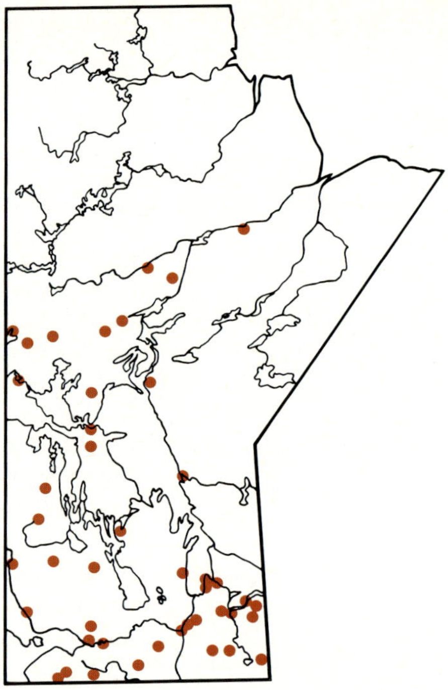

Manitoba Records: Agassiz Provincial Forest, Asessippi, Provincial Park, Aweme, Berens River, Birds Hill, Boissevain, Carberry, Cartwright, Cowan, Duck Mountain, Elm Creek, Flin Flon, Fort Alexander, Gillam, Gimli, Grahamdale, Grand Beach, Grand Rapids, Katimik Lake, Little Limestone Lake, Marchand, Max Lake, McCreary, Miami, Mile 200 Hudson Bay Railway, Miniota, Northwest Angle Provincial Forest, Norway House, Pikwitonei, Pine Ridge, Pointe du Bois, Ponton, Reed Lake, Rennie, Riding Mountain, Sandilands Provincial Forest, Seven Sisters, Simonhouse Lake, Spruce Woods Provincial Park, The Pas, Thompson, Victoria Beach, Wabowden, Whiteshell Provincial Park and Winnipeg.

Subspecies: No subspecies are recognized.

Remarks: The Tawny Crescent has a shorter flight period than the Northern Pearl Crescent and in Manitoba is more localized in distribution. The Tawny Crescent is also less abundant and more sedentary in its flight habits than the Northern Pearl Crescent. The two species are frequently seen together at Agassiz and Sandilands Provincial Forests where they can be best observed when feeding at flowers or taking moisture from puddles.

Anicia Checkerspot

Euphydryas anicia

Doubleday & Hewitson, 1848

= *Occidryas anicia*

Plate 19 No. 25, 26,

Description: 32-43 mm. This species is predominately dull orange dorsally. The wings contain alternate bands of brick-red or orange spots and whitish or cream spots heavily outlined in black. Ventrally the markings are similar but the spots are more distinct (the black outlines are thin and sharp) and the basal forewing pattern is suffused.

Life Cycle: The larval food plants of the Anicia Checkerspot include Beard tongue (*Penstemon* sp.) and Indian Paint Brush (*Castilleja* sp.). Little is known about the life history of this butterfly in Manitoba. Larvae feed gregariously within a silken shelter and enter into an overwintering diapause when half-grown. The mature larvae can vary in appearance and may be dull white and covered in bristly black tubercles or black, speckled with white and covered in orange tubercles (Howe 1975; Ferris and Brown 1981).

Habitat: Alpine and tundra ridges, pine forests, meadows and grasslands.

Range: Alaska, the Yukon and British Columbia to Manitoba, southward to Mexico.

Manitoba Records: Riding Mountain.

Subspecies: Twenty-two subspecies have been recognized in the literature however it is unclear to which subspecies the Manitoba specimen belongs.

Remarks: The nearest known colony of the Anicia Checkerspot outside of Manitoba is in the Cypress Hills of Saskatchewan. The Manitoba specimen was found in Riding Mountain National Park by J.F. May on July 19, 1933. Collecting is no longer permitted in Riding Mountain National Park and so it is probable that few people have come across the Anicia Checkerspot.

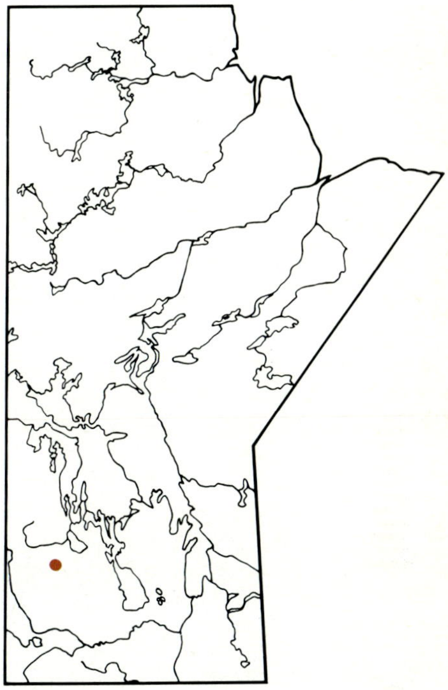

Baltimore

Euphydryas phaeton (Drury), 1773

Plate 19 No. 23, 24,

Description: 41-47 mm. The wings are black dorsally with small creamy-white spots, several orange-red spots basally and an orange-red border on each wing. The markings are similar on the underside of the wings with larger and more distinct white and orange spots. Females are larger than males.

Life Cycle: Turtlehead (*Chelone glabra*) is the preferred food plant of the Baltimore.

The pale yellow eggs are laid in masses of 100 to 700 under the leaves of the host plant. Larvae begin hatching after about three weeks and spin a silk shelter around the top of the host plant in which they feed communally. A heavier shelter is formed in the late summer. During the autumn the fourth instar larvae leave the host plant and enter an overwintering diapause within rolled leaves on the ground. Larvae return to the plant in the spring and resume feeding. If the host plant is entirely consumed before they mature, larvae will feed on other plants including White Ash (*Fraxinus americana*) and Common Lousewort (*Pedicularis canadensis*). The mature larvae are orange-red with transverse black stripes and a cuticle covered in black tubercles with long black branching spines. The white pupae are mottled with black and orange and have orange tubercles on the abdomen (Opler and Krizek 1981; Pyle 1981).

In Manitoba adults have been recorded from July 7 to July 12.

Habitat: Wet woodland meadows, open sphagnum bogs and marshes in the northern part of the Baltimore's range. In southern areas dry openings and hillsides in hardwood forests are preferred.

Range: Across southern Canada from southeastern Manitoba to Nova Scotia, southward to Nebraska, Arkansas and Georgia.

Manitoba Records: Agassiz and Sandilands Provincial Forests.

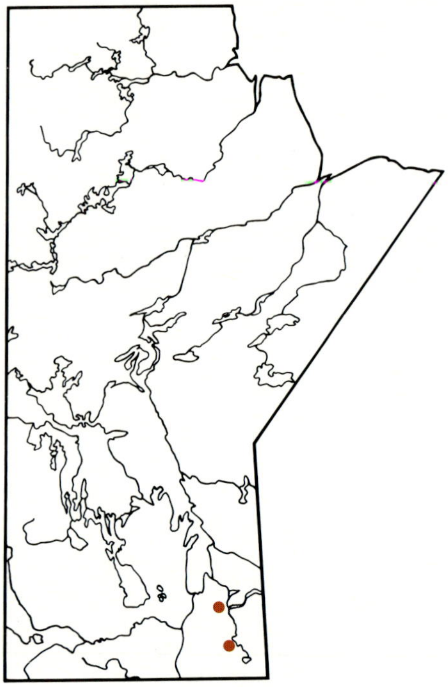

Subspecies: The number of Baltimore subspecies is still under investigation. The subspecies found in Manitoba is probably *Euphydryas phaeton phaeton*.

Remarks: Only three specimens of the Baltimore have been found in Manitoba, all males. These males were found feeding on Dogbane blossoms in a dry sandy area adjacent to wet forest and basking in the sun along a forest road within a Black Spruce bog. The Baltimore seldom strays far from the larval host plant Turtlehead, which is rare but occasionally found in southeastern Manitoba.

Subfamily

NYMPHALINAE

Members of the subfamily Nymphalinae are mostly confined to the temperate regions of the Old and New Worlds. In Manitoba the Nymphalinae are represented by three groups called Anglewings, Tortoiseshells and Thistle Butterflies. The Anglewings and Tortoiseshells are medium sized, usually predominantly orange although some species are black or dark brown dorsally, and have stout bodies and ragged-edged wings that are often angled. The eggs are laid singly or in clusters and larvae feed on nettles or composites. Most species have several generations per year and overwinter in the adult stage. Most species rarely visit flowers for nectar. Thistle Butterflies are medium-sized and have robust bodies. They are strong fliers, some are migratory and local populations can fluctuate dramatically from year to year.

Question Mark

Polygonia interrogationis (Fabricius), 1798

Plate 20 No. 1, 2, 3

Description: 58-71 mm. The wing margins of this Anglewing are jagged and the hindwings have distinct tails. The wings are orange dorsally with black spots, and violet margins and tails. Individuals from the first summer generation are strongly dimorphic and often have dark brown to black hindwings. Ventrally the wings are violet or brown and sometimes mottled. The hindwings contain a silvery dot accompanied by an off-set comma, forming a question mark or semicolon in appearance. This is the only Anglewing with pronounced tails, with a silvery dot opposite the comma and with violet wing margins.

Life Cycle: The larvae of the Question Mark feed on Nettle (*Urtica* sp.) and Hops (*Humulus lupulus*).

Females lay the pale green, keg-shaped eggs singly or stacked in rows on the leaves or stems of the host plant or on nearby plants. Ovipositing females have a bouncing flight, briefly touching their abdomens down on a number of plants, while searching for the correct host plant. Young larvae may feed gregariously for a short period, but spend most of the larval stage feeding alone. The mature larvae are variable in colour and may be black to yellow with yellow or red lines. They have numerous large tubercles varying in colour from yellow to red and two rows of bristly spines, including two on the head. The pupae range in colour from yellow to dark brown, have deeply notched heads and conspicuous narrow keels and sometimes eight metallic silver spots laterally. The pupae hang upside down from the food plant or nearby object. Adults that emerge late in the summer can hibernate during the winter (Klots 1951; Opler and Krizek 1981).

In Manitoba adults have been recorded from June 20 to August 27 and there are probably two generations per year.

Habitat: Open forests, damp meadows and fields and roadsides, nearly always near trees.

Range: Saskatchewan through southern Canada to the Maritime provinces southward through most of the United States except the Pacific coast and the Great Basin (Howe 1975; Morris 1980).

Manitoba Records: Aweme, Beulah, Cartwright, Culross, Killarney, Oak hammock, Riding Mountain, Sandilands Provincial Forest and Winnipeg.

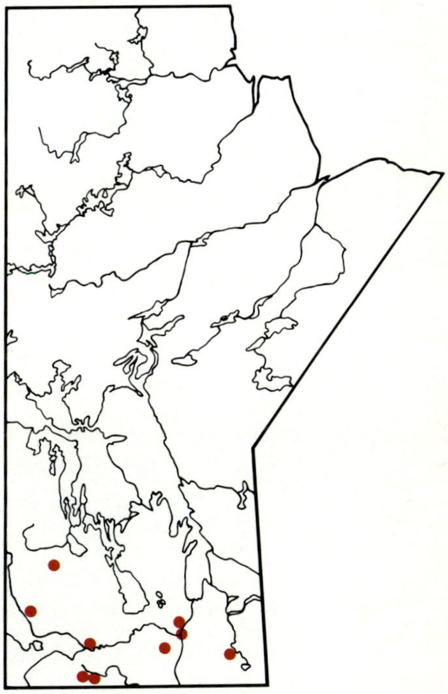

Subspecies: No subspecies are recognized.

Remarks: The Question Mark is uncommon in Manitoba and is partially migratory. Most of the adults found in June in the Winnipeg area have had dark hindwings indicating that they are the offspring of light hindwing overwintering individuals. As very few light hindwing overwintering adults have been collected, this probably indicates that the adults found in June have migrated into the Winnipeg area from more southerly breeding grounds. This tends to support the hypothesis that the Question Mark does not overwinter in the northern limits of its range. Adults may also lay dormant (aestivate) for a part of the summer. Individuals from the first summer generation are quite distinct from those of the second summer generation and at one time the two forms were considered different species. Males often perch on tree trunks, chasing other insects or even birds, then returning to the original perch. Adults feed on tree sap, rotten fruit, animal dung, carrion and rarely visit flowers.

Comma

Polygonia comma (Harris), 1842

Plate 20 No. 4, 5, 6

Description: 47-58 mm. The Comma is brownish-orange dorsally with black spots and dark margins. Like the Question Mark, the Comma is highly dimorphic: individuals from the first generation frequently have dark brown to black hindwings, compared to the much brighter orange of the second generation. Ventrally the wings are mottled in various shades of brown and yellow and are "washed-out" in females. On the hindwings the silvery comma is hooked at both ends. There may be considerable variation among individuals.

Similar Species: Satyr Anglewings are difficult to separate from the pale overwintering forms of the Comma. In the Satyr Anglewing the lower inner spot on the hindwings is double, being divided by a vein. In the Comma this spot is barely, if at all, extended above the vein. The Satyr Anglewing lacks the hindwing dark border and violet margin of the Comma. The Question Mark differs as described under that species.

Life Cycle: The larval food plants of the Comma include Nettle (*Urtica* sp.), Wood Nettle (*Laportea canadensis*), American Elm (*Ulmus americana*) and Hops, (*Humulus lupulus*).

Females usually oviposit about mid-day. The pale green, barrel-shaped eggs are laid either singly or stacked in columns of two or three on the underside of the leaves of the food plant. Newly hatched larvae feed on the underside of the leaves and as they grow larger construct a shelter by rolling the leaf together. Mature larvae are white, greenish-brown or black with white spines. The light brown pupae resemble a piece of wood and have small tubercles and metallic gold or silver spots on the abdomen.

In Manitoba adults have been recorded from May 17 to October 6. There are two generations per year. The first generation is the dark form and is the result of eggs laid by overwintering females. Adults from this first generation may spend part of the summer in aestivation. The second generation is the lighter form and emerges in the fall. Adults from this generation seek shelter in hollow trees or other protected sites where they pass the winter.

Habitat: Along forest streams, rivers and roads, forest edges and disturbed areas if the food plant is present.

Riverbottom forest with understory of Wood Nettle, La Barriere Park, Winnipeg, Manitoba. June 25, 1988.

Range: Southern Canada from Saskatchewan to Newfoundland, southward to Florida, the Gulf States and westward to Colorado.

Manitoba Records: Aweme, Beulah, Cartwright, Culross, Flin Flon, Glenboro, Grand Beach, Kelwood, Miami, Moose Lake, Pine Ridge, Portage la Prairie, Riding Mountain, Selkirk, Seven Sisters, Spruce Woods Provincial Forest, Teulon, The Pas, Turtle Mountain, Victoria Beach and Winnipeg.

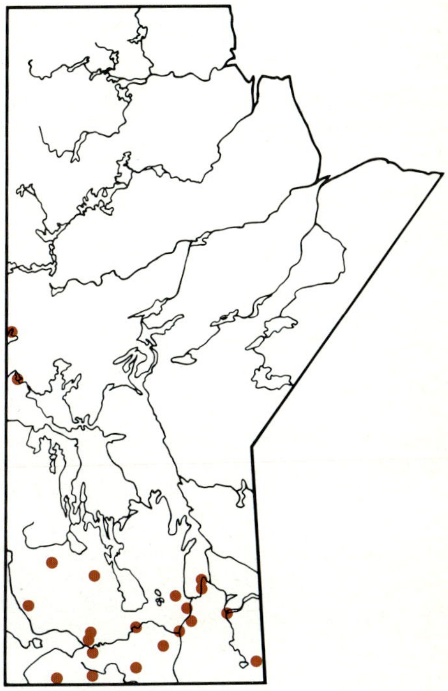

Subspecies: No subspecies are recognized.

Remarks: The Comma is like a small version of the Question Mark both in appearance and habits. It is uncommon in Manitoba and when found is most abundant in the fall.

Satyr Anglewing

Polygonia satyrus (W.H. Edwards), 1869

Plate 20 No. 7, 8, 9

Description: 49-54 mm. This Anglewing is yellowish-orange dorsally with black spots and brown forewing borders. The hindwing borders are pale, suffused with the ground colour and contain yellowish spots. In many females the dorsal wing borders are indistinct and broken into bars. Ventrally the wings of males are marked in shades of brown and yellowish-brown and contain small dots and striations. The hindwings contain a silvery comma, hooked or enlarged at the lower end. The ventral surface of the females is a uniform, reddish-brown with a brown band in the middle of each wing. The silvery comma is thinner and not as pronounced as in the males. Although the Satyr Anglewing has a number of forms, most authors do not consider them to be seasonally dimorphic such as those of the Question Mark and Comma.

Similar Species: The Question Mark and Comma differ as described underthose species. Other Manitoba Anglewings are gray ventrally.

Life Cycle: The primary larval food plant is Nettle (*Urtica* sp.). Females lay the ribbed, pale green eggs in groups of three to four on the underside of the leaves of the host plant. Larvae build shelters of folded or rolled leaves in which they feed. The mature larvae are black, mottled with greenish-white and have a broad, greenish dorsal stripe. Each body segment has a black V-shaped mark within the dorsal stripe. The cuticle has numerous light coloured branched spines and the head capsules are black and spiny. The light brown, angular pupae have thorn-like projections and are located some distance from the food plant on objects such as tree trunks or rocks (Emmel and Emmel 1973; Howe 1975; Dornfeld 1980; Pyle 1981).

In Manitoba adults have been recorded from April 20 to September 22. It is probable that the Satyr Anglewing has two generations per year in this province.

Habitat: Forest glades, streams, forest edges, disturbed areas and parks.

Range: Across southern Canada from British Columbia to Newfoundland southward to New York in the east and California in the west.

Manitoba Records: Aweme, Beulah, Birtle, Boggy Creek, Cartwright, Culross, Duck Mountain, George Lake, Gillam, Grand Beach, Hecla Island, Kelwood, Libau, Northwest Angle Provincial Forest, Norway House, Oak Hammock, Rennie, Riding Mountain, Sandilands Provincial Forest, The Pas, Victoria Beach, Whiteshell Provincial Park and Winnipeg.

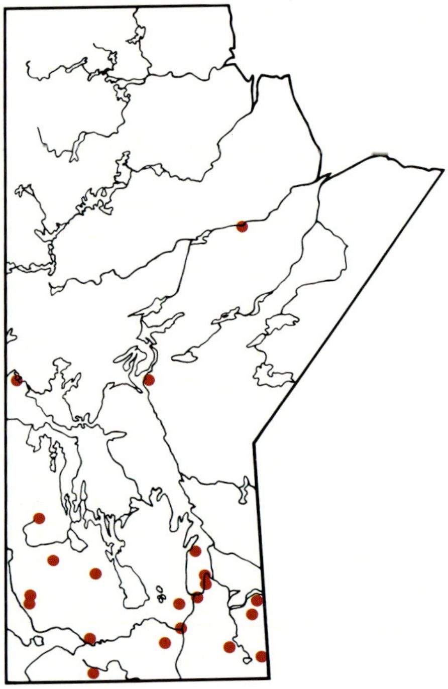

Subspecies: Some lepidopterists recognize two subspecies, while the majority feel there are none.

Remarks: This species is locally common in Saskatchewan but scarce in North Dakota. In Manitoba it does not seem to be very abundant and records indicate it was more common earlier in the century. The Satyr Anglewing is wary and has a swift, erratic flight. Adults are pugnacious, chasing large insects and other Anglewings. Males will perch on low vegetation or tree trunks in the late afternoon and evening waiting for females to pass by. Adults often perch with the head pointed downward. Late in the fall they seek crevices and other protected places where they hibernate.

Green Comma

Polygonia faunus (W.H. Edwards), 1862

Plate 20 No. 10, 11, 12, 15

Description: 45-50 mm. The wing edges of the Green Comma are very irregular and jagged. Dorsally they are brownish-orange, heavily marked with black spots and prominent dark brown borders. The wide hindwing borders enclose a row of yellowish spots and the wing fringes may be grayish-purple. Newly emerged adults have a greenish sheen on the dorsal borders. Ventrally the wings of males are variegated in contrasting grayish tones frequently dark basally with a row of submarginal mossy-green spots. There is a prominent silvery comma in each hindwing. Females are uniformly gray with a ''washed out'' appearance ventrally. The submarginal spots are reduced to black specks and the silvery comma is thin and small.

Similar Species: Gray and Hoary Commas are less heavily marked with black spots dorsally and the forewings are paler. Ventrally they are gray, not variegated and lack the greenish spots. All other anglewings have less jagged wings than the Green Comma.

Life Cycle: The larval food plants include Gray Willow (*Salix humilis*), Birch (*Betula* sp.), Alder (*Alnus* sp.), Currant and Gooseberry (*Ribes* sp.).

The pale green eggs are laid singly on the upper surface of the food plant leaf. Females generally lay only a few eggs per day. After hatching, the larvae skeletonize the upperside of the leaf, eventually consuming whole leaves when fully grown. The mature larvae are reddish or yellowish-brown with a white patch near the middle of the body and a broken, dull orange band laterally. There is a pale "W" mark on the front of the black head capsule. The pupae are pale brown with a keel-like protrusion and may be streaked with mossy-green or have a few metallic spots (Klots 1951; Harris 1972; Dornfeld 1977; Ferris and Brown 1981; Opler and Krizek 1984).

In Manitoba adults have been recorded from May 15 to August 20. There is one generation per year. Adults are seldom found in mid-summer and may have a life-span of up to 10 months.

Habitat: Strongly forest oriented, favouring boreal forests, sunny glades, forest roads and trails.

Range: The Pacific coast through the Yukon and the Northwest Territories eastward to Newfoundland, southward to California, Iowa and Georgia.

Manitoba Records: Agassiz Provincial Forest, Beulah, Birtle, Bissett, Cartwright, Cowan, Duck Mountain, Fort Alexander, Gillam, Grand Beach, Hecla Island, Husavik, Lynn Lake, Northwest Angle Provincial Forest, Riding Mountain, Sandilands Provincial Forest, South Indian Lake, Teulon, The Pas, Thompson, Victoria Beach, Wanless, Whiteshell Provincial Park and Winnipeg.

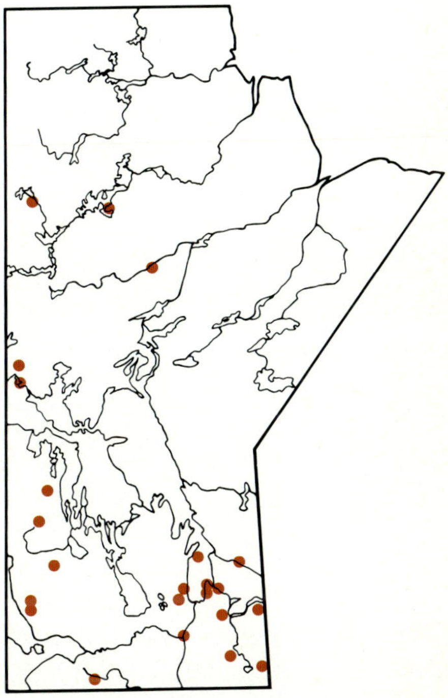

Subspecies: Four to five subspecies are recognized. The nominate subspecies *Polygonia faunus faunus* occurs in Manitoba.

Remarks: The Green Comma is sometimes referred to as "The Faun". Although never abundant, it is probably more common in Manitoba than present records indicate. Males perch on shrubs and rocks in the late afternoon and like other Anglewings, intercept passing intruders. These butterflies are attracted to sap, rotten fruit, carrion and dung.

Hoary Comma

Polygonia gracilis

(Grote & Robinson), 1867

Plate 20 No. 13, 14,

Description: 43-48 mm. This Comma is brownish-orange dorsally with relatively small black spots and dark borders. The hindwing borders enclose a row of submarginal yellowish spots. Ventrally the wings are two-toned, with dark gray inner halves and frosty-white or "hoary" outer halves (the wing margins may be darker). Each hindwing contains a silvery comma which is tapered at both ends. Females and males are similar in appearance.

Similar Species: Ventrally the Gray Comma lacks the hoary band across the hindwings and is more heavily striated.

Life Cycle: Larvae feed on currants. The Red Currant (*Ribes triste*) and Skunkberry (*Ribes glandulosum*) are the probable host plants.

The mature larvae are black with seven rows of spines on the cuticle. The spines on body segments three to six and the tops of the spines on segments seven to 12 are reddish-brown. The remaining spines are marked with white. There are a number of black markings which resemble arrowheads on the cuticle. The pupae are slender and salmon and olive coloured. The wing cases are elevated and there is a "nose-like" projection at the head. The pupal stage lasts approximately two weeks and the Hoary Comma overwinters in the adult stage (Klots 1951; Howe 1975).

In Manitoba adults have been recorded from May 31 to September 14. There are several generations per year.

Habitat: Forests, clearings and riverbanks.

Range: Alaska, the Yukon and the Northwest Territories across northern Canada to Prince Edward Island, southward to New England and the Great Lakes in the east and to California and New Mexico in the west (Opler and Krizek 1984).

Manitoba Records: Churchill, Gillam, Kelwood, Lynn Lake, Nueltin Lake, South Indian Lake, The Pas, Thompson and Wallace Lake.

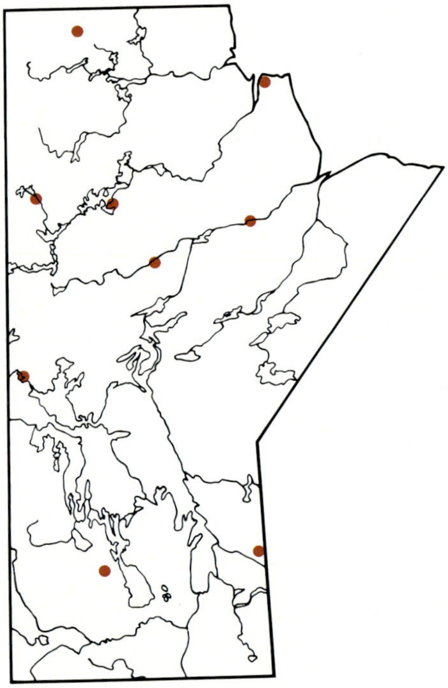

Subspecies: Our subspecies is probably *Polygonia gracilis gracilis*; although the underside is dark gray basally, not dark brown as in typical *Polygonia gracilis gracilis*.

Remarks: The Hoary Comma is not abundant in Manitoba. In addition to the locales listed, it is probably present in the eastern forests of the province. Adults feed on tree sap, rotten fruit and at mud puddles. They have also been observed taking nectar from Asters and Everlastings.

Gray Comma

Polygonia progne (Cramer), 1776

Plate 20 No. 16, 17, 18

Description: 41-51 mm. The Gray Comma is brownish-orange dorsally, with relatively small black spots and dark borders; the hindwing border encloses a submarginal row of yellowish spots. Ventrally the wings are dark gray and striated. There is a pale band in the forewings and the silvery comma, shaped like a wide-angled "L", is tapered at both ends. The dorsal hindwings of summer generation specimens are nearly completely dark brown and the spots are almost lacking. The undersides are brownish-gray and the lower arm of the silvery comma is short. Adults from both the overwintering and summer generation may be quite variable in colour and pattern.

Similar Species: The Hoary Comma differs as described under that species.

Life Cycle: Larval food plants include Currants (*Ribes* sp.), White Birch (*Betula papyrifera*) and American Elm (*Ulmus americana*).

The ribbed, pale green eggs are laid singly on the food plant leaves. After hatching, the young larvae feed on the underside of the leaves. When disturbed the larvae will move their head and posterior abdominal segments, holding on to the leaf with the prolegs in the middle of the body. The mature larvae have brown head capsules and yellowish-brown bodies covered in variegated olive-brown blotches and lines. The cuticle has numerous black and yellow branched spines, with a pair on the head capsule longer than the rest. The pupae are dark brown to tan and streaked with brown or black. The pupal stage lasts approximately 10 to 16 days.

In Manitoba adults have been recorded from May 5 to September 4. There are two generations per year in this province, with the adults from the late summer generation spending the winter in hibernation.

Habitat: Forests especially deciduous woods, clearings, farmyards and trails.

Range: Alaska, the Yukon and the Northwest Territories across Canada to Newfoundland, southward to Wyoming, Kansas, Missouri, Illinois and Virginia.

Manitoba Records: Agassiz Provincial Forest, Birds Hill, Birtle, Brokenhead, Cartwright, Culross, Duck Mountain, Fort Alexander, Gillam, Grand Beach, Hecla Island, Katimik Lake, Lynn Lake, Northwest Angle Provincial Forest, Norway House, Rennie, Riding Mountain, Ste. Rita, Sandilands Provincial Forest, Selkirk, Seven Sisters, Spruce Woods Provincial Forest, Teulon, Thompson, Treesbank, Victoria Beach, Wallace Lake, Whiteshell Provincial Park and Winnipeg.

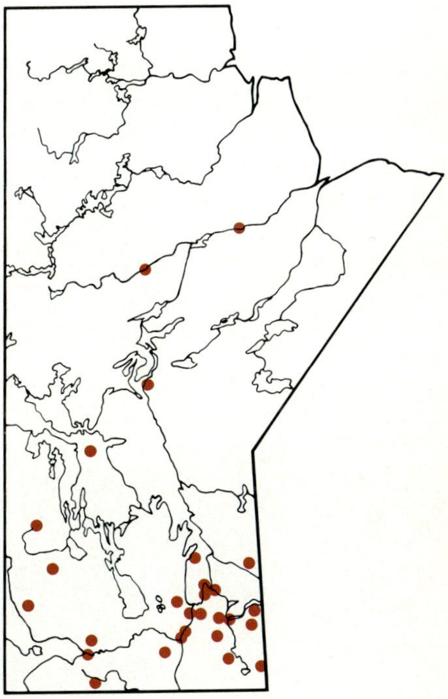

Subspecies: Until recently no subspecies were recognized. Scott (1984) recognized four subspecies, referring the specimens found in Canada to *Polygonia progne progne*.

Remarks: This is the only Anglewing that can be considered common in Manitoba. The Gray Comma is best observed in the Agassiz and Sandilands Provincial Forests in sunlit clearings or on forest trails. Although a slower flier than other Anglewings the Gray Comma is more wary and quite active. Adults visit rotten fruit, sap and carrion and will occasionally nectar at flowers.

Compton Tortoise Shell
Nymphalis vau-album
(Dennis & Schiffermüller), 1775
Plate 21 No. 1, 2

Description: 59-70 mm. Dorsally the wings are chocolate brown basally and yellowish-brown outwardly with brown borders. The forewings have large black spots and a whitish spot at the upper margins. The hindwings have a large black spot at the upper margins bordered by a whitish spot outwardly. Ventrally the wings are marbled with brownish-gray and are darker basally. The hindwings contain a small white bar or wide-angled "vee" (sometimes referred to as a "j"). Females are similar in appearance to males dorsally but ventrally females have a blurred or "washed-out" pattern. The wing margins are quite ragged in both sexes.

Similar Species: The California Tortoise Shell is smaller, paler, less heavily marked with black and has darker borders on the hindwings.

Life Cycle: Larval food plants include Willow (*Salix* sp.), Poplar (*Populus* sp.), Alder (*Alnus* sp.) and White Birch (*Betula papyrifera*).

Females mate in the spring after coming out of winter hibernation. The eggs are laid in clusters on the food plant. After hatching the larvae feed gregariously on the leaves. The mature larvae are pale green, mottled with yellowish-green and have numerous black branching spines. The pupae are green or brown with horned heads. They are usually formed on tree trunks or branches.

In Manitoba overwintered adults have been recorded from March 20 to June 4. Adult progeny of overwintering butterflies begin appearing by early June. Emergence continues throughout July and August with the last recorded observation of adults being October 2. The lifespan of the adult may be up to 10 months (Klots 1951; Howe 1975; Christensen 1981).

Habitat: Deciduous and coniferous forests, forest trails and roads and occasionally cities, towns or farms.

Range: Europe and Asia. In North America from Alaska and British Columbia through central and southern Canada to Newfoundland, southward to New York, Pennsylvania, Minnesota, North Dakota, Colorado and Oregon.

Compton Tortoise Shell chrysalis with parasitic wasp, Winnipeg, Manitoba. May 27, 1977.

Manitoba Records: Agassiz Provincial Forest, Aweme, Beulah, Birch River, Birtle, Brokenhead, Cartwright, Culross, Duck Mountain, Flin Flon, Fort Alexander, Grand Beach, Grand Rapids, Hecla Island, Little Grand Rapids, Northwest Angle Provincial Forest, Riding Mountain, Sandilands Provincial Forest, Schist Lake, Sharpe Lake, Spruce Woods Provincial Park, Thompson, Victoria Beach, Wallace Lake, Whiteshell Provincial Park and Winnipeg.

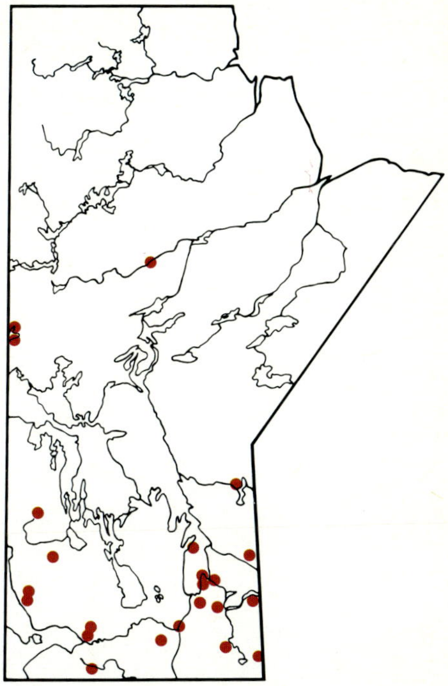

Subspecies: Two subspecies are recognized in North America. The subspecies that ranges through Manitoba is *Nymphalis vau-album j-album*.

Remarks: The Compton Tortoise Shell is usually one of the first butterflies to be seen in the spring and probably has the longest lived adult stage of any butterfly species found in Manitoba. Although never abundant, adults are observed every year, especially in forested areas. They frequent areas of mature trees, preferring to land on the trunks where the camouflaged ventral surfaces of the wings render them almost invisible against the bark. They are seldom attracted to flowers and prefer to feed on sap and rotten fruit or to congregate at mud puddles. In late fall adults search for hibernating sites such as hollows in trees and commonly find their way into unheated buildings where they pass the winter. In the early spring they have been observed to feed on the sap of Manitoba Maple (*Acer negundo*).

California Tortoise Shell

Nymphalis californica (Boisduval), 1852

Plate 21 No. 3, 4

Description: 48-60 mm. Dorsally the wings are yellowish-orange, basally suffused with brown. They contain both black spots and small white spots and have dark borders. Ventrally the wings are marbled with shades of grayish-brown paling outwardly.

Similar Species: The Compton Tortoise Shell as described under that species.

Manitoba Records: There are six records of the California Tortoise Shell in Manitoba. These records are for Cartwright, Kemnay, Miniota and Winnipeg.

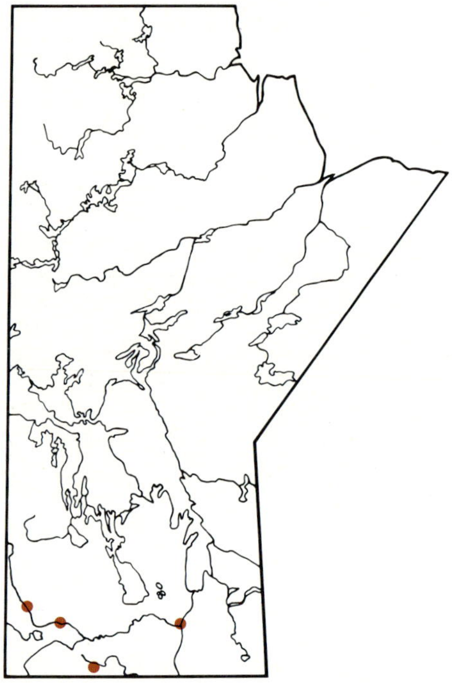

Remarks: All specimens were collected from September 14 to October 8. This species occasionally experiences population "explosions" and a great number migrate northward and westward from the west coast of North America. These migrations are probably responsible for the periodic occurrences in Manitoba.

Mourning Cloak

Nymphalis antiopa (Linnaeus), 1758

Plate 21 No. 5, 6

Description: 61-79 mm. This butterfly is dark reddish-brown dorsally with wide creamy-yellow borders (white in overwintering adults) and a submarginal band of blue spots. Ventrally the wings are black with black-speckled, dingy-white borders.

Life Cycle: The larvae of the Mourning Cloak feed on a wide variety of tree species including Sandbar Willow (*Salix interior*), Aspen (*Populus* sp.), Cottonwood (*Populus deltoides*), American Elm (*Ulmus americana*) and White Birch (*Betula papyrifera*).

After emerging from hibernation females lay green eggs in clusters around twigs or branches of the food plant. Feeding gregariously, the newly hatched larvae spin webs around the twigs and leaves of the host plant. As they mature the larvae spread over the host plant and if overcrowding occurs some may leave in search of other food sources. The mature larvae are black, speckled with white spots, have a row of red spots dorsally, orange-red prolegs and are covered in black, branched spines.

The angular pupae are brownish-gray with two horn like projections on the head and black-tipped tubercles on the abdomen. Like other Tortoise Shells the pupae are suspended from the end of the abdomen with head facing downward. The pupal stage lasts from 12 to 14 days.

In Manitoba adults have been recorded from April 6 to October 12. There is probably only one generation per year in in this province, but adults have a staggered emergence peaking in late summer.

Habitat: Glades, trails, stream banks and roads in forested areas are preferred, but adults are commonly found in farmyards, towns and cities.

Range: Europe and Asia. In North America throughout the subarctic and temperate regions. Rare in the southeast (e.g. Florida). Also found southward to Mexico and Venezuela.

Manitoba Records: Agassiz Provincial Forest, Beulah, Birds Hill, Boissevain, Carberry, Cartwright, Churchill, Cowan, Cromer, Culross, Deleau, Delta, Duck Mountain, Elm Creek, Flin Flon, Fort Prince of Wales, Gimli, Grand Beach, Little Grand Rapids, Lundar, Lyleton, Lynn Lake, McCreary, Melbourne, Norris Lake, Northwest Angle Provincial Forest, Oak Hammock, Onanole, Pine Ridge, Rennie, Riding Mountain, Sandilands Provincial Forest, Schist Lake, Selkirk, Seven Sisters, South Indian Lake, Sprague, The Pas, Thompson, Victoria Beach, Wallace Lake, Wattsview, Whiteshell Provincial Park and Winnipeg.

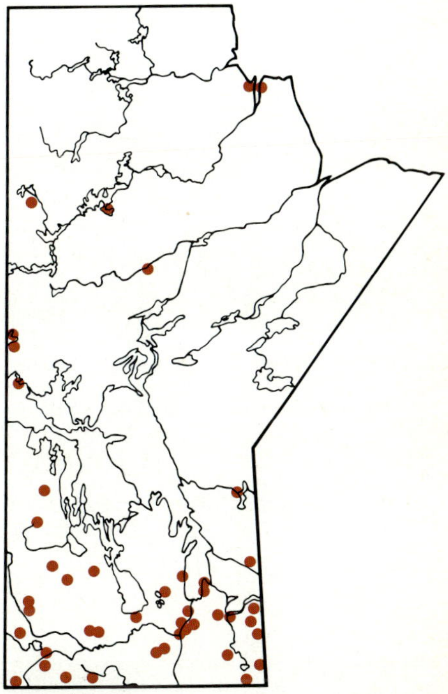

Subspecies: Two to three subspecies of the Mourning Cloak are recognized on a world wide basis. The subspecies found in most of North America, including Manitoba, is *Nymphalis antiopa antiopa*.

Remarks: This widespread butterfly is common in much of Europe and North America. In Britain it is a rare migrant and is known as the Camberwell Beauty. The Mourning Cloak is on the wing in early spring, often before all the snow has melted. Like the Compton Tortoise Shell the adult life span may last up to 10 months. It has a strong, swift flight. Males wait for females by perching on low branches or the ground and chase them when they pass by. Mating usually occurs in the early afternoon. Abandoned or unheated buildings are frequently used as overwintering sites for hibernating adults in Manitoba.

Milbert's Tortoise Shell

Nymphalis milberti (Godart), 1819
= *Aglais milberti*

Plate 21 No. 7, 8, 9

Description: 41-53 mm. Dorsally the wings are brownish-black basally with a submarginal yellow and orange band and black borders. The hindwings have a row of blue spots in the black borders. Ventrally both wings are brownish black with wide light brown borders.

Life Cycle: The larval food plant is Stinging Nettle (*Urtica dioica*).

In the spring the females lay clusters of several hundred (up to 900) pale green eggs on the underside of the leaves of the food plant. After hatching, the young larvae feed communally in a webbed shelter until the third instar. Older larvae feed singly and live in folded leaves. The mature larvae are usually black mottled with white, with orange stripes dorsally, green stripes laterally and seven rows of short spines. There are two whitish bumps on the head capsule. Larvae are very prone to parasitism by parasitic Hymenoptera in Manitoba. R. Westwood recorded rates of approximately 90 percent parasitism in colonies of Milbert's Tortoise Shell larvae from Winnipeg, Brandon and Souris reared from early instars between the years of 1972 and 1978. The pupae are off-white, gray, blackish or pale green with a golden sheen; they are speckled with dark brown and covered in short spines. This species overwinters in both the pupal and adult stages.

In Manitoba adults have been recorded from April 5 to November 4. Adults are most numerous from mid-June to early August and there are probably two generations per year.

Habitat: Glades, trails, roads, stream and river banks, and meadows usually near or in forested areas.

Range: The Yukon through central and southern Canada to Newfoundland, southward to West Virginia, Oklahoma and California.

Milbert's Tortoise Shell larvae on Stinging Nettle, Winnipeg, Manitoba. July 14, 1976.

Milbert's Tortoise Shell larvae on Stinging Nettle, Winnipeg, Manitoba. July 14, 1976.

Manitoba Records:

Agassiz Provincial Forest, Berens River, Beulah, Boundary Lake, Brandon, Carberry, Cartwright, Churchill, Cowan, Cromer, Culross, Delta, Duck Mountain, Elm Creek, Fort Alexander, Glenboro, Grand Beach, Grandview, Hecla Island, Little Grand Rapids, Lundar, Lyleton, Melbourne, Miami, Mile 200 Hudson Bay Railway, Moose Lake, Northwest Angle Provincial Forest, Oak Hammock, Pine Ridge, Ponton, Riding Mountain, St. Malo, Sandilands Provincial Forest, Sandy Hook, Selkirk, Simonhouse Lake, Souris, Sprague, Spruce Woods Provincial Forest, Stony Mountain, Teulon, The Pas, Thompson, Victoria Beach, Vivian, Wabowden, Westbourne, Westray, Whiteshell Provincial Park and Winnipeg.

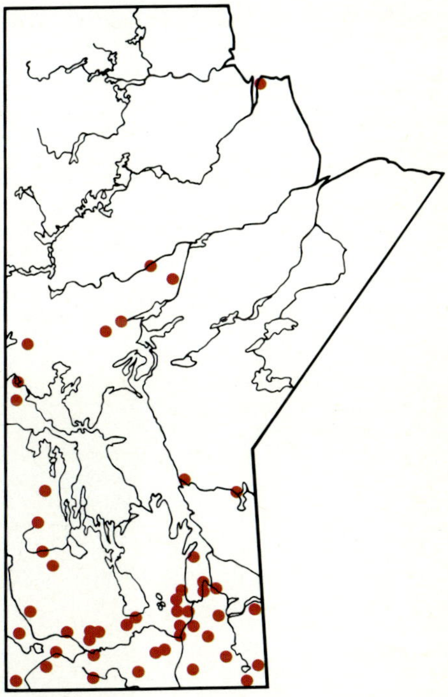

Subspecies:

Three subspecies are recognized. The nominate subspecies *Nymphalis milberti milberti* occurs in Manitoba.

Remarks:

Although primarily a woodland species this butterfly is found throughout the province and should be looked for wherever there are large stands of Stinging Nettle. It is on the wing very early in the spring and and has been observed taking sap from Manitoba Maple. Males are often seen perched on the ground waiting for passing females. Adults regularly visit a wide range of flowers including Thistles, Goldenrod and Lilac. In late fall prior to hibernation adults seek shelter in wood piles, hollow trees and unheated buildings.

American Painted Lady

Vanessa virginiensis (Drury), 1773

Plate 22 No. 1, 2, 3

Description: 44-59 mm. This butterfly is orange dorsally. The forewings have a brownish-black apex containing white spots. The hindwings have a submarginal row of blue-eyed black spots. Ventrally the wings are marked with brown, white and black and the lower part of the forewings is pink in colour. Each hindwing has two large black-ringed, blue-eyed spots. Overwintering adults are smaller and paler with reduced markings, while those from the early summer generation are larger and brighter.

Similar Species: The Painted Lady has five small submarginal eye-spots in each ventral hindwing.

Life Cycle: The larvae of the American Painted Lady feed on composites including Cudweed (*Gnaphalium* sp.), Plantain-leaved Pussy-toes (*Antennaria plantaginifolia*), Pearly Everlasting (*Anaphalis margaritacea*), Sagebrush (*Artemisia* sp.), Burdock (*Arctium* sp.) and Ironweed (*Veronia fasciculata*).

The females lay the yellowish-green ribbed eggs singly on the top of the leaves of the food plant. The newly hatched larvae feed on the leaves and build a shelter from silk and leaf parts at the top of the host plant. Older larvae will frequently feed on the flowers. The mature larvae are black with yellow cross-bands, have round white spots on each side of the abdominal segments and four rows of black branching spines with red bases. Pupation often takes place within the silk and leaf shelters. The pupae are brown or gray with orange-tipped tubercles; occasionally they may be golden green marked with purplish-brown. The American Painted Lady may overwinter either as an adult or in the pupal stage (Howe 1975; Orsak 1977; Dornfeld 1980).

Fields near Minnedosa, Manitoba. August, 1986.

Adults have been recorded from May 7 to September 5. The number of generations per year vary from one in Newfoundland to four farther south, with two generations per year in Manitoba.

Habitat: Forest openings, meadows, fields, stream banks, roads and farmyards.

Range: Central and southern Canada from coast to coast, the entire United States and southward to Colombia and the Galapagos Islands, off the west coast of South America (Ferris and Brown 1981; Pyle 1984).

Manitoba Records: Agassiz Provincial Forest, Beulah, Birtle, Cartwright, Churchill, Cromer, Culross, Elm Creek, George Lake, Grand Beach, Hadashville, Oak Hammock, Pine Ridge, Rennie, Riding Mountain, Sandilands Provincial Forest, Telford, Thompson, Turtle Mountain Provincial Park, Victoria Beach, Whiteshell Provincial Park and Winnipeg.

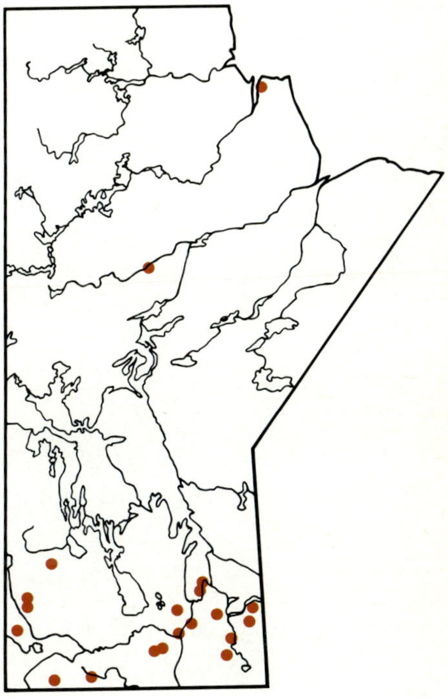

Subspecies: No subspecies are recognized.

Remarks: This species was once called Hunter's Butterfly and members of this genus are commonly called Thistle Butterflies. The American Painted Lady although found in many areas of the province is not common. Newly emerged males sometimes visit mud puddles and both sexes visit Dogbane, Milkweed, Vetch, Goldenrod, Marigold and Aster for nectar. The flight is swift and as there is no evidence of this species migrating into Manitoba, it probably overwinters here.

Painted Lady

Vanessa cardui (Linnaeus), 1758

Plate 22 No. 4, 5

Description: 45-67 mm. The Painted Lady is rosy orange dorsally. The forewings have black tips containing white spots, blackish borders and black blotches. The hindwings have black spotted margins and a submarginal row of black spots. Ventrally the wings are marked with brown, white and black. The forewings are dominated by large rosy pink patches while the hindwings contain a submarginal row of five eye-spots. The rosy hue is less obvious in worn specimens. Females are similar to males. Migratory individuals are smaller and duller than non-migratory adults.

Similar Species: The American Painted Lady differs as described under that species.

Life Cycle: The larval food plants are mostly composites including Thistle (*Cirsium* sp. and *Carduus* sp.), Knapweed (*Centaurea* sp.), Burdock (*Arctium* sp.), Groundsel (*Senecio* sp.), Sunflower (*Helianthus* sp.), Pearly Everlasting (*Anaphalis margaritacea*) and Cudweed (*Gnaphalium* sp.).

The pale green, ribbed eggs are laid singly on the host plant. The larvae feed within nests formed from silk and leaf parts. Although variable in appearance, mature larvae are yellowish-green mottled with black, with several rows of yellowish branching spines and hairy black heads. Occasionally larvae are purplish with yellow dorsal stripes. The pupae are brown, tan or gray with gold-tipped tubercles.

In Manitoba adults have been recorded from May 4 to October 10. The Painted Lady probably does not overwinter in Manitoba and populations consist of the progeny of adults or pupae overwintering in southern California and Mexico. There are two generations of the Painted Lady in Manitoba each year.

Habitat: Fields, meadows, open areas, towns, farmyards and forests.

Range: Europe, Asia, Africa and South America. In North America as far north as Chesterfield Inlet on the western coast of Hudson Bay.

Sunflower field, Glenboro, Manitoba. August, 1988.

Manitoba Records: Agassiz Provincial Forest, Beulah, Binscarth, Birds Hill, Brokenhead, Carberry, Cartwright, Churchill, Cowan, Culross, Cypress River, Deleau, Duck Mountain, Gillam, Grand Beach, Lyleton, McCreary, Oak Hammock, Onanole, Pine Ridge, Riding Mountain, Sandilands Provincial Forest, Selkirk, Sprague, Spruce Woods Provincial Forest, Teulon, The Pas, Thompson, Turtle Mountain, Victoria Beach, Whiteshell Provincial Park, Winnipeg and York Factory.

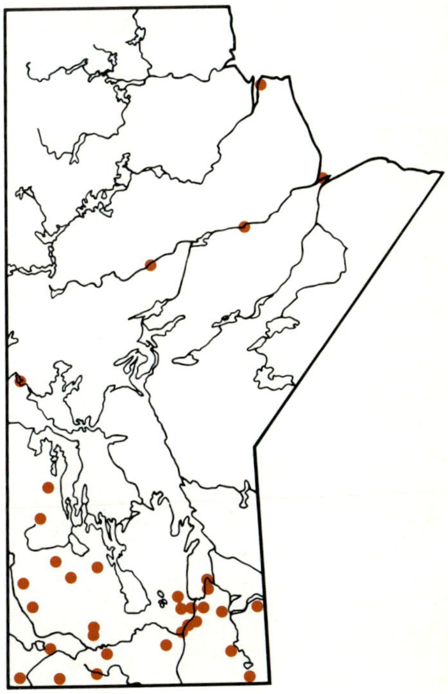

Subspecies: No subspecies are recognized.

Remarks: The Painted Lady, also known as the Thistle Butterfly, is the most widely distributed butterfly in the world. Although uncommon and in some years entirely absent, it occasionally becomes so abundant in Manitoba that it is a pest of sunflower crops. Periodic increases in the populations of the Painted Lady at the overwintering sites trigger mass migrations of adults northward. Large scale northward migrations from the southern wintering sites reached Manitoba in 1949, 1952, 1962 and 1973. In July 1973 migrating adults reached Churchill. Since 1973 no significant migrations are known to have reached this province. Adults have a swift, nervous flight and visit a wide variety of flowers for nectar. Males perch on the bare ground during the afternoon, repeatedly returning to a favourite site after chasing intruders.

Red Admiral

Vanessa atalanta (Linnaeus), 1758

Plate 22 No. 6, 7

Description: 43-57 mm. The Red Admiral is brownish-black dorsally. The forewing tips are black and contain white spots and a prominent orange-red band. Ventrally the forewings are marked with black, brown, blue, white and a pink band. Dorsally the hindwings have black-dotted orange-red borders and ventrally they are mottled with brown and black and have iridescent green and/or blue scales. Males and females are occasionally difficult to distinguish.

Life Cycle: The larval food plants include Stinging Nettle (*Urtica dioica*), Wood Nettle (*Laportea canadensis*) and Pellitory (*Parietaria pensylvanica*).

The pale green eggs are laid singly on the leaves of the larval food plant from midday to early afternoon. The young larvae build shelters from a single folded leaf. As the larvae mature they form larger shelters from several folded leaves. The larvae may be black with rows of yellow spots or entirely mottled with pale greenish, brown or white. The cuticle is covered in several rows of branched spines. The pupae are brown or gray with gold tubercles and may be formed on the host plant or an object nearby. The Red Admiral overwinters as a pupa or adult in the southern parts of its range and migrates to the northern United States and Canada in the spring (Klots 1951; Howe 1975; Bitzer et al. 1979).

In Manitoba adults have been recorded from May 4 to August 31. There are two generations during each summer in this province.

Habitat: Fields, meadows, open forests, farmyards, towns, parks and gardens.

Range: Europe, Asia and Africa. In North America from coast to coast from northern Canada, the Yukon, The Northwest Territories, southward through the United States and Mexico to Guatemala.

Manitoba Records: Agassiz Provincial Forest, Aweme, Beulah, Binscarth, Birds Hill, Black River, Carberry, Cartwright, Churchill, Cowan, Cromer, Culross, Deleau, Delta, Duck Mountain, Erinview, Fort Alexander, Grand Beach, Grand Marais, Grand Rapids, Gypsumville, Hecla Island, Katimik Lake, Libau, Lyleton, Margaret, McCreary, Melbourne, Moosehorn, Northwest Angle Provincial Forest, Oak Hammock, Pine Ridge, Pine River, Riding Mountain, Sandilands Provincial Forest, Sandridge, Sandy Hook, Sclater, Selkirk, Seven Sisters, Spruce Woods Provincial Forest, The Pas, Thompson, Tolstoi, Treesbank, Turtle Mountain Provincial Park, Victoria Beach, Whiteshell Provincial Park and Winnipeg.

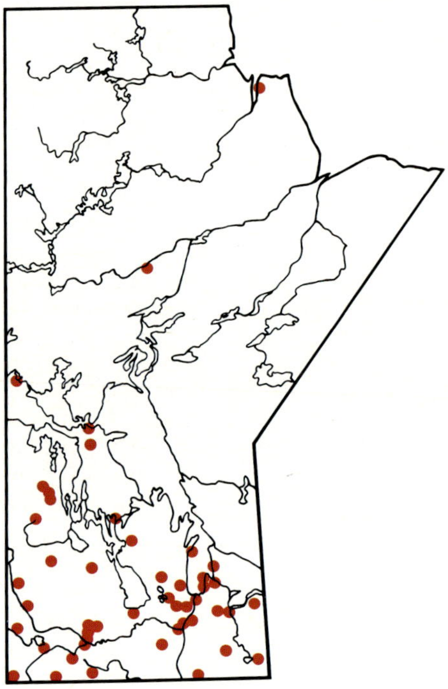

Subspecies: *Vanessa atalanta rubria* is the only subspecies recognized in North America.

Remarks: Although often common in Manitoba the Red Admiral may be nearly absent some years. Adults migrate in a fashion similar to that of the Painted Lady, but usually in much smaller numbers. The last recorded migration in Manitoba occurred on June 3, 1977 when large numbers of adults were observed flying northward throughout the area extending from Culross to Cowan, approximately 400 km. This migration lasted until June 16 when northward flying individuals were still numerous in the Elm Creek and Winnipeg areas. Adults feed on sap, rotting fruit, garbage and dung, and will occasionally take nectar from Thistle, Aster, Alfalfa, Red Clover, Milkweed and Dogbane. They have a swift jerky flight and are very wary. Males will perch on sidewalks, stones or bare ground, showing strong territorial behavior by chasing other butterflies, birds or even blowing leaves. The males are very mobile and if one leaves a preferred perching site it is quickly replaced by another.

Buckeye

Junonia coenia Hübner, 1822
= *Precis coenia*

Plate 22 No. 8

Description: 33-63 mm. The wings are brown dorsally. The forewings have two orange bars, a whitish band and two eye-spots, one near the apex and the other a little lower down. The hindwings have a prominent eye-spot near the upper margin and a smaller one beneath it. Ventrally the forewings are similar to, but paler than the upper surface. The hindwings are rosy brown or buff with small, vague eye-spots.

Life Cycle: Larval food plants include Ribgrass (*Plantago lanceolata*), Toadflax (*Linaria* sp.) and Snapdragon (*Antirrhinum* sp.). The larvae are blackish-gray, striped and spotted with orange and yellow. The cuticle is covered in short, branching black spines. The pupae are mottled pale brown. The Buckeye is a migratory species and cannot overwinter in the northern part of its range. Adults have been recorded in Manitoba from July 1 to July 25 (Klots 1951; Howe 1975).

Habitat: Open and cutover areas, fields and roadsides.

Range: Southern Manitoba, Ontario and Quebec and most of the United States, southward to northern Mexico.

Manitoba Records: Birtle, Husavik, Miniota, Riding Mountain, Sandilands Provincial Forest and Winnipeg.

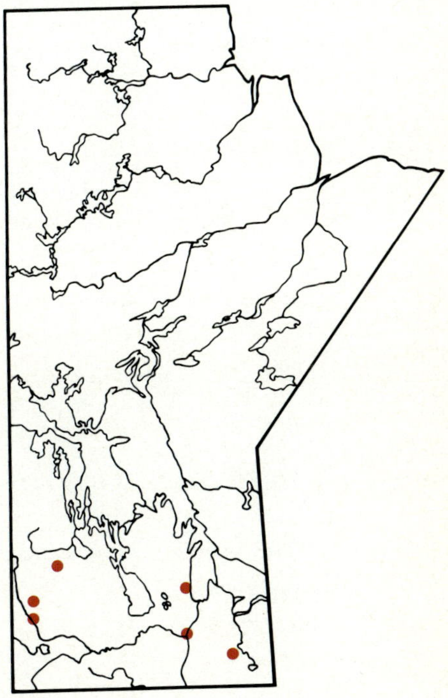

Remarks: Although the Buckeye does not normally breed in Manitoba, J. Polusny (pers. comm.) reported observing a colony at Sandilands Provincial Forest in early August 1976. In addition, there are records of nine specimens having been collected in this province between 1930 and 1941.

Subfamily

LIMENITIDINAE: ADMIRALS

In Manitoba there are two representatives of this subfamily. The Admirals are medium to large size butterflies and many of the species in North America often hybridize where their ranges overlap. The spines that cover the cuticle of fifth instar larvae are topped by a rosette of smaller spines. In some individuals the spines may be reduced to bristly tubercles.

White Admiral

Limenitis arthemis (Drury), 1773
= *Basilarchia arthemis*

Plate 22 No. 9, 10, 11

Description: 55-72 mm. The White Admiral is black dorsally, with a prominent white band across each wing. The hindwings contain a submarginal row of red spots and submarginal blue or green crescents. Ventrally the white bands are similar to the dorsal surface and the submarginal red spots are larger and may be fused to form a complete band. Females are similar to males in colouration but are generally larger.

Life Cycle: Aspen (*Populus* sp.), Balsam Poplar (*Populus balsamifera*) and Birch (*Betula* sp.) are the preferred host plants of the White Admiral.

The pale green eggs are laid at the tip of the leaf of the host plant, usually five to 15 metres from the ground. When they are partly grown, the larvae build shelters (hibernacula) composed of a rolled leaf tied with silk to the food plant. The larvae then enter an overwintering diapause within the shelters and resume feeding in the spring. The mature larvae are mottled with white, olive and greenish-yellow and have enlarged humps each containing two long dark bristles behind the head capsule. The larvae resemble bird droppings. The pupae are cream-coloured, with enlarged wing cases and a dark projection on the back resembling a ''saddle-horn'' (Opler and Krizek 1984).

Adults have been recorded in Manitoba from May 30 to September 9, being most common in late June. There is usually one generation per year in this province although occasionally a second generation occurs with adults emerging in late August.

Habitat: In or near deciduous forests, along trails, roads and in forest openings. Occasionally adults are seen in farmyards and towns.

Range: Alaska and the Yukon across southern Canada to Newfoundland, southward to New York, Pennsylvania, North Dakota and Montana.

Manitoba Records: Agassiz Provincial Forest, Anola, Asessippi Provincial Park, Assean Lake, Aweme, Berens River, Birds Hill, Boundary Lake, Brokenhead, Carberry, Cartwright, Cowan, Culross, Deleau, Duck Mountain, Elm Creek, Erinview, Flin Flon, Fort Alexander, Gillam, Grand Beach, Grand Rapids, Gypsumville, Hazel Creek at Hwy. 15, Katimik Lake, Komarno, Koostatak, Lauder Sandhills, Little Grand Rapids, Lundar, Lyleton, Lynn Lake, McCreary, Miami, Moosehorn, Norris Lake, Northwest Angle Provincial Forest, Norway House, Oscar Point, Overflowing River, Pictou, Pikwitonei, Pine Ridge, Pointe du Bois, Porcupine Provincial Forest, Reed Lake, Riding Mountain, Sandilands Provincial Forest, Sandy Hook, Schist Lake, Sclater, Seven Sisters, Simonhouse Lake, Sprague, Spruce Woods Provincial Park, Stead, The Pas, Thompson, Tolstoi, Turtle Mountain Provincial Park, Two Rivers, Victoria Beach, Wallace Lake, Waugh, Westbourne, Whiteshell Provincial Park, Whitemouth Lake, William River, Winnipeg and Winnipeg Beach.

Subspecies: *Limenitis arthemis arthemis* occurs in southeastern Manitoba and eastward to Newfoundland. *Limenitis arthemis rubrofasciata* occurs in the western and central parts of Manitoba and hybridizes with the eastern subspecies where their ranges overlap. The red spots in the hindwings of *rubrofasciata* are more developed dorsally and form complete, fused bands ventrally compared to the separate spots found in *arthemis*.

Remarks: The White Admiral is most common in forested areas in Manitoba. Populations fluctuate from year to year, becoming very abundant in some years. Adults have a strong flight, alternating flapping and gliding, as they follow forest trails or edges of woods. They frequently perch on branches quite high in trees and are best observed when sipping at mud puddles or feeding on dung. Males have a habit of slowly raising and lowering their outspread wings when at rest.

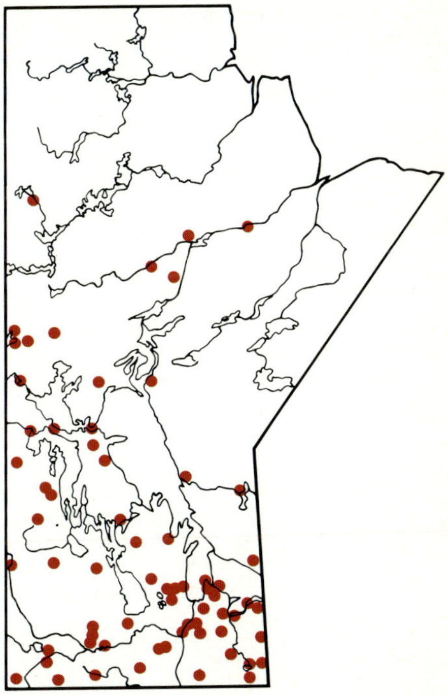

Viceroy

Limenitis archippus (Cramer), 1776

= *Basilarchia archippus*

Plate 22 No. 12, 13

Description: 56-80 mm. The dorsal and ventral surfaces of the wings of both sexes are orange with black veins and white-spotted black borders and a more or less developed black line across each hindwing. Females are generally larger than males.

Similar Species: The Monarch is larger and has two rows of submarginal spots in the black borders of the wings whereas the Viceroy has a single row of spots. The Monarch also lacks the black line across the hindwings.

Life Cycle: The larvae of the Viceroy feed on Willows (*Salix* sp.), Poplar and Aspen (*Populus* spp.).

The spherical pale-green eggs are laid singly on the tip of the food plant leaf, usually in mid-afternoon. Females prefer ovipositing on small trees and place only two or three eggs on each tree. The larvae consume the egg shells after hatching. They feed only at night, resting under the leaves or on twigs by day. While feeding, the larvae form a ball about the size of a pea, composed of bits of leaves. This ball dangles from the base of the leaf on which the larvae are feeding. The mature larvae are mottled brown or olive and are very similar to those of the White Admiral. Like the latter the larvae of the Viceroy construct a hibernaculum in which to spend the winter. The pupae also resemble that of the White Admiral.

In Manitoba, adults have been recorded from May 28 to September 4. There are two generations per year here but adults are on the wing all summer.

Habitat: Scrubby, wet areas, wet meadows, marshes, riverbanks, ponds and lakes. In southern Manitoba the Viceroy prefers roadside ditches.

Range: The Yukon, the Northwest Territories and every province of Canada, in most of the United States and in northern Mexico.

Manitoba Records: Agassiz Provincial Forest, Birds Hill, Cartwright, Culross, Deleau, Delta, Elm Creek, Libau, Lundar, Lyleton, Lynn Lake, McCreary, Melbourne, Miami, Moose Lake, Norris Lake, Northwest Angle Provincial Forest, Oak Hammock, Overflowing River, Pine Ridge, Riding Mountain, Sandilands Provincial Forest, Selkirk, Seven Sisters, Sipiwesk, Spruce Woods Provincial Park, Telford, The Pas, Tolstoi, Turtle Mountain Provincial Park, Victoria Beach, Wabowden, William River and Winnipeg.

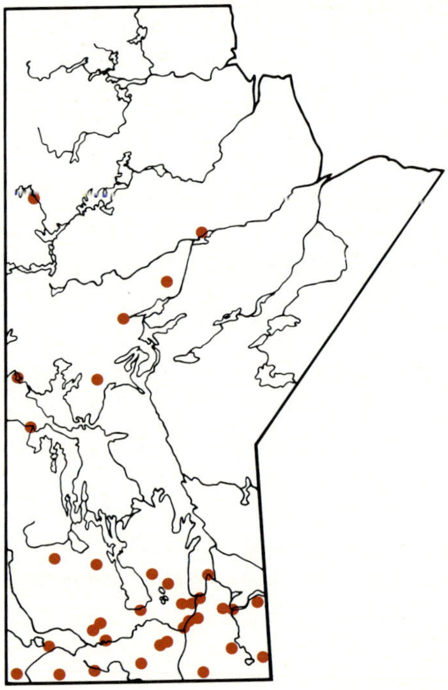

Subspecies: The nominate subspecies *Limenitis archippus archippus* occurs in Canada.

Remarks: The Viceroy, although found regularly in Manitoba, is not abundant. It is sometimes called the Mimic because of its resemblance to the Monarch. The Viceroy feeds on a wide variety of flowers preferring Asters. Adults also feed at mud puddles and on dung. Males often patrol a small area and perch on bare ground or on low willows, repeatedly returning to the same perch. Adults have a slow flapping and gliding flight.

Family

SATYRIDAE: SATYRS AND WOOD NYMPHS

There are about 3000 species in the family Satyridae worldwide. Approximately 50 species are found in North America, 30 in Canada and 19 in Manitoba. Members of this family are closely related to the Brush-footed butterflies (Nymphalidae) and some authors treat the Satyridae as a subfamily of the Nymphalidae. Like the Nymphalidae the forelegs of the butterflies in the Satyridae are poorly developed in both sexes. The conspicuously swollen veins at the base of the forewings in the Satyridae help distinguish them from other families. Manitoba species are dull brown to gray and often have a series of dark round spots, especially in the forewings. There are often patches of specialized scent scales (androconia) in either the fore or hindwings or both. Adults are sedentary, seldom moving far from host plants and often occurring in isolated colonies. Many species have cryptic colour patterns, which when combined with an erratic bobbing flight often makes observation difficult, especially in forest habitats. Adults seldom take nectar, but will feed on sap, rotting fruit or dung. The larvae feed on grasses and sedges and are usually green, striped and have forked tails.

Subfamily

ELYMNIINAE = LETHINAE

This subfamily has many members in eastern Asia, but few in North America. They are medium-sized brown butterflies with prominent eye-spots dorsally. Ventrally, the eye-spots are surrounded by shades of lavender and brown. Adults have a swift and erratic flight and prefer shady forests or open marshes.

Enodia anthedon

Northern Pearly Eye

Enodia anthedon (A.H. Clark), 1936
= *Lethe anthedon*

Plate 23 No. 1, 2, 3

Description: 45-54 mm. This butterfly is grayish-brown dorsally, with a purplish sheen on the underside. The forewings have five eye-spots on both the upper and lower surfaces. The hindwings have five eye-spots dorsally and six ventrally. The edges of the wings are slightly scalloped. The female is usually paler than the male.

Similar Species: The Eyed Brown is paler and more yellowish, especially on the underside. The eye-spots are smaller and the wing edges are not scalloped. The Little Wood Satyr is smaller and darker and has fewer eye-spots.

Life Cycle: The larvae of the Northern Pearly Eye feed on a number of different grass species including Purple Oat Grass (*Schizachne purpurascens*) and Reed Canary Grass (*Phalaris arundinacea*).

The greenish-white barrel-shaped eggs are laid singly on the host plant. Larvae hatch in the fall and enter into an overwintering diapause, resuming feeding in the spring. The mature larvae are yellowish-green striped with dark green and yellow. There are two red-tipped horns on the head capsule and two pink-tipped tails on the last abdominal segment. The pupae are glossy green or yellow-green and the top of the head and wing cases are cream (Klots 1951; Hopper 1973; Pyle 1981).

In Manitoba adults have been recorded from June 15 to August 8, being most common in July. Males emerge about a week before females. There is probably one generation per year in Manitoba.

Habitat: Damp deciduous forest edges, clearings, glades, roads and trails, especially where the underbrush is thick.

Range: Alberta across southern Canada to Prince Edward Island, southward to Georgia, Alabama, Arkansas, Kansas and North Dakota.

Northern Pearly Eye, Spruce Woods Provincial Park, Manitoba. July 13, 1974.

Manitoba Records: Agassiz Provincial Forest, Aweme, Berens River, Beulah, Birds Hill, Birtle, Boundary Lake, Brokenhead, Cartwright, Culross, Duck Mountain, Elm Creek, Eriksdale, Flin Flon, George Lake, Grand Beach, Hecla Island, Inglis, McCreary, Miami, Miniota, Norris Lake, Northwest Angle Provincial Forest, Pine Ridge, Riding Mountain National Park, Sandilands Provincial Forest, Schist Lake, Selkirk, Seven Sisters, Teulon, The Pas, Tolstoi, Victoria Beach, Waugh, Whiteshell Provincial Park and Winnipeg.

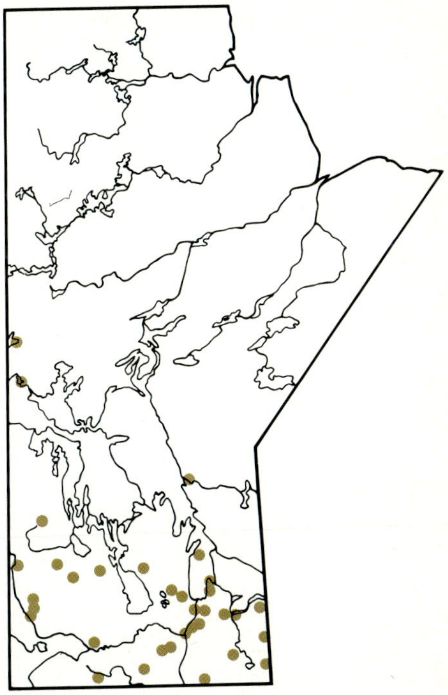

Subspecies: Two subspecies are recognized. *Enodia anthedon borealis* occurs in southern Manitoba.

Remarks: The Northern Pearly Eye is sometimes quite common in the forested areas of southern Manitoba. Adult observation is made difficult by their erratic flight and tendency to fly into heavy undergrowth. They are best observed when they congregate at moist patches on forest trails after showers or at carrion, sap or dung. The butterflies frequently perch on low shrubbery or tree trunks and when alarmed quickly disappear into heavy forest. The Northern Pearly Eye is common in the Sandilands and Agassiz Provincial Forests.

Eyed Brown

Satyrodes eurydice (Johansson), 1763

= *Lethe eurydice*

Plate 23 No. 4, 5, 6, 7

Description: 38-51 mm. The wings are mouse brown to very pale tan dorsally and usually somewhat darker basally. There are five occasionally poorly developed eye-spots on the upper and lower surfaces of the forewings. The hindwings usually have five eye-spots dorsally and six ventrally. The wings are paler ventrally and crossed by zig-zag lines. Females are larger than males and both sexes may be quite variable in appearance.

Life Cycle: Larval food plants include Awned Sedge (*Carex atherodes*) and Erect Sedge (*Carex stricta*).

The eggs are laid on the food plant or on nearby objects. Larvae hatch in the late summer and feed until they reach the third or fourth instar whereupon they enter into an overwintering diapause and resume feeding the next spring. The mature larvae are pale green with dark green stripes. The head capsule and the last abdominal segment each have a pair of red-tipped horn-like projections. The pupae are dark green, striped with buff and suspended by a cremaster from the host plant.

In Manitoba adults have been recorded from June 13 to September 2, being most common in July. Here the flight and emergence periods are quite prolonged and there is one generation per year.

Habitat: Open sedge marshes and wet meadows. In Manitoba adults are commonly found in wet grassy roadside ditches with scattered small willows.

Range: Southern Northwest Territories southeastward through southern Canada to Nova Scotia. Southward to Delaware, Illinois and North Dakota (Opler and Krizek 1984).

Manitoba Records: Agassiz Provincial Forest, Aweme, Beulah, Birds Hill, Birtle, Brandon, Carberry, Cartwright, Cooks Creek, Culross, Delta, Duck Mountain, Elm Creek, Eriksdale, Fort Alexander, Grand Beach, Grand Marais, Hazel Creek at Hwy. 15, Hecla Island, Inwood, Komarno, Libau, Lundar, Lyleton, Neelin, Northwest Angle Provincial Forest, Oak Hammock, Pine Ridge, Riding Mountain, Sand Ridge, Sandilands Provincial Forest, Seven Sisters, Sprague, Stuartburn, Telford, Teulon, The Pas, Tolstoi, Uno, Victoria Beach, Whiteshell Provincial Park and Winnipeg.

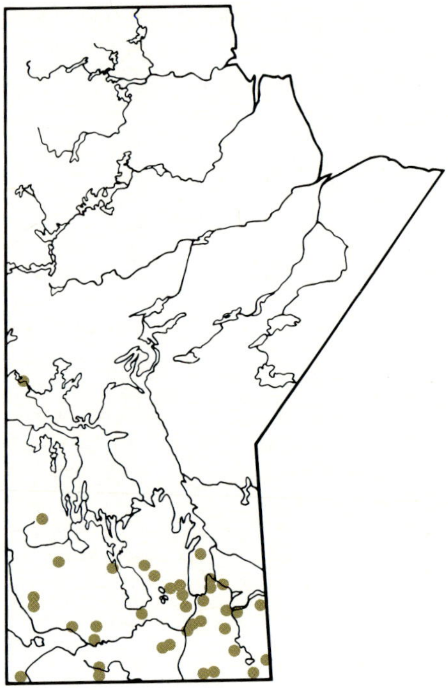

Subspecies: Two subspecies are recognized. Only *Satyrodes eurydice eurydice* occurs in Manitoba.

Remarks: The Eyed Brown is common in open areas, often far removed from forests. In Manitoba, populations are quite local, being concentrated in small tracts of suitable habitat. Although never found in large numbers, this species is common in roadside drainage ditches in many areas of southern Manitoba. Adults have a weak, "dancing" flight. Males search out females by frequently dipping down among grasses and vegetation where the more sedentary females remain concealed. Adults have been observed feeding on sap and on nectar from Swamp Milkweed and Joe-pye Weed.

Subfamily

SATYRINAE

In Manitoba, members of this family are mostly dull brown, grayish or blackish, often with fulvous or reddish flushes and a series of round eye-spots dorsally. Most have a cryptic colour pattern on the underside of the wings which renders them nearly invisible when they alight and close their wings. A few species are restricted to the northern tundra or to alpine summits. Most species have one generation per year but some may require two years to complete their life cycle. Most overwinter as larvae and adults rarely feed at flowers.

Little Wood Satyr

Megisto cymela (Cramer), 1777
= *Euptychia cymela*

Plate 23 No. 8, 9, 10

Description: 31-40 mm. The Little Wood Satyr is dark grayish-brown dorsally, with two eye-spots in each wing. The eye-spot on the upper hindwing is frequently much reduced. Ventrally the wings are paler with two prominent eye-spots on each wing. The hindwings usually contain an additional small eye-spot. Each eye-spot is ringed with yellowish scales and contains twin metallic "pupils". Females are often paler and larger than males.

Life Cycle: Larval food plants include Orchard Grass (*Dactylis glomerata*) and Kentucky Blue Grass (*Poa pratensis*).

The yellowish-green eggs are laid singly on the leaves of the host plant. Larvae usually hatch at night and in the fall, when partly grown, enter into an overwintering diapause. The mature larvae are pale greenish-brown with longitudinal stripes and are covered with small tubercles, each bearing a reddish brown hair. The head capsules are whitish and mottled with dark brown. The pupae are pale brown mottled with darker brown and have a strong curve at the end of the abdomen (Oliver 1982).

In Manitoba adults have been recorded from May 31 to July 23. There is one generation per year. Males peak in mid-June and females are most abundant in late June.

Habitat: Deciduous and open pine forests, glades and second growth areas. In Manitoba adults are common in areas of Hazel bushes.

Range: Saskatchewan through southern Canada to Nova Scotia, southward to Florida, Texas and Colorado.

Manitoba Records: Agassiz Provincial Forest, Aweme, Beulah, Birds Hill, Birtle, Carberry, Cartwright, Cowan, Culross, Elm Creek, Fort Alexander, Grand Beach, Gypsumville, Killarney, La Riviere, Miami, Pine Ridge, Riding Mountain, Ruthenia, Sandilands Provincial Forest, Selkirk, Seven Sisters, Spruce Woods Provincial Park, Stony Mountain, Tolstoi, Victoria Beach, Whiteshell Provincial Park and Winnipeg.

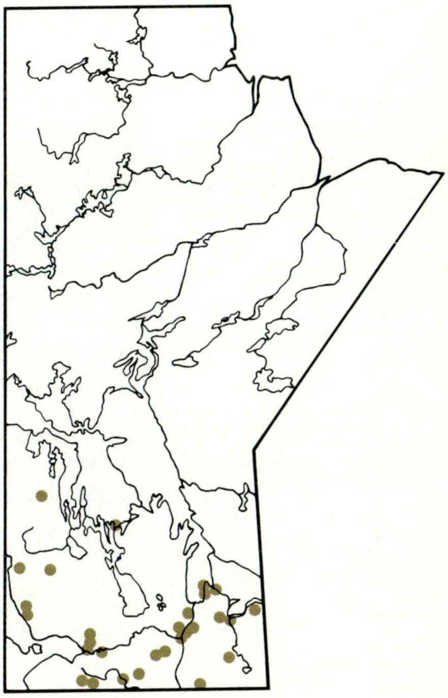

Subspecies: Two subspecies are recognized, of which *Megisto cymela cymela* occurs in Manitoba.

Remarks: This butterfly is our only representative of a large group of New World tropical butterflies. The Little Wood Satyr is common in the wooded areas of southern Manitoba, but seems to have disappeared from the intensely farmed areas. Adults bask in the sun with wings spread while perching on tree leaves or ground litter. Although observed feeding on aphid honeydew they rarely visit flowers. They have a dancing, skipping flight and as they weave through woods or underbrush, they often disappear from sight, only to reappear several metres away.

Ringlet

Coenonympha tullia (Müller), 1764 = *Coenonympha inornata* W.H. Edwards, 1861

Plate 23 No. 11, 12, 13, 14, 15, 16, 17

Description: 29-37 mm. The Ringlet is brownish-yellow to rich ochre dorsally. Sometimes there is a trace of an eye-spot near the apex of the forewings. Ventrally the forewings are brownish-yellow with gray tips which usually contain an eye-spot. The hindwings are gray with a greenish tinge basally and a variable broken whitish band across the middle. They also contain small, poorly developed eye-spots. Females are more brightly coloured than males which are usually suffused with darker scales.

Life Cycle: Larval food plants include various Grasses (Gramineae) and less commonly Sedges (Cyperaceae).

The pale green or yellowish barrel-shaped eggs are vertically ribbed. Females lay eggs on the host plant or on nearby objects. Larvae feed until they reach the third or fourth instar and then enter an overwintering diapause, resuming feeding in the spring. The mature larvae are brown, tan, green or olive with longitudinal stripes. The pupae are translucent green or brown, with darker stripes on the wing cases. They are usually suspended from the host plant (Klots 1951; Howe 1975; Dornfeld 1980).

In Manitoba, adults have been recorded from May 16 to July 20, being most common in June. Here there is one generation per year.

Habitat: Prairie, dry meadows, roadsides and abandoned grassy farmyards.

Range: Europe and Asia. In North America from Alaska through Canada to Newfoundland, southward to New England, Great Lakes states, the Great Plains and California.

Manitoba Records: Agassiz Provincial Forest, Asessippi Provincial Park, Berens River, Bellsite, Beulah, Birds Hill, Birtle, Binscarth, Brandon, Brokenhead, Carberry, Cartwright, Cooks Creek, Cowan, Cromer, Cypress River, Culross, Deleau, Delta, Duck Mountain, Elm Creek, Eriksdale, Flin Flon, Fort Alexander, Gillam, Gimli, Grahamdale, Grand Beach, Grand Rapids, Gypsumville, Hazel Creek at Hwy. 15, Inglis, Jacam, Katimik Lake, Kelwood, Killarney, Lauder Sandhills, Lundar, Lyleton, Marchand, Miami, Melbourne, McCreary, Miniota, Neepawa, Ninette, Norway House, Oak Hammock, Oak Lake, Oscar Point, Overflowing River, Paint Lake, Pine Ridge, Pointe du Bois, Ponton, Porcupine Provincial Forest, Riding Mountain, Roseisle, Sand Ridge, Sandilands Provincial Forest, Sandy Hook, Selkirk, Sprague, Spruce Woods Provincial Forest, Stonewall, The Pas, Thompson, Tolstoi, Treesbank, Victoria Beach, Whiteshell Provincial Park, William River, Winnipeg and York Factory.

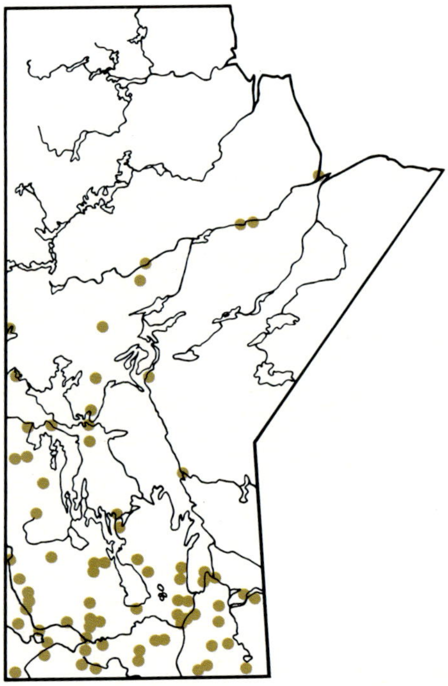

Mixed-grass prairie near Pine Ridge, Manitoba. May 26, 1988.

Subspecies: This complex and variable species has been divided into a large number of geographic races or subspecies. Nineteen have been recognized in North America. *Coenonympha tullia inornata*, (Inornate Ringlet) is found across Manitoba north of Riding Mountain. *Coenonympha tullia benjamini*, (Prairie Ringlet) is the dryland subspecies found in the prairie grasslands of southern Manitoba. The latter is brighter, has better developed eye-spots and ventrally is more brownish-gray while *inornata* is hoary gray. Hybrids representing mixtures of both subspecies are commonly encountered where their ranges overlap. A recently discovered colony of smaller and darker specimens at Gillam may constitute a new subspecies.

Remarks: The Prairie Ringlet is common over most of southern Manitoba and may be harboured on any patch of grass that has lain undisturbed for a few years. The Inornate Ringlet occurs throughout much of Manitoba north of Riding Mountain National Park. Adults have a slow, jerky and bouncy flight. Males often patrol across patches of grass for hours on end seeking females. Mating pairs are seen in the morning, with the females carrying the males when in flight. Unlike other Satyrs, the Ringlet avidly visits flowers, preferring yellow composites.

Common Wood Nymph

Cercyonis pegala (Fabricius), 1775

Plate 23 No. 18, 19, 20, 21

Description: 43-57 mm. This butterfly is dark brown dorsally, with two eye-spots in each forewing and frequently a poorly developed eye-spot in each hindwing. Ventrally the forewings have two eye-spots and the hindwings have from none to five small eye-spots. Females are larger and paler than males and have much larger eye-spots. In addition, those on the underside are conspicuously ringed with yellowish scales while on the dorsal surface these rings are somewhat paler yellow.

Life Cycle: The larvae feed on a wide variety of grasses, including Wild Oat (*Avena fatua*). The yellowish eggs are barrel shaped and vertically ribbed. They are laid singly on dried or live grass stems in the late summer. One female may oviposit up to 300 eggs at a rate of five to 30 eggs per day. Larvae begin to hatch approximately 14 to 25 days after the eggs have been laid and immediately enter into an overwintering diapause. Larvae begin feeding in the spring and take two and a half to three months to reach the pupal stage. The mature larvae are downy, yellowish green with four longitudinal paler stripes, green head capsules and reddish forked tails. Larvae pupate near the base of the food plant and the pupae are suspended from a blade of grass. The pupae are green with white-edged wing cases.

In Manitoba, adults have been recorded from June 22 to August 29, being most common in late July. There is one generation per year in this province. Males usually live two or three weeks while females have a much longer lifespan.

Habitat: Open grassy areas, meadows, old fields, roadsides and ditches.

Range: Southern Canada from British Columbia to Nova Scotia, southward through most of the Untied States.

Manitoba Records: Agassiz Provincial Forest, Arden, Asessippi Provincial Park, Aweme, Beulah, Binscarth, Birds Hill, Brereton Lake, Brokenhead, Carberry, Cartwright, Cooks Creek, Culross, Cypress River, Delta, Elm Creek, Eriksdale, Fort Alexander, Glenboro, Grand Beach, Hecla Island, Hilbre, Inglis, Killarney, La Salle, Libau, Lundar, Lyleton, Melbourne, Miami, Miniota, Neelin, Neepawa, Norris Lake, Northwest Angle Provincial Forest, Oak Hammock, Onanole, Pine Ridge, Pine River, Pipestone Creek, Ponton, Rennie, Riding Mountain, Russell, St. Lupicin, St. Malo, Ste. Rose du Lac, Sandilands Provincial Forest, Selkirk, Souris, Sprague, Spruce Woods Provincial Forest, Stony Mountain, Stuartburn, Teulon, Tolstoi, Treesbank, Turtle Mountain Provincial Park, Victoria Beach, Westbourne and Winnipeg.

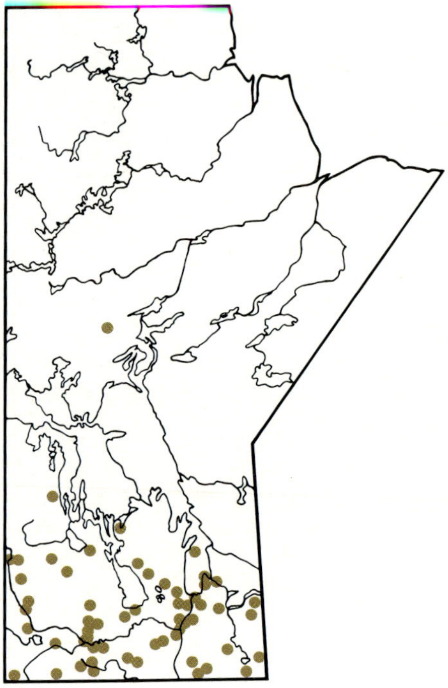

Subspecies: Many subspecies and forms have been described. The subspecies that occurs in Manitoba is *Cercyonis pegala ino*.

Remarks: The Common Wood Nymph is the largest and most common Satyr in Manitoba. Although much of its original prairie habitat is now intensively farmed, this species has successfully adapted to disturbed areas and is frequently abundant along roadsides. Males are seldom seen feeding, but females will take nectar from Alfalfa, Fleabane, Mint, Sunflowers and Spiraea. Males continually patrol for females in a dipping flight. Mating pairs can be found in the late morning or early afternoon and females carry males when in flight.

Ross' Alpine

Erebia rossi (Curtis), 1835

Plate 24 No. 1, 2, 3

Description: 38-47 mm. Ross' Alpine is brownish-black dorsally with two, three or four orange ringed eye-spots in each forewing. The top two spots are quite prominent. The hindwings occasionally have from one to four small eye-spots. Ventrally the forewings have two prominent eye-spots with white pupils, which may be accompanied by from one to three small, obscure spots. In Manitoba specimens the two prominent eye-spots are usually fused into one large, conspicuous double spot.

Similar Species: The Disa Alpine is paler and usually has an orange band containing four or rarely three eye-spots in the forewings both dorsally and ventrally. The lower two eye-spots are never smaller than the top two as in Ross' Alpine. The ventral hindwings have a white spot in the centre in Disa Alpine.

Life Cycle: Larval food plants are species of sedges including Dark Brown Sedge (*Carex atrofusca*) and Scant Sedge (*Carex rariflora*) (Scott 1986). Larvae are plain, usually unmarked or slightly striped with large head capsules and forked last abdominal segments. Larvae enter into an overwintering diapause in the third or fourth instar and resume feeding in the spring.

In Manitoba, adults have been recorded from June 3 to July 27, being most abundant at Churchill in late June or early July. There is one generation per year.

Habitat: Wet tundra and scrub tundra north of the treeline. Near Churchill this species is found on sedge-hummock tundra areas north of the treeline and in open tundra areas at the treeline.

Range: Eastern Siberia and in North America from the Arctic Ocean to Baffin Island, south to Alaska, the Yukon, British Columbia, Alberta and Manitoba.

Manitoba Records: Baralzon Lake, Caribou Lake, Churchill, Gillam and The Pas.

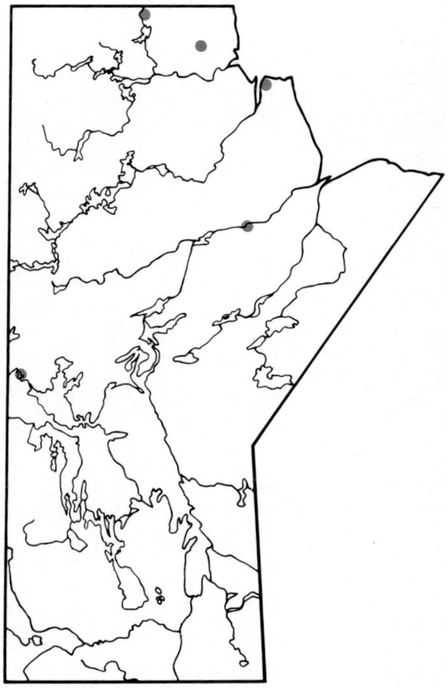

Subspecies: Four subspecies are recognized in North America, of which *Erebia rossi ornata* occurs in northern Manitoba.

Remarks: Ross' Alpine is a true inhabitant of the arctic tundra. It is relatively abundant in the Churchill region and usually the first butterfly on the wing in the spring. Adults occur in a variety of habitats, preferring wet tundra but avoiding heavy forest. The flight is leisurely and adults have not been observed feeding at flowers.

Disa Alpine

Erebia disa (Thunberg), 1791

Plate 24 No. 4, 5, 6

Description: 37-49 mm. The Disa Alpine is brownish-black dorsally. The forewings are flushed with red and contain four black eye-spots surrounded by orange or reddish-orange rings which may form diffuse bands. The top spot may be very small or lacking. Ventrally the eye-spots are similar to the upper surface and each hindwing has a white spot or "disa" spot in the center which distinguishes this Alpine from other Manitoban Alpines. Females are more heavily suffused with red than males.

Similar Species: Ross' Alpine differs as described under that species.

Life Cycle: Little is known about the biology of the Disa Alpine in Manitoba. In southern Manitoba adults have been recorded from May 24 to July 6, being most common in mid-June. In the northern part of the province adults occur from July 1 to July 23. Females emerge about one week after the males. The life cycle lasts two years since in some areas adults have been only observed in alternate years.

Habitat: Moist black spruce sphagnum bogs, usually where there are thick stands of trees. Adults occasionally stray into adjacent sedge marshes or open areas.

Range: Northern Europe and Asia. In North America from Alaska to Labrador, northward to the treeline and southward into Quebec, Ontario, northern Minnesota, the prairie provinces and British Columbia.

Manitoba Records: Aweme, Churchill, Cowan, Duck Mountain, Gillam, Lynn Lake, Miniota, Pikwitonei, Porcupine Provincial Forest, Riding Mountain, Sandilands Provincial Forest, The Pas, Thompson and Whiteshell Provincial Park.

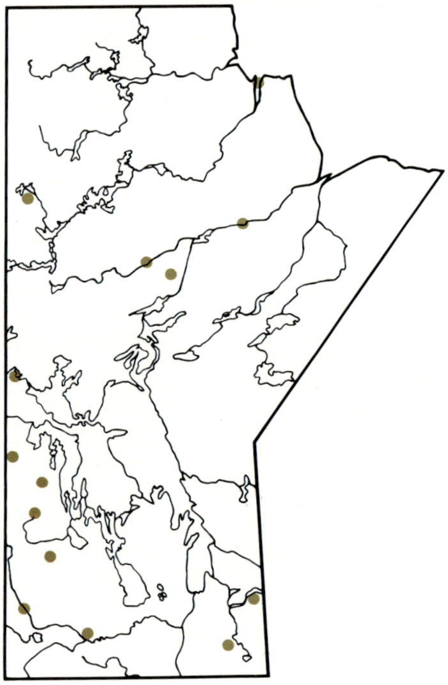

Subspecies: Three subspecies are recognized. *Erebia disa mancinus* is in Manitoba.

Remarks: Although the Disa Alpine is locally common it has been largely overlooked by lepidopterists in the past, probably due to its restricted habitat. In southern Manitoba adults are present in alternate, usually odd numbered years, however, at Churchill the Disa Alpine is found every year. It often occurs in association with the Jutta Arctic in glades and grassy runs. Adults have a slow leisurely flight, but when alarmed fly straight into tangled underbrush. This species only infrequently visits flowers but has been observed taking moisture from mud puddles.

Red Disked Alpine

Erebia discoidalis (W. Kirby), 1837

Plate 24 No. 7, 8, 9

Description: 34-45 mm. This butterfly is brownish-black dorsally and brown ventrally, with mottled gray towards the outer edges. The forewings' upper and lower surfaces are dominated by a large, diffuse, brownish-red patch. Females are paler than males.

Life Cycle: Krivda (pers. comm.) has reared larvae on Canby's Blue Grass (*Poa canbyi*). Scott (1986) noted that larvae feed on Alpine Blue Grass (*Poa alpina*) and Glaucus Speargrass (*Poa glauca*). In Manitoba adults have been recorded from May 1 to July 18. Adults are most abundant in mid to late May in the south and late June at Churchill. There is one generation per year and the flight period is short, usually about two weeks.

Habitat: Clearings in spruce bogs and pine forests, sedge marshes, forest edges and meadows. At Sandilands Provincial Forest adults prefer dry sandy ridges in open Jack Pine forests, in addition to boggy areas (Masters 1972).

Range: Asia and in North America south of the treeline from Alaska across the continent to Quebec, southward to Michigan, Wisconsin, Minnesota, North Dakota, Alberta and northern British Columbia (Pyle 1981).

Manitoba Records: Agassiz Provincial Forest, Aweme, Beulah, Birtle, Cartwright, Churchill, Duck Mountain, Hadashville, Hamiota, Lynn Lake, McCreary, Miniota, Norway House, Overflowing River, Piney, Richer, Riding Mountain, Sandilands Provincial Forest, Sprague, The Pas, Thompson, Victoria Beach and Whiteshell Provincial Park.

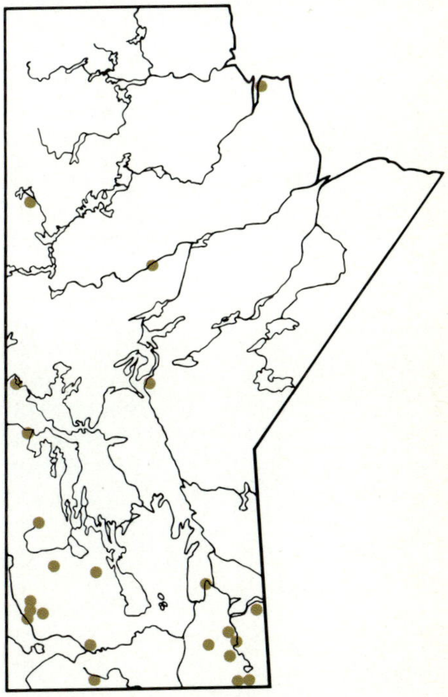

Subspecies: Two subspecies are recognized, but only *Erebia discoidalis discoidalis* occurs in Manitoba.

Remarks: The Red Disked Alpine is the most common member of the genus *Erebia* in Manitoba. Lepidopterists have overlooked this species in the past because of its earlier flight period and sedentary nature. Populations fluctuate greatly from year to year. Adults fly slowly and weakly, just above the ground, but when alarmed rise quickly and fly some distance before alighting. They prefer to perch in long grasses or on mossy ground. Males actively search for females, which are quite sedentary. This Alpine is best observed in Sandilands Provincial Forest and the Riding Mountain area.

Theano Alpine

Erebia theano (Tauscher), 1809

Plate 24 No. 10, 11, 12

Description: 31-39 mm. This butterfly is blackish-brown dorsally. The wings are crossed by a variable, dull reddish-orange band of spots which may merge into almost solid bands. The hindwing band is less well developed, occasionally being reduced to several spots. Ventrally the markings are similar to the upper surface, and the hindwing spots are cream-coloured or pale yellow. Females are usually paler than males.

Life Cycle: Host plants are probably Grasses (Gramineae), Sedges (Cyperaceae) and Rushes (Juncaceae). The early stages are probably similar to Ross' Alpine. Adults have been recorded from July 2 to August 8, being most common in mid to late July. Females emerge a week or more after males. At Churchill females have been observed ovipositing on Willow (Salicaceae) (Scott 1986). The life cycle lasts two years, although adults are on the wing every year.

Habitat: Bogs, meadows and lake shores near the treeline in mountainous areas. Grassy areas among Willow and Birch in the arctic. At Churchill adults prefer grassy ridges of wet tundra and raised meadows bordered by scrub willow.

Range: Siberia and Asia. In North America in widely distributed colonies from Alaska, the Yukon and the Northwest Territories to Manitoba.

Manitoba Records: Churchill and Fort Prince of Wales.

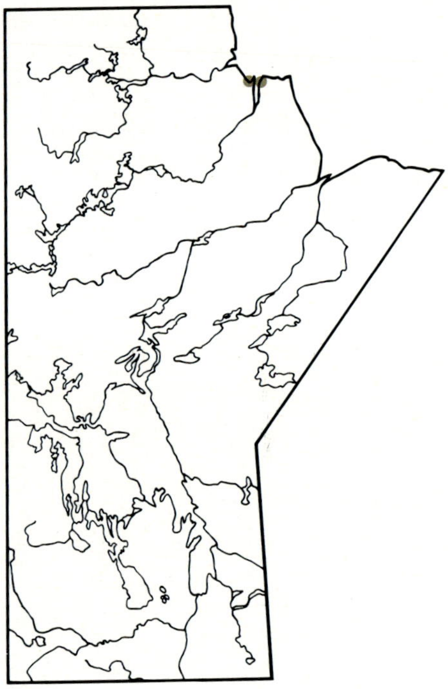

Subspecies: There are four subspecies in North America, of which *Erebia theano sophia* occurs in northern Manitoba.

Remarks: The Theano Alpine is the smallest Alpine found in Manitoba. Adults are on the wing later than other Alpine species and until recently were considered a rare find in this province. P. Klassen found the Theano Alpine to be locally common at Churchill from 1976 through 1981. Males are quite active and visit flowers including Milk Vetch, Locoweed and Everlasting. Females are more sedentary, mostly perching on low bushes and also have been observed visiting flowers in the Churchill area. Both sexes have a slow, weak flight but when alarmed frequently drop to the ground. Adults remain sheltered in small shrubs or tall grasses on windy days and can often be easily approached and picked up by hand.

Common Alpine

Erebia epipsodea Butler, 1868

Plate 24 No. 13, 14, 15, 16

Description: 32-44 mm. The Common Alpine is blackish-brown dorsally. The forewings have three to four (rarely two) eye-spots set in an irregular orange band. The hindwings usually contain three eye-spots ringed with orange; sometimes the orange rings may be merged, forming a complete band. Ventrally the wings are similar in appearance to the upper surface. The hindwings usually have a gray dusting outwardly. Females are slightly paler than males and their bands tend to be more yellowish-orange.

Life Cycle: The round, white eggs are laid singly or in small groups on the host plant. Food plants in Manitoba are undetermined but probably consist of one or more species of grasses. The larvae feed until the second or third instar and then enter an overwintering diapause. Larvae resume feeding in the spring and build a nest of grass blades tied together with silk in which to pupate. The mature larvae are light green with a dark strip dorsally and a dark olive green stripe laterally. The pupae are egg-shaped and pale brown with yellow and brown blotches.

In Manitoba, adults have been recorded from May 22 to July 16, being most common in the middle of June. Females emerge a week to two after the males. There is one generation per year.

Habitat: Grassy meadows, edges of marshes and ditches, clearings or meadows in forests and moist virgin prairie. Often found in association with aspens in the northern prairie parklands (Hooper 1973; Pyle 1981).

Range: Alaska, the Yukon and the Northwest Territories southeast to central Manitoba and southward to North Dakota, New Mexico and Oregon.

Manitoba Records: Aweme, Beulah, Birtle, Carberry, Cartwright, Duck Mountain, Mafeking, McCreary, Miniota, Overflowing River, Porcupine Provincial Forest, Riding Mountain, The Pas and Treesbank.

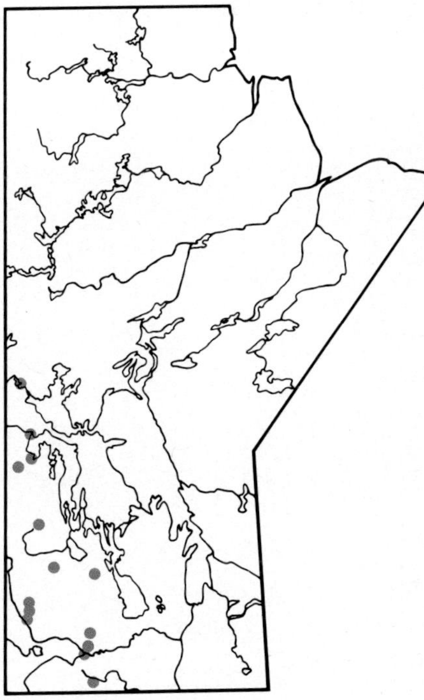

Subspecies: Four subspecies are recognized, but only *Erebia epipsodea freemani* occurs in this province.

Remarks: The Common Alpine is widely distributed in North America. It is sometimes locally abundant in western Manitoba. This species is the only Alpine not found in the most northern parts of the province. The Common Alpine was more abundant earlier before large amounts of prairie were intensively farmed. Adults have a slow zig-zag flight, and unlike most Alpines they readily visit flowers for nectar. In cool weather males frequently bask in the sun on rocks and roads with wings spread. On windy days adults take shelter in areas of long grass and when disturbed, rise swiftly into the air and fly downwind for considerable distances.

Riding's Satyr

Neominois ridingsii (W.H. Edwards), 1865

Plate 24 No. 17, 18, 19

Description: 38-48 mm. Riding's Satyr is pale grayish-brown dorsally with a wide band of pale elongated spots in each wing. The forewing bands contain two conspicuous black, white-centred eye-spots. Sometimes there is a third smaller spot and occasionally a single spot in the hindwings. The underside is grayer and striated with the dorsal pattern repeated less distinctly.

Life Cycle: The chalky-white eggs, laid directly on the host plant are barrel shaped, broader at the base and vertically ribbed. The larvae of Riding's Satyr feed on several species of grasses including Blue Grama Grass (*Bouteloua gracilis*) until partially grown and enter an overwintering diapause in the fall. The mature larvae have round head capsules, tapering cylindrical bodies and forked tails. The larvae are reddish-buff with pale green sides and a black dorsal stripe and are covered in short white hairs. Pupation occurs under the ground or in leaf litter and occasionally at the base of the food plant. The pupae are green, dull brown or reddish-brown, with green abdominal segments and wing cases (Hooper 1973; Howe 1975; Dornfeld 1980; Pyle 1981).

In Manitoba adults have been recorded from June 17 to August 10. This species usually has one generation per year but on occasion is double brooded.

Habitat: Dry short grass prairie hilltops, dry meadows with clump grasses and sage flats.

Range: Southern Alberta eastward to southern Manitoba, southward to North Dakota, Nebraska, New Mexico, California and Oregon.

Manitoba Records: Aweme, Onah and Riding Mountain.

Subspecies: Three subspecies are recognized. The subspecies found in Manitoba is *Neominois ridingsii ridingsii*.

Remarks: Riding's Satyr has not been found in Manitoba in recent years. The last record is July 2, 1953 and the species may no longer occur in this province. Wallis (1927) noted that Riding's Satyr was quite common in Manitoba in areas of sandy prairie. Hooper (1973) stated that it is locally common in southern Saskatchewan. Adults seldom fly, unless disturbed and then only for short distances with a swift and jerky flight. When alighting on bare ground, adults lean to one side, their camouflaged underside blending in with the background.

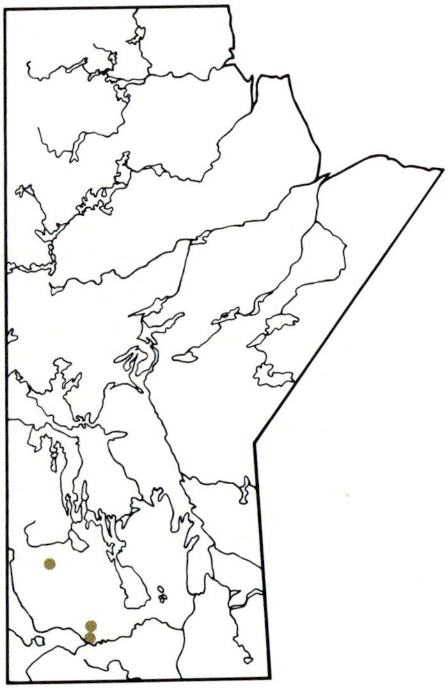

Macoun's Arctic

Oeneis macounii (W.H. Edwards), 1885

Plate 25 No. 1, 2, 3

Description: 46-61 mm. Macoun's Arctic is brownish-orange dorsally with blackish-brown margins. The forewings have two (sometimes one) prominent eye-spots but occasionally a third small spot may be present. The hindwings have one small spot, which may be faint or completely lacking. Ventrally the forewings are similar to the dorsal surface and the hindwings are striated with dark brown, crossed by a dark band and have slightly scalloped edges.

Life Cycle: Larval food plants include Grasses (Gramineae) and Sedge (*Carex* sp.).

The eggs are grayish-white when laid and the mature larvae are striped with bands of brownish-yellow, greenish-brown or red. The head capsule is round, the body tapered and the last abdominal segment is forked. The pupae are yellowish-brown. Macoun's Arctic requires two years to complete its life cycle.

In Manitoba, adults have been recorded from May 21 to July 6, being most common in the middle of June. Females emerge a week or more after males.

Habitat: Open Jack Pine forests, glades and clearing in mixed forests. In Manitoba adults prefer areas where Jack Pines are mature and there is an understory of ferns and shrubbery.

Range: The southern Northwest Territories, British Columbia and Alberta, southeastward to western Quebec, south to Michigan and Minnesota.

Manitoba Records: Agassiz Provincial Forest, Cowan, Duck Mountain, Marchand, McCreary, Rennie, Riding Mountain, Sandilands Provincial Forest, Schist Lake, Thompson, Victoria Beach and Whiteshell Provincial Park.

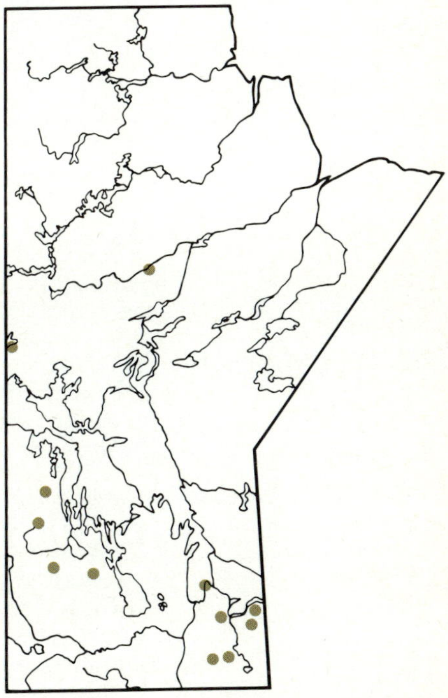

Subspecies: No subspecies are recognized.

Remarks: Macoun's Arctic is the largest and brightest Arctic found in Manitoba. This species has been found in even numbered years east of the Red River and Lake Winnipeg and in odd numbered years in western Manitoba. Males are very territorial, attacking intruders from perches on leaves, twigs or tree trunks in sunlit glades. Males also use these perches to intercept females as they fly through the forest. These butterflies are sometimes common in Sandilands and Agassiz Provincial Forests in even numbered years.

Mixed Jack Pine forest, Sandilands Provincial Forest, east of Richer, Manitoba. June 26, 1988.

Chryxus Arctic

Oeneis chryxus

(Doubleday & Hewitson), 1849

Plate 25 No. 4, 5, 6

Description: 39-50 mm. This butterfly is pale to dark reddish-brown dorsally. The forewings have zero to five eye spots, usually two or three and the hindwings have one to two eye-spots. The eye-spots are more developed in the forewings than the hindwings and are set in pale fulvous submarginal bands. Borders are gray and of moderate width. Males have gray forewing sex-patches that are largely suffused in dark specimens. Ventrally the forewings are similar to the dorsal surface and the hindwings are striated or mottled with dark brown and have whitish veins. Females are a little paler and more heavily marked than males. In Manitoba the Chryxus Arctic is extremely variable both in markings and colour.

Similar Species: The Alberta Arctic is smaller, grayer and usually paler, although occasional specimens are nearly impossible to separate. Uhler's Arctic is smaller, paler and dorsally the veins are more distinctly outlined and the eye-spots are more developed in the hindwings than the forewings.

Life Cycle: The larvae feed on various species of grasses including Poverty Oat Grass (*Danthonia spicata*), Northern Rice Cut Grass (*Oryzopsis pungens*) and Reed Canary Grass (*Phalaris arundinacea*). The white eggs are ridged. Larvae enter into an overwintering diapause in the third or fourth instar. The mature larvae are tan coloured with brown stripes laterally and have brown head capsules. The pupae are formed at the base of grass clumps and are tan with brown wing cases and heads (Opler and Krizek 1984).

In Manitoba, adults have been recorded from May 22 to July 11. Adults occur every year in this province, but in certain areas adults are present every second year. The Chryxus Arctic probably requires two years to complete its life cycle in Manitoba.

Habitat: Open pine forests, or open prairie in or near pine forests.

Range: Subarctic North America from Alaska to Quebec, southward to Ontario, Michigan, Wisconsin, the prairie provinces and in the west south to New Mexico.

Manitoba Records: Cowan, Gillam, Lynn Lake, Mile 349 Hudson Bay Railway, Riding Mountain and Thompson.

Subspecies: Six subspecies are recognized in North America. Only *Oeneis chryxus calais* occurs in Manitoba.

Remarks: The Chryxus Arctic is extremely local in Manitoba, being found in small widely scattered colonies. Like Macoun's Arctic this species is associated with pines. Adults prefer open, dry grassy areas and are not normally found in dense forest. Males are found on hills and ridges, spending much of their time perched on the ground or on grasses. When disturbed they rise abruptly and fly swiftly downwind for some distance before dropping back to the ground where their cryptic undersides render them almost invisible. Males often intercept one another and may rise to heights of 25 metres or more in aerial displays. Courtship often takes place in the late afternoon. At Cowan, Manitoba, Uhler's Arctic's flight period briefly overlaps that of the Chryxus Arctic.

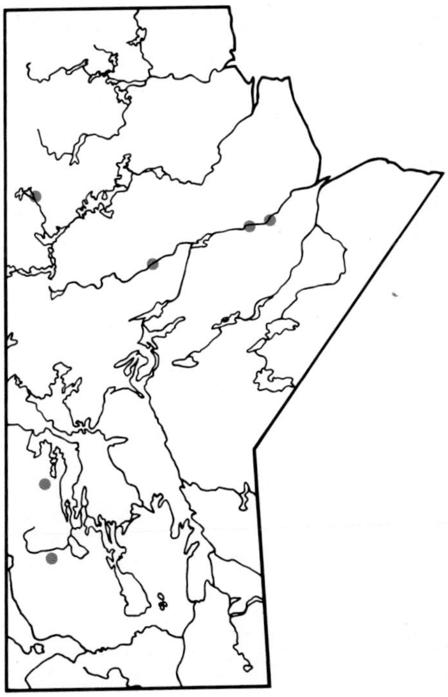

Uhler's Arctic

Oeneis uhleri (Reakirt), 1866

Plate 25 No. 7, 8, 9

Description: 35-45 mm. Uhler's Arctic is buff to grayish-brown dorsally, with narrow dark brown borders and usually dark brown veins. Each wing has one to five eye-spots which vary in size and number and are more developed in the hindwings. Some individuals lack eye-spots completely. Ventrally the eye-spots are repeated and the upper costal area of the fore and hindwings are striated with grayish-brown.

Similar Species: The Alberta Arctic although similar has pale submarginal bands. The inner edge of the forewing bands has a distinct angulate, beak-shaped projection, the eye spots are more developed in the forewings than the hindwings and the ventral veins are whitish. The Chryxus Arctic as described under that species.

Life Cycle: Larval food plants include several species of grasses. The eggs are white and vertically ribbed. Larvae feed until partially grown and usually during the fourth instar enter an overwintering diapause in the fall. The mature larvae are tan-coloured with dark brown longitudinal stripes and brown head capsules. Pupation occurs on or at the base of the food plant. The pupae are yellowish-brown and are slightly darker on the abdomen.

In Manitoba, adults have been recorded from May 17 to July 19, being most common in early June. There is one generation per year and females emerge about a week after males.

Habitat: Dry, sandy prairie and open grassy ridges in or near pine or scrubby oak woods.

Range: The Yukon, the Northwest Territories, Alberta, Saskatchewan and Manitoba, southward to South Dakota, Nebraska, and New Mexico in the west.

Manitoba Records: Aweme, Beulah, Birtle, Brandon, Carberry, Cartwright, Cowan, Cromer, Deleau, Elm Creek, Melbourne, Miniota, Morden, Onah and Stockton.

Subspecies: Five subspecies are recognized, of which *Oeneis uhleri varuna* occurs in Manitoba.

Remarks: Uhler's Arctic is still quite common in the remaining tracts of virgin prairie in southwestern Manitoba. Native grass pastures if not too badly overgrazed also offer acceptable habitat. Although restricted to prairie habitats this species has expanded its range in Manitoba and has spread to the Elm Creek area where it was first recorded in 1985. Uhler's Arctic prefers areas of bunch grass where the males perch on the crests of ridges or hover several metres above the ground, probably searching for females. For a short period at Cowan both Uhler's and Chryxus Arctics fly together, while further south Uhler's Arctic begins emerging at the end of the flight period of the Alberta Arctic. These species can be difficult to differentiate.

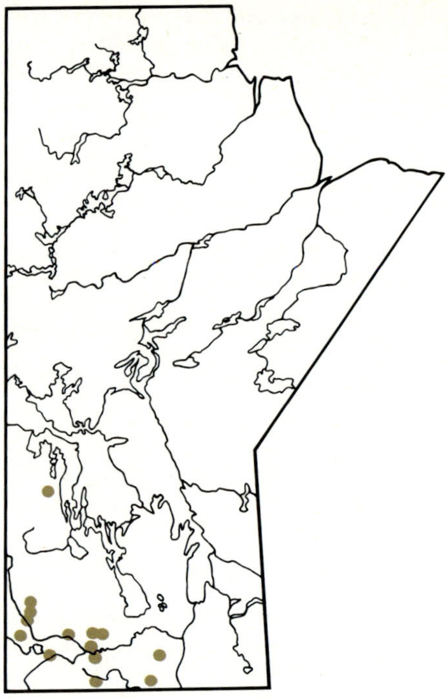

Alberta Arctic

Oeneis alberta Elwes, 1893

Plate 25 No. 10, 11, 12, 13, 14

Description: 34-44 mm. The Alberta Arctic is grayish-brown, yellowish-brown or reddish-brown dorsally. The forewings have one to four eye-spots and the hindwings have one or two eye-spots. Although eye-spots vary in number and size, occasionally completely lacking or missing they are always more developed in the forewings and are arranged in more or less developed bands. The inner margin of the pale band usually has a pointed beak-shaped projection. The eye-spot arrangement ventrally is similar to the dorsal surface. The forewings have a dark line outlining a beak-shaped projection and the hindwings have bands, dark brown striations and usually whitish veins. Females are larger, paler and more heavily marked than males. Those east of the Red River tend to be larger, more ruddy in colour, with more prominent bands and eye-spots.

Similar Species: Uhler's and Chryxus Arctics differ as described under those species.

Life Cycle: The larvae feed on species of Fescue (*Festuca* sp.). The eggs are white, rounded and ridged. Larval hatch requires about two weeks. Young larvae are grayish-tan with three darker stripes dorsally, brown head capsules and bodies tapering posteriorly.

In Manitoba, adults have been recorded from May 1 to June 21, being most common in late May. There is one generation per year and the females emerge about a week after the males.

Habitat: Dry virgin prairie hills and ridges. In Manitoba adults can be found in lightly grazed pastures.

Range: Alberta, Saskatchewan and Manitoba, southward to North Dakota and in the Rockies southward to New Mexico.

Manitoba Records: Aweme, Beulah, Birds Hill, Birtle, Brandon, Carberry, Carman, Cromer, Melbourne, Miniota, Oak Hammock, Onah, Pine Ridge, Rounthwaite, Sand Ridge, Shilo, Spruce Woods Provincial Park and Stockton.

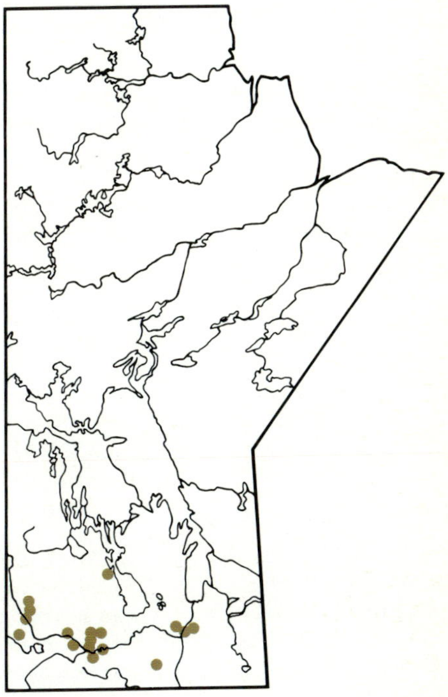

Subspecies: Four subspecies are recognized, of which *Oeneis alberta alberta* occurs in Manitoba, Saskatchewan and Alberta.

Remarks: The Alberta Arctic is on the wing very early in the spring. The best time to observe these butterflies is when the last Prairie Crocuses are in bloom. Although extremely localized, the species is sometimes abundant when found. The Alberta Arctic was not found east of the Red River until 1940. A large colony exists east of Winnipeg in the gravel deposits at Pine Ridge, although due to strip mining this habitat is shrinking. A male and a female collected by J. Masters at Pine Ridge in 1968 are held in the American Museum of Natural History. Masters considered these specimens to belong to a supspecies distinct from *alberta*. Adults are wary and when disturbed rise vertically into the wind and fly some distance before alighting. Like other Arctics, adults perch at right angles to the sun with their wings closed. Males are found on hilltops and ridges while females are often observed near the perimeter, or lower slopes, of their habitat.

Arctic Grayling

Oeneis bore (Schneider), 1792

Plate 26 No. 1, 2, 3

Description: 37-46 mm. This butterfly is grayish-brown dorsally. The males have a diffuse triangular patch of black scales (sex patch) in the middle of each forewing. Ventrally the forewings are yellowish. The hindwings are dark at the base and outer margin, with a distinct brown median band bordered by hoary white scales. The veins are more or less distinctly outlined in white or pale gray. Females are larger, paler and more yellowish than males.

Similar Species: The Melissa Arctic is grayer dorsally, the males have no sex patch and both sexes are heavily mottled with dark blackish-brown ventrally. The Polixenes Arctic is paler and more yellowish and males have no sex patches. Ventrally the veins of the Polixenes Arctic are not white and the median bands are less distinct, giving the wings a washed-out appearance. Some individuals are very difficult to separate and are best distinguished by dissection and comparison of male genitalia.

Life Cycle: Little is known about the biology of the Arctic Grayling in Manitoba. In Europe this species feeds on Fescue grass (*Festuca* sp.). Scott (1986) indicated that this species feeds on Nodding Sedge (*Carex misandra*) at Churchill. The larvae are very similar in appearance to other Arctic larvae such as Jutta Arctic. Adults have been recorded from June 15 to July 22 and are only present in even numbered years. The Arctic Grayling requires two years to complete its life cycle.

Habitat: Wet hummock tundra, moist tundra meadows and low sandy or gravelly ridges surrounded by wet grassy margins.

Range: Europe and northern North America from Alaska, the Yukon and the Northwest Territories to Hudson Bay, southward to Churchill, Manitoba.

Manitoba Records: Caribou Lake and Churchill.

Subspecies: Two subspecies are recognized in North America. *Oeneis bore hanburyi* occurs in the Churchill area.

Remarks: The Arctic Grayling has been found only at Caribou Lake and in the Churchill region in this province. Earlier observers confused it with the Polixenes Arctic. Males perch on ridges or patrol moist areas in search of females that frequently perch on mossy ground. Like other Arctics, this species is wary and when disturbed will fly a considerable distance upwind before alighting. Adults have been observed taking nectar in the Yukon but this behavior was not apparent at Churchill.

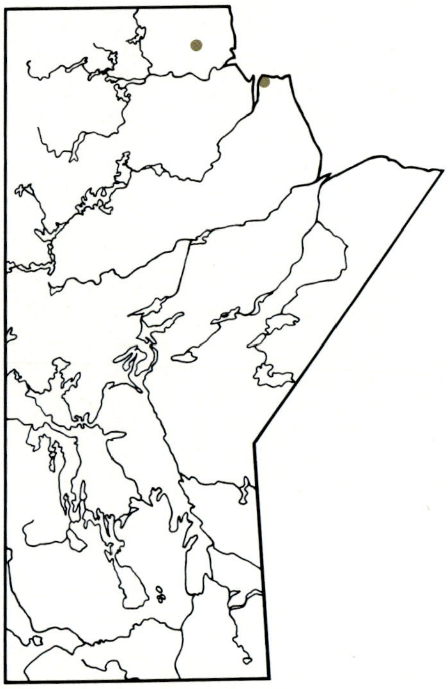

Jutta Arctic

Oeneis jutta (Hübner), 1805-1806

Plate 26 No. 4, 5, 6

Description: 42-54 mm. The Jutta Arctic is dark blackish-brown dorsally, with yellowish patches and bands enclosing black eye-spots. The eye-spots may vary in size and number from one to four in the forewings with three eye-spots being the most common. Occasionally specimens are found that completely lack eye-spots in the hindwings, but most have one or two. The markings are more developed in females than males. Males have a triangular dark gray sex-patch in the forewings. Ventrally the forewings are similar to the dorsal surface but the hindwings are heavily mottled with blackish-brown. Females are larger than males.

Life Cycle: The larvae feed on Cotton-grass (*Eriophorum spissum*) and Rush (*Juncus* sp.).

The whitish barrel-shaped eggs are laid on or near the host plant. This species enters into an overwintering diapause as young larvae the first year and as nearly mature larvae the second winter. Occasionally the Jutta Arctic will overwinter in the pupal stage. The mature larvae are pale olive green, with darker green longitudinal stripes and olive green head capsules. The pupae are yellowish-green with green wing cases, brown abdominal markings and amber heads.

Adults have been recorded from May 27 to July 6 in southern Manitoba and June 25 to July 27 in the Churchill area. They are most abundant in mid-June in southern Manitoba and in mid-July in the north. In the southwestern part of the province adults are present in even numbered years and in the southeast in odd numbered years. Adults occur every year at Churchill. The Jutta Arctic requires two years to complete its life cycle (Masters 1972a; Howe 1975; Morris 1980).

Habitat: Black Spruce and Tamarack Sphagnum bogs. In Manitoba adults prefer areas with moderate stands of trees over sparse or heavy growth. Labrador Tea, Leather Leaf, Cottongrass, Sphagnum Moss and Feather Moss predominate in their habitat.

Range: Europe and Asia. In North America from Alaska to Newfoundland southward to Maine, Michigan, Wisconsin, Minnesota and in the Rockies to Utah and Colorado.

Manitoba Records: Aweme, Birds Hill, Churchill, Cowan, Douglas, Duck Mountain, Fort Alexander, Gillam, Hargrave River, Lynn Lake, McCreary, Miniota, Patricia Beach, Pine Ridge, Riding Mountain, Sandilands Provincial Forest, The Pas, Thompson and Whiteshell Provincial Park.

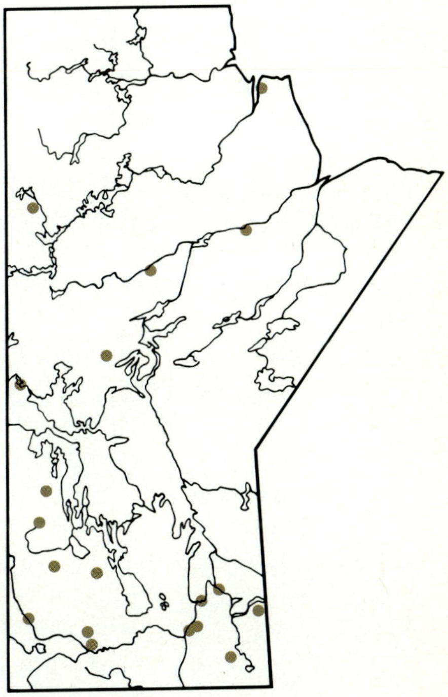

Subspecies: Six to eight subspecies are recognized in North America. Three subspecies occur in Manitoba. *Oeneis jutta ascerta* is found from southeastern Manitoba to Nova Scotia and is quite dark. *Oeneis jutta ridingiana* occurs in the southwestern part of the province and is brighter with more developed spots and bands than *ascerta*. *Oeneis jutta harperi* is found in northern Manitoba. The subspecies *harperi* is smaller and duller than the other two species and the wing markings are somewhat intermediate.

Remarks: The Jutta Arctic is widely distributed and although restricted to Spruce and Tamarack bogs in Manitoba it occurs over most of the province. Adults seldom venture far from breeding areas. Males perch in grassy runs or glades and will return to the same perch after chasing away intruders. Females are frequently found near the edges of bogs or flying through open areas adjacent to the breeding habitat. Adults visit flowers for nectar, preferring Labrador Tea in eastern Manitoba. Sandilands Provincial Forest and Churchill are areas where the Jutta Arctic is common.

Melissa Arctic

Oeneis melissa (Fabricius), 1775

Plate 26 No. 7, 8, 9

Description: 34-45 mm. This butterfly is gray to grayish-brown dorsally, normally lacking eyespots on the wings. Ventrally the forewings are similar to the upper surface and the hindwings are heavily mottled with dark blackish-brown. The wings are translucent and usually checkered with white fringes. Females are more brownish or yellowish than males.

Similar Species: The Arctic Grayling differs as described under that species. The Polixenes Arctic is more yellowish or tan and has a distinct band on each ventral hindwing.

Life Cycle: Larvae feed on various grass species and sedges, including Stiff Sedge (*Carex bigelowii*) and Rock Sedge (*Carex rupestris*).

The eggs are oval, flattened dorsally, heavily ridged and usually grayish-white to pale green. Females oviposit on the litter at the base of the food plant. Larvae are nocturnal feeders, hiding by day. The mature larvae are stout, green or brownish with longitudinal darker stripes. The head capsules may be yellowish-brown to greenish-brown. The pupae are brown or blackish-olive with darker wing cases and are suspended from the cremaster. In the first year the Melissa Arctic overwinters in an early larval stage and in the second winter as a mature larva (Morris 1981; Ferris and Brown 1981).

In Manitoba adults have been recorded from June 20 to July 20 peaking in numbers in early July. The Melissa Arctic requires two years to complete its life cycle.

Habitat: Dry raised tundra meadows and sandy eskers.

Range: Europe and Asia. In North America from Alaska to Newfoundland in the Arctic, southward in the mountains to New Hampshire in the east and through the Rockies to New Mexico in the west. The Melissa Arctic is absent from the Maritime provinces and Saskatchewan.

Manitoba Records: Caribou Lake and Churchill.

Subspecies: Seven subspecies are recognized in North America, of which *Oeneis melissa semplei* occurs in the Churchill area.

Remarks: In Manitoba the Melissa Arctic has only been found at Caribou Lake and in the Churchill area, preferring areas of dry tundra. Adults are wary and on windy days tend to fly on sheltered sides of ridges. They seldom visit flowers for nectar. Males frequently perch on ridges or patrol rocky areas in search of females. At Churchill the Melissa Arctic is most abundant in odd numbered years.

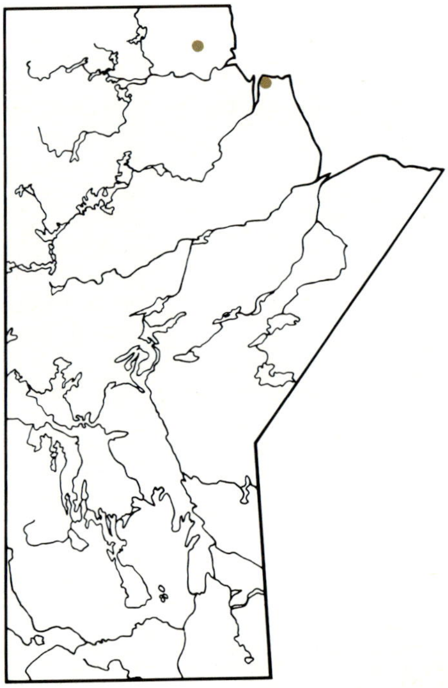

Polixenes Arctic

Oeneis polixenes (Fabricius), 1775

Plate 26 No. 10, 11, 12

Description: 37-47 mm. Dorsally the wings are pale yellowish-brown to reddish-brown, paler outwardly. Occasionally a row of submarginal diffuse yellow spots may be present. Ventrally the forewings are similar to the dorsal surface and the hindwings are brown with darker bands. Some specimens may have one to two small eye-spots dorsally or ventrally. Manitoba specimens have translucent wings and the females are paler than males. Some may have the ventral veins outlined in pale gray, similar to the Arctic Grayling. In these cases examination of the genitalia is necessary for correct identification.

Similar Species: Arctic Grayling and Melissa Arctic differ as described under those species.

Life Cycle: The larval food plants are Nodding Sedge (*Carex misanbra*) and probably species of grass at Churchill. The ridged, oval white eggs are laid directly on the food plant or on objects nearby. This species enters into an overwintering diapause as young larvae the first year and again as nearly mature larvae in the second year, thus requiring two years to reach maturity. The mature larvae are pale brown with dark longitudinal stripes and brown head capsules. The stout pupae are also brown.

In Manitoba adults have been recorded from June 2 to July 27 and are most abundant in early July. Females emerge a week or more after males.

Habitat: Moist sedge tussock tundra and other open areas.

Range: Across the Arctic from Alaska to Labrador, southward to Maine in the east and New Mexico in the Rockies. Absent from Saskatchewan, Ontario, New Brunswick, Nova Scotia and Prince Edward Island.

Manitoba Records: Caribou Lake and Churchill.

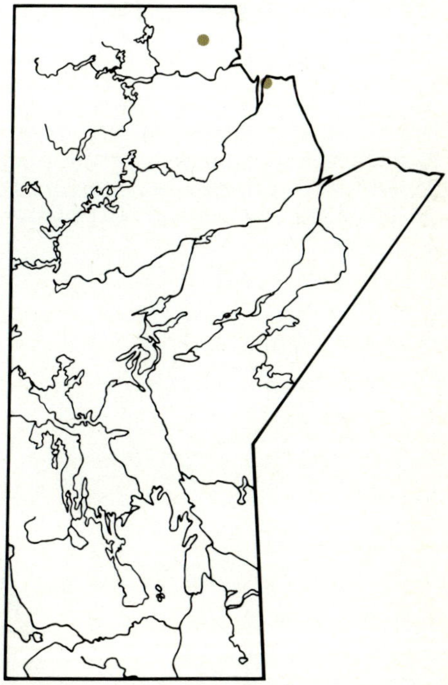

Subspecies: Six subspecies are recognized in North America. *Oeneis polixenes polixenes* occurs from the eastern arctic westward into northern Manitoba.

Remarks: The Polixenes Arctic is most common in Churchill in odd numbered years. Although preferring moist areas adults range widely over the tundra. When abundant males may be found perching on nearly every tussock and aerial skirmishes occur when males intrude on each other's territory. Females have an extended flight period and outnumber males towards the end of the flight season.

Family

DANAIDAE: MILKWEED BUTTERFLIES

Only a few species of Milkweed Butterflies exist in the New World (300 species world wide, four in North America and one in Canada). This is primarily a tropical family and many species feed on plants that confer distasteful properties to the adults. Predators learn to avoid these foul-tasting butterflies. Interestingly, other families of butterflies have developed colouration similar to many members of the Danaidae to take advantage of this protection. Some authors treat the Danaidae as a subfamily of the Nymphalidae.

Subfamily

DANAINAE: MILKWEED MONARCHS

Members of this subfamily have four walking legs. The forelegs in males are stunted and reduced to small knobs in females. Near the knobs are specialized organs that can detect the chemical make-up of candidate host plants. When ovipositing the females scratch the leaf of the plant with the knob-like projections and with the specialized organs determine if they have the correct host plant.

Danaus plexippus

Monarch

Danaus plexippus (Linnaeus), 1758

Plate 27 No. 1, 2, 3

Description: 78-102 mm. The wings are orange dorsally, with black veins and black outer margins containing a double row of small white spots. There are larger white or light orange spots near the tips of the forewings. Ventrally the wings are paler with markings similar to the upper surface. The females are duller with heavier black markings. Males have a pad of black scales (sex-pad) below the hindwing cell.

Similar Species: Viceroy differs as described under that species.

Life Cycle: The larval food plants include Common Milkweed (*Asclepias syriaca*), Swamp Milkweed (*Asclepias incarnata*), Green Milkweed (*Asclepias viridiflora*) and Dogbane (*Apocynum* sp.).

The white or pale green eggs are conically shaped and ridged. The females lay the eggs singly on the undersides of the leaves of the host plant. The fifth instar larvae are nearly five centimetre in length when full grown and require about two weeks from hatch to pupation. The mature larvae are dull white with yellow and black cross-stripes on each segment. There are a pair of fleshy black filaments behind the head capsule on the first thoracic segment and another pair near the end of the abdomen. The stout, rounded pupae are green with gold spots. The pupal stage lasts about a week. Adults overwinter in the southern United States and Mexico and their progeny migrate northward in the spring. Many of the individuals produced in Manitoba during the summer migrate southward in the fall to the overwintering areas (Howe 1975; Opler and Krizek 1984).

In Manitoba, adults have been recorded from May 19 to October 19, being most abundant in late summer. There are two generations produced in Manitoba each summer if conditions are favourable.

Habitat: Almost any area where milkweeds are found. Although strong breeding populations become established in large milkweed patches in meadows or ditches, adults will oviposit on single plants in the middle of grain fields. Adults overwinter in areas of pine or cypress or in eucalyptus groves in the south.

Monarch larva on milkweed, Brokenhead, Manitoba. July 28, 1973.

Range: Hawaiian Islands and Australia. In North America from Alaska, the southern Yukon and the Northwest Territories, eastward to Newfoundland. Through most of the United States and Central America to South America.

Manitoba Records: During the summer the Monarch occurs throughout southern and central Manitoba to The Pas and Cowan in the north.

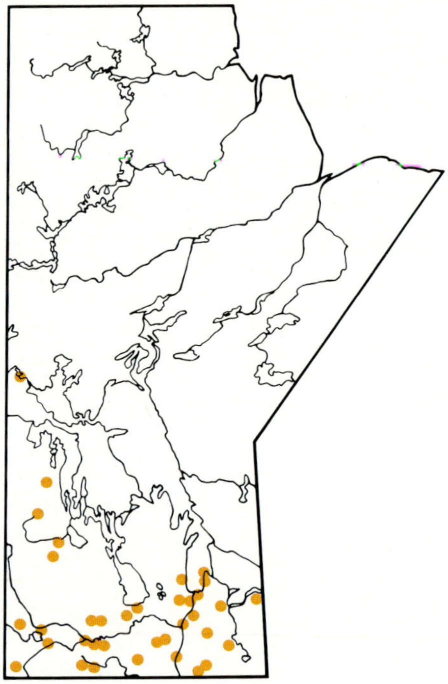

Subspecies: The only subspecies occurring north of Mexico is *Danaus plexippus plexippus*.

Remarks: Populations of the Monarch in Manitoba fluctuate from year to year and are dependent on the strength of the migration from overwintering areas. Adults have a strong, soaring flight and females are often seen flying low over the ground in search of food plants. Both sexes feed on flowers and prefer Milkweed and Composites. The fall migration covers huge distances, for example one individual tagged in Alberta was recovered later in Mexico, a distance of over 3800 km. Overwintering populations concentrate by the millions in small areas and often cover entire trees. Wintering sites have been found in southern Florida, Texas, Arizona, California and Mexico.

Hypothetical Species List

The authors have grouped those butterfly species that have not been collected, but may occur in Manitoba.

Family

HESPERIIDAE: SKIPPERS

Afranius Dusky Wing

Erynnis afranius (Linter), 1876
Plate 1 No. 22

Description: 24-32 mm. This skipper is blackish-brown dorsally, paler outwardly. The male forewings are overcast with white scales but lack the raised white hairs found in *Erynnis persius*. The forewings of both sexes have a series of small, white translucent dots in a band. The hindwings are suffused with tan spots which are more prominent toward the outer edges of the wings. Ventrally the wings are brown and have two rows or bands of tan spots. Males have a tibial tuft on the hindlegs and a costal fold on the forewings.

Similar Species: Juvenal's, Persius and Columbine Dusky Wings differ as described for those species.

Life Cycle: Larvae feed on legumes, including Milk Vetch (*Astragalus* sp.).

The early stages resemble those of the Dreamy Dusky Wing. Mature larvae are pale green with small, white points, a dark line dorsally and yellow lines laterally. The head capsule and collar on the first thoracic segment are black. There are small white dots on the head capsule and the front may be orange. The pupae are green in colour (Scott 1986). There are two generations per year in Saskatchewan and North Dakota.

Habitat: Dry prairie, open woodland and ravines.

Range: Montana, Alberta, and Saskatchewan, southward into Mexico.

Remarks: This species was formerly considered a subspecies of the Columbine Dusky Wing. Although records from northern Manitoba are erroneous, the Afranius Dusky Wing may occur in southwestern Manitoba (Scott 1986).

Common Sooty Wing

Pholisora catullus (Fabricius), 1793
Plate 2 No. 7, 8, 9

Description: 22-32 mm. This butterfly has rounded wings that are uniformly coal-black or brownish black dorsally with small white spots frequently arranged into two rows on each forewing. Occasionally the hindwings may also contain white spots. Ventrally the wings are dark brown with white spots similar to the upper surface. Males have a costal fold and lack hind tibial tufts.

Life Cycle: Larvae feed on Pigweed (*Amaranthus* sp.) and Lamb's-quarters (*Chenopodium album*).

The small white or yellowish eggs are laid directly on the food plant. Larvae form webbed leaf shelters on the plant and individuals from the second generation overwinter within these shelters. The mature larvae are light green, covered in pale dots and have dark brown head capsules. The pupae are purplish-brown with a bluish waxy flush. In North Dakota the flight period lasts from June 5 until late October (Opler and Krizek 1984).

Habitat: Roadsides, ditches, vacant lots, farms and gardens.

Range: British Columbia through southern Canada to Quebec, southward through most of the United States (Klots 1951; Hooper 1973; Howe 1975).

Remarks: Klots (1951) has stated that the Common Sooty Wing occurs in Manitoba. The authors were unable to locate any specimens of this species from Manitoba, however it is their opinion that this species probably does occur here but has been overlooked. It has been found in nearby North Dakota and northwestern Ontario and its host plants are commonly found in southern Manitoba. Adults feed on White Clover, Dogbane, Milkweed and other flowers.

Family

PAPILIONIDAE: SWALLOWTAILS

Spicebush Swallowtail

Papilio troilus Linnaeus, 1758
= *Pterourus troilus*
Plate 8 No. 4

Description: 89-114 mm. This Swallowtail is black dorsally with a submarginal band of creamy-white or creamy-yellow spots in each forewing. The hindwings of the male have a submarginal band of pale blue-green spots and are broadly suffused with blue-green scales. The female hindwings have a submarginal band of lime-green spots and are broadly suffused with blue and green scales. Both sexes have an orange spot on the upper margin and one in the inner margin of the hindwings. Ventrally, the wings are blackish-brown with cream spots on the forewings and two bands of orange spots enclosing a blue band on the hindwings, which have paddle-shaped tails.

Similar Species: The Black Swallowtail lacks the orange spot in the upper margin of the hindwing and the paddle-shaped tails.

Remarks: Klots (1951), Howe (1975) and Scott (1986) stated that the Spicebush Swallowtail ranged into southeastern Manitoba. Wallis (1927) and Brooks (1942) did not include this species in their lists of Manitoba butterflies. The authors have found no definite records or specimens from Manitoba. As the larval host plants do not occur here it is doubtful that this species is found in Manitoba.

Family

PIERIDAE: WHITES AND SULPHURS

Northern Marble

Euchloe creusa (Doubleday), 1847

This species was apparently collected in Gillam in 1961. (Chermock and Chermock, 1968). The authors have not seen these specimens.

Little Sulphur

Eurema lisa (Boisduval & Leconte), 1829
= *Pyrisitia lisa*

This species was recorded from Sandilands Provincial Forest by J. Masters. There is no reason to doubt this record as the species is easily distinguished from other Manitoban Sulphurs (Masters 1972e).

The wing span is 25-38 mm. Dorsally the rounded wings are bright yellow, with black borders that are very wide at the forewing tips and narrow in the hindwings. Ventrally the wings are yellow with obscure dark spots and a rusty-orange spot at the upper margins of the hindwings.

The larvae feed on legumes including clovers (*Trifolium* sp.). This species occurs in South America, the West Indies, the southern United States and strays northward to southeastern Canada.

Family

LYCAENIDAE: GOSSAMER WINGS

American Copper

Lycaena phlaeas (Linnaeus), 1761

This species was reported by Gregory (1975) and Scott (1986) but no specimens have been located. Scott (pers. comm.) indicated that southwestern Manitoba is included on the distribution maps in Scott (1986) because specimens have been collected in Minnesota and Saskatchewan.

Family

NYMPHALIDAE: BRUSHFOOTED BUTTERFLIES

Western Painted Lady

Vanessa carye (Hübner), 1812
= *Vanessa annabella* (Field), 1971

At times this species may stray into Manitoba as it has been seen in northern North Dakota and southeastern Saskatchewan, at Indian Head. Scott (pers. comm.) indicated that southwestern Manitoba is placed on locality maps in Scott (1986) because of the North Dakota and Saskatchewan records.

Dubious Manitoba Records

The authors regard these records as dubious since it is believed that there may have been errors in identification or labelling.

Lace-winged Roadside Skipper

Amblyscirtes aesculapius (Fabricius), 1793
= *Amblyscirtes textor* (Hübner), 1827-1831

Description: 25-32 mm. This skipper is dark grayish-brown dorsally with a curved band of buff spots (whitish in the female) on the forewings and a vague band on the hindwings. Ventrally the wings are dark grayish-brown. The forewings have a whitish band and the hindwings are distinctively marked with irregular whitish spots criss-crossed with whitish veins. The hindwing "cobweb" pattern distinguishes this species from other Skippers, except the Uncas Skipper which is tawny-orange dorsally. The wing fringes are checkered and males have long, narrow obscure brands.

Life Cycle: Little is known about this skipper's life history in northern areas of its range. There are successive generations from January to September in the south, but only one in the north.

Habitat: Glades and trails in heavily wooded areas.

Range: Connecticut to Florida, west to Missouri and New Mexico.

Manitoba Records: Minto.

Subspecies: None are recognized.

Remarks: The only Canadian record for this easily recognized species is a freshly emerged male collected at Minto in 1947 by W.D. Leathers. It is currently held in the Wallis Collection in the Museum of Natural History, Regina, Saskatchewan. As Minto is so far out of this species' range it is a doubtful record. The specimen in the Wallis collection may have been mislabelled or brought in accidently in plant material.

Northern Broken Dash

Wallengrenia egeremet (Scudder), 1864

Although included in the 1974 Field Season Summary of the Lepidopterists' Society, this specimen had been misidentified.

Bairdii Swallowtail

Papilio bairdii W.H. Edwards, 1869

Those reported by Brooks (1942) from Beulah were misidentified Kahli Swallowtails (*Papilio kahli*).

Anise Swallowtail

Papilio zelicaon Lucas, 1852

This species was reported by Wallis (1927) and Brooks (1942) as occurring in Beulah and Miniota, but all specimens examined were misidentified Kahli Swallowtails.

Nitra Swallowtail

Papilio nitra W.H. Edwards, 1883

Those reported for Riding Mountain by Brooks (1942) were misidentified Kahli Swallowtails.

Becker's White

Pieris beckerii W.H. Edwards, 1871
= *Pontia beckerii* (W.H. Edwards), 1871
= *Pontia chloridice* Hübner, 1808

This species was erroneously reported by Gregory (1975), (pers. comm.).

Blueberry Sulphur

Colias pelidne Boisduval & Leconte, 1829

This species was reported by Gregory (1975) and Scott (1986). It may occur in Manitoba as it has been collected in the Northwest Territories and northern Ontario. Specimens in the Canadian National Collection, Ottawa, recorded Fort Churchill, May 26, 1952, collected by P.R. Ehrlich, were obviously mislabeled as it is still winter at Churchill in May. The locality data may be erroneous.

Heath's Hairstreak

Satyrium heathii (Fletcher), 1903

This species was reported by Wallis (1927) and Brooks (1942), but is now considered to be an aberration of the Banded Hairstreak (*Satyrium calanus*).

Thicket Hairstreak

Callophrys spinetorum (Hewitson), 1867
= *Mitoura spinetorum*

Although this species is recorded by Gregory (1975) no specimens were located by the authors. Gregory (pers. comm.) indicated that they were in the Canadian National Collection, Ottawa. Unfortunately these could not be found. O. Shields (1965 and pers. comm.) stated that there were no Manitoba records for this Hairstreak.

Dingy Arctic Fritillary

Boloria improba (Butler), 1877
= *Clossiana improba*

Although this species was recorded by Gregory (1975) no specimens could be located by the authors.

Arctic Fritillary

Boloria chariclea (Schneider), 1794
= *Clossiana chariclea*

This species was reported by Wallis (1927) and Brooks (1942) who referred all *Boloria titania* to *Boloria chariclea*. A few *Boloria titania* from northern Manitoba resemble *Boloria chariclea*. Some authors believe the two taxa represent subspecies of a single species.

Field Crescent

Phyciodes campestris (Behr), 1863
= *pratensis* (Behr), 1863

This species has been reported for Manitoba but no valid specimens have been found. Locality records for specimens in Dos Pasos and Gunder's collections in the American Museum of Natural History, New York are considered unreliable (Rindge pers. comm.). Northern Pearl Crescent (*Phyciodes morpheus*) specimens in the Manitoba Museum of Man and Nature were erroneously identified as *Phyciodes campestris* by Masters (1973).

Zephyr Angle Wing

Polygonia zephyrus (W.H. Edwards), 1870

This species was reported by Wallis (1927), Brooks (1942), Howe (1975) and Gregory (1975) based on misidentified specimens. This "species" is now considered a subspecies of *Polygonia gracilis* by some authors. The grayer underside of western Canadian material has led some to identify it as *zephyrus* rather than *gracilis*.

Fasciata Alpine

Erebia fasciata Butler, 1868

This species was erroneously reported by Gregory (1975) (pers. comm.).

Taygete Arctic

Oeneis taygete Geyer, 1830

This species was recorded by a number of authors, including Brooks (1942) and Gregory (1975). The Taygete Arctic is now considered to be a subspecies of the Artic Grayling.

References

Allen, W.R. 1963. A history of the Entomological Society of Manitoba. Proc. Ent. Soc. Man. **19**: 4-6.

Bates, H.W. 1915. The naturalist on the river Amazons. J. Murray, London. 394 pp.

Berenbaum, M. 1978. *Taenidia integerrima* a new food plant record for *Papilio polyxenes* (Papilionidae). J. Lep. Soc. **32 (4)**: 303-304.

Bird, C.D. 1940. Some new diurnal Lepidoptera from the Riding Mountains and the Sand Ridge, Manitoba. Can. Ent. **74 (4)**: 81-83.

Bird, C.D. 1956. A collection of Rhopalocera from the Whiteshell Forest Reserve, Manitoba. Lep. News, **10 (3-4)**: 107-108.

Bitzer, R.J. and K.B. Shaw. 1979. Territorial behavior of the Red Admiral, *Vanessa atalanta* (L.) (Lepidoptera: Nymphalidae). J. Res. Lep. **18 (1)**: 36-49.

Bland, R.G. and H.E. Jaques. 1978. How to know the insects. 3rd ed. W.C. Brown Co., Dubuque. 262 pp.

Borror, D.J., D.M. DeLong and C.A. Triplehorn. 1976. An introduction to the study of insects. 4th ed. Holt, Reinhart and Winston, New York. 852 pp.

Brewer, J. and D. Winter. 1986. Butterflies and moths: a companion to your field guide. Prentice Hall, New York. 194 pp.

Brodie, H.J. 1969. Lepidoptera of Victoria Beach, Manitoba (as Taken by Myself up to Aug. 1925). Bulletin Association Minnesota Entomologists. **2 (4)**: 70-73. (A reprint of Brodie 1926.)

Brooks, G.S. 1942. A check list of the butterflies of Manitoba. Can. Ent. **74**: 31-36.

Brown, F.M. 1974. The butterfly called *ismeria* by Boisduval and LeConte (with a neotype for *Eresia carlota* Reakirt). Bull. Allyn Mus. No. **16**: 1-12.

Catling, P.M. and J.D. Lafontaine. 1986. First documented record of *Oarisma powesheik* (Lepidoptera: Hesperiidae) in Canada. Great Lakes Ent. **19 (2)**: 63-66.

Chermock, F.H. and R.L. Chermock. 1940. Some new diurnal lepidoptera from the Riding Mountains and the Sand Ridge, Manitoba. Can. Ent. **72 (4)**: 81-83.

Chermock, P.W. and F.H. Chermock. 1968. Churchill. Bulletin Association Minnesota Entomologists. **2 (2)**: 33-39.

Christensen, J.R. 1981. A field guide to the butterflies of the Pacific Northwest. University Press of Idaho, Moscow. 116 pp.

Dana, R.P. 1981. An unusual oviposition substrate for *Hesperia ottoe* (Hesperiidae) in southwestern Minnesota. J. Lep. Soc. **35 (1)**: 77-78.

Danks, H.V. ed. 1978. Canada and its insect fauna. Mem. Ent. Soc. Can. No. **108**: 1-573.

Davies, J.F., B.B. Bannatyne, G.S. Barry and N.R. McCabe. 1962. Geology and mineral resources of Manitoba. Dept. of Mines and Natural Resources, Winnipeg. 190 pp.

Dornfeld, E. 1980. The butterflies of Oregon. Timber Press, Forest Grove, Oregon. 276 pp.

Dos Passos, C.F. 1964. A synonymic list of the Nearctic Rhopalocera. Lep. Soc. Mem. **1**: 1-145.

Ehrlich, P.R. and A.H. Ehrlich. 1961. How to know the butterflies W.C. Brown Co., Dubuque. 262 pp.

Emmel, J.F., O. Shields and D.E. Breedlove. 1970. Larval food plant records for North American Rhopalocera, Part 2. J. Res. Lep. **9** (4): 233-242.

Emmel, T.C. and J.F. Emmel. 1973. The butterflies of southern California. Science Series, No. 26. Los Angeles County Museum of Natural History. 145 pp.

Ferris, C.D. and M.S. Fisher. 1973. *Callophyrs* (*Incisalia*) *polios* (Lycaenidae): distribution in North America and description of a new subspecies. J. Lep. Soc. **27** (**2**): 112-118.

Ferris, C.D. and F.M. Brown. 1981. Butterflies of the Rocky Mountain States. U. of Oklahoma Press, Norman. 442 pp.

Ferris, C.D., C.F. dos Passos, J.A. Ebner, and J.D. Lafontaine. 1973. An annotated list of the butterflies (Lepidoptera) of the Yukon Territory, Canada. Can. Ent. **115**: 823-840.

Freeman, T.N. 1950. Field season summary. Lep. News. **4** (**8-9**): 106

Gregory, W.W. 1975. Checklist of the butterflies and skippers of Canada. Lyman Ent. Museum and Res. Lab. Mem. **3**. (Spec. Publ. 10.): 1-44.

Gregory, W.W. 1983. A revised checklist of the butterflies and skippers of Canada. Lyman Ent. Museum and Res. Lab. Mem. **14**: 1-39.

Hardy, G.A. 1959. On the life history of *Incisalia eryphon* (Lycaenidae) on southern Vancouver Island. J. Lep. Soc. **13** (**2**): 70.

Harris, L. Jr. 1972. Butterflies of Georgia. U. of Oklahoma Press, Norman. 326 pp.

Hayes, J.L. 1980. Some aspects of the biology of the development stages of *Colias alexander* (Pieridae). J. Lep. Soc. **34** (**4**): 345-352.

Heath, E.F. 1895. Butterflies of southern Manitoba. Can. Ent. **27** (**11**): 310-314.

Heitzman, J.R. 1964. The early stages of *Euphyes vestris*. J. Res. Lep. **3** (**3**): 151-153.

Heitzman, J.R. and J.E. Heitzman 1974. *Atrytonopis hianna*: biology and life history in the Ozarks. J. Res. Lep. **13** (**4**): 239-245.

Holland, W.J. 1905. The butterfly book. Doubleday, Page and Co., New York, 382 pp.

Hooper, W.J. 1973. Butterflies of Saskatchewan: a field guide. Museum of Natural History. Saskatchewan Dept. of Natural Resources, Regina. 216 pp.

Hooper, R.A. 1969. Butterflies Collected at Lynn Lake, Manitoba. Bulletin Association Minnesota Entomologists. **3** (**1**): 11-12.

Howe, W. H. 1975. The butterflies of North America. Doubleday and Co., Garden City, New York. 633 pp.

Huber, R.L. 1981. An updated checklist of the Minnesota butterflies. Minn. Ent. Assoc. Newsletter. **14** (**3**): 15-25.

Kendrew, W.G. and B.W. Currie. 1955. The climate of central Canada. Queen's Printer, Ottawa. 194 pp.

Klassen, P. 1984. Checklist of Manitoba butterflies (Rhopalocera). J. Lep. Soc. **38** (**1**): 32-39.

Knapton, R.W. 1977. Observations on some butterflies and skippers from the Lyleton-Gainsborough region, Manitoba-Saskatchewan. Blue Jay **35** (**3**): 142-144.

Kohler, S. 1977. Revision of North American *Boloria selene* (Nymphalidae) with description of a new subspecies. J. Lep. Soc. **31** (**4**): 243-268.

Klots, A.B. 1951. A field guide to the butterflies of North America east of the Great Plains. Houghton Mifflin Co., Cambridge, Mass. 349 pp.

Krivda, W. 1976. The European Skipper (*Thymelicus lineola*) a new Manitoban butterfly. News of Lep. Soc. **5**: 5.

Longley, R.W. 1972. The climate of the Prairie Provinces. Climatological Studies. No. 13. Environment Canada, Toronto. 79 pp.

Looman, J. and K.F. Best. 1979. Budd's flora of the Canadian Prairie Provinces. Res. Br. Agriculture Canada. Pub. 1662. Agriculture Canada, Ottawa. 863 pp.

Manitoba Mineral Resources Division. 1979. Geological map of Manitoba. Scale 1 = 1,000,000 Map 79-2.

Martin, J.E.H. 1977. Collecting, preparing and preserving insects, mites and spiders. The insects and arachnids of Canada. Part 1. Research Br., Canada Dept. of Agriculture. Publ. 1643. Canada Dept. of Agriculture, Ottawa. 182 pp.

Masters, J.H. 1968. Notes on the occurrence of the Bog Copper, *Lycaena epixanthe*, in Manitoba. Blue Jay **26** (**3**): 146-148.

Masters, J.H. 1971a. The butterfly collecting expeditions of George Shirley Brooks to Churchill, Manitoba, and an unpublished manuscript concerning them. Blue Jay **29** (**2**): 94-96.

Masters, J.H. 1971b. The butterflies of Churchill, Manitoba. Mid-Cont. Lep. Ser. **2** (**25**): 1-13.

Masters, J.H. 1972a. Habitat: *Oeneis jutta ascerta* Masters and Sorensen. J. Res. Lep. **11** (**2**): 94.

Masters, J.H. 1972b. The butterflies of Manitoba's provincial parks. I. Whiteshell Provincial Park. Blue Jay **30** (**2**): 113-118.

Masters, J.H. 1972c. A list of butterflies taken at Northwest Angle Provincial Forest, Manitoba. Blue Jay **30** (**2**): 118-119.

Masters, J.H. 1972d. The butterflies of Manitoba's provincial parks. II. Grand Beach Provincial Park and Belair Forest Reserve. Blue Jay **30** (**3**): 161-166.

Masters, J.H. 1972e. A list of butterflies taken at Sandilands Provincial Forest, Manitoba. Blue Jay **30** (**2**): 166-167.

Masters, J.H. 1973. The collection of butterflies made by Jack Dennis at Beulah, Manitoba. J. Lep. Soc. **27** (**1**): 33-39.

Masters, J.H. 1974. Biennialism in *Oeneis macounii* (Satyridae). J. Lep. Soc. **28**: 237-242.

Masters, J.H. 1975. Variation in *Colias alexander* Edwards (Pieridae) in southwestern Manitoba. J. Res. Lep. **14** (**3**): 148-157.

McCabe, T.L. 1981. The Dakota Skipper, *Hesperia dacotae* (Skinner): range and biology, with special reference to North Dakota. J. Lep. Soc. **35** (**3**): 179-193.

McCabe, T.L. and R.L. Post. 1977. Skippers (Hesperioidea) of North Dakota. North Dakota Insects Pub. No. 11. North Dakota State University, Agricultural Experiment Station, Fargo. 70 pp.

McGugan, B.M. 1958. Forest lepidoptera of Canada. Vol. I. Forest Biology Division. Canada Dept. of Agriculture. Pub. 1034. Canada Dept. of Agriculture, Ottawa. 76 pp.

McKillop, W.B. 1978. Observations of a dermestid infestation in Manitoba Museum of Man and Nature. Man. Ent. **12**: 63-67.

McKillop, W.B. 1986. Induced colour fading in entomological specimens. In Proceedings of the 1985 Workshop on Care and Maintenance of Natural History Collections, ed. J. Waddington and D.M. Rudkin. Life Sci. Misc. Pub. Royal Ontario Museum, Toronto: 101-104.

Miller, L.D. and F.M. Brown. 1981. A catalogue/checklist of the butterflies of America north of Mexico. Lep. Soc. Mem. **2**: 1-280.

Morris, R.F. 1980. Butterflies and moths of Newfoundland and Labrador: The Macrolepidoptera. Res. Branch, Agriculture Canada. Publ. 1691. Agriculture Canada, Ottawa. 407 pp.

Muller, J. 1969. Collecting and observing *Thymelicus lineola* form "pallida" (Hesperiidae) in New Jersey. J. Lep. Soc. **23** (**4**): 249-250.

Nielsen, M.C. 1958. Observations of *Hesperia pawnee* in Michigan. Lep. News **12** (**1-2**): 37-40.

Oliver, C.G. 1979. Experimental hybridization between *Phyciodes tharos* and *P. batesii* (Nymphalidae). J. Lep. Soc. **33** (**1**): 6-20.

Oliver, C.G. 1982. Experimental hybridization between *Phyciodes tharos* and *P. phaon* (Nymphalidae). J. Lep. Soc. **36** (**2**): 121-131.

Opler, P.A. (In preparation). Field guide to the butterflies. Houghton Mifflin Co. Boston.

Opler, P.A. and G.O. Krizek. 1984. Butterflies east of the Great Plains: an illustrated natural history. Johns Hopkins University Press, Baltimore. 294 pp.

Oosting, D.P. and D.K. Parshall. 1978. Ecological notes on the butterflies of the Churchill region of northern Manitoba. J. Res. Lep. **17** (**3**): 188-203.

Orsak, L.J. 1978. The butterflies of Orange County, California. Museum of Systematic Biology. Res. Ser. No. 4. University of Calif., Museum of Systematic Biology, Irvine. 349 pp.

Preston, W.B. 1979. Winnipeg butterflies. Manitoba Nature **20** (**3**): 12-17.

Preston, W.B. and A.R. Westwood. 1981. The European Skipper, *Thymelicus lineola* (Lepidoptera: Hesperiidae), in Manitoba and Northwestern Ontario. Can. Ent. **113**: 1123-1124.

Pyle, R.M. 1974. Watching Washington butterflies. Seattle Audubon Society, Seattle. 109 pp.

Pyle, R.M. 1981. The Audubon Society field guide to North American butterflies. Chanticleer Press, New York. 916 pp.

Pyle, R.M. 1984. The Audubon Society handbook for butterfly watchers. Charles Scribner's Sons, New York. 274 pp.

Reeks, W.A. 1959. Early collectors and collections of insects in Manitoba. Proc. Ent. Soc. Man. **15**: 48-54.

Reist, J.D. 1979. *Callophrys niphon* (Lycaenidae) in Alberta with notes on identification of *C. niphon* and *C. eryphon*. J. Lep. Soc. **33** (**4**): 248-253.

Riegert, P.W. 1980. From arsenic to DDT: A history of entomology in Canada. University of Toronto Press, Toronto. 357 pp.

Royer, R.A. 1988. Butterflies of North Dakota; an atlas and guide. Science Monograph No. 1, Division of Science, Minot State University, Minot, North Dakota. 192 pp.

Scoggan, H.J. 1957. Flora of Manitoba. Biol. Ser. 47. Can. Nat. Museum. Bull. 140. National Museum of Canada, Ottawa. 619 pp.

Scott, J.A. 1984. A review of *Polygonia progne* (*Oreas*) and *P. gracilis* (*Zephyrus*) (Nymphalidae) including a new subspecies from the southern Rocky Mountains. J. Res. Lep. **23** (**3**): 197-210.

Scott, J.A. 1986. The butterflies of North America: a natural history and field guide. Stanford University Press, Stanford, Calif. 583 pp.

Scott, J.A. and R.E. Stanford. 1981. Geographical variation and ecology of *Hesperia leonardus* (Hesperiidae). J. Res. Lep. **20** (**1**): 18-35.

Shields, O. 1965. *Callophrys* (*Mitoura*) *spinetorum* and *C.* (*M.*) *johnsoni*: their known range, habits, variation and history. J. Res. Lep. **4** (**4**): 233-250.

Sperling, F.A.H. 1987. Evolution of *Papilio machaon* species group in western Canada (Lepidoptera: Papilionidae). Quaestiones Entomologicae. **23** (**2**): 198-315.

Teller, J.T. ed. 1984. Natural heritage of Manitoba: legacy of the ice age. Manitoba Museum of Man and Nature, Winnipeg. 208 pp.

Tilden, J.W. and A.C. Smith. 1986. A field guide to western butterflies. Houghton Mifflin Co., Boston. 370 pp.

Thomas, M.K. 1954. Climatological atlas of Canada. Division of Building Research, National Research Council and the Meteorological Division, Canada Dept. of Transport, Ottawa 253 pp.

Wallis, J.B. 1954. Pioneers of entomology in Manitoba. Proc. Ent. Soc. Man. **10**: 45-49.

Wallis, J.B. 1927. A colour key to the Manitoban butterflies. Natural History Society of Manitoba, (Winnipeg). 31 pp.

Weir, T.R. ed. 1960. Economic atlas of Manitoba. Dept. of Industry and Commerce, Winnipeg. 81 pp.

Wolley Dod, F.H. 1916. The Heath Collection of Lepidoptera. Can. Ent. **48 (5)**: 161-167

Wright, D.M. 1983. Life history and morphology of the immature stages of the Bog Copper butterfly, *Lycaena epixanthe* (Bvd. and LeC.) (Lepidoptera: Lycaenidae). J. Res. Lep. **22 (1)**: 47-100.

Glossary

abdomen–the most posterior of the three main body divisions.
aestivate–to spend a certain period of time in a dormant state. e.g. warm or dry season.
anal fold–the portion of the hindwing that folds against the abdomen when a butterfly's wings are closed.
androconia–specialized scales that produce sex attractant pheromones (chemical messengers).
antennae–paired segmented appendages located on the head above the mouth parts and usually sensory in function.
apex–see apical.
apical–the end, tip or outermost part.
apiculus–the slender portion of the antenna, beyond the club, in some skippers.

bifid–forked or divided into two parts.

cell–refers to discal cell (see discal cell).
chevron–V-shaped pattern.
cline–a gradual change of physical characteristics across a species's geographical range.
conspecific–belonging to the same species. e.g. *O. jutta ascerta* and *O. jutta ridingiana* are conspecific.
costal area–portion of the wing immediately behind the anterior margin.
costal fold–a fold at the costal margin or leading edge of the forewing of the males of some skippers which contains scent scales.
cremaster–hooked projections at the tip of the abdomen of the pupa that hook into the silken pad spun by the larva.
crepuscular–active at dusk or twilight.
cuticle–the noncellular outer layer or skin of an insect.

diapause–period of arrested development, often induced by environmental factors.
dicotyledon–a plant whose seeds contain a pair of cotyledon seed leaves which are always opposite to one another.
dimorphic–two different forms existing in one population of a species (or subspecies).
discal cell–an enlarged cell in the basal or central area of the wing.
discocellular spot–spot in the discal cell (large central wing cell).
dorsal–top or uppermost, pertaining to the back or upperside.

emarginate–notched or indented.
epiphysis–movable pad or lobe like process on the inner surface of the front tibia.

facies–external appearance of the upper or lower surfaces of the wings, e.g. size, shape, color, pattern etc.
family–a subdivision of an order, suborder or superfamily and containing a group of related genera, tribes or subfamilies; family names end in "-idae".
foreleg(s)–the most anterior pair of legs.
forewing(s)–the first or anterior pair of wings.
forewing brand–a patch of scent scales on the forewing of many male skippers and hairstreaks.
fulvous–reddish brown.
fuscous–grayish brown or tawny in color.

generation–from any given stage in a lifecycle to the same stage in the offspring.
genitalia–sexual organs and associated structures.

head capsule–anterior body region, which bears eyes, antennae and mouthparts.
hindwing(s)–the posterior set of wings.
hybridization–an offspring produced by a female and male of different species.

instar–the development stage between larval moults.

labrum–upper lip.
lateral–on or pertaining to the side (right or left).

maxillae–pair of mouth structures behind the mandibles.
monocotyledon–a plant with one cotyledon or seed leaf only.

nominate subspecies–has the same name as the species. e.g. *Colias philodice philodice.*

order–a subdivision of a class or subclass containing a group of related families.
osmeterium–a fleshy, tubular, eversible, usually Y shaped scent gland at the anterior end of certain caterpillars.
oviposition–the act of egg laying, to oviposit.

palpus–segmented mouthpart born by the maxilla or labrum.
proboscis–extended beak or tube-like mouthparts used for sucking liquids.
prothorax–the anterior of the three thoracic segments.

species–a group of individuals or populations that are similar in structure and physiology and are capable or interbreeding and producing fertile offspring and which are different in structure and (or) physiology from other such groups and normally do not interbreed with them.
stigma–see forewing brand.
stridulate–to make a noise by rubbing two structures or surfaces together.
subconic–rounded cone-shaped.
subfamily–a major subdivision of a family containing a group of related tribes or genera; subfamily names end in "-inae".
submarginal–directly behind or paralleling the margin of the wing.
subspecies–a subdivision of a species, usually a geographic race. The different subspecies of a species are ordinarily not sharply differentiated and intergrade with one another and are capable of interbreeding.
suffuse–to overspread or mix in with. For example one color intermixed with another.
superfamily–a group of closely related families; superfamily names end in "-oidea".

tarsal claw–a claw at the apex of the tarsus.
tarsus–part of the leg beyond the tibia, consisting of one or more segments or subdivisions.
tegula–a small scale like structure overlying the base of the front wing.
thorax–a body region behind the head which bears the wings and legs.
tibia–the fourth segment of the leg, between the femur and tarsus.
tibial spur–a large spine on the tibia, usually located at the lower end of the tibia.
tibial tuft–a tuft of long hair-scales on the tibia.
tubercle–a raised, wartlike projection which may contain spines.

ventral–lower or underneath; the underside of the body.

Appendix I:

Collecting Butterflies

In order to catch butterflies a net is required. The net should consist of strong, yet soft, netting made into a bag about two and one half times as long as the hoop diameter. The bag should be rounded, not pointed and green or brown in color rather than white. A sleeve of muslin approximately five cm. in diameter should be attached to the top of the bag to receive the hoop. The hoop should have a diameter of 35 to 45 cm. and be of stiff wire approximately three mm. in thickness. Coat hanger wire may suffice. The ends of the hoop are bent at right angles, in the plane of the hoop, for attachment to the handle. One end is made a little longer than the other and both ends bent inward at right angles to allow insertion into holes drilled in the handle (Fig. 1). A wood dowel of 16 mm. diameter is a suitable handle, but a broom handle will suffice. Two holes, the diameter of the hoop wire, are drilled through the handle to receive the bent ends of the hoop (Fig. 2). Grooves cut from these holes to the end of the handle receive the hoop wire. The hoop may be attached to the handle with one or two hose clamps, which will enable easy removal of the net for travel or for bag replacement.

A variety of techniques are used to kill butterflies. Some collectors merely pinch the thorax and place the specimen immediately into a glassine envelope, on which the collecting data are written. This method requires some practice to avoid damaging the specimen. Butterfly wings should not be touched with the fingers, but handled with forceps. Alternately, the specimen may be placed directly into a glassine envelope and later the envelopes can be placed in a freezer with the day's catch. Many collectors, however, prefer to use a killing jar. Traditionally this was the cyanide jar, which did not need constant recharging and since it was dry, caused little damage to the specimens. Potassium cyanide was commonly used and these jars usually lasted about two years. However it is now very difficult to obtain cyanide. Cyanide killing jars must be used with great caution as the cyanide fumes are highly poisonous. Furthermore, if the jar should break there is the extreme danger of being cut and receiving an injection of cyanide. A much safer, yet efficient, killing jar can be made using ethyl acetate. Some absorbent material such as cotton batting is placed in the bottom of the jar and held in place with a tight-fitting disc of cardboard. A few drops of ethyl acetate are placed on the cotton and the jar is ready for use. The jar must be kept closed and recharged frequently, since ethyl acetate evaporates quickly.

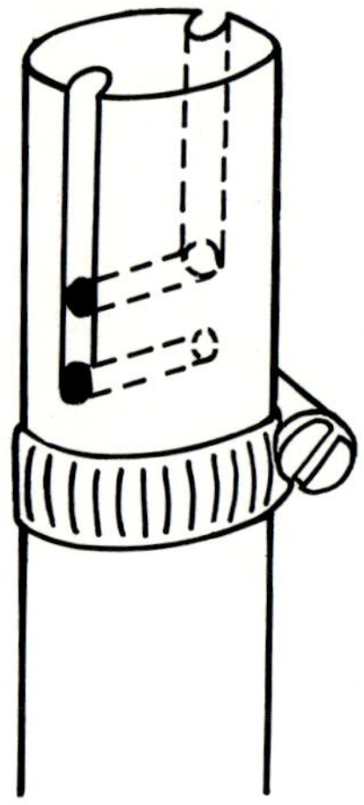

Figure 1

Figure 2

Nail polish remover may be substituted for ethyl acetate, although it works slowly. A more elaborate killing jar may be constructed by placing one or two centimetres of sawdust in the bottom of the jar. A short piece of glass or polyethylene tubing is placed upright in the sawdust and plaster of paris mixed with water poured over the sawdust, leaving the top of the tubing exposed. After the plaster has dried the jar may be charged by injecting ethyl acetate using a syringe or eye-dropper through the tubing into the sawdust. A jar of this type may retain its potency for several days. The fumes from a killing jar should never be inhaled as they are dangerous and are often inflammable.

Several pieces of equipment are needed to pin and spread butterflies. Insect pins are available in a number of sizes from 000 to 7 with the most useful sizes of 1 to 3 for Manitoba butterflies. These are available from biological supply houses, as is most of the equipment required. The spreading board (Fig. 3) consists of two pieces of soft wood, like pine, separated by a groove slightly larger than the body of the butterfly. These are attached at either end to a stand and have upper surfaces planed at an angle so that they slope slightly downward toward the groove. Beneath the groove a strip of cork or balsa wood is glued to receive the insect pin. A thin wood or hardboard base may be attached beneath the end stands to protect the protruding pins of the pinned specimens. Also needed are sharp pins, strips of translucent paper, forceps and a setting needle. The latter can be made by inserting the blunt end of a fine insect pin, with the head cut off, into a wood handle, for example a match stick.

Butterflies are best spread when fresh, however frequently it may be necessary to store specimens in their envelopes for a long period of time. In this case they must be relaxed before attempting to pin and spread them. A relaxing chamber can be made from a polyethylene box with a tight-fitting lid. A piece of foam or other water absorbent material is placed in the bottom of the polyethylene box. The absorbant material is then saturated with water. A few drops of carbolic acid, or a few flakes of paradichlorobenzene added to the foam, will prevent mold. A piece of aluminum window screen placed over the absorbant material will keep the specimens away from the moisture. The envelope containing the specimen is placed in the chamber and after 24 hours the specimen should be checked to see if it is soft enough to pin and spread. Large specimens may require two to three days in the chamber. Data should be written on the envelope with either permanent ink or pencil, or it may be obliterated by the moisture in the chamber.

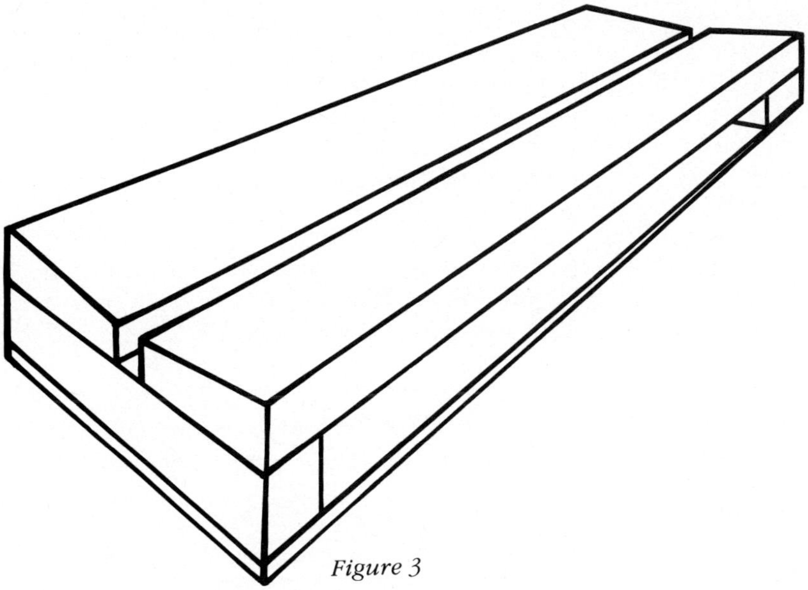

Figure 3

To pin and spread a butterfly, select a pin of appropriate size, for example a number 3 pin for a Monarch or Tiger Swallowtail, and a number 1 pin for a Blue. The pin is pushed through the center of the thorax and adjusted so that the head of the pin is 9 mm. above the thorax. A pinning block (Fig. 4) may be used to check this and to attain uniformity among specimens. The same block is used to space the labels at uniform levels on the pins after the specimen has dried. Uniformity provides for neatness in appearance of the collection. The pin is then pushed into the cork at the bottom of the groove, with the butterfly's body in the groove, until the wings are level with the surface of the spreading board. The left wings are held down with a strip of paper, and using the setting needle the forewing is moved gently forward until its trailing edge is at right-angles to the axis of the body. The paper strip is then pinned to the board around the wing to hold it in place. The hindwing is then teased forward in a similar fashion until its leading edge is beneath the trailing edge of the forewing, and the remainder of the paper strip pinned to the board to hold it in place. The right wing is then spread in similar fashion. While spreading the left wing the body of the butterfly may have a tendency to swing to the left. This may be prevented by inserting a pin into the cork next to the thorax on the left side of the body, behind the wings. The abdomen may be prevented from sagging by crossing pins beneath it to hold it up. The antennae should be symmetrically arranged in the same plane as the body and held in place with pins. The data labels should be pinned next to the specimen on the board. Drying may require one to two weeks for fresh specimens and several days for relaxed, stored specimens. When the specimen has dried it should be carefully removed from the board and the labels spaced on the pin using the pinning block.

Specimens are best stored in a pest-proof box or drawer with a bottom that will accept pins, for example cork or polyethylene foam. Do not use styrofoam as it may react with certain fumigants. A small piece of dichlorvos strip (for example Vapona) will help keep the box pest free. Insert a stout pin through the strip and pin it into one corner of the box or drawer. If the container has a glass lid it should be kept in a dark place away from sunlight to prevent fading of the butterfly wings.

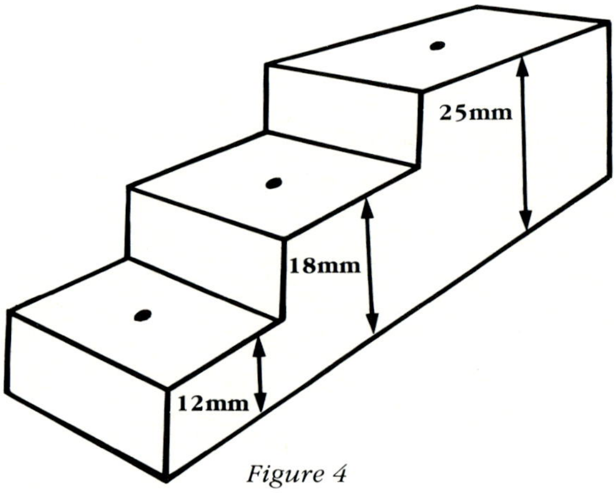

Figure 4

Appendix II:

List of Larval and Adult Food Plants

***The larval food plants are indexed. The names are based on Looman and Best* (1979) *and Scoggan* (1957)**

Alder–*Alnus* spp. 83, 208, 212
Alfalfa–*Medicago sativa* 13, 70, 71, 72, 79, 106, 113
Alpine Blue Grass–*Poa alpina* 237
Alpine Milk Vetch–*Astragalus alpinus* 73
Alpine Smartweed–*Polygonum viviparum* 131, 139
Alsike Clover–*Trifolium hybridum* 114
American Elm–*Ulmus americana* 206, 211, 214
Annual Wild Rice–*Zizania aquatica* 47
Apple–*Malus* spp. 97
Arctic Daisy–*Chrysanthemum arcticum*
Arctic Sagebrush–*Artemisia arctica*
Arrow Wood–*Viburnum rafinesquianum*
Ash–*Fraxinus* spp. 83
Aspen–*Populus spp.* 214, 224, 225
Aster–*Aster* spp.
Awned Sedge–*Carex atherodes* 229

Balsam Poplar–*Populus balsamifera* 59, 224
Barnyard Grass–*Echinochloa crusgalli* 44
Basswood–*Tilia americana*
Beaked Sedge–*Carex rostrata* 47
Bean–*Phaseolus* spp. 104, 106
Bearberry–*Arctostaphylos uva-ursi* 98, 99, 137
Beardtongue–*Penstemon* spp. 202
Beggarticks–*Bidens* spp. 81
Beggar's lice–*Desmodium canadense* 12
Bent Grass–*Agrostis* spp. 36, 52
Big Bluestem–*Andropogon gerardi* 45, 50
Birch–*Betula* spp. 14, 135, 208, 224
Bird Rape–*Brassica campestris* 67
Black Crowberry–*Empetrum nigrum* 111
Black-eyed Susan–*Rudbeckia serotina*
Blazing Star–*Liatris* spp.
Blue Grama Grass–*Bouteloua gracilis* 31, 37, 240
Blue Grass–*Poa* spp. 26, 32, 43, 44, 46
Blueberry–*Vaccinium* spp. 97, 98, 100, 108, 116
Bluestem–*Andropogon* spp. 45
Bog Bilberry–*Vaccinium uliginosum* 78, 136, 137
Borage–*Borago officinalis*
Bristly Black Current–*Ribes lacustre*
Broccoli–*Brassica oleracea* var. *italica* 66
Brome Grass–*Bromus* spp. 23, 32
Buffalo Berry–*Sheperdia argentia*
Bur Oak–*Quercus macrocarpa* 16, 17, 95, 96
Burdock–*Arctium* spp. 218, 220
Butternut–*Juglans* spp. 96

Cabbage–*Brassica oleracea* var. *capitata* 66, 65
Camas–*Zygadenus* spp.
Canby's Blue Grass–*Poa canbyi* 237
Carrot–*Daucus carota* 55, 56
Cauliflower–*Brassica oleracea* var. *botrytis* 66
Cherry–*Prunus* spp. 91
Chicory–*Cichorium intybus*
Chickweed–*Stellaria media* 81
Choke Cherry–*Prunus virginiana* 91, 97
Cinquefoil–*Potentilla* spp.
Cloudberry–*Rubus chamaemorus* 21, 135, 137
Clover–*Trifolium* spp. 13, 79, 107, 255
Colt's-foot–*Petasites* spp.
Columbine–*Aquilegia* spp. 19
Common Lousewort–*Pedicularis canadensis*
Common Milkweed–*Asclepias syriaca* 251

Appendix III:
Checklist of the Butterflies in Manitoba

Superfamily Hesperioidea: Skippers

Family Hesperiidae: Skippers

Subfamily Pyrginae

Epargyreus clarus–Silver Spotted Skipper
Thorybes pylades–Northern Cloudy Wing
Erynnis icelus–Dreamy Dusky Wing
Erynnis brizo–Sleepy Dusky Wing
Erynnis juvenalis–Juvenal's Dusky Wing
Erynnis martialis–Mottled Dusky Wing
Erynnis lucilius–Columbine Dusky Wing
Erynnis persius–Persius Dusky Wing
Pyrgus centaureae–Grizzled Skipper
Pyrgus communis–Common Checkered Skipper

Subfamily Heteropterinae

Carterocephalus palaemon–Arctic Skipper

Subfamily Hesperiinae

Ancyloxypha numitor–Least Skipper
Oarisma powesheik–Powesheik Skipper
Oarisma garita–Garita Skipper
Thymelicus lineola–European Skipper
Hesperia uncas–Uncas Skipper
Hesperia comma–Comma Skipper
Hesperia ottoe–Ottoe Skipper
Hesperia leonardus–Leonardus Skipper
Hesperia pawnee–Pawnee Skipper
Hesperia dacotae–Dakota Skipper
Hesperia sassacus–Indian Skipper
Hesperia nevada–Nevada Skipper
Polites coras = *Polites peckius*–Peck's Skipper
Polites themistocles–Tawny-edged Skipper
Polites mystic–Long Dash
Atrytone logan = *Atrytone delaware*–Delaware Skipper
Poanes hobomok–Hobomok Skipper
Poanes viator–Broad-winged Skipper
Euphyes ruricola = *Euphyes vestris*–Dun Skipper
Atrytonopsis hianna–Dusted Skipper
Amblyscirtes hegon = *Amblyscirtes samoset*–Pepper and Salt Skipper
Amblyscirtes vialis–Roadside Skipper

Superfamily Papilionoidea: True Butterflies

Family Papilionidae: Swallowtails and Parnassians

Subfamily Papilioninae: Swallowtails

Battus philenor–Pipevine Swallowtail
Papilio polyxenes–Black Swallowtail
Papilio kahli–Kahli Swallowtail
Papilio machaon–Old World Swallowtail

Papilio cresphontes = *Heraclides cresphontes*–Giant Swallowtail
Papilio glaucus = *Pterourus glaucus*–Tiger Swallowtail

Family Pieridae: White, Marbles and Sulphurs
Subfamily Pierinae: Whites
Pontia protodice = *Pieris protodice*–Checkered White
Pontia occidentalis = *Pieris occidentalis*
= *Pieris callidice*–Western Checkered White
Pieris napi = *Artogeia napi*–Veined White
Pieris rapae = *Artogeia rapae*–Cabbage White

Subfamily Anthocharinae: Marbles and Orange Tips
Euchloe ausonides = *Euchloe ausonia*–Ausonides Marble
Euchloe olympia–Olympia Marble

Subfamily Coliadinae: Sulphurs
Colias philodice–Common Sulphur
Colias eurytheme–Alfalfa Sulphur
Colias alexandra–Christina Sulphur
Colias hecla–Arctic Sulphur
Colias nastes–Nastes Sulphur
Colias gigantea–Giant Sulphur
Colias interior–Pink Edged Sulphur
Colias palaeno–Palaeno Sulphur
Colias cesonia = *Zerene cesonia*–Dogface
Eurema mexicana–Mexican Sulphur
Nathalis iole–Dainty Sulphur

Family Lycaenidae: Gossamer Wings
Subfamily Miletinae = Subfamily Liphyridae
Feniseca tarquinius–Harvester

Subfamily Lycaeninae: Coppers
Lycaena xanthoides = *Gaeides xanthoides*–Great Copper
Lycaena hyllus = *Hyllolycaena hyllus* = *Lycaena thoe*–Bronze Copper
Lycaena epixanthe = *Epidemia epixanthe*–Bog Copper
Lycaena dorcas = *Epidemia dorcas*–Dorcas Copper
Lycaena helloides = *Epidemia helloides*–Purplish Copper

Subfamily Theclinae: Hairstreaks and Elfins
Harkenclenus titus = *Satyrium titus*–Coral Hairstreak
Satyrium acadica–Acadian Hairstreak
Satyrium edwardsii–Edwards' Hairstreak
Satyrium calanus–Banded Hairstreak
Satyrium liparops–Striped Hairstreak
Callophrys augustus = *Incisalia augustus*
= *Incisalia augustinus*–Brown Elfin
Callophrys polios = *Incisalia polios*–Hoary Elfin
Callophrys henrici = *Incisalia henrici*–Henry's Elfin
Callophrys niphon = *Incisalia niphon*–Pine Elfin
Callophrys eryphon = *Incisalia eryphon*–Western Pine Elfin
Strymon melinus–Gray Hairstreak

Subfamily Polyommatinae = Plebejinae: Blues
Hemiargus isola–Reakirt's Blue
Everes comyntas–Eastern Tailed Blue

Everes amyntula–Western Tailed Blue
Celastrina argiolus = *Celastrina ladon*–Spring Azure
Glaucopsyche lygdamus–Silvery Blue
Lycaeides idas = *Plebejus idas* = *Plebejus argyrognomon*–Northern Blue
Lycaeides melissa = *Plebejus melissa*–Orange Bordered Blue
Plebejus saepiolus–Greenish Blue
Vacciniina optilete = *Plebejus optilete*–Yukon Blue
Agriades glandon = *Plebejus franklinii*–Arctic Blue

Family Heliconiidae
Dione vanillae = *Agraulis vanillae*–Gulf Fritillary

Family Nymphalidae: Brush-footed Butterflies
Subfamily Argynninae: Fritillaries or Silverspots
Euptoieta claudia–Variegated Fritillary
Speyeria cybele–Great Spangled Fritillary
Speyeria aphrodite–Aphrodite Fritillary
Speyeria idalia–Regal Fritillary
Speyeria edwardsii–Edwards' Fritillary
Speyeria callippe–Callippe Fritillary
Speyeria atlantis–Atlantis Fritillary
Speyeria electa–Northwestern Fritillary
Speyeria mormonia–Mormonia Fritillary
Boloria eunomia = *Proclossiana eunomia*–Bog Fritillary
Boloria selene = *Clossiana selene*–Silver Bordered Fritillary
Boloria bellona = *Clossiana bellona* = *Boloria toddi*–Meadow Fritillary
Boloria frigga = *Clossiana frigga*–Frigga Fritillary
Boloria polaris = *Clossiana polaris*–Polaris Fritillary
Boloria freija = *Clossiana freija*–Freija Fritillary
Boloria titania = *Clossiana titania*–Purple Lesser Fritillary

Subfamily Melitaeinae: Checkerspots and Crescents
Chlosyne gorgone = *Charidryas gorgone*–Gorgone Checkerspot
Chlosyne nycteis = *Charidryas nycteis*–Silvery Checkerspot
Chlosyne harrisii = *Charidryas harrisii*–Harris' Checkerspot
Phyciodes tharos–Pearl Crescent
Phyciodes morpheus = *Phyciodes pascoensis* =
= *Phyciodes selenis*–Northern Pearl Crescent
Phyciodes batesii–Tawny Crescent
Euphydryas anicia = *Occidryas anicia*–Anicia Checkerspot
Euphydryas phaeton–Baltimore

Subfamily Nymphalinae: Anglewings
Polygonia interrogationis–Question Mark
Polygonia comma–Comma
Polygonia satyrus–Satyrus Anglewing
Polygonia faunus–Green Comma
Polygonia gracilis–Hoary Comma
Polygonia progne–Gray Comma
Nymphalis vau-album–Compton Tortoise Shell
Nymphalis californica–California Tortoise Shell
Nymphalis antiopa–Mourning Cloak
Nymphalis milberti = *Aglais milberti*–Milbert's Tortoise Shell
Vanessa virginiensis–American Painted Lady
Vanessa cardui–Painted Lady

Vanessa atalanta–Red Admiral
Junonia coenia = *Precis coenia*–Buckeye

Subfamily Limenitidinae: Admirals
Limenitis arthemis = *Basilarchia arthemis*–White Admiral
Limenitis archippus = *Basilarchia archippus*–Viceroy

Family Satyridae: Satyrs and Wood Nymphs
Subfamily Elymniinae
Enodia anthedon = *Lethe anthedon*–Northern Pearly Eye
Satyrodes eurydice = *Lethe eurydice*–Eyed Brown

Subfamily Satyrinae
Megisto cymela = *Euptychia cymela*–Little Wood Satyr
Coenonympha tullia = *Coenonympha inornata*–Ringlet
Cercyonis pegala–Common Wood Nymph
Erebia rossi–Ross' Alpine
Erebia disa–Disa Alpine
Erebia discoidalis–Red Disked Alpine
Erebia theano–Theano Alpine
Erebia epipsodea–Common Alpine
Neominois ridingsii–Riding's Satyr
Oeneis macounii–Macoun's Arctic
Oeneis chryxus–Chryxus Arctic
Oeneis uhleri–Uhler's Arctic
Oeneis alberta–Alberta Arctic
Oeneis bore–Arctic Grayling
Oeneis jutta–Jutta Arctic
Oeneis melissa–Melissa Arctic
Oeneis polixenes–Polixenes Arctic

Family Danaidae: Milkweed Butterflies
Subfamily Danainae
Danaus plexippus–Monarch

Appendix IV:

Geographic Locations of Collection Sites

Ref.	Site	LAT		LONG	
77*	AGASSIZ PROVINCIAL FOREST	50	00	96	09
104	ALTONA	49	06	97	33
	ANOLA	49	53	96	38
	ARBORG	50	54	97	13
	ARDEN	50	17	99	16
	ASESSIPPI PROVINCIAL PARK	50	59	101	20
	ASHVILLE	51	10	100	18
17	ASSEAN LAKE	56	13	96	30
	AUBIGNY	49	27	97	15
84	AUSTIN	49	57	98	56
	AWEME	49	43	99	36
	BADGER	49	11	95	58
2	BARALZON LAKE	60	00	98	03
	BEAVER CREEK	49	57	98	56
	BELAIR	50	37	96	35
39	BELLSITE	52	35	101	04
40	BERENS RIVER	52	22	97	03
	BERESFORD LAKE	50	52	95	14
	BEULAH	50	16	101	02
	BINSCARTH	50	37	101	17
	BIRCH RIVER	52	24	101	06
	BIRDS HILL PROVINCIAL PARK	50	01	96	53
69	BIRTLE	50	25	101	03
51	BISSET	51	02	95	41
	BLACK RIVER	50	49	96	21
	BOGGY CREEK	51	32	101	21
101	BOISSEVAIN	49	14	100	03
	BOUNDARY LAKE	49	00	100	12
42	BOWSMAN	52	14	101	12
82	BRANDON	49	50	99	57
	BRERETON LAKE	49	54	95	31
76	BROKENHEAD	50	14	96	30
	BUFFALO LAKE	53	25	99	17
	CAMP MORTEN	50	43	97	00
13	CAPE TATNAM	57	16	91	00
83	CARBERRY	49	52	99	22
3	CARIBOU LAKE	59	21	96	10
	CARMAN	49	30	98	00
	CARTWRIGHT	49	06	99	20
	CHATFIELD	50	47	97	34
6	CHURCHILL (MILE 509.8 HUDSON BAY RAILWAY)	58	47	94	11
	CLANWILLIAM	50	22	99	49
	COOKS CREEK	50	01	96	47
	CORMORANT LAKE	54	15	100	50
43	COWAN	52	02	100	39
25	CRANBERRY PORTAGE	54	35	101	23
81	CROMER	49	44	101	14
	CULROSS	49	43	97	55

*REFERENCE NUMBERS TO MAP 2

		LAT		LONG	
	CYPRESS RIVER	49	34	99	05
55	DAUPHIN	51	09	100	03
	DAWSON BAY	52	53	100	49
	DEER RIVER (MILE 200 HUDSON BAY RAILWAY)	58	23	94	13
	DELEAU	49	35	100	34
75	DELTA	50	11	98	19
37	DENBEIGH POINT	52	53	99	46
	DOUGLAS	49	53	99	42
45	DUCK MOUNTAIN PROVINCIAL PARK AND FOREST	51	40	100	55
94	ELM CREEK	49	41	98	00
	ELVA	49	13	101	07
105	EMERSON	49	00	97	12
62	ERIKSDALE	50	52	98	06
	ERINVIEW	50	22	97	29
	FAIRFORD	51	36	98	42
	FALCON LAKE	49	41	95	19
49	FISHER BRANCH	51	05	97	37
23	FLIN FLON	54	46	101	53
68	FORT ALEXANDER	50	37	96	18
5	FORT PRINCE OF WALES	58	48	94	13
	GARDENTON	49	05	96	42
	GARSON	50	05	96	42
19	GILLAM (MILE 326.1 HUDSON BAY RAILWAY)	56	21	94	40
66	GIMLI	50	38	96	59
74	GLADSTONE	50	13	98	57
	GLENBORO	49	33	99	17
	GRAHAMDALE	51	23	98	30
	GRAND BEACH	50	33	96	38
	GRAND MARAIS	50	32	96	37
36	GRAND RAPIDS	53	10	99	18
54	GRANDVIEW	51	10	100	42
	GRASS RIVER PROVINCIAL PARK	50	40	100	50
46	GYPSUMVILLE	51	46	98	38
88	HADASHVILLE	49	40	95	55
71	HAMIOTA	50	11	100	36
	HARGRAVE RIVER	54	24	98	48
	HAZEL	49	53	96	15
50	HECLA ISLAND	51	06	96	43
11	HERCHMER (MILE 412 HUDSON BAY RAILWAY)	57	23	94	11
47	HILBRE	51	30	98	36
	HOROD	50	39	100	18
	HUSAVIK	50	34	97	00
	INGLIS	50	57	101	15
64	INWOOD	50	30	97	30
33	ISLAND LAKE	53	52	94	40
20	JACAM	56	27	94	24
	KATIMIK LAKE	52	53	99	21
	KELWOOD	50	37	99	28
	KEMNAY	49	51	100	08
	KETTLE RAPIDS (MILE 333.5 HUDSON BAY RAILWAY)	56	25	94	32
102	KILLARNEY	49	11	99	40
	KINOSOTA	50	55	98	52
	KOLA	49	51	101	22
	KOMARNO	50	30	97	15

		LAT		LONG	
	KOOSTATAK	51	26	97	22
	LA RIVIERE	49	14	98	40
	LA SALLE	49	42	97	16
	LAKE WILLIAM	49	02	99	59
99	LAUDER SANDHILLS	49	29	100	40
9	LEAF RAPIDS	56	28	100	00
	LIBAU	50	16	96	43
41	LITTLE GRAND RAPIDS	52	03	95	28
	LITTLE LIMESTONE LAKE	53	45	99	20
63	LUNDAR	50	42	98	02
97	LYLETON	49	03	101	11
8	LYNN LAKE	56	51	101	03
	MAFEKING	52	41	101	06
	MARCHAND	49	27	96	23
	MARCO	50	43	100	36
	MARGARET	49	24	99	51
	MASKWA RIVER	50	33	96	08
60	McCREARY	50	46	99	29
	McMUNN	49	38	95	42
	MELBOURNE	49	52	99	12
98	MELITA	49	16	101	00
	MIAMI	49	22	98	14
7	MILE 473 HUDSON BAY RAILWAY (CROMARTY)	58	03	94	09
	MILLWOOD	50	42	101	25
70	MINIOTA	50	08	101	02
48	MOOSEHORN	51	17	98	25
103	MORDEN	49	11	98	06
	MULVIHILL	50	58	98	11
	NARCISSE	50	41	97	32
73	NEEPAWA	50	14	99	28
14	NELSON HOUSE	55	47	98	51
	NINETTE	49	24	99	38
	NORGATE	50	41	99	28
	NORRIS LAKE	50	27	97	24
96	NORTHWEST ANGLE PROVINCIAL FOREST	49	17	95	22
32	NORWAY HOUSE	53	59	97	50
1	NUELTIN LAKE	60	00	99	50
	OAK HAMMOCK MARSH	50	12	97	08
	OAK LAKE	49	46	100	38
	OBERON	50	03	99	29
	ODEI RIVER	56	06	96	54
	ONAH	49	48	99	31
59	ONANOLE	50	37	99	58
16	ORR LAKE	56	07	97	11
35	OSCAR POINT	53	06	100	25
34	OVERFLOWING RIVER	53	08	101	06
	O'HANLY RIVER	50	50	96	19
	PAINT LAKE	55	30	98	00
	PARTRIDGE LAKE	49	02	100	21
	PASQUIA	53	45	101	38
	PATRICIA BEACH	50	25	96	36
	PIERSON	49	11	101	15
22	PIKWITONEI (MILE 213.3 HUDSON BAY RAILWAY)	55	35	97	09
	PINE FALLS	50	34	96	13

		LAT		LONG	
	PINE RIDGE	50	00	96	50
44	PINE RIVER	51	47	100	32
	PINEY	49	04	95	59
	PIPESTONE CREEK	49	42	100	48
	PIPUN	54	50	98	45
	PISEW FALLS	55	12	98	24
	POINT DU BOIS	50	18	95	33
27	PONTON (MILE 107.1 HUDSON BAY RAILWAY)	54	38	99	10
38	PORCUPINE PROVINCIAL FOREST	52	30	101	25
85	PORTAGE LA PRAIRIE	49	59	98	18
	PRAWDA	49	39	95	47
	RATHWELL	49	39	98	33
	RED ROCK LAKE	50	00	95	32
	REED LAKE	54	38	100	30
79	RENNIE	49	51	95	33
	RICHER	49	39	96	27
58	RIDING MOUNTAIN NATIONAL PARK	50	50	100	00
53	ROBLIN	49	10	99	20
	ROSEBANK	49	22	98	07
	ROSEISLE	49	30	98	21
	ROSENBURG	51	06	97	12
57	ROSSBURN	50	40	100	49
90	ROUNTHWAITE	49	40	99	48
56	RUSSELL	50	47	101	17
93	ST. CLAUDE	49	40	98	20
	ST. LAZARE	50	27	101	18
	ST. MALO	49	19	96	57
	ST. NORBERT	49	46	97	09
	STE. RITA	49	53	96	18
61	SAND RIDGE	50	46	99	16
	SAND RIVER	49	13	96	17
95	SANDILANDS PROVINCIAL FOREST	49	22	96	07
	SANDRIDGE	50	35	97	30
	SANDY HOOK	50	32	96	59
	SANDY LAKE	49	02	100	28
	SANFORD	49	41	97	27
24	SCHIST LAKE	54	40	101	47
	SCLATER	51	56	100	37
4	SEAL RIVER	59	04	94	48
	SELKIRK	50	09	96	52
78	SEVEN SISTERS	50	07	96	01
	SHARPE LAKE	49	03	100	20
	SHILO	49	49	99	38
	SIMONHOUSE LAKE	54	33	101	10
21	SIPIWESK	55	27	97	24
26	SNOW LAKE	54	53	100	02
89	SOURIS	49	37	100	15
10	SOUTH INDIAN LAKE	56	47	98	56
18	SPLIT LAKE	56	15	96	06
108	SPRAGUE	49	02	95	38
92	SPRUCE WOODS PROVINCIAL PARK	49	43	99	05
	STEAD	50	26	96	27
	STOCKTON	49	35	99	27
	STONEWALL	50	08	97	19

		LAT		LONG	
	STONY MOUNTAIN	50	05	97	13
72	STRATHCLAIR	50	24	100	24
	STUARTBURN	49	08	96	46
	TELFORD	49	51	95	23
	TEULON	50	23	97	16
30	THE PAS	53	50	101	15
15	THOMPSON	55	45	97	52
	THORNHILL	49	12	98	14
106	TOLSTOI	49	05	96	49
	TRANSCONA	49	54	97	00
91	TREESBANK	49	38	99	36
100	TURTLE MOUNTAIN PROVINCIAL PARK	49	03	100	15
	TWO RIVERS LAKE	52	31	98	57
	UNO	50	14	101	06
	VALLEY RIVER	51	15	100	08
67	VICTORIA BEACH	50	42	96	34
107	VITA	49	08	96	34
87	VIVIAN	49	53	96	27
28	WABOWDEN (MILE 136.4 HUDSON BAY RAILWAY)	54	55	98	38
52	WALLACE LAKE	51	00	95	21
	WANIPIGOW	51	11	96	18
29	WANLESS	54	10	101	22
	WASKADA	49	06	100	48
	WATTSVIEW	50	22	101	13
	WAUGH	49	37	95	12
	WESTBOURNE	50	08	98	35
31	WESTRAY	53	36	101	24
	WHITEMOUTH LAKE	49	15	95	40
80	WHITESHELL PROVINCIAL PARK	50	00	95	30
	WHITEWATER LAKE	49	14	100	19
	WILLIAM RIVER	53	52	98	58
86	WINNIPEG	49	53	97	09
65	WINNIPEG BEACH	50	30	96	58
12	YORK FACTORY	57	00	92	18

Map 2: Major Collecting Sites

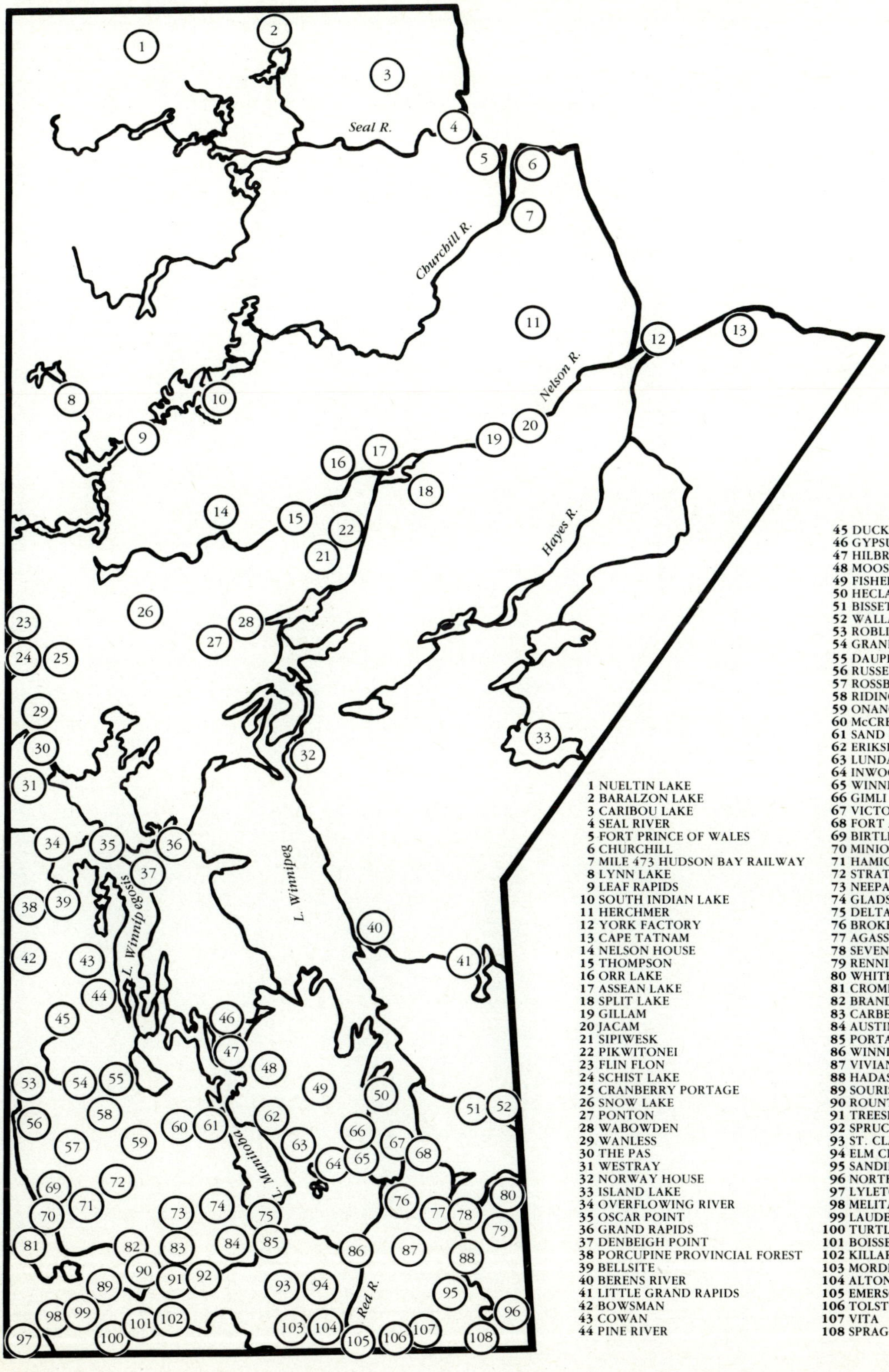

1 NUELTIN LAKE
2 BARALZON LAKE
3 CARIBOU LAKE
4 SEAL RIVER
5 FORT PRINCE OF WALES
6 CHURCHILL
7 MILE 473 HUDSON BAY RAILWAY
8 LYNN LAKE
9 LEAF RAPIDS
10 SOUTH INDIAN LAKE
11 HERCHMER
12 YORK FACTORY
13 CAPE TATNAM
14 NELSON HOUSE
15 THOMPSON
16 ORR LAKE
17 ASSEAN LAKE
18 SPLIT LAKE
19 GILLAM
20 JACAM
21 SIPIWESK
22 PIKWITONEI
23 FLIN FLON
24 SCHIST LAKE
25 CRANBERRY PORTAGE
26 SNOW LAKE
27 PONTON
28 WABOWDEN
29 WANLESS
30 THE PAS
31 WESTRAY
32 NORWAY HOUSE
33 ISLAND LAKE
34 OVERFLOWING RIVER
35 OSCAR POINT
36 GRAND RAPIDS
37 DENBEIGH POINT
38 PORCUPINE PROVINCIAL FOREST
39 BELLSITE
40 BERENS RIVER
41 LITTLE GRAND RAPIDS
42 BOWSMAN
43 COWAN
44 PINE RIVER
45 DUCK MOUNTAIN PROVINCIAL FOREST
46 GYPSUMVILLE
47 HILBRE
48 MOOSEHORN
49 FISHER BRANCH
50 HECLA ISLAND
51 BISSETT
52 WALLACE LAKE
53 ROBLIN
54 GRANDVIEW
55 DAUPHIN
56 RUSSELL
57 ROSSBURN
58 RIDING MOUNTAIN NAT. PARK
59 ONANOLE
60 McCREARY
61 SAND RIDGE
62 ERIKSDALE
63 LUNDAR
64 INWOOD
65 WINNIPEG BEACH
66 GIMLI
67 VICTORIA BEACH
68 FORT ALEXANDER
69 BIRTLE
70 MINIOTA
71 HAMIOTA
72 STRATHCLAIR
73 NEEPAWA
74 GLADSTONE
75 DELTA
76 BROKENHEAD
77 AGASSIZ PROVINCIAL FOREST
78 SEVEN SISTERS
79 RENNIE
80 WHITESHELL PROVINCIAL PARK
81 CROMER
82 BRANDON
83 CARBERRY
84 AUSTIN
85 PORTAGE LA PRAIRIE
86 WINNIPEG
87 VIVIAN
88 HADASHVILLE
89 SOURIS
90 ROUNTHWAITE
91 TREESBANK
92 SPRUCE WOODS PROVINCIAL PARK
93 ST. CLAUDE
94 ELM CREEK
95 SANDILANDS PROVINCIAL FOREST
96 NORTHWEST ANGLE PROV. FOREST
97 LYLETON
98 MELITA
99 LAUDER
100 TURTLE MOUNTAIN PROV. PARK
101 BOISSEVAIN
102 KILLARNEY
103 MORDEN
104 ALTONA
105 EMERSON
106 TOLSTOI
107 VITA
108 SPRAGUE

Appendix V:

Summary of Butterfly Flight Periods in Manitoba

	APR	MAY	JUN	JUL	AUG	SEPT	OCT	NOV
Epargyreus clarus		– – –	– – –	– – –				
Thorybes pylades		– –	– – –	– – –				
Erynnis icelus		– – –	– – –	– –				
Erynnis brizo		– – –	– –					
Erynnis juvenalis		– –	– – –					
Erynnis martialis		– –	– –					
Erynnis lucilius			–	– – –				
Erynnis persius		–	– – –	– –				
Pyrgus centaureae		– –	– – –	– –				
Pyrgus communis		–	– – –	– – –	– – –	– – –	–	
Carterocephalus palaemon		– –	– – –	–				
Ancyloxypha numitor			–	– – –	– – –			
Oarisma powesheik			–	–				
Oarisma garita			– – –	– – –	–			
Thymelicus lineola			– – –	– – –	–			
Hesperia uncas			–					
Hesperia comma			–	– – –	– – –	– –		
Hesperia ottoe				–				
Hesperia leonardus					– – –			
Hesperia pawnee				–	– – –			
Hesperia dacotae			–	– –				
Hesperia sassacus			– – –	– – –				
Hesperia nevada			– –		–			
Polites coras			–	– – –	–			
Polites themistocles			– – –	– – –				
Polites mystic			– – –	– – –	– –			
Atrytone logan			–	– – –				
Poanes hobomok		– –	– – –	– –				
Poanes viator			–					
Euphyes ruricola			–	– – –	– –			
Atrytonopsis hianna		–	– – –					
Amblyscirtes hegon		– –	– – –	–				
Amblyscirtes vialis		– –	– – –	– –				
Battus philenor						–		
Papilio polyxenes		– –	– – –	– – –	– –	– –		
Papilio kahli		– –	– – –	– – –	– –			
Papilio machaon		– –	– – –	– – –				
Papilio cresphontes					–	–		
Papilio glaucus		– –	– – –	– – –	– –			
Pontia protodice				– – –	– – –	– – –		
Pontia occidentalis	–	– – –	– – –	– – –	– – –	– – –		
Pieris napi		– – –	– – –	– – –	– – –			
Pieris rapae	–	– – –	– – –	– – –	– – –	– – –	– –	

Note: Each dash represents on the average a ten day period. Flight periods will vary from southern to northern Manitoba and from year to year. Some species fly in alternate years in the north.

	APR	MAY	JUN	JUL	AUG	SEPT	OCT	NOV
Euchloe ausonides		– – –	– – –	– – –				
Euchloe olympia		–						
Colias philodice		– – –	– – –	– – –	– – –	– – –	– – –	–
Colias eurytheme		– –	– – –	– – –	– – –	– – –	– – –	– –
Colias alexandra			– –	– – –	–			
Colias hecla				– – –	–			
Colias nastes			–	– – –	– –			
Colias gigantea			– – –	– – –	–			
Colias interior			– – –	– – –	– – –			
Colias palaeno			–	– – –	–			
Colias cesonia						NO DATE		
Eurema mexicana				– – –	– – –	– – –		
Nathalis iole				–	– – –	– – –		
Feniseca tarquinius		– –	– – –	– – –	– –			
Lycaena xanthoides			–	– – –	– –			
Lycaena hyllus			– – –	– – –	– – –	– –		
Lycaena epixanthe				–				
Lycaena dorcas				– – –	– – –			
Lycaena helloides			– – –	– – –	– – –	– – –		
Harkenclenus titus			–	– – –	– – –			
Satyrium acadica			– –	– – –	– –			
Satyrium edwardsii			–	– – –	– – –			
Satyrium calanus			–	– – –	– – –			
Satyrium liparops			– – –	– – –	– –			
Callophrys augustus		– –	– – –					
Callophrys polios		– – –	– – –					
Callophrys henrici		– –	– –					
Callophrys niphon		– – –	– –					
Callophrys eryphon			– –					
Strymon melinus					– –			
Hemiargus isola						NO DATE		
Everes comyntas		– –	– – –	– – –	– – –	–		
Everes amyntula		– –	– – –	– – –	– – –			
Celastrina argiolus	– –	– – –	– – –	– – –	– –			
Glaucopsyche lygdamus	–	– – –	– – –	– – –	– –			
Lycaeides idas			–	– – –	– – –			
Lycaeides melissa		– –	– – –	– – –	– – –	– – –		
Plebejus saepiolus		– –	– – –	– – –				
Vacciniina optilete				– – –				
Agriades glandon		–	– – –	– – –	– –			
Dione vanillae						NO DATE		
Euptoieta claudia		– –	– – –	– – –	– – –	– – –	–	
Speyeria cybele			– – –	– – –	– – –			
Speyeria aphrodite			–	– – –	– – –	– –		
Speyeria idalia				– –	– –			
Speyeria edwardsii			– –	–				
Speyeria callippe			– –	– – –				
Speyeria atlantis			– – –	– – –	– – –			
Speyeria electa			– – –	– – –	– – –			
Speyeria mormonia			– – –	– – –	– – –			
Boloria eunomia			– – –	– – –	– –			
Boloria selene		–	– – –	– – –	– – –			

	APR	MAY	JUN	JUL	AUG	SEPT	OCT	NOV
Boloria bellona		– – –	– – –	– – –	– – –	– –		
Boloria frigga		–	– – –	– – –	–			
Boloria polaris			– –	– – –	–			
Boloria freija		– –	– – –	– – –				
Boloria titania			– – –	– – –	– – –			
Chlosyne gorgone		– –	– – –	–				
Chlosyne nycteis			– –	– –				
Chlosyne harrisii			– – –	– –				
Phyciodes tharos			– – –	– – –	– – –			
Phyciodes morpheus		–	– – –	– – –	– – –	–		
Phyciodes batesii		–	– – –	– – –	– –			
Euphydryas anicia				–				
Euphydryas phaeton				– –				
Polygonia interrogationis			– –	– – –	– – –			
Polygonia comma		– –	– – –	– – –	– – –	– – –	–	
Polygonia satyrus	–	– – –	– – –	– – –	– – –	– – –		
Polygonia faunus		– –	– – –	– – –	– –			
Polygonia gracilis		–	– – –	– – –	– – –	– –		
Polygonia progne		– – –	– – –	– – –	– – –	–		
Nymphalis vau-album	– – –	– – –	– – –	– – –	– – –	– – –	–	
Nymphalis californica						– –	–	
Nymphalis antiopa	– – –	– – –	– – –	– – –	– – –	– – –	– –	
Nymphalis milberti	– – –	– – –	– – –	– – –	– – –	– – –	– – –	–
Vanessa virginiensis		–	– – –	– – –	– – –	–		
Vanessa cardui		– – –	– – –	– – –	– – –	– – –	–	
Vanessa atalanta		– – –	– – –	– – –	– – –			
Junonia coenia				– – –				
Limenitis arthemis		–	– – –	– – –	– – –	–		
Limenitis archippus		–	– – –	– – –	– – –	–		
Enodia anthedon			– –	– – –	–			
Satyrodes eurydice			– –	– – –	– – –	–		
Megisto cymela		–	– – –	– – –				
Coenonympha tullia		– –	– – –	– –				
Cercyonis pegala			–	– – –	– – –			
Erebia rossi			– – –	– – –				
Erebia disa		–	– – –	– – –				
Erebia discoidalis		– – –	– – –	– –				
Erebia theano				– – –	–			
Erebia epipsodea		–	– – –	– –				
Neominois ridingsii			– –	– – –	–			
Oeneis macounii		–	– – –	–				
Oeneis chryxus		–	– – –	– –				
Oeneis uhleri		– –	– – –	– –				
Oeneis alberta		– – –	– – –					
Oeneis bore			– –	– – –				
Oeneis jutta		–	– – –	– – –				
Oeneis melissa			– –	– –				
Oeneis polixenes			– – –	– – –				
Danaus plexippus		– –	– – –	– – –	– – –	– – –	– –	

Appendix VI:

The Lepidopterists' Society

Statement of the Committee on Collecting Policy

Preamble

Our ethical responsibility to assess and preserve natural resources, for the maintenance of biological diversity in perpetuity, and for the increase of knowledge, requires that lepidopterists examine the rationale and practices of collecting Lepidoptera, for the purpose of governing their own activities.

To this end, the following guidelines are outlined, based on these premises:

0.1 Lepidoptera are a renewable natural resource.

0.2 Any interaction with a natural resource should be in a manner not harmful to the perpetuation of that resource.

0.3 The collection of Lepidoptera

- 0.31 is a means of introducing children and adults to awareness and study of their natural environment;
- 0.32 has an essential role in the elucidation of scientific information, both for its own sake and as a basis from which to develop rational means for protecting the environment, its resources, human health and the world food supply;
- 0.33 is a recreational activity which can generally be pursued in a manner not detrimental to the resource involved.

Guidelines

PURPOSES OF COLLECTING (consistent with the above):

1.1 To create a reference collection for study and appreciation.

1.2 To document regional diversity, frequency, and variability of species, and as voucher material for published records.

1.3 To document faunal representation in environments undergoing or threatened with alteration by man or natural forces.

1.4 To participate in development of regional checklists and institutional reference collections.

1.5 To complement a planned research endeavor.

1.6 To aid in dissemination of educational information.

1.7 To augment understanding of taxonomic and ecologic relationships for medical and economic purposes.

RESTRAINTS AS TO NUMBERS:

2.1 Collection (of adults or of immature stages) should be limited to sampling, not depleting, the population concerned; numbers collected should be consistent with, and not excessive for, the purpose of the collecting.

2.2 When collecting where the extent and/or the fragility of the population is unknown, caution and restraint should be exercised.

COLLECTING METHODS:

3.1 Field collecting should be selective. When consistent with the reasons for the particular collecting, males should be taken in preference to females.

3.2 Bait or light traps should be live-traps and should be visited regularly; released material should be dispersed to reduce predation by birds.

3.3 The use of Malaise or other killing traps should be limited to planned studies.

LIVE MATERIAL:

4.1 Rearing to elucidate life histories and to obtain series of immature stages and adults is to be encouraged, provided that collection of the rearing stock is in keeping with these guidelines.

4.2 Reared material in excess of need should be released, but only in the region where it originated, and in suitable habitat.

ENVIRONMENTAL AND LEGAL CONSIDERATIONS:

5.1 Protection of the supporting habitat must be recognized as the *sine qua non* of protection of a species.

5.2 Collecting should be performed in a manner such as to minimize trampling or other damage to the habitat or to specific foodplants.

5.3 Property rights and sensibilities of others must be respected (including those of photographers and butterfly-watchers).

5.4 Regulations relating to publicly controlled areas and to individual species and habitats must be complied with.

5.5 Compliance with agricultural, customs, medical and other regulations should be attained prior to importing live material.

RESPONSIBILITY FOR COLLECTED MATERIAL:

6.1 All material should be preserved with full data attached, including parentage of immatures when known.

6.2 All material should be protected from physical damage and deterioration, as by light, molds, and museum pests.

6.3 Collections should be made available for examination by qualified researchers.

6.4 Collections or specimens, and their associated written and photographic records, should be willed or offered to the care of an appropriate scientific institution, if the collector lacks space or loses interest, or in anticipation of death.

6.5 Type specimens, especially holotype or allotype, should be deposited in appropriate scientific institutions.

RELATED ACTIVITIES OF COLLECTORS:

7.1 Collecting should include permanently recorded field notes regarding habitat, conditions, and other pertinent information.

7.2 Recording of observations of behaviour and of biological interactions should receive as high priority as collecting.

7.3 Photographic records, with full data, are to be encouraged.

7.4 Education of the public regarding collecting and conservation, as reciprocally beneficial activities, should be undertaken whenever possible.

TRAFFIC IN LEPIDOPTERAN SPECIMENS:

8.1 Collection of specimens for exchange or sale should be performed in accordance with these guidelines.

8.2 Rearing of specimens for exchange or sale should be from stock obtained in a manner consistent with these guidelines, and so documented.

8.3 Mass collecting of Lepidoptera for commercial purposes, and collection or use of specimens for creation of saleable artifacts, are not included among the purposes of the Society.

(Published in the NEWS of the Lepidopterists' Society, No. 5, Sept/Oct 1982. May be reproduced without permission.)

Index to Species

Design: **Terry McIntyre**
Typesetting: **Linda Nelson**
Separations: **Image Color**
Negative Stripping: **Image Graphics**
Printing: **Friesen Printers**

Photo Credits:
J.E. Dubois, p. 79
K.L. Johnson, p. 22, 88
W.B. McKillop, p. 5, 32, 57, 72, 115, 135, 218
W.B. Preston, Cover, p. 8, 11, 25, 29, 35, 45, 53, 61, 80, 82, 84, 91, 94, 97, 106, 119, 120, 127, 194, 201, 206, 212, 216, 217, 220, 227, 228, 233, 242, 250, 251
A.R. Westwood, p. 62

Plate Photography: **Robert Barrow**

With the exceptions of Plate 1, no. 22 and Plate 4, no. 23, all specimens illustrated in the plates are from the collection of Paul Klassen.